This book provides an outline of the development of eschatological thought in the first seven centuries of Christianity. It is the first attempt, in any language, to give a comprehensive description of the origins of Christian eschatology, as it grew from its Jewish roots and from Jesus' preaching, and as it drew upon the philosophical and folkloric notions of death and the afterlife held by the peoples of the Mediterranean. Basing his study on the original texts, Father Daley considers not only the eschatology of the Greek and Latin Fathers, but also what can be known from early Syriac, Coptic and Armenian Christian literature. Concise and clearly focused in its range of subjects, this book provides an accessible historical survey of a centrally important aspect of early Christian doctrine.

THE HOPE OF THE EARLY CHURCH

THE HOPE OF THE
EARLY CHURCH

A HANDBOOK OF
PATRISTIC
ESCHATOLOGY

BRIAN E. DALEY, S. J.

ASSOCIATE PROFESSOR
WESTON SCHOOL OF THEOLOGY

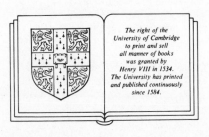

The right of the
University of Cambridge
to print and sell
all manner of books
was granted by
Henry VIII in 1534.
The University has printed
and published continuously
since 1584.

CAMBRIDGE UNIVERSITY PRESS

CAMBRIDGE
NEW YORK PORT CHESTER
MELBOURNE SYDNEY

Published by the Press Syndicate of the University of Cambridge
The Pitt Building, Trumpington Street, Cambridge CB2 1RP
40 West 20th Street, New York, NY 10011, USA
10 Stamford Road, Oakleigh, Melbourne 3166, Australia

First published 1991

Printed in Great Britain
at the University Press, Cambridge

British Library cataloguing in publication data

Daley, Brian E. (Brian Edward), 1940–
The hope of the early Church: a handbook of Patristic
eschatology.
1. Christian doctrine. Eschatology. Theories, history
1. Title
236.09

Library of Congress cataloguing in publication data

Daley, Brian, 1940–
The hope of the early Church: a handbook of Patristic eschatology
/ Brian E. Daley.
p.   cm.
Includes bibliographical references.
ISBN 0 521 35258 4
1. Eschatology – History of doctrines – Early church, *ca.* 30–600.
1. Title.
BT819.5.D34 1990
236'.09'015–dc20   90–32317 CIP

ISBN 0 521 35258 4 hardback

In memory of my brother John
(1936–1986)
who taught me, by example,
both scholarship and hope.

"Fleant ergo, qui spem resurrectionis habere non possunt . . ."
(Ambrose, *De Excessu Fratris* 1.70)

CONTENTS

Contents

PREFACE

This book, like its subject, has had a long and somewhat tortuous history. I was asked, in the early 1970s, to contribute the section on Patristic eschatology to the multi-volume *Handbuch der Dogmengeschichte* being published in Germany by Herder-Verlag. When, after a long delay due to doctoral studies, I began research on the project in earnest, I discovered that despite the breadth and obvious importance of the subject, and despite the enormous mass of scholarly literature on eschatological themes in various Patristic authors and periods, no single large-scale survey exists of the whole development of ancient Christian eschatological hope. The most ambitious treatment of the subject to date, Ludwig Atzberger's *Geschichte der altchristlichen Eschatologie innerhalb der vornicänischen Zeit* (Freiburg 1896), stops, as its title indicates, with the Council of Nicaea (325), and is not only obsolete in its information but hopelessly narrow in the range and organization of material it considers. Other, much briefer surveys are available in various languages, but most of them do not exceed article or chapter length, most stop at the time of the Council of Chalcedon (451) or earlier, and all restrict their concern to Latin and Greek Patristic literature.

As I worked on my own survey, I became more and more convinced of the need for something much more comprehensive: a broad sketch, such as this, of the various aspects of early Christian hope for the future of individual, Church and planet; a study directly based on all available Patristic texts that deal with eschatological themes, starting with the writings of the apostolic period and reaching to the authors usually thought of as "the last of the Fathers," Gregory the Great and John Damascene; and one which would include not only Latin and Greek material, but the Syriac, Coptic and Armenian traditions as well. This book is a first attempt to fill that need.

As a historical theologian – a student of the Christian tradition, who is convinced of its living value for faith today – I truly believe that the hope of people in our own age can be nourished and inflamed by an informed acquaintance with the hopes of earlier generations. I am certainly aware of the limitations of what I have produced – of the narrowness of focus that undoubtedly results from considering only textual evidence for ancient religious faith, and even more of the hermeneutical questions raised by a study which treats simply the history of religious ideas, without constant parallel examination of their cultural and social contexts. I have tried to limit these shortcomings as much as possible, by suggesting how the early Church's developing eschatological hope was enmeshed in other aspects of faith and practice, and by at least pointing, in passing, to wider issues of context and culture. The result, however, is still very much a historically ordered handbook on one aspect of early Christian thought, rather than a theological encyclopaedia or a broad, interpretative historical synthesis. I hope that the very limits of this study, as well as the information and interpretation it offers, will be a spur to further research on the many aspects of ancient Christian hope which urgently need further consideration.

A considerably abbreviated version of this book appeared, a few years ago, in German translation as part of volume IV/7a of the *Handbuch der Dogmengeschichte* (Freiburg: Herder 1986). I am deeply grateful to Herder-Verlag, and especially to Dr. Franz Johna, who oversaw the editing and production of that fascicle, for their permission to allow the full English text of my contribution to appear independently. I am also very grateful to Prof. Aloys Grillmeier, S.J., my friend and mentor from the Hochschule Skt. Georgen in Frankfurt-on-Main and one of the general editors of the *Handbuch*, for originally inviting me to undertake the research. I am grateful, too, to Prof. Michael Seybold, of the Katholische Universität Eichstätt, the *Handbuch*'s managing editor, for his patient but relentless prodding and cajoling through the early years of this book's gestation; without his occasional reminders of my tardiness, the project might still be unfinished.

Part of the early research for this book was done at Dumbarton Oaks, in Washington, D.C., while I was a fellow there in 1981/82. I should like to thank the Fellows of Harvard College, who are also the Trustees of Dumbarton Oaks, and Prof. Giles Constable, who at that time was its director, for making it possible for me to begin this work, under such gracious conditions, in one of the world's great Byzantine libraries. I should also like to thank my colleagues there in 1981/82 for their friendship and their readiness to share with me their knowledge of the spiritual and intellectual world of early Byzantium.

Most of the research for this book, however, and all of the writing, was done in the excellent joint library of the Weston School of Theology and the Episcopal Divinity School, in Cambridge, Massachusetts, where I teach. I owe a large debt of thanks to the staff of the library, who have been so helpful through the years, and especially to the library's director, Dr. James M.

Dunkly. More deeply still, I am grateful to my colleagues and students at the Weston School of Theology for their constant encouragement, their patient example and their unstinting good humor during the years that Patristic eschatology has occupied much of my own academic horizon. I am especially grateful to the administrators of both the Weston School of Theology and its Jesuit community, who have supported me materially and spiritually with unfailing and unquestioning generosity. On a more personal level, I am perhaps most grateful of all to two scholarly friends who have followed this project with constant interest since its beginning, and have supplied me with advice, information, good judgment and sympathy at every turn: Prof. John W. O'Malley, S.J., of the Weston School of Theology, and Prof. Lloyd G. Patterson, of the Episcopal Divinity School. Scholarship and authorship depend on friends such as these.

For generous help in the production of the manuscript, I am deeply grateful to Prof. Joan M. Nuth, of John Carroll University in Cleveland, Ohio, who edited and typed the first draft for me during her student days in Boston, and to Ms. Theresa Busher, presently of the Weston staff, who helped me a great deal in producing its revised versions. Finally, I am very grateful also to the staff of the Cambridge University Press who have patiently shepherded this book through its revision and production: to Mr. Richard Purslow, Dr. Robert Williams, Ms. Ulrike Hellen and Mr. Alex Wright. It has been a privilege and a great pleasure for me to work with such careful and distinguished publishers in bringing this study of the Church's early conceptions of "Christian finality" to what I hope is a happy and fruitful conclusion.

A NOTE ON ABBREVIATIONS

In referring to periodicals and serials, I have used the standard abbreviations listed in S. Schwertner, *International Glossary of Abbreviations for Theology and Related Subjects* (= *Internationales Abkürzungsverzeichnis für Theologie und Grenzgebiete* [*IATG*] Berlin 1974). When referring to the individual works of Greek Patristic authors, I have usually adopted the abbreviations of G. W. H. Lampe, *A Patristic Greek Lexicon* (Oxford 1961) ix–xliii, except in the case of some familiar works, for which simpler abbreviations seem more appropriate.

The following abbreviations for Patristic *corpora* and major reference works appear frequently throughout this book:

ACO   *Acta Conciliorum Oecumenicorum* (Berlin 1914–)
CCG   *Corpus Christianorum, Series Graeca* (Turnhout/Louvain 1977–)
CCL   *Corpus Christianorum, Series Latina* (Turnhout 1953–)
CSCO *Corpus Scriptorum Christianorum Orientalium* (Louvain 1903–)
CSEL *Corpus Scriptorum Ecclesiasticorum Latinorum* (Vienna 1866–)
DSp   *Dictionnaire de spiritualité* (Paris 1932–)
DThC *Dictionnaire de théologie catholique* (Paris 1903–72)
GCS   *Die griechischen christlichen Schriftsteller der ersten drei Jahrhunderte* (Berlin 1897–)
PG   *Patrologia Graeca* (Paris 1857–66)
PL   *Patrologia Latina* (Paris 1841–55)
PLS   *Patrologiae Latinae Supplementum* (Paris 1958–70)
PO   *Patrologia Orientalis* (Paris 1907–)

Introduction

Eschatology is a word with many meanings. Essentially, as religious doctrine about "last things," it is faith in final solutions. It is the hope of believing people that the incompleteness of their present experience of God will be resolved, their present thirst for God fulfilled, their present need for release and salvation realized. It is faith in the resolution of the unresolved, in the tying-up of all the loose ends that mar the life of the believer in the world. It is the expectation, despite uncertainties, that our choices and patterns of action in this present human life will find lasting relevance in the retribution – for good or ill – administered by a God who is good and wise and powerful, the expectation that God's provident action in history will be shown, in the end, to have a consistency and purposefulness that reflect his goodness.

This kind of faith – more properly, this kind of hope – has taken many forms in the history of Christianity. For people living under oppression or persecution, eschatological hope has often meant simply the overriding, radically optimistic sense that the present intolerable order of things is about to end. This sense of crisis, of challenge and promise, has usually been expressed by Christians in apocalyptic images: dramatic expectations of cosmic violence that will destroy the world and its institutions completely and let God begin again, powerfully saving his own. For people living in times of social or economic strain, eschatological hope has meant a similarly strong conviction that the world is "growing old," running out of resources, facing depletion from within, and a similar trust that the end of its natural processes will mean the beginning of a new world, and for humanity a fresh start.

For others, living in periods of greater public security and of individual freedom and competitiveness, eschatological hope has often been something quite different: an ordered doctrine of the "last things," personal expectation of final justice and retribution, a personal longing for rest and satisfaction in a new life that will begin at death. For the philosophically cultivated believer, eschatology can be the expression in future terms of underlying assumptions about the true nature of the mind, the person and the material world. For the intensely religious person – the ascetic or the mystic – it can mean a trust that union with God in knowledge and love, which has already begun in this present life of faith, will someday be consummated in an existence free from all the limits earthly life imposes: a union of ecstatic, mutual self-giving between creator and creature, for which this life's religious experience can only provide hints and shadows.

At its heart, eschatology can be called a derived or secondary aspect of theology, for the Jew or the Christian, in that it reflects other, more fundamental convictions about God, the world and human existence. This is not to say that it is unimportant – indeed, eschatological hope has often strongly colored all faith and practice, and can easily dominate the religious sensibilities of an age, as it seems to have done in late Palestinian Judaism and at various points in Christian history. But eschatology is secondary, in Jewish and Christian faith at least, because it is the hope that grows from faith and leads to love: a projection on to an unknown future of the understanding of God and God's workings with which believers presently live, a drawing into final convergence of the incomplete arcs presently described by their doctrine of God, their understanding of God's saving activity, their conception of the human person and the faithful community.[1]

So eschatology includes, among other things, the attempt to construct a theodicy: a justification of faith in God, a hope in the final revelation of God's wise and loving activity throughout history, with a longing for final reckonings. It is the logical conclusion of the biblical doctrine of creation, in the attempt to foresee the fulfillment of creation's purpose. For the Christian, eschatology is the final stage of Christology, provided it is conceived in historical or dynamic terms – provided, in other words, that it sees the person of Jesus not simply as the incarnate Word of God, but as the revelation of "what was from the beginning" (I Jo 1.1): God's saving design for all humanity. So eschatology also represents, as something hoped for, the stage of final achievement implied by Christian belief in human salvation; it draws out the ultimate implications of a theology of grace; it provides the meeting-point of an ever-unrealized ideal of the believing community with the ambiguities of the Church's present historical exis-tence; it imagines the "Mystery," in all its fullness, at which all the "mysteries" of worship and symbol now merely hint obscurely. There is, or at least there can be, an eschatological dimension to every aspect of Christian faith and reflection, as the believer looks from the community's tradition, and from his or her own religious experience, to the uncertainties and threats of the collective and individual future. In a word, eschatology "applies" a conviction about the ultimate character of reality, in hope, to that unknown which lies ahead.

Because it touches so many of the central themes of faith, then, the early history of Christian eschatology, which this book proposes to survey, is a complex and elusive subject, yet one of enormous synthetic importance for our understanding of how the Christian faith, in its formative stages, came to be articulated in rational thought. To see the development of Christian doctrine in the first several centuries, as Martin Werner tried to do several decades ago,[2] as essentially the by-product of a failed eschatological hope – a way of coping intellectually with the non-fulfillment of first-century apocalyptic fantasies – is surely to reverse the order of religious priorities suggested in early Christian literature, and confirmed in our own reflective faith.[3] The first Christians believed the end was near, almost certainly, and they hoped for a radically better life for themselves, because they believed Jesus had risen from the dead, and because they were convinced that the community's new experience of the charisms of the Spirit was a first taste of the Kingdom of God. The fulfillment of their early hopes was surely delayed, and the delay required – just as surely – a constant reconception and re-expression of the community's conviction that it was called to share in the divine life and power that had been bestowed on the risen Lord. But this reorientation of the time-line of its eschatological hope, if we are to trust the evidence at hand, seems to have caused no more of an upheaval for the Christians of the first and second centuries than it does for modern believers, whose predictions of the end of the world repeatedly prove to be mistaken. Christians, in fact, have almost always looked forward to the second coming of Christ, with all that it signifies, as something "very near, even at the gates" (Mark 13.29); and the disappointment of this hope, in a temporal sense, seems to have strikingly little effect on the overall character and content of faith – doubtless because the nearness of God Christians hope for is, in the most fundamental sense, a nearness that transcends history.

Clearly, the early Church's understanding of the hope implied in its faith grew and changed as rapidly as the rest of its theology. A comprehensive study of the documents of that faith, however, suggests that the development was much more complex and cyclical than Werner's thesis presupposes. Eschatological emphases in the early Church varied, apocalyptic hopes died and were revived, and individual or cosmic or ecclesiological or mystical perspectives succeeded one another, not so much in a direct line of development as in response to the social and ecclesial challenges met by Christian communities in each generation, and as an outgrowth of the personal theological interests and allegiances of individual writers.

In the midst of such change, the content of eschatological teaching was usually drawn from a variety of sources: biblical and apocryphal traditions; popular, semi-Christian beliefs about the fate of the human person after death; the myths and the reasoned convictions of Hellenistic philosophy; and a good deal of simple speculation. Necessarily, this Christian hope for a world yet to come was expressed in images: the "stuff of dreams," rather than the products of observation. Yet it was rooted – empirically, if one takes spiritual experience with any seriousness – in the witness of the first disciples of Jesus that "the Lord is truly risen, and has appeared" (Lk 24.34), and in the conviction of their hearers that the Kingdom of God, whose coming Jesus had proclaimed, had actually begun to be a world-transforming reality in the new, transformed life of Jesus. So the early baptismal creeds proclaimed, in various turns of phrase, a faith not only in the Easter kerygma, with its news about the one God of history and his Son, Jesus, but also in "the resurrection of the body and life everlasting" for the believer and the whole community. Baptism and the Eucharist, by offering believers, through the Spirit, a share in the very life and mind of the risen Jesus, became promises, as well, of a final salvation that still lay ahead, beyond death and the collapse of human history: types or symbols of "the life of the world to come."

The history of eschatology in the Patristic age, then, which this book attempts to sketch out in its most general lines, cannot be separated from the whole development of early Christian reflection on the mystery of salvation in Jesus. It is that underlying faith in Jesus crucified and risen, and in the saving implications of his death and life for the believer, that gives early Christian hope its consistency and continuity.[4] As early Christian preachers and writers looked towards the future in hope, they could only express their expectations by using and adapting the metaphors and categories that the Scriptures and their own cultural traditions provided. The result, at first sight, seems to be simply a patchwork. But it was the Christian author's underlying conviction about God and Christ, and about the world and the individual as objects of God's saving action in Christ, that provided the final shape of his or her hope for the end of things, and that drew future expectation into the untidy yet vitally interconnected whole we call Christian theology.

Visions of a new day: early Semitic Christianity and Christian apocalyptic

The history of Christian eschatology begins, by any reckoning, in the apocalyptic hopes of salvation cherished by the earliest Palestinian Christian communities. Although the expectation of a bodily resurrection and of the restoration of Israel in a transformed material world seems to have had little importance in the Hellenized Judaism of the Mediterranean Diaspora,[1] it was apparently a cherished hope of a large number of Jews in Palestine, as both the Old Testament pseudepigrapha and several of the Qumran documents demonstrate, and it left its mark on the teaching of Jesus, as well.[2] Inevitably, then, much of what is known today as "Jewish Christianity" – both in the narrow sense of the hybrid faith of certain early Jewish heretical sects that recognized Jesus as Messiah, and in the broader sense of an early orthodox Christianity whose theology was expressed in Semitic rather than Hellenistic concepts and images[3] – was also deeply colored by apocalyptic expectations of salvation.

Jewish Christian sects

Little is known with certainty about the theology and religious practices of "Jewish Christians" in the narrow sense. The term undoubtedly covers a variety of groups, most of which seem to have led a shadowy, increasingly marginal existence in Palestine, Syria, Mesopotamia or Western Asia Minor in the first four centuries of our era.[4] Although they recognized Jesus as Messiah, these communities seem to have continued to observe Jewish dietary and ritual practice, to have cultivated good relations with their Jewish fellow believers, and to have promoted an adoptionist Christology. Some, apparently, were also strongly influenced by Gnostic conceptions of salvation, and were interested in astrology and magic.[5] Their eschatological hope seems to have been focused on the return of Christ in glory and the

5

resurrection of all the dead at the end of history, which they believed to be imminent. Eusebius (*HE* 2.23.13) quotes the second-century writer Hegesippus in attributing both of these doctrines to those Jews converted by James, brother of the Lord. Epiphanius (*Pan* 29.7) speaks of "Nazoreans" in his own day, who lived in the region east of the Jordan and who followed the Old Law; "they also accept the resurrection of the dead and hold that everything has its origin in God. They proclaim one God and his Son Jesus Christ" (*ibid.*, 29.7.3). The "Ebionites," the sect (or perhaps caricature) of Jewish Christians to whom the Fathers refer most frequently, were said to have preferred to refer to Jesus as "Son of Man" rather than as "Christ," a practice which may suggest an apocalyptic Christology,[6] and they may well have been the "excommunicate Jews" (*posh'ei Yisrael*) referred to in *Midrash Tehillim* 31.24, who are praised by the rabbinic authors for acknowledging at least the resurrection of the dead.[7]

The Pseudo-Clementine *Recognitions* and *Homilies*, in their present state probably a compilation of at least two fourth-century reworkings of earlier Syriac and Jewish Christian material, are usually taken as our main direct source for "Ebionite" theology, even though their complex origin makes it clear that this source has been mingled with several others.[8] These works present history as divided into "two kingdoms": the present short age, under the rule of the "Evil One," and the great and eternal age to come, reserved for "the Good One" (*Hom* 20.2; *Rec* 1.24; cf. Epiphanius, *Pan* 30.16.2). The human believer is capable of becoming immortal and incorruptible, if he or she acknowledges God with faith and love (*Hom* 3.37). At the resurrection of the dead, our bodies will be changed into light and we will become like angels, so that we will then be able to see God directly and live (*Hom* 17.16). That time of transformation, in which "a separation of souls from things shall take place," will also be a day of judgment: not only shall the good be rewarded with eternal life and ineffable blessings, but the wicked "shall be handed over to eternal fire for their sins" (*Rec* 1.24). Until then, the dead are apparently "stored" in Hades, the "place of souls" (*Hom* 3.33).

There is no direct evidence in these texts to confirm Schoeps's assertion that the "Ebionites" were millenarians.[9] Indeed, the only ancient evidence for such a view is a remark of Jerome (*In Esaiam* 66.20) that the "Ebionites," who are "heirs of Jewish error," share with the Jews a materialistic expectation of a coming kingdom of luxury that will last a thousand years. Jerome's other caustic allusions to millenarian hopes (e.g., *In Esaiam* 11.15–16; 35.10; 60.1; *In Jer* 31.28; *In Zach* 14.18) identify them with Jews and "the Judaizers among us (*nostri Judaicantes*)," a phrase which seems to refer to the Christian millenarians of his own day.

Early biblical apocrypha

Although it is usually difficult to specify the original home of the many apocryphal gospels, apocalypses, and pseudo-apostolic letters and narratives composed by Christian groups in the second century, most of them represent a style of symbolic, dramatic theological thinking that belongs to the world of Jewish apocalyptic. Their pseudepigraphic identification with central figures of the Old or New Testament, the urgent, moralizing tone of their exhortations, the cosmic judgment and salvation they usually announce, and their sense of rapidly approaching doom for Greco-Roman civilization all link them in spirit and literary technique with the Jewish apocalyptic literature of the period. Like Jewish apocalyptic works, these Christian writings reflect not only the hopes of biblical faith, but the sense of frustration and insecurity shared by a people living without political or religious freedom, a people for whom persecution was always a real possibility. In some cases, in fact (e.g., *IV Ezra*, the *Ascension of Isaiah* or the first five books of the *Sibylline Oracles*), originally Jewish works have been rewritten to convey a Christian message. Some of these Christian apocrypha may be the work of marginal, syncretistically Jewish Christian communities such as the so-called "Ebionites," but even apocalyptic works of unambiguously Christian origin represent, in the second century, what we have referred to as "Judaeo-Christian" features.[10]

The most important early Christian apocrypha for our understanding of Judaeo-Christian eschatology are the following: The *Apocalypse of Peter* (*Apoc Pet*), probably composed about 135 in Syria but well known also in Egypt during the second century – a work especially notable for its detailed and graphic description of the kinds of eternal punishment reserved for sinners;[11] the *Ascension of Isaiah* (*Asc Is*), a work probably of Syrian origin from the mid second century, incorporating an older Jewish account of the martyrdom of the prophet Isaiah into an apocalyptic Christian account of the origin, death and second coming of Jesus;[12] the *Epistula Apostolorum* (*Ep Ap*), a "letter" purportedly from all twelve apostles addressed to the universal Church, reporting a long revelatory discourse of the risen Lord on Easter night – a work that seems to have been composed in a Jewish Christian community in Asia Minor about 160;[13] and the so-called *Fifth and Sixth Books of Ezra*, chapters 1–2 and 15–16 of the Latin translation of the Jewish apocryphon *IV Ezra*, which seem to have been written in Asia Minor or Syria at the end of the second or the beginning of the third century, and which portray in remarkable detail the future rewards of the just (*V Ezra 2*) and the tribulations that will accompany the end of the world (*VI Ezra*).[14] To these works – some of which may include material from older Hebrew or

7

Aramaic apocalypses – must be added books VII and VIII of the *Sibylline Oracles* (*Or Sib*): Christian, probably Alexandrian, compositions in Greek hexameters from the latter half of the second century – as well as the Christian interpolations in book II, which may come from the mid third century.[15] Though not biblical apocrypha in the strict sense, the Christian Sibylline poems make wide use of biblical and apocalyptic themes and continue the style of cosmic Wisdom-theology found in the earlier, purely Jewish sections of the same collection.

Although these works differ widely in the details of their eschatological hope, the picture of impending deliverance and retribution that they paint is fairly consistent in its broad outlines. Human history, for their authors, is in its last days. Jesus proclaimed "the end of ages and the final day" when he descended into Hades after his death (*Or Sib* VIII, 310f.); *Ep Ap* 17 foretells the coming of the end 150 years after Jesus' resurrection;[16] and *Or Sib* VIII (65–72) predicts it will arrive during the last years of the reign of Antoninus Pius (147–61). The signs of the imminent end are familiar from the New Testament and Jewish apocalyptic: first discord, corruption and false teaching within the community (*Asc Is* 3.21–31; *Ep Ap* 37; *Or Sib* II, 168ff.); then strife among families (*Ep Ap* 34; *Or Sib* VIII, 84f.), war among nations (*Ep Ap* 37; *VI Ezra* 15.28–45), widespread disease, crop failure, famine and the resulting depopulation of the inhabited world (*Ep Ap* 34; *VI Ezra* 15. 57f.; 16.20–35; *Or Sib* II, 154–61). Catastrophic changes in the structure of the universe will accompany these natural disasters: the sequence of day and night will be reversed (*Asc Is* 4.5; *Ep Ap* 34; *Or Sib* VIII, 337–40), storms and earthquakes will shake the earth (*Ep Ap* 34; *VI Ezra* 16.10–12), stars will fall into the sea (*Ep Ap* 34; *Or Sib* VIII, 190–93), and fire will rain down from heaven to consume the earth (*Apoc Pet* 5; *Or Sib* VII, 120–27; VIII, 225f.; 243; II, 96–205), until all natural motion ceases and the world becomes silent (*Or Sib* VIII, 342–48; II, 208–13). "Beliar, the great prince" will then appear (*Asc Is* 4.2ff; *Or Sib* II, 167f.) – according to some accounts, as *Nero redivivus* (*Asc Is* 4.2; cf. *Or Sib* VIII, 68–72) – to lead the persecution of the faithful; but Christ will also appear in glory, riding on the clouds and preceded by a cross of light (*Ep Ap* 16; cf. *Or Sib* VIII, 244–46), to defeat Beliar and lead the saints and angels in a procession of triumph (*Apoc Pet* 6; *Asc Is* 4.14–16; *Or Sib* II, 238–48).

At the coming of Christ, the gates of Hades will be opened and the shadowy dead kept there will be released (*Or Sib* VIII, 226f.; II, 214–37; cf. *V Ezra* 2.23, 31). Souls will be reunited to their bodies, and all men and women will rise again in their flesh to incorruptible life (*Apoc Pet* 4; *Ep Ap* 19, 21–25).[17] Christ will then join his Father in making a final, righteous judgment of all who have lived (*Ep Ap* 26; *Or Sib* II, 42–55, 238–44; VIII,

218–21). Everything will be revealed in this judgment, even a person's most secret deeds (*Or Sib* VIII, 219–30; *VI Ezra* 16.54–68). In several passages, God executes his judgment by making all the risen pass through a stream of fire (*Apoc Pet* 5–6; cf. *Or Sib* II, 252–54, 313–16; VIII, 411), "and the righteous shall all be saved, but the impious shall perish" (*ibid*.).[18]

Eternal fire will be the lot of those found to be sinners (*Or Sib* VII, 119–28); "the abyss of torture" will be opened (*Or Sib* VIII, 241), and after being tormented by angels wielding flaming whips, sinners will be plunged into its depths forever, to burn without hope of release (*Or Sib* II, 285–310). *Apoc Pet* 7–13 describes in vivid detail the specific punishments to be assigned to different classes of sinners; fire, however, is the element common to them all. *Or Sib* II, 330–38, presents an alternative to the doctrine of eternal punishment for all sinners: God will allow the just to intercede for those whom they wish to save, and they will be brought to share in the comforts of the Elysian fields. This same hope may be represented in the "Rainer Fragment," related to *Apoc Pet* 14, but the text is uncertain.[19]

To the just, however, God will give rest (*Ep Ap* 19; *V Ezra* 2.29, 34), everlasting light (*ibid*., 35), and the delights of a Paradise abundant with fruits and flowers of every kind (*ibid*., 19; *Apoc Pet* 16), where they will put on shining garments and join in God's everlasting banquet (*V Ezra* 2.38–40, 45), or be fed with heavenly manna (*Or Sib* VII, 148f.).[20] There Christ himself will crown them (*ibid*., 43–47), and they will live with him a life of eternal comfort in one endless day (*Or Sib* II, 325–29), free from divisive earthly concern for status or possessions (*Or Sib* VIII, 205–16; II, 316–29).[21] It will be a new creation, a restoration of humanity's "pure mind," as it was in the beginning (*Or Sib* VII, 144f.).

In all of these documents, then, the dramatic sense of crisis and the powerfully imaginative expectation of a wholly new order of space and time, a world of justice and judgment and powerfully restored relationships between God and creation, bear close resemblance to the Jewish apocalyptic literature current since the Book of Daniel. The distinctive element is the role of the glorified Christ as executor of the judgment of God and divinely sent inaugurator of the new age. Though the imaginative tools of the authors of these works were known from a sectarian tradition within Jewish religious thought, the grounds of their hope were decidedly Christian, and grew out of the gospel kerygma of Jesus' resurrection and Lordship.

The "Apostolic Fathers"

Although their language and method, as well as their theological interests, are also dominated by the literature of biblical and post-biblical Judaism, the

Greek-speaking Christian writers of the first half of the second century who have traditionally been termed the "Apostolic Fathers" present a wide variety of themes and emphases in their eschatological message.

(a) The so-called *First Letter of Clement* is the earliest of these documents that can be dated with any certainty. It was written apparently by Clement, one of the chief presbyters of the Church of Rome, to the Church in Corinth about the year 96; its chief aim is to urge respect for Church order and established authority on a group of young, dissident Christians. Understandably, Clement's ecclesiological perspective leads him to stress the continuity of sacred history and its institutions rather than to repeat the world-shattering challenge of apocalyptic hope. Eschatology is not a strong concern for him. The traditional themes of New Testament eschatology that he does preserve – the imminent coming of the Kingdom, for instance (42.3; 50.3), or the suddenness of the Lord's return (23.3–5) and the universal certainty of his judgment (28) – are presented as being in continuity with creation, the expected culmination of the orderly process of history rather than a crisis that has suddenly come upon us.[22]

The main eschatological section of the work, cc. 23–28, seems to be, like the New Testament's II Peter, a kind of apology for the Church's traditional expectations of resurrection and judgment in the face of the delay being experienced by believers. The "double-minded" and "doubters" are reminded that the crops, too, take time to grow to ripeness, but that they do mature in their own time (23.3–4). The passage of day and night, the growth of plants from apparently lifeless seeds (24), even the legend of the phoenix (25) all testify, within God's created order, to the possibility of resurrection. "Nothing is impossible to God save lying . . . Not one of the things he has decreed will fail" (27.3,5). Therefore the right attitude for the Christian is to fear God's coming judgment and lead a holy life (28.1–29.1). The aim of this section, aside from the obviously paraenetic element at its end, may be to counteract an exaggeratedly "realized" eschatology that may have been current in the Corinthian community, parallel to that rejected by Paul in his own first letter to the Corinthians. Clement, like Paul in I Cor 15, attacks this understanding of an already-assured salvation by defending the temporally future character of resurrection and judgment, and implying the necessity of both life and death in the present historical order before the blessings promised in the gospel can be realized.[23]

For the author of *I Clement*, in any case, both the future punishment of the unfaithful and the future reward of the just are guaranteed by God's fidelity to his promises (11.1; 34.3, 7; 35.2–3), even though their details exceed our present comprehension. The saints "who have been made perfect in love" will be revealed to all when Christ's Kingdom comes and they are raised from their graves (50.3–4); but the martyrs and the faithful leaders of the Church who have died already enjoy "a secure place" of glory (5.4, 7; 6.2; 44.5). Indeed, Clement follows Jewish apocalyptic tradition in suggesting that the number of the elect is already fixed by God (2.4; 59.2), and that any person who keeps the commandments humbly will be enrolled in that number (58.2).[24]

(b) The *Epistle of Barnabas*, a pseudepigraphic work of Judaeo-Christian origin, probably written in Alexandria in the 130s, shows, in contrast, a much stronger eschatological intent; it sets its urgent moral exhortation and its bitter criticism of rabbinic faith and exegesis against a backdrop of intense apocalyptic hope. "Let us pay attention in these last days," the author writes (4.9), for "the final stumbling-block is approaching" (4.3) and the "Black One," the "wicked prince," is preparing his assault on the faithful (4.10, 13). In this time of crisis, "there are three teachings of the Lord: hope for life, which is the beginning and end of our faith; righteousness, the beginning and end of judgment; and cheerful, joyous love, a testimony that our works are just" (1.6).[25] The author's expectation of the Lord's coming reminds him of the certainty of judgment and retribution for both the just and sinners (21.1); "for this reason there will be a resurrection," and for this reason, too, Jesus has revealed our resurrection in his own flesh (*ibid.*; 5.6f.). The "Kingdom of God" is clearly a future reality for Barnabas (e.g., 21.1), yet it is present among us in a hidden way even now, undergoing "evil and polluted days" and sharing in the contradiction of the cross of Jesus (8.5f.). For Jesus, by establishing a new covenant with us, has already "redeemed our hearts from darkness" (14.5) and has let us "taste the first-fruits of what is to come" (1.7). The community to which the letter is addressed is already forgiven, already a new creation (6.11–13); when its members have been "perfected," they will rule over the earth (6.17–19).

As part of his criticism of Jewish ritual practice, the author interprets even the institution of the Sabbath, in Gen 2.2, in an eschatological sense: the end of history will come six "ages," or six thousand years, after creation (15.1–4), since "with the Lord, a thousand years is as a day" (Ps 90.4; cf. II Pet 3.8). The second coming of the Son, he continues, will bring not only judgment but drastic cosmic changes, and will inaugurate a seventh age of rest (15.5). After that, at the dawning of the "eighth day" or age, a new world will begin (15.8). Although this interpretation of sacred history is not Christian millenarianism in its usual, highly concrete second-century form, it marks the first use by a Christian author of the traditional pagan conception of history as a "week" of ages, a borrowing that was to have a long life in early Christian art, liturgical prayer and biblical interpretation.[26]

(c) The brief patchwork of catechetical, liturgical and homiletic material known as the *Didache* or *Teaching of the Twelve Apostles* was probably put into its present form in Palestine or Syria towards the middle of the second century, but it contains passages that may be older by half a century or more, including some sections with a strongly eschatological flavor. Its Eucharistic prayer (9–10) twice asks that the Church "be brought together from the ends of the earth" into the Kingdom God has prepared (9.4; 10.5), and concludes with several fervent acclamations calling on the Lord Jesus to "come" (10.6). Its final chapter – possibly woven out of several strands of apocalyptic and didactic material[27] – urges the community to watchfulness in the "final days" (16.1, 3) and warns of the coming of "the world-deceiver [disguised] as God's Son," who will rule over the earth and oppress the faithful (16.4–5). The signs proclaiming Christ's final victory over this tyrant will be three classically apocalyptic events: "a stretching-out [of a cross?] in the heavens,"[28] a trumpet-blast, and finally the resurrection of the saints, who will join the Lord in his triumphal procession across the sky.[29]

(d) Opinions vary as to the importance of eschatological themes in the seven Epistles of *Ignatius of Antioch* which are generally accepted as authentic.[30] These letters were written to various churches in Asia Minor, about the year 110, as Ignatius made his way, under arrest, to Rome and to martyrdom. Traditional elements of Christian apocalyptic expectation are certainly present: the assertion that "the last days are here," for instance, the consequent call for radical ethical choice (*Eph* 11.1; *Magn* 5.1), and the expressed conviction that all who fail to accept in faith "the grace we have" – even the heavenly powers – are doomed to destruction in eternal fire (*Eph* 11.1; 16.2; *Smyrn* 6.1). Yet there are clear suggestions in the letters, too, of a "realized eschatology" at odds with such a future-oriented hope: Ignatius remarks, for instance, that at the birth of Jesus all the dark powers of "the ancient kingdom" came to an end, for "what God had prepared was now beginning" (*Eph* 19.3). The gospel of Jesus' "coming" ($\pi\alpha\rho o\upsilon\sigma\iota\alpha$),[31] death and resurrection is, in itself, already "the realization of incorruptibility" (*Philad* 9.2).

Behind the elusive conceptual content of Ignatius' eschatological hope stands, surely, the very personal character of the letters. They are not, in the first instance, documents of instruction or even of church order; they are, if one may take them as genuine, impassioned, hastily written messages of encouragement to sister-churches from a captive bishop convinced he will soon be laying down his life for Christ. The prospect and ideal of martyrdom dominates all seven letters.[32] This, for Ignatius, and only this, is his way to become a "real disciple" (*Eph* 1.2; *Rom* 4.2; 5.1, 3), his means to "get to

God" (*Rom* 1.2; 2.2; etc.)[33] or "to Jesus Christ" (*Rom* 5.3; cf. 6.1). Such a death is "death into Jesus Christ," a means of personal union with him who died and rose "for us" (*Rom* 6.1). On the other side of martyrdom stands life, union with God, the fulfillment of Ignatius' humanity (*Rom* 6.2): "the pangs of birth are at hand for me" (*Rom* 6.1).

Into the context of this deeply personal hope for union with Christ, Ignatius assimilates the general Christian expectation of resurrection: just as Christ, in the full reality of his humanity, was "truly raised from the dead," so too "the Father will raise us, who believe in him, according to his likeness – in Christ Jesus, apart from whom we do not have real life" (*Trall* 9.2). Resurrection, in fact, is a central and prominent part of Ignatius' hope (*Eph* 11.2; *Trall* Intro; *Rom* 2.2; 4.3); but he seems to see it as a promise restricted to those who believe in the full reality of Jesus, fleshly as well as spiritual (*Magn* 9.2; *Smyrn* 5.2f.). In fact, he describes the punishment destined for those who deny Jesus' corporeal reality not only as "unquenchable fire" (*Eph* 16.2) but as a continuing, wraith-like, bodiless existence (*Smyrn* 2.1).

Ignatius sees the resurrection of the dead simply as part – although undeniably a very important part, for embodied beings – of the "prize of incorruptibility and eternal life" which lies ahead for "God's athlete" (*Pol* 2.3). "Incorruptibility" is the "ointment" Christ pours on his Church (*Eph* 17.1); the reason he died for us was "that we might believe in his death and so escape dying ourselves" (*Trall* 2.1). So the Eucharist, in which the physical reality of Jesus, and especially the memory of his Passion, is celebrated most concretely, is both the "medicine of immortality" (*Eph* 20.2) and the means by which those who partake in it (ἀγαπᾶν) are prepared to share in his resurrection (*Smyrn* 2.1). Eschatological renewal, in Ignatius' eyes, is not merely a wonderful transformation of the material world reserved for some dramatic future day, but a gift of life that has already begun for those who genuinely believe in the risen Lord.

(e) In the *Letter of Polycarp to the Philippians*, closely connected with the Ignatian corpus and probably written soon afterwards,[34] the author's concerns are presented in the same eschatological perspective we find in Ignatius' letters. Resurrection and judgment are part of an accepted central body of Christian teaching, based on "the sayings of the Lord," which also includes the reality of Jesus' human flesh and the "testimony of the cross." Whoever denies any of these things "is the firstborn of Satan" (7.1). Christian compassion and mutual forbearance should be motivated by the certainty that God sees us all and will judge us all (6.2); yet resurrection is a promise held out only to the worthy (5.2), to those individuals who "do his will and follow his commandments and love what he loved" (2.2).[35]

Ignatius and his fellow martyrs are already "in their deserved place with the Lord" (9.2), but Polycarp offers no further speculations about the state of their bodies, the character of their reward or the fate of apostates. The hope of Christians for the future, its images and its supposed conditions are not yet the object of reflection and explanation; it is simply part of the Easter kerygma at the heart of the community's life and worship.

(f) The *Martyrdom of Polycarp*, apparently composed shortly after the bishop's execution in 156, is the oldest extant account of a Christian martyr's death, written in the name of the church at Smyrna to the church at Philomelium in Phrygia. It makes skillful use of the eschatological horizon that will become commonplace in martyr-acts, drawing a sharp contrast between the biased human trial Polycarp has undergone and the coming divine judgment, between his brief sufferings for the faith and his hope of eternal reward. This prospect of punishment and reward, in fact, is presented as a key motivating force behind the martyr's remarkable endurance. To all the martyrs of the recent persecution, the letter observes, "the fire of their inhuman tortures was cold; for they set before their eyes escape from the fire that is everlasting and never quenched, while with the eyes of their heart they gazed upon the good things reserved for those who endure patiently" (2.3). When the proconsul Quadratus threatens him with burning, Polycarp retorts: "You do not know the fire of the coming judgment and everlasting punishment that is laid up for the impious" (11.2). Yet reward and punishment are not simply postponed to the end of human history; after Polycarp's death, the community is convinced he has already been "crowned with the wreath of immortality and has borne away an incontestable prize" (17.1). The apocalyptic imagery of the Jewish and Christian apocrypha is here being applied directly to the faith and the sufferings of the individual martyr.

(g) The anonymous homily traditionally referred to as the *Second Letter of Clement* – probably delivered in some Hellenistic community before 150 – presents, in contrast to Ignatius' letters or *I Clement*, the expectation of an unambiguously apocalyptic transformation of the world in the near future. The message of the work is, essentially, a simple exhortation to lead a holy and upright life. But this is given a tone of seriousness and urgency by the repeated warning that "our stay in this world of the flesh is slight and short" (5.5; cf. 5.1; 7.1; 8.1–3), and we cannot be certain when God's Kingdom will come (12.1). Indeed, the author implies that the coming of the Kingdom has only been delayed in order to train us in uprightness (20), and to give people a chance to repent from their sins, especially those of a sexual character (12.2–6). Jesus' coming as judge will bring a full revelation of both human righteousness and human sin, as corroborating evidence for his own justice and glory (16.3; 17.4–7). On that day, heaven will be dissolved and earth "will be like lead melting in fire" (16.3); the faithless will then be punished with "endless torments and undying fire" (17.7; cf. 6.7; 7.6), while the just will "gather the immortal fruit of the resurrection" (19.3) and receive, as their due reward, the everlasting blessing of the Kingdom (11.7; 19.4).

In chapter 9, the author gives his own apologetic argument against those who think a bodily resurrection is impossible. If we have been saved and enlightened as incarnate beings, he insists, we must consider our flesh to be God's temple; and "just as you were called in the flesh, you will come [i.e., to fulfillment] in the flesh" (vv. 3–5). Secondly, if Christ saved us by taking on human flesh, then "we, too, in this flesh will receive our reward" (v. 5). Chapter 14, which distinguishes between a "fleshly" and a "spiritual" Church, nevertheless concludes that "the flesh is able to share in so great a life and immortality, because the Holy Spirit cleaves to it" (v. 5). The author seems uninterested in arguing to the possibility of a resurrection from natural analogies, as his namesake Clement of Rome has done; his apology rests, rather, on the experience of the Holy Spirit in the present life of Christians, which confers a dignity on the human constitution that is incompatible with annihilation.

(h) Another Greek homily in this same Judaeo-Christian style of thought, dating probably from the late 160s, is *Melito of Sardis'* recently discovered discourse *On the Pasch*. This richly typological meditation on the paschal mystery focuses its attention almost exclusively on the meaning of the death of Jesus for the present Christian community. Except for a promise of resurrection, put into the mouth of Jesus as part of his final invitation to baptism and the salvation it imparts (103), the homily shows no direct concern for the specifically eschatological dimension of Christian faith.

The *Odes of Solomon*

The earliest collection of Christian liturgical poetry which we still possess is the so-called *Odes of Solomon*, composed almost certainly in Edessa, in either Greek or Syriac, in the first half of the second century. The language and theology of these sublime, mysterious hymns is classically representative of Semitic rather than Hellenistic Christianity; yet the apocalyptic element is almost entirely lacking, and the poems' vision of eschatological salvation is normally presented rather as something already experienced in the charismatic, poetic inspiration of the speaker and in the worship of his community.[36]

So the odist speaks in rich detail of having already tasted the Lord's light and rest, and having been taken himself to Paradise (11.11–16; 38); as "priest of the Lord," he invites his hearers to follow him there (20.7–9). He says that he has composed the *Odes*, in fact, as a consequence of being lifted up in the Spirit to heaven (36.1–2; cf. 21.6–8). The results of this kind of ecstatic experience, in both the speaker's life and in that of the community, are described in terms normally associated with God's future promises: Christ calls forth "those who have been afflicted," as if from their tombs, to possess joy and immortality and the gracious gift of their own souls (31.6f.); death is destroyed, "eternal life . . . has been given to all who trust in him" (15.9f.; cf. 11.11f.). The speaker has "removed his garments of skin" (25.8) and "put on incorruption" (15.8); he has been "crowned" by God and given justification, salvation and freedom (17.1–4).[37] The reason for this transformation is made clear in several places in the *Odes*: it is because he is united to Christ in love (3.7–9), because he "abides in the love of the Lord" (8.20–22; cf. 5.13–15), that the odist knows he already shares in eternal life. Indeed, it is the Incarnation of the eternal Word that has made this loving identification possible: "He became like me, that I might receive him. In form he was considered like me, that I might put him on" (7.4; cf. 7.6).

Striking, in any case, is the fact that the consciousness of salvation already won by Christ for his disciple so dominates the poet's consciousness that there is no direct mention in the *Odes* of the end of the world, judgment, or resurrection as future realities. These hymns are themselves a celebration of the Christian experience of ecstatic worship as a foretaste of the eschaton; as such, they are appropriately styled the "odes of the Lord's rest."[38]

The *Shepherd* of Hermas

The *Shepherd* of Hermas occupies a unique place in the development of second-century eschatology. Composed in its present form probably by the year 140, and possibly incorporating material (*Vis.* 1–4) from as early as the end of the first century, the work is essentially a compassionate and hopeful exhortation to do penance, addressed to the Church of Rome. It is cast in the form of five allegorical "visions," twelve paraenetic sections or "mandates," and ten parables or "similitudes." As P. Vielhauer has observed, "the book is an Apocalypse in its form and style, but not in its contents, since it includes no disclosures of the eschatological future or of the world beyond."[39] In fact, it explicitly refuses to offer even symbolically veiled information on the time or character of a coming crisis. In his vision of the building of the tower – an obvious allegory for the growth of the Church – the narrator asks specifically "in regard to the ages, if now there is the conclusion." His angelic visitor's reply sets the tone as well as the content of the whole work:

"Foolish man! do you not see the tower yet building? When the tower is finished and built, then comes the end; and I assure you it will be soon finished. Ask me no more questions. Let you and all the saints be content . . . with my renewal of your spirits" (*Vis.* 3.8.9).

In one sense, Hermas considers the eschaton to have begun already; it is this that gives peculiar urgency to his call for reform. Christ's coming as a human being, he observes, began "the last days of the consummation" (*Sim.* 9.12.3). The end is not far off; yet the completion of the "tower" has been delayed (*Sim.* 9.5.1), to allow those "stones" or structured members which have been made unfit by sin time to repent and be included in the building (*Sim.* 9.14.2; 10.4.4).[40] Stones that do not fit into the tower are ultimately to be cast aside (*Vis.* 3.2.7,9; 3.7.1–2); so "the heathen and the sinners" will be burned like dry branches in "the world to come" (*Sim.* 4.2–4). Some sinners are capable of repentance, but for those who are not, eternal destruction lies ahead (*Sim.* 6.2.4; 8.7.3; 8.8.2–5; 8.11.3). The righteous, on the other hand, are guaranteed life in the world to come (*Vis.* 2.3.2f.; 4.3.5); they will "dwell with the Son of God" (*Sim.* 9.24.4), and "their place is already with the angels" (*Sim.* 9.27.3; cf. 9.25.2; *Vis.* 2.2.7). Significantly, Hermas does not mention a resurrection, and gives little concrete description of the rewards of the blessed life, except for the detail that those who have been persecuted will sit on the Lord's right in a place of special honor (*Vis.* 3.1.9–2.3). His concern is to motivate repentance rather than to offer solace in persecution.

This allegorical tract, then, is more a call for the reform of the present Church than a proclamation of the future God is about to bring; still, the Church of its vision is clearly an eschatological as well as a historical reality. In the *Vision* with which the work begins, she is the first of God's creatures (*Vis.* 2.4.1), who grows younger and more radiant through the courage and holiness of her members, until she finally appears as a virgin bride (*Vis.* 4.2.1–2). It is only this last, youthful personification of the Church who is able to reassure the seer that the "beast" who confronts him (hostile secular authority) is harmless, and that he can escape "the great tribulation" to come by sincere repentance (*Vis.* 4.2.3–5).[41] It is the Church herself, in her present and her future form, the community where conversion and penance are possible, which has become for Hermas the central eschatological sign.

Millenarian Christianity in Asia Minor

The central and western mountains of Asia Minor had been a center of ecstatic cults long before the coming of Christianity;[42] it was no surprise, then, that early Christian communities there should be touched by the "enthusiasm" of local pagan traditions, as well as by Jewish influences. Our

17

evidence for early Asiatic theology is second-hand and fragmentary, but it suggests that at least some Christian communities in this region cherished the hope of a coming "millennium" similar to that expressed in the Johannine Apocalypse (20.1–21.5): the expectation of a period of a thousand years to follow the return of Christ and the resurrection of the saints, in which members of the Christian sect, now persecuted, will enjoy a richly endowed Paradise on earth before the final defeat of Satan and the transformation of this world into a totally new creation. *Cerinthus*, an early Gnostic leader of apparently Jewish Christian background[43] who was probably active in western Asia Minor about the year 100, was universally supposed by later writers to have proclaimed the coming of such a millennial kingdom, in which all sorts of luxury and sensual delights would be available for its members.[44] According to Epiphanius (*Pan* 28.6.1), Cerinthus also taught that Christ had not yet truly risen, but would only do so at the time when all the dead are raised (cf. Augustine, *De Haer* 8). In third-century Egypt, opponents of the canonicity of the Johannine Apocalypse apparently attributed the book to Cerinthus (Dionysius of Alexandria, quoted by Eusebius, *HE* 7.25.1–3) – probably because of the millenarian passage in ch. 20 and perhaps also because of its Asiatic origin.

Papias, bishop of Hierapolis in Phrygia in the early second century, apparently also had had close contact with the community in which the Johannine writings were produced. He is known to have collected material about Jesus and his disciples from oral sources, and to have arranged it in five books entitled *Explanations of the Words of the Lord* ($\Lambda o \gamma i \omega \nu$ $K \upsilon \rho \iota a \kappa \hat{\omega} \nu$ $\dot{\epsilon} \xi \eta \gamma \dot{\eta} \sigma \epsilon \iota \varsigma$). According to Irenaeus (*AH* 5.33.3–4), book 4 of Papias' collection contained, among teachings attributed to Jesus, a vivid description of a coming millennial kingdom, in which the fruitfulness of the earth will be increased to staggering proportions for the sake of the risen saints. Papias' authority became the basis of Irenaeus' own millennial expectations at the end of the second century; Eusebius, however (*HE* 3.39.13), found Papias' millenarianism proof of his "very small intelligence."[45]

Montanism, the prophetic sect that originated in this same region (Phrygia) about 170, is also generally thought to have been dominated by a vivid expectation of the Parousia, as well as by a sense of the active presence of the Spirit within the believing community. Aside, however, from one saying attributed by Epiphanius (*Pan* 48.2–4) to the Montanist prophetess Maximilla – "After me there will be no more prophets, but only the consummation" – and from the celebrated Montanist belief that the new Jerusalem, when it descended from heaven, would descend on the Phrygian village of Pepuza, there is nothing in the ancient sources to suggest the sect had any marked apocalyptic character, or that its eschatological hope differed substantially from the general sense of second-century Christians that the end was near. The criticism directed against the Montanist community by orthodox writers centers on the anti-institutional implications of its reliance on post-biblical prophecy, rather than on any of its explicit doctrines.[46]

2

Making history intelligible: eschatology and the apologists

The first Christian theologians who attempted to address the social and intellectual establishment of the pagan Hellenistic world, and to articulate Christian beliefs and defend Christian religious practice to them on their own terms, were the second-century writers now known as the apologists. Their works give a central place to the Christian hope in a bodily resurrection, and often mingle the eschatological expectations of apocalyptic Judaeo-Christianity with mythical and philosophical speculation on the rewards and punishments that can be justly expected to follow this life.

Aristides

The earliest apologist whose work we possess is Aristides, who addressed a defense of Christianity to the Emperor Hadrian (117–138). Aristides repeatedly emphasizes the ethical uprightness of Christians, which he attributes to their expectation of a resurrection, followed by divine judgment and recompense for their deeds (*Apology* 15f.). When a member of their community dies who was known to be virtuous, Aristides asserts, the Christians "rejoice and thank God . . . as if he were only being transferred from one place to another"; but when a sinner dies, they weep bitterly over him, because they know he is sure to be punished (*ibid.*).

Justin

The most important and innovative of the apologists, Justin, composed his two *Apologies* and his *Dialogue with Trypho* between 155 and 165. These works were aimed at convincing the Roman and the Hellenized Jewish worlds, respectively, of the moral uprightness of Christians and the truth of their gospel; in both cases, Justin's argument is centered on an appeal to the fulfillment of biblical prophecy in the person and the works of Jesus. Because his interests are both biblical and apologetic, Justin frequently lays great stress on the Christian expectation of coming judgment and reward, and does so in the familiar terms of Jewish apocalyptic.

Christians are marked out from the rest of pleasure-loving human society, he argues, by their conviction that the wicked will be punished in eternal fire, and the Christ-like just united with God, free from suffering (*II Apol* 1; cf. *I Apol* 14). This is the reason Christians are truthful in affirming their faith (*I Apol* 8), as well as the ground of their good citizenship (*ibid.*, 12) and their ultimate fearlessness before the threat of persecution (*ibid.*, 17). But the relevance of the Christians' vision of the end is not simply for their own comfort, in Justin's view. It is the just judgment of a provident and all-knowing God, not the necessity of fate, that provides the final intelligibility of history (*I Apol* 43f.). He is convinced that God's day of reckoning, over which the triumphant Christ will preside, is coming very soon (*Dial* 28; 32; 40). This "great and terrible day" (*ibid.*, 49) will mean judgment of the whole world by a fire that will consume all things (*II Apol* 7; cf. *I Apol* 20) and purify the just (*Dial* 116). Christ will then "appear in Jerusalem" (*Dial* 85) and destroy all his enemies (*I Apol* 45; *Dial* 121), including the "man of sin" foretold by Daniel (*Dial* 32). In several places, Justin suggests that the end has been delayed until his time of writing because the "number of the just" to be included in the Kingdom is still incomplete (*I Apol* 28; 45; *Dial* 39). It is in this sense, probably, that he asserts "the seed of the Christians" is the reason God now refrains from destroying the world (*II Apol* 7).

Until the time of resurrection and judgment comes, Justin foresees some kind of provisional reward for the just and punishment for sinners after death. Although not strictly immortal – because their existence is not eternal like God's – human souls do survive with sensation after death, "the souls of the pious remaining in a better place, while those of the unjust and wicked are in a worse one" (*Dial* 5; cf. *ibid.*, 105; *I Apol* 18, 20). However, according to Justin every true Christian expects that "we will receive again our own bodies, though they be dead and cast into the earth, for we maintain that with God nothing is impossible" (*I Apol* 18; cf. *ibid.*, 19; *Dial* 80; 85: "the mystery of our own regeneration").

The beatitude of the saved, for Justin, will be enjoyed in two stages. Initially, they will possess the land that formerly was Canaan (*Dial* 113, 139), and will reign there with Christ for a thousand years in a renewed Jerusalem, enjoying all the peace and prosperity prophesied in Isaiah 65.17–25 (*ibid.*, 80f.). This millennial Kingdom, according to one passage (*ibid.*, 81), is only a prelude to Christ's final judgment and retribution: "thereafter the general, and, to put it briefly, eternal resurrection and judgment of all will . . . take place." Other passages, however, speak of an eternal possession of the Holy Land by the saints "after the holy resurrection" (*ibid.*, 113; cf. 139). The heart of the reward of the saints, for Justin, in any case, is "incorruption and fellowship" with God (*I Apol* 10), an immortality (*ibid.*, 21; *Dial* 45) and vitality that includes the body and its natural environment as well as the "inner" faculties. Sinners, on the other hand, will receive back "the same bodies" they now have, in order to undergo eternal punishment (*I Apol* 8) with Satan and the demons (*ibid.*, 28; 52) in Gehenna (*ibid.*, 19). Justin almost invariably describes this punishment as everlasting fire (*I Apol* 12; 17; 28; 52; 57; *II Apol* 1f.; 7f.; *Dial* 45).

All of this forms the eschatological perspective of Justin's two *Apologies* and his *Dialogue with Trypho*; other works were also attributed to him in antiquity, including several long fragments of a treatise *On the Resurrection*, found chiefly in the *Sacra Parallela* associated with John Damascene. Although probably not by Justin,[1] this work confronts the typical objections raised against the Christian hope for a bodily resurrection in Greek intellectual circles – pagan and Christian – during the late second and third centuries: it is physically impossible, given the constant flux of matter; it is inappropriate, because the body is sinful; most of all, it is unnecessary if the soul, which is the core of human identity, is immortal. The author handles these objections in a forthright apologetic manner, along lines of argument similar to those later followed by Athenagoras, Tertullian and Augustine (3–8), and then goes on to argue to the certainty of our resurrection from the reality of Christ's risen body (9), and from the consistent Christian proclamation that the whole human person is called to salvation (10). The work is probably part of an anti-Gnostic tract composed during the century after Justin's death.

Tatian

In his *Address to the Greeks*, probably composed soon after 165, Justin's pupil Tatian also emphasizes the Christian hope of resurrection and judgment in his proclamation of the gospel to cultured pagans. For Tatian, the human person was originally created both with his own soul or $\psi v \chi \acute{\eta}$ and with a share in the Spirit ($\pi v \epsilon \hat{v} \mu a$) of God (12; 15); it was this higher Spirit that made humans into God's image and likeness, notably by letting them share in God's distinctive characteristic of immortality (7). Of its own nature, the human soul, like the body, is mortal (13). After its creation, the soul chose to submit to the "laws of death" implied in its material surroundings, and lost its share in the Spirit that made it immortal (15). After the fiery "consummation" ($\sigma v v \tau \acute{\epsilon} \lambda \epsilon \iota a$)[2] of the world and its history (6; 17), however, the souls and bodies of all human beings will be reconstituted and restored to immortality, though both have been "dissolved for a time" (13). Sinners will be raised to "receive death by punishment in immortality" (*ibid.*), while the just will receive the "blessed immortality" of knowing God (*ibid.*; 14) and being reunited with his Spirit (15). Then, in a place beyond the limitations of the world we know, "the spirit, together with the soul, will acquire a clothing for its mortality . . . It is possible," Tatian adds, "for everyone who is naked to obtain this apparel, and to return to the soul's ancient kindred" (20).[3] The way to attain such immortality is by "submitting to death in faith" – presumably faith in the risen Jesus – and so overcoming the sinful subjection to matter that is death's ultimate source (15).

Athenagoras

The apologist Athenagoras, known in Christian antiquity as "the Athenian philosopher," probably composed his *Plea for the Christians* about the year 177. Like Justin, Athenagoras stresses the moral importance for Christians of their hope for resurrection and a future life, both because it entails the prospect of judgment (12) and because it affirms so concretely the value of human existence (31). Only divine being is eternal of its own nature (4); but the Christian expects to share in God's imperishability, "since we shall abide near God and with God, free from all change or suffering in the soul – not as flesh, even though we shall all have flesh, but as heavenly spirit" (31). Humans who "fall" in the coming judgment will also endure "in fire"; no one will simply be annihilated (*ibid.*).

The authorship of the treatise *On the Resurrection of the Dead* which is associated with Athenagoras' name has been questioned by some modern scholars, but the weight of present opinion seems to be in favor of the attribution.[4] If genuine, the work is perhaps the earliest full-fledged apology, on philosophical grounds, for Christian hope in the resurrection of the body; the work could also be called the earliest essay in Christian anthropology. The author insists both that it is possible for God to raise the disintegrated bodies of the dead (2–11) and that the purpose of creation, the nature of human existence, and simple justice require God to do so (12–23).

The author assumes that resurrection means the reconstitution of the bodies in which we now live, and the reuniting of them to the same souls we now have (25). The difficulties in such a reconstitution are obvious, especially when one considers the constant process of transformation which matter undergoes, and the possibility that the same particles of matter can be assimilated in succession by different organic beings (4). Aside from insisting that God's knowledge and creative power are both sufficient to effect such a reconstitution (9), the author argues that the matter which truly belongs to the essence of an individual human body can never be assimilated by another being to become part of its central identity, too (7f.).

In the second part of the work, the author argues from the acknowledged immortality of the soul that human beings were created to live forever (13);

since the human person is a composite of body and soul, this end will be vitiated if both aspects of his or her nature do not endure together (15). The discontinuity introduced into this life by death is no more permanent than the daily discontinuity of sleep (16). So the moral necessity of judgment and recompense are not, for this author, the only rational arguments in favor of resurrection (14); nevertheless, our moral choices are incoherent without such a future reckoning (19), and justice requires the survival of the whole person to take final responsibility for his or her actions (20–21).

Theophilus of Antioch

Theophilus of Antioch's apologetic treatise *To Autolycus*, probably written *c.* 180, deals with the Christian eschatological hope in a less philosophical, more biblical way than does the treatise we have just discussed. Central in Theophilus' hope, too, is a sense of the appropriateness of a final divine recompense after death: justice demands that the believer be "made immortal" in body and soul and "see God worthily" in a new and incorrupt life (1.7; 1.14; cf. 2.26), while the unbeliever is to be consigned to everlasting fire (1.14).

Theophilus finds "vestiges" or analogies of the promised resurrection of the body in the succession of seasons, the growth of seeds, and the waxing and waning of the moon (1.13). Human nature, however, has no intrinsic claim on immortality, which, for Theophilus as for Tatian, is proper only to God (1.4). The human person is "neither immortal nor mortal, but capable of both, so that if he should incline to the things of immortality, keeping the commandment of God, he should receive as reward from him immortality and become God; but if he should turn to the things of death, disobeying God, he should himself be the cause of death to himself" (2.27; cf. 2.24). So immortality is at once a pure gift, and yet something one "procures for oneself" by faith and action (2.27).

Theophilus is also the first Christian theologian to speak of Christian fulfillment expressly in terms of divinization. The place of this transformation from a human to a divine mode of life will be Paradise, a place "intermediate between earth and heaven" (2.24); there those who have sought for God and kept his commandments will rediscover the original harmony of created nature (2.17), and receive new, unparalleled gifts that will allow them to share in the nature of God (2.26).

3

Regaining the light: eschatology in the Gnostic crisis (150–200)

By the middle of the second century of our era, the existence of Gnostic groups, alongside and within the larger bodies of Christians throughout the Empire, posed a serious problem both to the interpretation of the gospel and to the life and worship of the communities. The challenge of Gnostic views of God, the world and human salvation prompted Christian writers and leaders to reflect in new depth on the shape of authentic Christian tradition, as well as on the criteria for determining its content.

Gnosticism was not simply a Christian heresy, nor was it a unified, theologically coherent religious movement. It was rather a type of elitist religious thought, present in Jewish and philosophical pagan circles as well as in a fairly wide range of Christian ones, which claimed privileged access to a kind of knowledge that could revolutionize the believer's understanding of existence. Gnostics generally regarded the world of ordinary experience and work as having only a low grade of reality, and promised escape from matter and union with the transcendent source of being to the favored few who accepted the esoteric knowledge that the group possessed. Although our knowledge of Gnostic doctrine formerly depended, for the most part, on hostile Christian sources like Irenaeus, Hippolytus and Epiphanius, the recent publication of the collection of Coptic Gnostic documents found at Nag Hammadi in Egypt in 1947[1] has made available a wealth of original documents that are only beginning to be studied. The dates of composition of these works, however, seem to range between the mid second and mid fourth centuries; their sectarian origin is often unclear, their language heavily veiled in the symbols of cult and cosmic myth, and their teaching sometimes obscure to the point of unintelligibility. It is impossible, therefore, to give an exposition of Gnostic eschatology that is completely consistent or universally representative of our ancient sources.

Practically all Gnostic groups, Christian, Jewish or pagan, seem to have taught, through elaborate mythic narratives of the origins of things, that the present world is only an accidental by-product of a much larger, more complex history: the work of ignorant and subordinate cosmic forces, which is destined to pass away when their time of power comes to an end. Our bodies, like the rest of material creation, were generally considered by Gnostics as a prison for the true, immaterial self, rather than a constitutive part of that self (e.g., *Apocryphon of John* 30.25–31.4) – a coarse and illusory shell untouched by redemption. So Christian writers often accused the Gnostics of denying both the relevance of the world and our actions to future salvation, and the Christian hope for the resurrection of the body (e.g., Irenaeus, *AH* 1.24.5 [Basilides]; 1.27.3 [Cerdo and Marcion]; Epiphanius, *Pan* 42.5.1 [Marcion]; Tertullian, *Adv Marc* 5.10 [Marcion]).

In reality, Gnostic eschatology seems to have been a good deal more complex than this. Salvation, in virtually all Gnostic teaching, is certainly conceived as the restoration of the luminous elements in this world that belong to the highest, least material, realms of reality – namely, the souls of the initiate – to their place in the *pleroma* or original "full complement" of hierarchically ordered divine beings. For Valentinian Gnosis, this was simply a "restoration" (*apokatastasis*) of heavenly reality to its original state (so *Treatise on the Resurrection* [*Ep to Rheginus*] 44.31; cf. Irenaeus, *AH* 1.8.4; 1.14.1 [Marcosians]; *Origin of the World* 127.14–17; *Gospel of Philip* 67.15–18; *Trip Tract* 122.19–23). Basilides, however, the early second-century Alexandrian Gnostic teacher, taught that even the "seed" of this future life, which is to saved from this world, was made by the supreme God from nothing, and that it grows to a state of full sonship which is infinitely beyond its origins. Those creatures who are not blessed with this degree of fulfillment – a fulfillment Basilides conceived in terms of unitive knowledge and love – will at least be consoled by "enormous ignorance," so that, in the end, every member of the cosmos will be content to remain within the limitations of its own nature (so Hippolytus, *Elench* 6.27.1–4).[2]

Within the framework of their "enlightened" depreciation of the material cosmos, some Gnostic sects seem to have made free use of apocalyptic traditions about the end of the world. According to Irenaeus (*AH* 1.7.1), the Valentinians held that when the souls of the righteous reach their final place of rest, "that fire which lies hidden in the world will blaze forth and burn" until all matter, and the fire itself, is destroyed. Several of the Nag Hammadi documents, notably *On the Origin of the World* and *The Concept of our Great Power* (both probably fourth-century works), as well as the non-Christian tract from the same collection called *The Paraphrase of Shem*, contain descriptions of this destruction of the universe in the grand apocalyptic style. Amid thunder and earthquakes (*Origin* 125.33f.; *Concept* 44.5; *Paraphrase* 44.11) and disturbances in the cosmic order (*Origin* 126.10–14; *Concept* 45.31–46.5; *Paraphrase* 45.9–31), the "archons," or leaders of the opposition to truth, will stir up confusion and war (*Concept* 43.35–44.31;

Origin 126.5–8; *Paraphrase* 44.22–26) on earth at the climax of human history. An "imitator" of the Savior will deceive many into following him (*Concept* 45.1–24) and there will be widespread disease and depopulation (*Origin* 126.3f.; *Concept* 44.6–10). In the end, however, the forces of the primeval Pleroma will vent their wrath on the earth (*Origin* 126.19–21; *Concept* 46.22–47.9), cast the hostile powers into a fiery abyss (*Origin* 126.22–35; *Concept* 46.29–33; cf. *Paraphrase* 45.14–30) and lead the faithful into eternal light (*Origin* 126.35–127.14; *Concept* 47.9–26).

The fate of human individuals is usually not clearly distinguished, in Gnostic documents, from the fate of the "light" or "dark" elements in the cosmos as a whole.[3] The *First Apocalypse of James* (33.2–36.1) tells, in folkloric style, of a kind of trial held at each person's death by three demons acting as toll-collectors;[4] normally, however, Gnostic writings conceive of death as a blessed release. The reward of the enlightened, who have accepted the saving knowledge revealed to them by the sect, is described in the following terms: as rest (e.g., *Gosp Truth* 22.9–12; 24.14–21; 41.28f.; *Treatise on Res* 44.1ff.; *Gosp Philip* 71.14f.), light and glory (*II Treatise of Great Seth* 67.10; 68.7f.; *Gosp Philip* 85.24–86.5; *Concept* 46.8–12), close fellowship with the rest of the saved (*II Treatise of Great Seth* 67.32–68.5; 68.9–13), and loving union with the Father of all things (*Gosp Truth* 41.30–34). The *Gospel of Philip* describes the goal of salvation as the consummation of a mystical marriage between the soul and truth or light, foreshadowed on earth in the community's liturgy of initiation (67.14–30; 84.20–86.8; cf. *II Treatise of Great Seth* 57.7–27; 67.5–18).

Positive punishment for those who reject the saving *gnosis* is less often described in the Gnostic treatises. The *Book of Thomas the Contender*, however, describes the fate of apostates from the initiate community as fire, a continually frustrated concern for the things of the flesh, and immersion in an abyss of bitterness (141.4–18; 141.32–142.2; cf. *Pistis Sophia* 147), and gives a vivid description of the imprisonment and torture of each apostate in Tartarus (*ibid.*, 142.11–143.7; cf. *Apocryphon of John* 30.25–31.4, equating Hades with "the prison of the body"). Other Gnostic documents speak, more encouragingly, of a purifying punishment of each soul after death, "until she is liberated from forgetfulness and acquires knowledge" (*Apocr John* 27.4–11; cf. *Concept* 46.23–33); the *Pistis Sophia* describes in some detail the purification of all departed souls – even sinless ones – in fire, until they are judged worthy to drink the "water of forgetfulness" (144–47).[5]

Some Gnostic documents emphasize the future character of this eschatological fulfillment, while others stress its present availability through the sect's tradition of revealed knowledge. The *Tripartite Tractate*, for instance, suggests that much time will be needed for the perfection that has been achieved in the Logos to be accomplished in his members; only when all are perfected will the Logos and his body be "restored" to the Pleroma (122.25–124.3; cf. 136.7–24). The *Gospel of Truth*, on the other hand, refers, in Johannine terms, to a "judgment" that has already been accomplished (25.25–26.26). The *Treatise on the Resurrection (Ep to Rheginus)*[6] pointedly interprets the traditional Christian hope of resurrection as being a call to disregard fleshly existence and "enter into the wisdom of those who have known the Truth" (46.30ff.; 47.2–12). Resurrection, as an event in history, is for this author simply the anthropological phenomenon of enlightenment, "the disclosure of those who have risen" (48.5f.). "Therefore do not think in part," he urges his reader, "or live in conformity with the flesh for the sake of unanimity, but flee from the division and the fetters, and already you have the resurrection" (49.9–16; cf. 49.22ff.).

Those Gnostic groups that made use of sacramental rites seem to have found in liturgical symbols a way to express a fruitful tension between the present, typological communication of saving enlightenment and a fuller realization of that salvation after death (so especially *Gosp Phil* 66.7–23; 67.14–19; cf. Irenaeus on the initiation rites of the Marcosians: *AH* 1.21.3). The *Gospel of Philip* refers to this tension in a more general way when it remarks with characteristic vagueness: "The mysteries of truth are revealed, though in type and image. The bridal chamber, however, remains hidden. It is the holy in the holy . . . If anyone becomes a son of the bridal chamber, he will receive the light. If anyone does not receive it while he is in these places, he will not be able to receive it in the other place" (84.20–23; 86.4–7). In so far as we may speak of a single eschatological hope in Gnosticism at all, its heart is expressed here, in the promised continuity between the present enlightenment claimed by the sect and an eternal sharing in a saving, but largely hidden, truth.

Irenaeus

The broad, synthetic theological vision of Irenaeus of Lyons, including his presentation of the Christian hope, must be seen above all as a polemical response to the typical Gnostic understanding of God, the world and human salvation. Irenaeus' theology is essentially a plea for the validity of ordinary Christian life and tradition, in the ordinary world. As a result, Irenaeus stresses unities: the unity of God as creator and savior, in contrast to the Marcionite and Gnostic tendency to see in the world continuing conflict between warring supercosmic forces; the personal unity of Christ, as both the eternal Word, the agent of creation, and a full participant in our fleshly, human life; the unity of every person, as a single composite of spirit and flesh who is called, as such, to salvation through Christ; and the unity and continuity of all human history, which begins in its creation by a loving

God, endures the temporary defeat of sin, and is now – thanks to the Incarnation of the Word – drawing near to the lasting union of the human race with God that was history's goal from the start.

Salvation, for Irenaeus, is not so much God's unexpected intervention in history to rescue his faithful ones from destruction as it is the end-stage of the process of organic growth which has been creation's "law" since its beginning. So eschatology, in the apocalyptic sense of the expectation of a wholly new age, is replaced in Irenaeus' theology by a grand, continuous conception of salvation-history, whose final achievement lies in the not-too-distant future.[7] A famous passage in book IV of his *Adversus Haereses* (written in Lyons about 180 as a polemical tract against local varieties of Gnostic Christianity) summarizes biblical history in the following terms: "It was necessary that the human person should in the first instance be created; and having been created, should receive growth; and having received growth, should be strengthened; and having been strengthened, should abound; and having abounded, should recover [from the disease of sin]; and having recovered, should be glorified; and being glorified, should see his Lord. For God is the one who is yet to be seen, and the beholding of God is productive of immortality, but immortality renders one near unto God" (*AH* 4.38.3).

In this perspective, immortal and incorruptible life appears as the goal of God's plan for humanity from its very creation. Immortality is clearly a gift of God, not a right of nature: for "the soul itself is not life, but partakes in that life bestowed upon it by God" (*AH* 2.34.4). Yet the gift is as old as its recipients, in Irenaeus' scheme; the first humans lost it by breaking God's commandment (*Demonstration of the Apostolic Teaching* 15), but God remains with his creation and gradually renews it for the sake of his human creatures, "so that coming to maturity in them, he may produce the fruit of immortality" (*AH* 4.5.1). The heart of this work of renewal, for Irenaeus as for his Gnostic opponents, is revelation, carried on by the activity of the Word and by the enlivening presence of the Holy Spirit. Its fruit is the vision of God (*AH* 4.20.5–7), the knowledge of God (*ibid.*, 5.12.4) that confers immortality and incorruptibility on the human person; this has already been communicated to us in scriptural prophecy and in the "portion" of the Spirit given to us in the Church (*ibid.*, 3.24.1). "We do now receive a certain portion of his Spirit," Irenaeus writes, "tending towards perfection and preparing us for incorruption, being little by little accustomed to receive and bear God" (*ibid.*, 5.8.1). It is through the "fellowship with God" involved in this charismatic gift of knowledge, ultimately, that we "partake of incorruption" (*Dem* 40; cf. *AH* 5.27.1).

Within the context of this providentially directed process of the human race's maturing, Irenaeus sketches out a clear, distinctive picture of the eschatological future humanity can hope for. Rejecting the doctrine of some Gnostic groups that the recipients of sectarian knowledge have thereby already experienced resurrection, he insists that all of us must "observe the law of the dead," as Christ did (AH 5.31.1–2). Our souls will be separated from our bodies, and "go away to the invisible place allotted to them by God" (ibid., 5.31.2), where – as shades – they will retain the "form" of their body and memory of their existence on earth, but not its fleshly substance (ibid., 2.34.1–2). Irenaeus paints the end of human history – which he clearly expects soon[8] – in traditional and vivid apocalyptic colors. The Antichrist will appear in Jerusalem, endowed with all the powers of the devil, and usurp the place of God, persecuting all the saints and "recapitulating in himself the whole history of sin" (ibid., 5.25; 5.28–30). Then Christ will come again in glory as judge (ibid., 4.33.1) and will cast the Antichrist and his followers into "the lake of fire" (ibid., 5.30.4). Christ's judgment will be a "winnowing," a sifting of wheat from chaff (ibid., 4.4.1; 4.33.1); it will be terrible (ibid., 4.33.13; 4.36.3), yet utterly necessary if God's constant providence and Christ's return to the earth are to be seen to have a meaning (ibid., 5.27.1). It will be the "day of retribution" prophesied by Isaiah as the end of the "acceptable year of the Lord," in which salvation is available to all (ibid., 2.22.1–2). Destructive as they will be for the wicked, the tribulations of the end will only refine and purify the just (ibid., 5.28.4; 5.29.1).

Central to Irenaeus' hope is the resurrection of the body, which he expects at the time of Christ's return. Hope in such a resurrection is an integral part of the Christian tradition of faith Irenaeus is concerned to protect (see AH 1.10.1; 1.22.1; 3.16.6 – all formulaic passages; cf. 3.12.3, where "the resurrection of the dead" is made the content of apostolic preaching). His argument is essentially a moral one: for adequate retribution to be possible, divine justice requires that both the just and the unjust should rise in "their own bodies" as well as "their own souls" (AH 2.33.5).[9] Consistent with this, Irenaeus insists on the fleshly reality of risen bodies: only such a hope can take seriously God's continued involvement with his creation (AH 5.2.2), the biblical promise of "the salvation of the flesh," and the double reality of the Church – at once spiritual and worldly – that is reflected in our celebration of the Eucharist (ibid., 4.18.5; 5.2.3; cf. 4.38.1).

The long section AH 5.1–15, in fact, is an apologia for the material reality of the resurrection of the body, based mainly on passages in Scripture. Beginning from the fleshly reality of Jesus' own humanity (1–2), Irenaeus stresses that the ability to raise the dead is implicit in God's creative power (3). To suggest that the God who saves us will not also raise our bodies is to suggest, as the Gnostics do, that the material world is made by a lesser God (4). If the whole human person is made by God to be the temple of his Spirit (6), and if Christ rose in the flesh (7), then our own bodies – transformed, certainly, and made spiritual by the gift of Christ's Spirit – must also rise (7–8). In chapters 9–15 of this section, Irenaeus refutes the Gnostic interpretation of the important text I Cor 15.50 ("Flesh and blood cannot inherit the Kingdom of God"), making use of many other scriptural passages to underline his central argument: namely, that "the Word has saved that which really was the humanity that had perished, effecting by means of himself that communion which should be held with it, and seeking out its salvation. But the thing which had perished possessed flesh and blood" (5.14.2); so that which will be saved must also possess them!

At the end of book 5 of *Adversus Haereses*, Irenaeus goes on, in his apologetic for the future of the material cosmos, to defend the millenarian hope represented by Papias and the "elders" of earlier Asiatic Christianity (cf. 5.33.3–4). Here he presents a prospect of human resurrection in two stages, arguing that "it is fitting for the righteous first to receive the promise of the inheritance which God promised the fathers, and to reign in it, when they rise again to behold God in this creation which is renewed, and that the judgment should take place afterwards" (*ibid.*, 32.1). Irenaeus supports this interpretation by referring to many biblical passages that promise salvation to Israel in typical terms of peace, prosperity and material restoration (*ibid.*, 33–35), and he insists that these may not be allegorized away (*ibid.*, 35.1–2). The purpose of such a millennial kingdom, he suggests, is to allow the just time, in the familiar setting of a renewed earth, to become gradually accustomed "to partaking of the divine nature" (*ibid.*, 32.1). Once again, however, Irenaeus' underlying concern seems to be to defend the inclusion of the material side of creation in the unified plan of God's salvation.[10]

At the end of this thousand-year period of preparation, Irenaeus foresees God's final judgment and retribution in terms of Apoc 20 and 21. All the dead will be raised, the unjust will be cast into the eternal fire of Gehenna, and "a new heaven and a new earth" – timeless and incorruptible – will be created as the abode of the just (*AH* 5.35.2; 5.36.1). The physical nature of the saved will be preserved, but transformed into a thing of inconceivable beauty (*ibid.*, 4.39.2; cf. 4.33.11). In accord with Jesus' promise that the seed of God's Word, falling on fertile ground, will bear fruit "a hundredfold, sixtyfold and thirtyfold" (Matt 13.23), Irenaeus foresees different grades of beatitude for the just, according to each one's merit: the most worthy will be taken to "heaven," the next will be taken to "Paradise" (presumably a place between heaven and earth), and the least worthy will "possess the splendor of the city" (*AH* 5.36.1–2).[11] Yet Irenaeus seems to imply the possibility of growth and advancement toward closer union with God even after the judgment, until at last all distinctions disappear (*ibid.*, 2; cf. 2.28.3, on our eternal capacity to "learn the things taught us by God"). Just as the real punishment for sinners will be separation from God – a separation which they have "chosen of their own accord"[12] – so the real reward of the just is "communion with God" (*ibid.*, 5.27.2; cf. 4.37.7; 4.38.3), "receiving God" (*ibid.*, 3.20.3) as life and light (*ibid.*, 5.27.2), and being made anew in God's image (*ibid.*, 5.36.3).[13] Such a relationship, Irenaeus implies, is neither static nor limited by human finitude: it is part of a history of growth, whose term is participation in the glory which is God's own life.

4

Senectus Mundi: eschatology in the West, 200–250

The first three decades of the third century were a period of political stability and cultural cohesion in the Roman Empire. It was not until the death of Alexander Severus in 235 that barbarian attacks, economic disasters, and conflicts over the imperial succession began a new period of violence and corruption which would last until the accession of Diocletian in 284. The relative prosperity and peace of the Severan period, however, did not make life any easier for the expanding network of Christian communities throughout the Empire. Christians continued to be despised by the intellectual elite and were considered suspicious by imperial bureaucrats; there were even occasional outbreaks of actual persecution, such as that in Egypt and North Africa during the reign of Septimius Severus (193–211). The social base of the Christian Church seems still to have been among "ordinary" people: uneducated merchants and laborers, who probably had little time for philosophical fashion and Roman cultural ideology. So the extant religious writings of the Western Church, especially, from this period show decidedly sectarian and anti-intellectual tendencies. Apology gives way to controversial theology; the efforts of apologists like Justin and Athenagoras to present Christianity to the cultured Hellenistic world in attractive and irenic terms are replaced now by bitter attacks on classical paganism, on Jewish and Judaeo-Christian teachings, and on the occult speculations of the Gnostics. A spirit of cultural criticism and a strong, often rigorist moral tone dominate most of the works produced within the main Christian community at this time.

This sense of social alienation and religious competition, understandably, had its effect on the articulation of the Christian eschatological hope. Popular expectation of an immediate end of the world seems to have reached fever pitch in many areas of the Western Roman Empire, especially during periods of persecution.[1] Christian writers concerned themselves more and more to reflect ordinary people's beliefs about the afterlife, and used popular expectations of future reward and punishment as an instru-

33

ment for reinforcing their own social and moral message. Irenaeus' integration of eschatology into a sweeping view of salvation-history that culminated in the Incarnation of the Word came now to be replaced – despite the lasting influence of Irenaeus' work – by an eschatology preached more for its own sake: one that organized biblical images and popular lore into a more and more comprehensive doctrine of life after death.

Tertullian

The Carthaginian lawyer Tertullian (*c*. 160–*c*. 220), who left the Catholic communion to join the Montanist sect by 207, represents the beginning of this subtle yet far-reaching change. Impassioned and brilliant in his rhetoric, often obscure and elusive in his ideas, Tertullian drew freely on biblical eschatology and on the writings of earlier Christian writers, particularly Justin and Irenaeus. He used these sources, however, for his own polemical and moralistic purposes, and colored them noticeably, in his later works, with Montanist shadings. For Tertullian, the coming end of history is above all to be a time of reckoning: the settling of accounts between God and those who have come to deserve reward or punishment (see *De Poen* 2.11). Thus Christian eschatological faith, as he formulates it, is caught in a tension between fear of judgment and dread of the suffering that the end of the present order will involve, and a longing to be free of the injustices and limitations of this age.[2]

Though he nowhere develops the subject at great length, Tertullian sees the end of the world, the *transactio mundi*, as both violent and very near (*Apol* 32; cf. *De Cult Fem* 2.6). The "spectacle" is approaching when "the world, hoary with age, and all its many products, shall be consumed in one great flame" (*De Spect* 30; cf. *De Bapt* 8). The Antichrist is "now close at hand and gasping for the blood, not for the money, of Christians" (*De Fuga* 12; cf. *De An* 50; *De Res* 25 for passing references to the Antichrist).

As part of his polemic against both skeptical pagans and dualist Gnostics, Tertullian emphasizes that Christians look forward to a universal resurrection when the material body of every person will rise again to share in the reward or punishment of its soul. In the *Apologeticum* (48), he incorporates this teaching into an attack on the pagan doctrine of metempsychosis; he argues that the reason for the universal resurrection is to enable all human beings to undergo judgment and retribution, "for the soul is not capable of suffering without solid substance."[3] Tertullian's explanation of the possibility of resurrection is based on the now-standard appeal to God's power: if God is capable of creating us out of nothing, he is surely able to reassemble us out of a state of material disintegration.

In *Adversus Marcionem* 5.9–10, Tertullian's main concern is to assert the reality of the flesh of the risen body, relying mainly on I Cor 15 and other scriptural proof texts. His treatise *De Carnis Resurrectione* is directed against Christian "heretics" – Gnostics or Marcionites – who deny the materiality of the risen body. After remarking on pagan and Jewish inklings of such a belief (1–3), Tertullian first defends the dignity and goodness of the flesh in general (5–10), then argues that God *can* reassemble the bodies he has created (11), that there are analogies for such an event in nature (12–13), and that justice requires God to do so (14–17). After a lengthy section assembling scriptural proofs for the coming resurrection (18–50), Tertullian argues powerfully for the identity of the risen body with this present one (51–56), appealing both to the example of the risen Jesus (51, 53) and to philosophical considerations on the identity of substances within change (55). He then speculates on the characteristics the risen body will have (57–62), insisting on its perfection (57–58) and integrity (59–61), even though many of its limbs and organs will no longer be needed for their present purposes. In short, the risen will be "like the angels" (so Luke 20.36), and so will experience, in this same substance of flesh, the characteristics of spiritual beings (*spiritalem subeant dispositionem* [62]; cf. *De An* 56, where Tertullian asserts that the state of the risen body will be determined by the "standard of the angels").[4]

Although he does not give it much emphasis in his works, Tertullian also defends, in a chapter of his treatise against Marcion (3.24), the millenarian tradition previously espoused by Justin and Irenaeus. He offers as confirmation the report that neutral eyewitnesses have recently seen something shaped like a city, suspended in the dawn sky over Judaea. Against the critics of the millenarian hope, Tertullian argues that the rewards promised to the faithful in the restored earthly Jerusalem are simply "a recompense for those which, in the world, we have either despised or lost." In his version of the tradition, the just will rise at various times during this millennium of reward, depending on their deserts. Only at the end of the thousand years "will ensue the destruction of the world and the conflagration of all things at the judgment." In other passages, however, he attacks a materialistic interpretation of the rewards promised to the just in the Old Testament and takes a more allegorical line of interpretation: for example, *De Res* 26, which identifies the "promised land" foretold by the prophets as "the Lord's flesh, which in all those who put on Christ is thenceforward the holy land."

The prospect of a future judgment, Tertullian insists, like the prospect of life after death, is something every reasonable person spontaneously assumes, as part of his or her innate sense of a morally concerned God (*De Test Animae* 2.6;4). So the classical poets and philosophers expected judgment and recompense after this life (*Apol* 47). Such things are implied by the naturally accessible conception of a God who sees all things (*De Spect*

20); Christian revelation only adds the clarification that Christ is the judge who is to come (*Adv Marc* 4.29; 4.39; 5.4; cf. *Apol* 18; 23).

Although he does not spend much time describing the rewards of the blessed,[5] Tertullian asserts that the final "Kingdom in heaven" will be of a very different order from the earthly millennial Kingdom that precedes it: "We shall then be changed in a moment into the substance of angels, even by the investiture of an incorruptible nature" (*Adv Marc* 3.24; cf. *De Res* 58). Tertullian understands Gehenna, however, where sinners will be punished, as real, if everlasting, fire (*De Res* 35; *Apol* 45; 47; *De Carne Christi* 14; *De Poen* 12). The paradoxical character of this fire, by which God "is able to destroy both body and soul in hell" (Matt 10.28), is that it "kills" without annihilating either of those substances: it brings about a "never-ending killing . . . more formidable than a merely human murder" (*De Res* 35). Punishment in that fire will be suited to each person's crimes (*De Spect* 30), and part of the joy Tertullian himself expects to share with the blessed is the sight of this "spectacle" of divine retribution (*ibid.*). Not until the universal resurrection and judgment, in any case, will final reward and punishment begin to be fully realized, according to Tertullian, since such final retribution demands, in justice, the participation of our bodies (*De Res* 17).

Even so, Tertullian elaborates more clearly than any Christian writer before him a theory of an "interim state," in which the souls of the dead await and even anticipate their final punishment or reward. He hints, in fact, that this picturesque conception of the beginnings of the afterlife before the resurrection is one of the charismatically inspired doctrines of the Montanist sect. So, at the end of his *De Anima* (cc. 55–58), he sketches out in some detail a picture of Hades, "an enormous subterranean space, hidden deep in the bowels of the earth," which serves as a "reception room" (*hospitium*) for all the dead, villains and heroes alike (55). Both the parable of Dives and Lazarus (57) and the tradition of Jesus' *descensus ad inferos* after his death, he argues (55), attest the existence of such a place. There souls live "in exile" (56) until the time of their resurrection, unchanged in age and form from the time of their death (*ibid.*) and unable to escape, even in response to the summons of sorcerers (57). Tertullian conjectures that "the soul undergoes punishment and consolation in Hades in the interval, while it awaits its alternative of judgment, in a certain anticipation of gloom and glory" (58). Such a foretaste is only just, since the soul is also capable of heroism or sin without the cooperation of the flesh (*ibid.*); and it is possible, he argues elsewhere, because the soul itself possesses a genuine, if subtle and very limited, corporeality (*De An* 7; *De Res* 17).

So Tertullian conceives of Hades as having "two regions," one for the good and one for the wicked (*De An* 56). The just are received into "Abraham's bosom . . . a temporary receptacle of faithful souls, where we find drawn, even now, an image of the future" (*Adv Marc* 4.34).[6] Sinners, on the other hand, begin already in Hades to suffer for their sins – especially the sins committed through the soul alone (*De Res* 17; *De An* 58). In two passages of the *De Anima* (35; 58), Tertullian applies to this pre-resurrection period of suffering in Hades the reference in Matt 5.26 to the "prison" from which the unforgiving believer will not be released until he has "paid the last farthing." This does not imply, for him, a limited suffering of purgation, but rather a temporary anticipation, in the sinner's soul, of the eternal fate of his whole person (so *De An* 58).[7]

Tertullian's vivid conception of the fate of individuals after death, then, grew from a variety of related sources: his apologetic and polemical concerns, his adherence to the Montanist prophecies, and his lawyer's zeal for the full enactment of divine justice. Despite his idiosyncrasies and the archaically picturesque quality of his thought, it was he who really laid the foundation for Latin Christendom's doctrine of "the last things."

The *Passio Perpetuae*

A similarly imaginative conception of life in Hades after death, as well as of the special rewards of martyrs, meets us in the *Passio Perpetuae et Felicitatis*, a contemporary account of the martyrdom of several Montanist Christians in Carthage, in March 203, which may have been edited by Tertullian himself. The account tells of several visions of the afterlife experienced by the young Christian matron Perpetua in prison, shortly before her death. In one series of such visions (7–8), Perpetua's pagan brother Dinocrates, who had died of cancer as a child, is seen progressing from a state of wretchedness and suffering to one of healing and refreshment, because of the prayers of the martyr.[8] Two other visions (4:11–12) reported in the *Passio* depict the future bliss of the martyrs as a life of joy and repose in a lush garden, where the angels are their companions and where God himself welcomes them and gives them refreshment. These visions, like the later works of Tertullian, reflect the Montanists' strong preoccupation with the prospect of life and retribution immediately after death, and give examples of the vivid images, drawn from both apocalyptic and classical sources, in which they gave that hope expression.

Minucius Felix

The apologetic dialogue *Octavius*, written by the Roman lawyer Minucius Felix, seems also to be roughly contemporary with the work of Tertullian and shows signs of dependence on Tertullian's works, especially his *Apologeticum* and *Ad Nationes*. As part of his defense of the reasonableness of

Christian beliefs, Octavius, the Christian spokesman in the dialogue, points to the similarity of the Christian eschatological hope to the speculations of pagan literature and philosophy about the future. Stoics and Epicureans, as well as Plato, share in the Christian conviction that the world will be consumed by fire (34); classical mythology, too, tells of the fiery torments of the underworld (35). Yet Christianity brings new clarity and purity to these ancient notions, according to Minucius Felix: so it replaces the unworthy theory of metempsychosis with the hope of a bodily resurrection – a doctrine which has its analogues in the natural world, but which is only explainable by the power of the creator God as he is known from the Bible (34). The Christian realizes that the "wise fire" of Hades – so called because it can discriminate between what is to be consumed and what is to be preserved for further burning, and so can torture some of its victims without destroying them – is reserved for those who do not know the true God (35).

So the Christian faces death with tranquillity, "since we, being both moderate and secure in the liberality of our God, are animated to hope in future felicity by the confidence of his present majesty. Thus we both rise again in blessedness, and are already living in contemplation of the future" (38). The tension between present and future in the Christian consciousness of salvation has been transferred here by Minucius Felix to the psychological level, and has become simply the present assurance of eternal life in a world to come.

Hippolytus

Hippolytus, traditionally thought to have been the Greek-speaking bishop of a schismatic church in Rome, who died as a martyr around 235, has been the subject of energetic controversy over the past forty years: the details of his career, and the extent of the corpus of writings to be attributed to him, are questions not yet entirely resolved.[9] Even if we assume unity of authorship for all but the certainly spurious fragments in that corpus – as we shall do here, for lack of compelling evidence to the contrary – a striking discontinuity is apparent in Hippolytus' eschatology, between the strongly apocalyptic predictions of his *Commentary on Daniel*, his treatise *De Christo et Antichristo*, and several of his exegetical and dogmatic fragments, on the one hand, and the more "realized" eschatology, emphasizing the divinization of the Christian, of the final section of the brief exposé of Christian faith appended to his *Refutation of all Heresies* (= *Elenchus*), on the other.

The treatise *De Christo et Antichristo* is in reality little more than a florilegium of apocalyptic passages – or passages capable of an apocalyptic interpretation – drawn from the Old and New Testaments and arranged in a dramatic sequence. According to Hippolytus' reconstruction, the end of history will be heralded unwittingly by a violent tyrant, who will imitate Christ in his attempt to win over all nations to himself (6.49). He will rebuild the temple in Jerusalem (6), but the political base of his rule will be the Empire of Rome, the "new Babylon" (30–36). This Antichrist will summon all people to follow him, and, by persuading them with false promises, will win most of them over for a time (54–58). The Church will then undergo great persecution (59–63); but at its height the Lord – preceded by two prophetic forerunners, John the Baptist and Elijah (64; cf. 44ff.) – will come in majesty, gather his faithful together on the site of Paradise (64), and "bring the conflagration and just judgment on all who have refused to believe in him" (ibid.). Then all the dead will rise, the just to enter the Kingdom and sinners to be cast into everlasting fire (65). Despite his desire to provide a cohesive and concrete narrative of history's final chapter, Hippolytus is cautious here in interpreting the traditional apocalyptic hints, given in Apoc 13 and 17, about the name of the Antichrist and the time of his coming: he is content simply to advance Irenaeus' tentative suggestions as the best interpretations available.

In his *Commentary on Daniel*, the oldest extant scriptural commentary, Hippolytus reaffirms this general scheme for conceiving history's end, and espouses the tradition that the reign of the Antichrist and the end of the world will come six thousand years after creation. Advancing several scriptural passages to prove Christ was born midway through the last millennium of history, he concludes that the end is not due until five hundred years after Christ's birth (4.23f.). After this will come a "Sabbath": "the future Kingdom of the Saints, when they will reign with Christ after his coming from heaven, as John narrates in the Apocalypse" (4.23). Despite his dependence on Irenaeus, Hippolytus does not develop this millenarian hope any further. His interest, in fact, in the *Commentary on Daniel*, is as much Christological as apocalyptic. It is Christ who will "give us power when all the strength and glory of this life is gone, will give us his hand and raise us, 'as living people from the dead,' from Hades for a resurrection to life" (4.39; cf. 4.56). It is Christ, too, who will judge the world when he comes at the end of time, overturning the present cosmic order to establish a new one (4.10). Nor does Hippolytus interpret the traditional apocalyptic hope in an exclusively cosmic direction; in one sense, he affirms, each of us reaches the end of the world at death. So our sense of moral responsibility will be reinforced if "each one recognizes that on the day when he leaves this world he is already judged; for the consummation has come upon him" (4.18).

Another important witness to Hippolytus' more apocalyptic strain, if it is genuine, is a sizeable fragment of his treatise *Against Plato, on the Cause of the Universe*.[10] Here the author sketches out what he understands as the

Christian view of the afterlife, using colorful, popular expectations in contrast to the Platonic doctrines of the immortality of the soul and metempsychosis. The similarity of the fragment's vision to Tertullian's picture of the underworld is striking in many respects. Souls after death are led by angel guardians to Hades, a dark and vast subterranean vault in which they are to be confined until the day of resurrection. Some of them – presumably sinners who have deserved damnation – undergo "temporary punishment for their ways" (*PG* 10.796A9f.), in anticipation of eternal punishment later on. Kept near the "lake of fire," which is Gehenna, they see its flames and smell its smoke, and so suffer already in fear of their coming condemnation (*PG* 10.797B10–C7). The just, on the other hand, are led to a much brighter, more pleasant part of the underworld called "Abraham's bosom." where they enjoy the company of the angels and patriarchs and rejoice in the vision of the rewards which are to come (*ibid.*, A13–B10).

Hippolytus then defends the Christian hope for a bodily resurrection, appealing simply to God's power to remake what he has created (*PG* 10.800A12–B9). The risen bodies of the just, unlike their present bodies, will be "pure and no longer corruptible" (*ibid.*, B13f.); but the unjust will rise just as they are, with all their present burden of disease and passion and without glory (*ibid.*, C6–10). After the resurrection, Christ will come to judge in his Father's name (*PG* 10.800D3–801A3), and will send sinners into eternal fire, where they will suffer without respite or hope of mitigation (*ibid.*, 801A9–15). The just will enter "the Kingdom of heaven," where they will remember their good deeds of the past (*ibid.*, B2–4) and enjoy free access to a hospitable universe, nourished by the fruits which the earth will spontaneously produce for them (*ibid.*, B10–C4). Although the features of this Kingdom strongly resemble those of the traditional millennium, Hippolytus does not portray it here as a passing era, but identifies it with ultimate beatitude.

In sharp contrast to these vivid images of temporary confinement and of punishment and reward after death, the concluding section of Hippolytus' heresiological work called the *Elenchus* (10.34) promises to the orthodox believer a more spiritual and internal fulfillment: he shall escape "the threat of fiery judgment" and "the ever-threatening eye of Tartarus' punishing angels" (10.34.2), to become "a familiar companion of God and a fellow-heir of Christ." The redeemed believer can expect to become immortal and incorruptible in body and soul, "no longer enslaved by desires, passions or disease, for he will become God" (10.34.3). For the Christian, in fact, the proverb "Know thyself" should lead to the recognition that one is already known and called by God in this life (10.34.4), already renewed by Christ and enabled to "imitate him" by "being made God" (10.34.5), for God's greater glory. The promise here is less concrete, perhaps, than the hope held out in the other writings attributed to Hippolytus, yet it reflects an early stage of a theological tradition whose roots are already to be found in Irenaeus. This very point may strengthen the case for seeing the *Elenchus* as the work of a different author from the Hippolytus of the exegetical and dogmatic treatises. In any event, this work anticipates more clearly than anything before it the human hope for an ultimate share in God's own life that will characterize the eschatology of the later Greek Fathers.[11]

Cyprian

For Cyprian, bishop of Carthage during the turbulent decade 248–58, the political disasters and the internal ecclesiastical crises of his own time provided the two principal spurs to theological thought. The persecutions of Decius (250) and Valerian (257–58), and the plague that ravaged the West in 252–54, provide the dark background for Cyprian's fluent, urgent reflections on Church unity and structure, on asceticism and the reconciliation of sinners, and on the details of the Christian's hope for the future which he offers as encouragement. Echoing the Stoic theme of the *senectus mundi*[12] with all the pathos of a trained rhetor, Cyprian often expresses the conviction that human history has reached its evening (*Ep* 63.16); the world was dying from a general depletion of its natural forces, and so showing the cumulative effects of sin (*Ad Dem* 3–8; cf. *Ep* 58.2). The sufferings of his own time were proof that "the world is failing, passing away, and it witnesses to its ruin not now by the age, but by the end of things" (*De Mort* 25; cf. *Ep* 61.4; 67.7). The six thousand years allotted to history since creation were nearing their term, by Cyprian's reckoning (*Ad Fort, praef.* 2); all the catastrophes of his own world had indeed been prophesied in the Bible for "the last times," and were proof that "the reward of life, and the rejoicing of eternal salvation, and the perpetual gladness and possession of paradise once lost are now coming, with the passing away of the world" (*De Mort* 2). The Christian should know from the Bible that "still more terrible things are imminent" (*De Mort* 25), but he or she also knows that even greater consolation lies beyond them.

Indeed, Cyprian stresses more than any previous Latin writer the greatness of the reward promised those who remain faithful in adversity. Yet lyrical descriptions of the beatitude of the just, either in spiritual or in millennial terms, are generally missing from Cyprian's works. Instead, he stresses to a striking degree the social and interpersonal dimensions of the hoped-for fulfillment. In heaven, which each Christian should regard as his or her true homeland, "a great number of our dear ones are awaiting us," along with the patriarchs, apostles and martyrs (*Ad Dem* 26; cf. *Ep* 58.10);

we can expect there nothing less than "the embrace and kiss and sight of the Lord" (*Ep* 6.4; cf. *Ep* 37.3) and the honor of standing beside him, as friend and fellow heir, when he sits in judgment (*Ad Fort* 13).

Cyprian also stands apart from previous Fathers in insisting that all those who live and die in fidelity to their Christian vocation will be admitted to the Kingdom immediately (e.g., *Ad Fort* 13). Many second- and third-century writers, as we have already seen, promised that martyrs would gain direct access to beatitude. Cyprian echoes this hope emphatically (e.g., *Ep* 31.3; 58.3), but adds to their number anyone who proves his or her discipleship by "having forsaken and condemned all his possessions," and who "stands in the firmness of the faith and in the fear of God" (*Ad Fort* 12). As a consequence, Cyprian constantly stresses the connection between merit and heavenly reward: "one does not attain the Kingdom of heaven," he observes in *De Unitate Ecclesiae*, "unless he walks in the observance of the right and just way" (*De Unit* 15; cf. *De Zelo* 18). Further, one must belong to the "peace of the Church" – must be in communion with the legitimately recognized Christian community – to "attain to the Kingdom"; even the martyr who dies outside the Church's communion will not be "crowned" (*De Unit* 15; cf. *Ep* 60.4). There are degrees of reward in heaven, too: the longer a martyr or confessor must suffer, "the loftier will be [his] crown" (*Ep* 37.3), while those who consecrate themselves to God by a life of virginity on earth will receive "a double glory," the hundredfold fruit of which the gospel speaks (*Ep* 76.6).[13] Yet for all his stress on merit, Cyprian is careful to point out, in *Ad Donatum* 14, that our salvation cannot be won by either bribery or exertion: "it is a gratuitous gift from God, and it is accessible to all."

Cyprian gives less emphasis to the punishment of sinners after death, and describes it in more conventional terms: they will be consigned to Gehenna, body and soul, "devoured with living flames" eternally, without hope of escape (*Ad Dem* 24; *Ep* 58.10).[14] Nor does he seem to have envisaged the possibility of a temporary, purgative suffering for certain classes of sinner after death. A passage in *Ep* 55.20 referring to the purgation of sins by "long suffering" and "fire," which leaves the sinner "in suspense till the sentence of God at the day of judgment," apparently refers, in its context, to the public penance practiced by *lapsi* who have been readmitted to Church life.[15] Cyprian stresses elsewhere, in fact, that once we have departed from this life, "there is no longer any place for repentance, and no possibility of making satisfaction" (*Ad Dem* 25).

In general, Cyprian's use of the Church's earlier eschatological tradition reinforces his urgent call to Christians to look beyond this world for their security in a difficult time (*ibid.*; *Ad Dem* 14), "since being Christian is, for us, essentially a matter of faith and hope" (*De Bono Pat* 13). It is through their hope that the rewards of the future can become a present force in the lives of the Christian confessors and virgins to whom Cyprian writes. "That which you shall be, you have already begun to be. You possess already in this world the glory of the resurrection" (*De Hab Virg* 22; cf. *Ep* 37.2). Eschatology here is "realized" in the gracious, astounding fact of Christian endurance.

5

A school for souls: Alexandrian eschatology and its critics (185–300)

Clement of Alexandria

It is always difficult to characterize the theological position of Clement of Alexandria (d. before 215), the first representative of the Alexandrian tradition of Greek Christian thought. A complex, subtle thinker as well as a learned, allusive writer, Clement draws on both the intellectualist, anthropocentric speculations of Platonic and Stoic cosmology, and on the esoteric, mythically couched revelations of the New Testament apocrypha and the Gnostic documents, in elaborating his understanding of the Christian eschatological hope. The importance he assigns to the traditional features of that hope, and the interpretations he suggests for them, vary with the character of the work he is writing and with the kind of audience – popular or intellectual – for which it is intended. Nevertheless, the general characteristics of Clement's eschatology are remarkably consistent, both with themselves and with his general theological style.

Thoroughly convinced of the role of discipline and acquired control in the fulfillment of the human ideal, Clement tends to conceive of the Christian life in terms of painstaking development rather than of eschatological crisis and decision. The serious believer can *learn* perfection. "It is in your power," Clement assures his more advanced Christian readers, "not to be a son of disobedience, but to pass from darkness to life" (*Strom* 1.27.173.6). Indeed, the "true Gnostic," who combines the highest Christian virtue and learning in a life of contemplation and lived faith, has reached such a level of freedom that he "even forms and creates himself" (*ibid.*, 7.3.13.1). In a life so conceived, the death of the body is unquestionably a change for the better, a "liberation for the Lord" (*ibid.*, 4.11.80.1; cf. 7.13.83.1); the ascetical practices by which the Christian learns to share in the life-giving cross of Christ are indeed, in Plato's phrase, "practice for death" (μελέτη θανάτου, an allusion to *Phaedo* 81A: *ibid.*, 2.20.109.1).[1] So death never comes to the Christian disciple as an unwelcome surprise. Although not rejecting the body and its physical surroundings as evil, Clement's "Gnostic" has trained himself to be thoroughly free of the passions or susceptibilities that come from embodiment (*ibid.*, 6.9); he has learned to live as a stranger and pilgrim in the world, "giving thanks for his sojourn and blessing God at his departure, welcoming his dwelling place in heaven" (*ibid.*, 4.26.166.1; cf. 7.12.78.3, 79.4).

The goal of Christian endeavor is the eternal contemplation of God, the "transcendently clear and absolutely pure, insatiable vision which is the privilege of intensely loving souls" (*Strom* 7.3.13.1). This promised life of vision will involve the transformation of our present nature, sanctification, sonship and friendship with God (*ibid.*, 5.6.39–40), and ultimately "assimilation to God" (*ibid.*, 2.23.136.6, alluding to Plato, *Theaet* 176B; cf. *ibid.*, 134.2). Its full realization clearly lies beyond the limiting confines of this life.

So Clement sketches out, near the end of his notes on Old Testament passages (*Eklogai Prophetikai*), a description of the events to be looked for after Christ's second coming, when all the just will be taken up into a life of contemplation with the angels, in the glorious light of heaven (56–67). Explaining the verse "he has pitched his tent in the sun" (Ps 18.6) as a reference to the place of eschatological fulfillment, Clement here identifies the "sun" with the abode of the "commanding angel" (*Ecl Proph* 56.4), or perhaps even with God himself (if 'El = $\dot{\eta}\lambda\iota os$) (57.3). There the angels, who have been given various tasks to perform in the present age of creation, will again be reunited "in their first home" and will have no other cares except contemplating God (56.6f.). And there, "in the true restoration ($\dot{\alpha}\pi o\kappa\alpha\tau\dot{\alpha}$-$\sigma\tau\alpha\sigma\iota s$),"[2] human beings will join the "thrones and dominations" and also have God "resting in them," according to the varying degrees of their knowledge of him (57.1f.). The most advanced among them will become pupils of the angels for a thousand years, and will then in turn teach other humans what they have learned, having become angels themselves (57.4f.).

In *Strom* 6.13f., Clement repeats this hierarchical view of heaven, suggesting that human beings will receive differing degrees of glory in heaven according to the knowledge of God they have manifested in their lives. So human fulfillment, in all its richness, "is reserved until the resurrection of those who believe" (*Paed* 1.6.28.3). Yet even in this life, the perfected Christian believer or the "Gnostic" is allowed a foretaste of what he will possess, in fullness, after death and resurrection (*ibid.*, 29.3; cf. *Strom* 7.11.63.1f.). The Gnostic's love of God, transforming his faith, allows him now to "anticipate hope by knowledge ... having, as far as possible, the very thing he desires" (*Strom* 6.9.73.4). "Through love, the future is for him already present" (*ibid.*, 77.1).[3]

This highly spiritual and personal view of human fulfillment, with its stress on the possibility of a mystical anticipation of eternal beatitude in a life of contemplation and good works, appears mainly in Clement's private notes and esoteric writings, such as *Stromateis*. In his works of a more popular nature, Clement alludes occasionally, although without a great deal of elaboration, to more traditional Christian expectations of an afterlife. So his homily, *Who is the Rich Man who will be Saved?*, ends with a tableau of "the resurrection for which we hope: when, at the end of the world, the angels, radiant with joy, singing hymns and opening the heavens, shall receive into the celestial abodes those who truly repent, and, before all, the Savior himself goes to meet them, . . . conducting them to the Father's bosom, to eternal life, to the Kingdom of heaven" (42). So, too, in the *Paedagogos*, his manifesto for the education of less advanced Christians, Clement portrays the resurrection of the body as the final realization of human "enlightenment" (1.6.28.3–5). Christ, the Tutor and Shepherd, "wishes to save my flesh by wrapping it in the robe of incorruptibility" (1.9.84.3); for this reason he took on flesh himself, revealing the immortality that is its true beauty (3.1.2.3; 3.1.3.3).

Traces of the apologetic tradition that began in Athenagoras' *De Resurrectione*, as well as striking anticipations of Gregory of Nyssa's conception of the resurrection, are evident in Clement's brief comments (*Adumbrationes*) on I Peter, extant only in the Latin translation made by Cassiodorus. There Clement observes that the soul is not, after death, simply reunited to a body "in this life," lest it find in it a new opportunity to sin. In the resurrection, however, both the just (who have become "angelic") and sinners will receive their bodies again, each in "its appropriate form (*iuxta genus proprium*)," the soul seeking out its own flesh "by a kind of kinship" (*quadam congruentia*), and reassembling it "like a network or a building made of stones" (*Adumb in I Pet* 1.3). The soul, he adds, is not naturally immortal, "but is made incorruptible, by God's grace, through its faith, its righteousness and its intelligence" (*ibid.*, 1.9).

Although he alludes in one place, at least, to "the punishment of eternal fire" (*Quis Dives* 33), Clement generally views punishment after death as a medicinal and therefore temporary measure. It is proper, after all, for the providence that guides and judges the universe to administer punishment only as a means of correction (*Strom* 1.27.173.5); no other kind of punishment by a good God is intelligible (*ibid.*, 4.24.154.1–2; 6.12.99.2; 7.16.102). So Clement repeatedly interprets the traditional image of Tartarus – a conception that Greek philosophy "borrowed," in his view, from the Hebrew Gehenna – as meaning "corrective torture for discipline" (*Strom* 5.14.91.2f.; cf. 5.1.9.4). "The Christian teaching," he asserts, "is that the fire sanctifies not flesh or sacrifice, but sinful souls – understanding by fire not the all-devouring flame of everyday life but the discerning

($\phi\rho\acute{o}\nu\iota\mu o\nu$) kind, that pierces through the soul that walks through fire" (*Strom* 7.6.34.4).[4] For this reason, the Christian "Gnostic" can think with compassion on "those who undergo discipline after death and are brought to repentance against their will by means of punishment" (*Strom* 7.12.78.3): he understands both the cost and the loving purpose of their suffering. In fact, the progress of every soul towards the knowledge of God seems to involve, in Clement's eschatological vision, a long and painful purification, involving the discipline of "divesting oneself of the passions" (*Strom* 6.14.109.5). Only when this knowledge has been acquired and has purified the soul of its sinful inclinations can the soul be said to reach perfection: the eternal contemplation of God, "with understanding and certainty," that Clement calls "restoration" (*apokatastasis*: *Strom* 7.10.56.5; cf. 57.1).[5]

In this consistent interpretation of all punishment, including punishment after death, as purification rather than retribution, Clement can be considered the first Christian exponent of the doctrine of purgatorial eschatological suffering; he thus paves the way for centuries of speculation and controversy on the subject of "Purgatory" among Christian theologians.[6] He is also the first Christian writer to suggest, with great caution, the related prospect of universal salvation for all intelligent creatures (e.g., *Strom* 7.2.12.2–3.13.1).

Origen

Without a doubt the most controversial figure in the development of early Christian eschatology – and one of the thinkers who most influenced its development as an integral part of Christian theological reflection – was Origen (d. 253/54). Although his exact relationship to Clement, personal as well as theological, remains unclear, Origen was certainly steeped in the same rich mixture of religious intensity and classical learning that characterized both Jewish and Christian Alexandria. But while Clement generally tried to present the eschatological hopes of the second-century Church in a way that would harmonize with the cosmology and the ethical ideals of enlightened Greeks, Origen's approach, here as everywhere in his theological enterprise, was more complex. An ambitious and prodigiously learned student of both Christian Scripture and Greek philosophy, a speculative thinker as well as a preacher and catechist, Origen was always concerned – in his eschatology as in all his theological thought – to be both a bearer and an imaginative interpreter of Christian tradition: a man of critical intelligence, unafraid of bold speculation, but also a man of the Church. He was not a systematic theologian by later standards; yet there is unquestionably a shape to his way of interpreting Christian tradition, including its eschatology, that remains coherent despite many variations in detail, style and emphasis, and many suggestions that are frankly tentative and incomplete.

With only a touch of anachronism, one might characterize Origen's eschatological thought as an attempt to de-mythologize the accepted apocalyptic tradition of the Scriptures and popular Christian belief in a constructive, reverent and pastorally fruitful way. While affirming the Church's traditional "rule of faith" as the norm of belief (for instance, in the preface to *De Principiis*), Origen is also aware of the broad field for free speculation outside its boundaries, and of the responsibility of the intelligent believer to struggle for clearer understanding. He is always in search of a "deeper" meaning in biblical texts and in the categories of traditional doctrine, which will be applicable to the day-to-day spiritual and ethical life of Christian believers. As a result of this pastoral concern, Origen tends, even more than Irenaeus or Clement, to emphasize the continuity between the present Christian life and its eschatological τέλος or goal, to assume that eschatological statements must have a present as well as a future relevance, and to see the fundamental historical pattern of all creation – cosmic and individual – as one of free, yet providentially guided growth towards union with God.

Origen's underlying attitude towards the accepted eschatological tradition of his day is perhaps best observed in his handling of apocalyptic passages in the New Testament. In commenting on the cataclysmic signs predicted by Jesus in the Synoptic Gospels for the end of the world, he first puts forward what he considers plausible narrative interpretations for these cosmic events, explanations in historical or natural terms that he realizes are important for the "little ones in Christ." He then attempts a "moral" or spiritual interpretation, however, for those capable of more substantial religious thought.[7]

Origen's longest discussion of this synoptic apocalyptic material comes in the *Commentariorum Series in Matthaeum* 32–60. Here he is careful to explain the literal sense of Matt 24.3–44 as modestly as possible, pointing to the "false prophets" and persecutions of his own time, and to the accepted view that the world's resources were being depleted (36–37; cf. Cyprian's theme of the *senectus mundi*), as indications that "the end of the world" was, in fact, a dimension of contemporary life. For the "more advanced," however, Origen offers a parallel, allegorical line of interpretation of the passage in terms of the personal spiritual growth of the serious, devout student of the Bible. So one can speak of another "second coming of Christ," in which he becomes present to the souls of those *viri perfecti* who can understand his divine beauty;[8] "to this second coming is joined the end of this world in the one who reaches maturity" (32). The famine that precedes Christ's coming, in this spiritual sense, is the Christian's hunger for a deeper meaning beneath the surface of Scripture (37); the plagues are the "noxious harangues" of Gnostics and heretics (38); the persecutions are the false doctrines of teachers who pervert Christian truth (39). The "abomination of desolation, standing in the holy place" is any false interpretation of Scripture (40–42); indeed, the Antichrist himself is a symbol for all spurious Christian doctrine and virtue (33; see esp. *GCS* 11.62.15–73).[9] The clouds on which the triumphant Christ appears are the writings of the "apostles and prophets" (50), the "heavens" are the books in which sacred truth is found (51), and the final trumpet is the gospel proclaimed throughout the world (52).

The few extant passages in which Origen comments on the Apocalypse of John – a work generally avoided by Greek commentators until the sixth century – also offer sober, literal interpretations of the book's dramatic imagery in terms of known historical events; but Origen's interest is centered, appropriately enough, on the work's Christology rather than on the content of its predictions of the future.[10] Similarly, he is scornful towards those millenarians who, in his opinion, interpret the scriptural prophecies of the eschatological Jerusalem "in a Jewish sense," by taking them to imply an extended period of idealized earthly beatitude (*Princ* 2.11.2; *Comm in Matt* 17.35). Clearly the most important part of the Church's traditional images of the future, for Origen, is what they can tell us, in a symbolic way, about the individual Christian's growth towards salvation.

For this reason, Origen's chapter "On the Consummation of the World" in the *De Principiis* stresses that "this should not be understood to happen suddenly, but gradually and by steps, as the endless and enormous ages slip by, and the process of improvement and correction advances by degrees in different individuals" (*Princ* 3.6.6; cf. 3.6.9). The process of eschatological fulfillment has already begun, but is by no means complete; the Church experiences a tension, not only between present and future, but also between the salvation of the individual saint and that of the whole body of Christ. So, in explaining the meaning of the Kingdom of God, Origen likes to stress that God's rule is already a reality in those who obey his word (*Or* 25.1). One might also call the virtues, taken together, the Kingdom of heaven, since each of them is a "key" to that Kingdom, and Christ, who is the revealer of all divine knowledge and virtue, has brought the Kingdom near to us (*Comm in Matt* 12.14). On the other hand, the Kingdom cannot reach its full realization until this God-given order of knowledge and virtue has reached perfection in each human being (*Or* 25.2). The blessings of this life are only a "shadow of the good things to come," as the Epistle to the Hebrews reminds us (Hebr 10.1: *Hom in Num* 28.3). Ultimately, the Kingdom of God is "the assembly of the firstborn and of the unspotted members of the Church that has no spot or blemish" (*Hom in Luc* 17): it is a collective reality, which is now achieved in individuals to varying degrees, but which will only be fulfilled at the end of human history. So the joy of Christ and his apostles in the Kingdom is not yet full, "as long as I remain in sin; . . . they are waiting until I can partake in their joy" (*Hom in Lev* 7.2: *GCS* 6.374.20f.; 377.16f.).

The heart of this "joy" of the Kingdom, in Origen's view, is the contemplation of God as ultimate truth and beauty. This is apparent, he argues in his essay "On the Promises" in *De Principiis* 2.11, from the human mind's "proper and natural yearning to know the truth of God and to recognize the causes of things. We did not receive this yearning from God in order that it remain unfulfilled, let alone incapable of fulfillment" (2.11.4). So the heavenly banquet promised in the Scriptures (e.g., Prov 9.1–5) is to be understood as "the contemplation and understanding of God," according to "the measures that are appropriate and suited to this nature, which is created" (2.11.7). "There shall be one activity," Origen writes in the *Commentary on John*, "for those who have come to be with God ($\pi\rho\grave{o}s$ $\Theta\epsilon\acute{o}v$) through the Word who is with him: to apprehend God ($\kappa\alpha\tau\alpha\nu o\epsilon\hat{\imath}\nu$ $\tau\grave{o}\nu$ $\Theta\epsilon\acute{o}v$)" (*Jo* 1.16.92). "Then," he argues later in the same work, "one will see the Father and the things of the Father for oneself, just as the Son does, no longer merely recognizing in the image the reality of the one whose image it is. And I think this will be the end ($\tau\grave{o}$ $\tau\acute{\epsilon}\lambda os$), when the Son hands over the Kingdom to God his Father, and when God becomes all in all" (*Jo* 20.7.47f.).

Because of the limitations of the human mind and the incomprehensibility of God, such knowledge will never be complete, Origen observes in *Homily 17 on Numbers*. We can never speak of our knowledge of God as coming to rest, "reaching home." Those who "follow the way of God's wisdom" should think of themselves, rather, as living in "tents," "with which they always walk and always move on, and the farther they go, so much more does the road still to walk grow long and stretch out endlessly . . . For it never happens that a mind, enkindled by the spark of knowledge, can come to quiet repose; it is always called to move on, from the good to the better and from the better to still higher things" (*Hom in Num* 17.4: *GCS* 7.160.11–26). "I must progress beyond this world," Origen adds some lines later, "to be able to see what these 'tents' are, which the Lord has made" (*ibid.*, 162.10–12). Here Origen sketches out a picture of the eschatological contemplation of God as constant spiritual movement and growth, a view which Gregory of Nyssa will later develop into his own theory of beatitude as eternal self-transcendence or $\grave{\epsilon}\pi\acute{\epsilon}\kappa\tau\alpha\sigma\iota s$.

Just as there are many different "places" in the earthly Promised Land, Origen believes "that in the heavenly places themselves Jesus our Lord will establish each person in this or that part of heaven to dwell, not without regard for his merits" (*Hom in Num* 28.3; *GCS* 7.284.2–4). Yet the reality of beatitude is for Origen, above all, the fulfillment of the whole Church's growth as the Body of Christ, and the union of that eschatological body in joy and glory will be even greater than its present unity (*Jo* 10.36.236–38). The whole eschatological Church will know God as the Son now knows him, "so that all, in the knowledge of the Father, will be formed literally into a [single] son" (*Jo* 1.16.92). This knowledge, which is truly a "mingling and union" with God in love (*Jo* 19.4.24), is for Origen the key to understanding Paul's promise that "God will be all in all" (I Cor 15.28): God will ultimately be the totally satisfying object of every mind's activity, "the measure of every motion," and so the personal, immediate basis for the unity of creation (*Princ* 3.6.3; cf. Jerome, *Ep* 124 *ad Avitum* 9f.).

One of the most debated points in Origen's eschatology has been his understanding of the Christian hope for resurrection. In the preface to the *De Principiis*, Origen includes among the doctrines that are "defined in the preaching of the Church" both the belief that "the soul has its own substance and life," which continues after death in order to experience immediate reward or punishment for its actions, and the expectation that "there will come the time of the resurrection of the dead" (*praef.* 5). Later in the same work, he argues forcefully that belief in resurrection only has meaning if it refers to our own individual bodies, existing in some recogniz-able form (*aliquo habitu*: *Princ* 2.10.1–2). On the other hand, he is equally concerned to stress Paul's teaching, as expressed in I Cor 15.35–50, that the body which will rise will be a "spiritual" body, utterly different in form (*habitus*) from its present state (*Princ* 2.10.2). He vigorously denies Celsus' charge that Christians simply expect the reconstitution of their present material bodies (*Cels* 5.18–23), and shows nothing but contempt for overly materialistic conceptions of the risen life: "our hope is not one of worms, nor does our soul desire a body that has rotted . . ." (*ibid.*, 5.19).[11]

Origen realizes that the form and constitution of the risen body is both a difficult issue to discuss with clarity and a highly sensitive one, because of the Church's concern to defend the importance of the body against Gnostic mythification and because of the practical relevance of the subject to the lives of "the multitude" (*Cels* 5.19). As part of his explanation of Christian hope for personal resurrection, he develops his insistence on the immortality of the spiritual and intellectual soul. This doctrine, taken by itself, sounded to third-century Greek Christian ears dangerously close to Celsus' brand of philosophical paganism. So Origen is quick, in his *Dialogue with Heracleides*, to add qualifications to his admission that he teaches such a doctrine and to show that immortality, in the sense of personal continuity, is required by the Christian expectation of a just retribution after death (24f.). In the final chapter of *De Principiis* (4.4.9f.), he also argues positively for the immortality of the soul, by insisting it would be "impious" to hold that a substance which is *capax dei*, like the human mind, should be able to perish utterly. And in the *Commentary on Matthew* (17.29), he remarks frankly that "a person who rejects the resurrection of the dead as it is believed in the Church, even though he is mistaken in rejecting it, has not simply 'hoped in Christ for this life only' [see I Cor 15.19]," provided he holds at least that the soul "lives and survives": for the soul "does not receive this body [in the resurrection], but one of an ethereal, superior kind." Clearly, for Origen the real conflict is not between a hope in resurrection and a belief in the immortality of the soul, but between the materialistic, popular conception of risen life current among Christians of his day and a more spiritual one.[12]

When he comes to give a positive explanation of the qualities of the risen body, Origen is understandably tentative. For him, as for anyone sympathetic to the Platonic tradition, the body and its material world are only a "shadow" cast by the more substantial reality of the spirit (*De Orat* 17.1). Yet he argues, in the *De Principiis*, that only God is utterly incorporeal, and that every living creature, although essentially spiritual, needs some kind of body to "support its life and contain its movements" (2.2.1f.; cf. 3.6.1; *praef.* 9f.). Bodies, however, exist with a wide range of characteristics, suited to the environment in which their souls find themselves (*Cels* 7.32; *Frag on Psalm* 15 [PG 12.1093c11–1096a3]). So the soul admitted to the contemplation of God will need a very different kind of body for the "purer, ethereal and heavenly regions" from that which it bears on earth (*Cels* 7.32).[13] A further implication is that the risen bodies of sinners destined for punishment will also be different from those of people who have been "purified in this life" and rise to be united with God (*Princ* 2.10.2). The former will manifest the "darkness of ignorance" which now characterizes their minds (*ibid.*, 2.10.8), while the latter will be so much "like the angels" in radiance and refinement that their owners can be said to have *become* angels (*Comm in Matt* 17.30; *Hom in Lev* 9.11).

The principle of continuity between present and future forms of the human body is clearly the soul, which acts throughout life as an "inherent principle of intelligibility (*insita ratio*)"; like the λόγος σπερματικός of Stoic theory, it holds the body together, gives it recognizable form, and will actively reassemble it at the resurrection (*Princ* 2.10.3). In this sense, it is more correct to say – as Scripture does – that the incorruptible soul "clothes" the body with its own permanence than that the body, as the garment of the soul, is itself made immortal (*Princ* 2.3.2; cf. *Jo* 13.61 [59].429–31; *Cels* 7.32). Our new form of bodily existence at the resurrection will be the "spiritual body" of I Cor 15 (*Princ* 2.2.2): a transfiguration of the present material body, free of the features that suit it only for life in this material world, and "subtle, pure and resplendent . . . as the rational creature's situation demands and as its merits suggest" (*Princ* 3.6.4).[14]

Origen's most thorough discussion of the physical characteristics of the risen body, at least in his extant works, is found in a long fragment of his *Commentary on Psalm* 1.5 (LXX: "Therefore the impious will not rise in the judgment"), quoted by Methodius in his own *De Resurrectione* 1.20–24 and preserved in Greek by Epiphanius (*Panarion* 64), along with a large section of Methodius' work. Origen begins by rejecting the notion, which he ascribes to the "simpler members of the faithful," that our bodies will rise again "in their whole substance (οὐσία)," just as they now are. Against such an idea, he raises the standard philosophical criticisms, already familiar from the apologetic replies marshaled against them by Athenagoras and Tertullian. Will these risen bodies include even the blood, even the hair and other bodily parts, which they have lost during life? What will become of human flesh eaten by carnivorous birds and animals, when those animals are in turn eaten by other humans – to whom will such flesh belong? Such questions, justified in themselves, show the "depth of silliness" in a purely material understanding of the risen body (20). Yet Origen complains that his opponents merely answer – as Athenagoras and Tertullian did – that "everything is possible with God," and offer as proof of their interpretation a literal reading of such scriptural passages as Ezekiel 37 (the raising of the valley of bones), Matt 8.12 (in Gehenna there will be the "gnashing of teeth"), Matt 10.28 ("fear him who can destroy both soul and body in Gehenna"), and Rom 8.11 ("he will give life to your mortal bodies") (21). The skilled exegete, he implies, must do better.

Origen begins to explain his own conception of the risen body by remarking that in handing on "the tradition of the ancients" we must "be careful not to fall into the silliness of impoverished thoughts, which are both impossible and unworthy of God" (22). The key to his explanation is his insistence – also borrowed from Stoic science – that the body, of itself, is like a "river," constantly in flux; its underlying materiality (πρῶτον ὑποκείμενον) is constantly being assimilated and discharged, so that its matter is never the same for two days in a row. Despite this fluidity of matter, individuals do remain the same – not only in their interior life or soul (ψυχή) but also in the unique form (εἶδος), imposed by the soul, that shapes and integrates the material body. This is the reason why Peter and Paul remain recognizable – still bearing the scars of childhood, for example, into old age – even though their actual flesh is constantly changing.

It is this εἶδος of the body which is again produced by the soul at the resurrection, and which builds for itself a new body, better in every way than the present one, yet recognizable as the same corporeal individual. The risen body's characteristics will be different from those of the present one, Origen explains, because the soul always forms for itself a body suited to its physical environment. Just as we would doubtless have gills if we lived in water, so "those who are going to inherit the Kingdom of heaven . . . will necessarily make use of spiritual bodies. But the form of the former body will not disappear, even if its style changes to become more glorious . . ."(22).

Origen then replies to the scriptural arguments of his opponents in some detail (23–24), insisting that "not everything should be understood according to the literal text (κατὰ τὸ κείμενον)" (24). The "bones" of Ezekiel 37 clearly refer to Israel, in its hope of restoration. And the "gnashing of teeth" in Matt 8.12 must be understood as the soul's faculty of assimilating knowledge, since the risen body, which will no longer need food, will certainly not have teeth (24). Origen concludes the discussion by likening the εἶδος of the body to the dynamic principle in any living organism, the creative form that the Stoics called its "intelligible seed-structure" (σπερμα-τικὸς λόγος). Just as this vital principle in a grain of wheat makes growth possible, by interacting with the various kinds of material around the seed, so the form of our own bodies will create our materiality anew in the resurrection. Scripture, however, makes it clear "that the underlying materiality (πρῶτον ὑποκείμενον)" of our present body – taken as a particular set of material particles – "does not rise" (24).

It is unclear whether or not Origen sees the glorified body as an integral part of final human fulfillment, or simply as a penultimate stage, to be realized before all the redeemed are united with the incorporeal God, who in the end will become "all in all." Several passages in the De Principiis – all in Rufinus' admittedly favorable translation of the work – assert that some kind of body, however "spiritual" in quality, is an irreducible part of created existence: e.g., 1.6.4; 2.3.2f.; 3.6.5. Less favorable translations of some of these same passages (2.3.2f.; 3.6.1) by Jerome, however, as well as hostile allusions by Theophilus of Alexandria and by Origen's sixth-century critics,[15] portray Origen as teaching that all bodily existence will eventually pass away. Even in Rufinus' translation of De Principiis 2.3.7, Origen offers three hypotheses "about the end of all things and the ultimate beatitude": it will be either a totally incorporeal state, or a state of ethereal and spiritualized corporeality, or else a state of such stability and balance that corporeality, as we know it, will lose its labile character and come to rest in a part of the universe beyond all motion. Origen expressly leaves it to his reader to judge which of these interpretations of the resurrection seems to accord best with a reasonable faith. Other passages in the work, however, as well as the passages from his Treatise on the Resurrection and sources quoted by Pamphilus (Apol pro Origene 1.7: PG 17.594A6–601B2), suggest his own sympathies lay with the third hypothesis.[16]

Two final remarks must be made about Origen's doctrine of the resurrection. First, he is not content to consider the resurrection exclusively as a promise for the future, but sees it, too, as already anticipated "in part" in the life of the baptized Christian (*Jo* 1.27 [25] 181f.; *Comm on Rom*, Greek fr. 29: *JTS* 13 [1912] 363). This experience of the power of the resurrection in grace is the "first resurrection" mentioned in Apocalypse 20, the "baptism in water and the Holy Spirit" that will deliver the faithful from a "baptism of fire" at the "second" resurrection (*Hom in Jer* 1.3).[17] Secondly, Origen stresses that the final resurrection will be the eschatological fulfillment of the whole Church, rather than simply the salvation of individual believers. In this perspective, distinctions between society and individual became blurred. After the resurrection, the faithful will radiate divine light as a single sun (*Comm in Matt* 10.3); they will be built into a single temple (*Cels* 8.19f.), and all invidious diversity among individuals will come to an end (*Princ* 3.6.4). "The temple will be created, the body raised on the third day," he writes in the *Commentary on John*, "after the day of evil which has now begun in it, and the day of consummation to follow. For the third day will begin in the new heaven and the new earth, when these bones, the whole house of Israel, are wakened on the great day of the Lord, and death is conquered. So the resurrection of Christ from his suffering on the cross, which has already occurred, contains a symbol of the resurrection of the whole body of Christ" (10.35 [20].229).

Origen's view of the "interim" state between death and resurrection resembles Clement's revised reading of older Christian traditions. The soul does not remain near the body after death, as some pagans thought, but goes to a place reserved for "souls unclothed by bodies" (*Jo* 28.6 [5].44; *Cels* 2.43; *Dial Her* 23). In some places, Origen repeats the popular dual conception of Hades, familiar to us from Tertullian, in which there is both a place of comfort for the just (the "bosom of Abraham") and a place of anticipatory punishment for sinners (so apparently *Princ* 4.3.10). Before the death of Christ, all the dead waited for salvation in such an underworld (cf. *Homily on the Witch of Endor* [I Sam 28.8ff.]).[18] It is unclear, however, what Origen imagines Hades to be in the present age; so he suggests, in other passages, that the souls of the just go directly to Paradise at death, to be "with Christ" (*Hom in Lk*, fr. 253; *Dial Her* 23) and to share immediately in the contemplation of truth that is beatitude (*Mart* 47).

In a fragment of an unknown work – possibly the *Treatise on the Resurrection* – quoted by Methodius (*De Res* 3.17) and referred to also by Photius (*Bibl* 234: ed. R. Henry V [Paris 1967] 105f.), Origen seems to suggest that the soul in Hades possesses a subtle, wraithlike body, of the same shape as its former earthly one, as a "vehicle" (ὄχημα) for its continuing activity. Similarly, he explains the appearance of ghosts in the world "by the fact that the soul is subsisting in what is called a luminous body" (*Cels* 2.60; cf. the fragment quoted by Procopius of Gaza, *Catena on Genesis* 321 [*PG* 87.221], which may be from Origen, referring to a "subtle" and "sparkling" body of Adam before the fall). This notion of an "astral" body or "body of light," borne by souls when outside the material parameters of this world, is familiar from Neoplatonism and fits well with Origen's supposition that only God is truly incorporeal.[19]

Wherever they are, the souls of the just, in Origen's view, still take an active interest in the living (*Comm in Matt* 15.35; *Jo* 13.58 [57] 403). By their prayers at the heavenly altar, the martyrs – and indeed all the just who have died – intercede for the living and help Christ in his work of purifying them (*Mart* 30, 38; *Hom in Num* 24.1; *Hom in Cant* 3 [GCS 8.191.12–15]). The "former fathers," who are now with the Lord, "have their promised reward and are at rest," he writes in one of the *Homilies on Joshua*; "still even now they fight and are involved in the struggle for those who serve under Jesus" (16.5).

Another controversial aspect of Origen's eschatology, and one on which his own thought is not entirely clear, is the subject of the nature and duration of punishment after death.[20] In many passages, particularly in his homiletic works, he refers to the need for divine punishment of sinners (so *Hom in Jer* 12.5) and paints the prospect of "eternal fire" in thoroughly traditional terms (e.g., *ibid.*, 19 [18].15; *Hom in Lev* 14.4). The existence of this "fire of Gehenna" is taught by both Scripture and "the preaching of the Church" (*Princ praef*, 5; 2.10.1); it is invisible, burning the invisible parts of our natures (*Comm Ser in Matt* 72), and may well give heat without producing light (*Hom in Ex* 13.4). Those condemned to this fire will become companions of the devil, who will continually accuse them of their sins (*Hom in Lev* 3.4; cf. *Comm Ser in Matt* 72). Origen even speaks approvingly, in *Homilies on Ezekiel* 4.8, of the "common understanding" that this punishment is final, in contrast with the "foolishness of some," who believe that anyone can be saved from Gehenna by the prayers of holy intercessors.

In several passages, however, Origen cautiously introduces modifications in this traditional doctrine of eternal punishment. One such modification is his tendency towards a "moral" or psychological explanation of the fire of hell. In *De Principiis* 2.10.4, for instance, he asserts that "every sinner himself lights the flames of his own fire, and is not immersed in some fire that was lit by another or existed before him." This fire is the "fever" within him that results from the unhealthy imbalance of his passions, and its pain is the consequent accusation of a troubled conscience (*ibid.*, 5–6; cf. *Comm in Rom* 7.5).[21] It is a fire wholly of the sinner's own making (*Hom 3 in Ezek* 7; *Hom in Lev* 8.8).

Secondly, and more important, Origen at least raises serious questions about the eternity of the punishment of sinners. In the *Commentary on John* (28.8 [7].63–66), for instance, he declares himself unsure whether those who are "bound and cast into outer darkness" will remain there forever, or will someday be released; "it does not seem safe to me to pass judgment," he remarks, "since I have no knowledge at all, especially since nothing is written [i.e., in Scripture] on the subject." Origen is careful to point out, in several places, that Scripture designates "eternal fire" expressly "for the devil and his angels," as if implying that it is not meant for human souls (so *Hom in Jos* 14.2; cf. *ibid.*, 8.5). And "eternal" (αἰώνιος), as he uses it, seems to refer to long but limited periods of time or "ages" (αἰῶνες), rather than to eternity in the Augustinian sense of timeless existence, or even to endless duration.[22]

Origen is aware that the issue of the eternity of punishment is a sensitive one, because of the enormous importance of the "deterrent" of eternal fire in shaping the ordinary Christian's moral behavior (*Hom in Jer* 12.4; 19 [18].15; 20 [19].4). Indeed, he writes in one passage, "to communicate these things (i.e., speculations on Gehenna) openly and at length, by ink and pen and parchment, seems to me incautious" (*Comm Ser in Matt* 16). Yet he is convinced, like Clement, that "all the torments of a good God are designed for the benefit of those who endure them" (*Hom I in Ezek* 3); this medicinal, corrective character has been concealed from "those who are still 'little ones' with respect to their spiritual age" (*ibid.*), but must nevertheless be acknowledged at times in order to refute the "heretical" Gnostic picture of a cruel and judging God (*ibid.*; *Hom in Jer* 20 [19].3).

In fact, Origen insists, all souls need to be purified by "fire" from the "lead" intermingled with their natural "gold," in order to be saved (*Hom in Ex* 6.4; cf. *Hom in Num* 25.6).[23] In the human creature, this fire will torture both soul and body, "not without great suffering" (*Comm Ser in Matt* 20; cf. *Jo* 13.23.138; *Hom in Jer* 20 [19].8); the degree and duration of suffering for those confined in it will vary, depending on their guilt (*Hom in Jer* 19 [18].15; *Comm in Prov*, fr. [in Pamphilus, *Apologia*: PG 17.615A10–616A11). This is the "wise fire," the "debtor's prison," which God has established for sinful humans "as a benefaction, to cleanse them from the evils committed in their error" (*Or* 29.15). It is the "baptism of fire" destined for those not previously cleansed by a "baptism in the Holy Spirit" (*Hom in Ezek* 1.13; *Hom in Jer* 1.3; 2.3; *Hom in Luc* 24); it is the "fiery sword" of the cherub stationed at the gate of Paradise (*Hom in Ezek* 5.1; *Mart* 36; *Comm in Cant* 3 [GCS 8.238.23–29]).[24]

This process of purification seems to include, for Origen, not only the negative experience of detachment from the passions and the effects of sin, but also a positive growth in knowledge and wisdom, as a preparation for the eternal vision of God (*Princ* 3.6.9). So he suggests, in the *De Principiis*, that a long period of instruction will intervene, for human souls, between death and resurrection – that they will be sent to a "school for souls," situated somewhere "in the heavenly regions" (2.11.6–7), where they will learn from the angels (cf. *Comm Ser in Matt* 51) "the explanation for all that happens on earth" (*Princ* 2.11.5), the meaning of difficult passages in Scripture (*ibid.*), the nature of the heavenly powers (*ibid.*), and ultimately the plan (*ratio*) behind all the "movements" of the created universe (2.11.6). This *schola animarum* is what the Bible calls "Paradise" or "the Heavenly Jerusalem" (2.11.3,6); what souls will learn there will be simply a propaedeutic for a more mystical knowledge, aimed at preparing them "to receive the things that the Son will teach," when they have been finally united with him (*Comm Ser in Matt* 51).

Behind this conviction that all punishment is ultimately medicinal and educational stands – in Origen's thought as in Clement's – the equally strong conviction that all human souls will ultimately be saved, and will be united to God forever in loving contemplation. For Origen, universal salvation is an indispensable part of the "end" promised by Paul in I Cor 15.24–28, when Christ will destroy all his enemies, even death, and hand over all things in "subjection" to his Father, who will be "all in all."[25] Evil then will totally come to an end (*Jo* 1.16.91), and "all Israel will be saved" (*Hom in Jos* 8.5; *Comm in Rom* 8.9; *Princ* 2.3.7).

Origen sometimes refers to this final state of universal salvation by the term ἀποκατάστασις, "restoration," which he suggests is already a familiar concept to his readers (*Jo* 1.16.91). Although the word seems simply to have meant the "attainment" or "realization" of a goal in most second-century Christian works, Origen clearly understands it to have a retrospective as well as a prospective dimension: to mean not merely human fulfillment, but the re-establishment of an original harmony and unity in creation (so, e.g., *Hom in Jer* 14.18).[26] Behind this conception of the eschaton is the assumption, expressed several times in *De Principiis*, that "the end is always like the beginning" (1.6.2; cf. 3.6.1, 3), that human fulfillment is really the restoration of the soul to a unity with God that it possessed before its fall and embodiment. The context of these passages, however, suggests that Origen regarded this as an attractive theological hypothesis rather than a sure doctrine, and that his concern was more to develop a theory of human origins, based on the Church's eschatological hope and compatible with God's goodness and with human freedom, than it was to canonize a cyclic view of history (so *Princ* 3.6.1).[27] Although Origen seems to have regarded the reincarnation of souls and the existence of at least some other, future worlds as a theoretical possibility (*Comm Ser in Matt* 96; *Princ* 2.3.1–2), he also seems to have assumed that salvation ultimately means the permanent stability of rational creatures in loving union with God (*Dial Her* 27; *Jo* 10.42 [26]. 295; *Hom in I Kg* 1.4). An endless cycle of alternating falls and redemptions is almost certainly foreign to his thought.[28]

A further dimension of Origen's belief in universal salvation that scandalized many ancient authors was the suggestion, implied in at least some passages of his works, that it would include even Satan and the other evil spirits. So he stresses, in the *Commentary on John* (32.3.29f.), that Christ's final triumph will mean an end to all "struggle" against the "principalities, powers and virtues" (cf. *Princ* 3.6.5). In *De Principiis* 1.6.2 he emphasizes that "all beings who, from that single beginning, have been moved, each by their own motion, through various stages allotted them for their deserts," will ultimately be restored to unity with God through subjection to Christ (see also *Comm in Rom* 5.10 [*PG* 14.1053A13–B7]; 9.41 [*ibid.*, 1243C4–1244A15]). In other passages, however, he speaks of the "destruction" of the demonic powers in "eternal fire" (*Hom in Jos* 8.5; 14.2), hinting that the devil, by his long career of deception, may have become a "liar by nature" and so have condemned himself to destruction (*Jo* 20.21 [19]. 174; cf. *Comm in Rom* 8.9 [*PG* 14.1185B8f.]: "as for him who is said to have fallen from heaven, not even at the end of the ages will a conversion take place").

In his apologetic "Letter to Friends in Alexandria," written at the time of his expulsion by Bishop Demetrius in 231, Origen strongly denies that he ever taught the redemption of the devils, accusing his enemies of adulterating his writings (cf. Jerome, *Apol adv Ruf* 2.18f.; Rufinus, *De Adult Libr Orig* [*PG* 17.624A2–625A2]).[29] In *De Principiis* 1.6.3 (Rufinus' translation), he leaves the question open to his readers' judgment, insisting that, in any case, nothing will disrupt the final unity and harmony of God's creation. This uncertainty in the extant texts of his works may well mean that Origen himself remained undecided on the subject. He was sharply attacked for his leniency towards the devil, however, both in his own time and in later centuries.[30]

Throughout his discussion of all these aspects of the Christian hope, Origen shows himself remarkably consistent, not only in his doctrinal concerns, but also in his conception of the theologian's task. His aim is to give an explanation of the meaning of Scripture and Church tradition that is both true to those sources and intellectually responsible in terms of the science and philosophy of his own day (*Princ.* 1. *praef.* 2–10). Equally opposed to contemptuous pagans like Celsus, to Gnostics who made light of the Church's public teaching and to fundamentalists within the Christian community, Origen was, perhaps, the first fully professional Christian thinker. He was not afraid to offer his own imaginative opinions, on subjects for which tradition gave no clear guidelines to Christian teaching; yet he remained, in his intentions at least, the faithful exegete of the preached word, reverently trying to integrate each detail of the community's tradition into the wider context of a unified biblical faith and spirituality. His optimistic, deeply religious way of interpreting the eschatological images of that tradition would arouse violent contradiction from the more literal-minded, and enthusiastic support from those of a more mystical bent, both in the East and in the West, for centuries to come. For Origen himself, eschatology was simply part of a larger picture: the grace-filled finality of the mystery of growth towards God that is already the heart of Christian faith and practice. It was not simply bold theological speculation, but reflection on a more practical, everyday hope: "what we think to be the blessed end with God in Christ, who is the Logos, wisdom, and every virtue, which will be the experience of those who have lived purely and blamelessly, and have recovered their undivided and unbroken love for the God of the universe – [an end] which will be bestowed by God's gift" (*Cels* 3.81).

Origen's admirers and critics

Greek theology of the late third and early fourth centuries, until the time of the Council of Nicaea (325), was generally dominated by Origen's powerful synthesis. Then, as to a lesser degree ever since, one was either an admirer and defender of Origen or one was a critic; one could hardly be neutral, or unaware of his achievement. In the eschatology of the later third century, however, it is an odd fact that neither Origen's friends nor his enemies seem to have understood more than the superficial features of his hope for future salvation. No one adopted, in a consistent way, his radically spiritual, internalized reinterpretation of the eschatological tradition.

Origen's devoted pupil, Gregory "the Wonderworker" and later bishop of Neocaesaraea in Pontus (d. *c.* 270), in the florid panegyric of his master that is attributed to him, describes the end (τέλος) of all human asceticism and spiritual growth as "to draw near to God, being made like him in the purity of one's mind, and to abide in him" (*Pan* 12.149). To develop oneself in prudence or practical wisdom, seeing in one's own intellectual virtue a mirror of the divine mind, is to "walk an ineffable path towards diviniza-tion" (*ibid.*, 11.142) – a path that Origen himself had trodden successfully, according to Gregory (*ibid.*, 2.10, 13). Curiously, Gregory's *Paraphrase of Ecclesiastes* projects a different hope, showing traces of the traditional expectation of the "day of the Lord" as a coming catastrophe within human history, without any attempt to find deeper allegorical meaning in the apocalyptic passages of Scripture.[31]

Despite Origen's criticism, the millenarian hope apparently remained strong in the Alexandrian world throughout the third and early fourth centuries.[32] Eusebius (*HE* 7.24f.) summarizes two pamphlets written against such "materialistic" eschatological ideas by Dionysius, bishop of Alexandria (d. 264/65) and a loyal pupil of Origen. Entitled "On the Promises" (like Origen's treatise on eschatological reward in *De Principiis* 2.11), Dionysius' two essays were directed against the ideas of an Egyptian bishop named Nepos, who had himself written a tract *Against the Allegorists*. Nepos, who was recently dead at the time of Dionysius' criticism and who therefore must have been a contemporary of Origen, seems to have formulated his attack against allegorical exegesis in order to defend the traditional, literal interpretation of the millenarian promises in Apocalypse 20 and 21. By the time of Dionysius' episcopate, followers of Nepos – led by a certain Korakion – had formed a schismatic group in the Fayyum, whose main differences from the official Church seem to have been in their Christology and their eschatological hope (so Eusebius, *HE* 7.24.1f.). The theology of this sect probably rested on a strongly literalist exegesis and an anthropomorphic, possibly even unitarian view of God which would have implied a "lower" Christology than Origen's.[33] The first book of Dionysius' response was directed against an overly worldly understanding of the Kingdom of God (so Eusebius, *ibid.*, 24.3); the second attempted to prove the genuine Johannine authorship of the Apocalypse of John, as justification for finding in it "some deeper meaning" behind the millenarian promise of chapter 20 (Eusebius, *ibid.*, 25.2–5).

The learned Palestinian chronographer Sextus Julius Africanus (d. after 240) was also a friend and correspondent of Origen (Eusebius, *HE* 6.31.1). Nevertheless, he seems to have adopted the familiar apocalyptic notion of a "world week" of seven thousand years as the underlying structure of his *Chronography* (*PG* 10.65A10–B2). According to the usual form of this scheme, history will come to an end six thousand years after creation, and will usher in a "Sabbath" of a thousand years. It is not clear, however, whether Julius Africanus also subscribed to the other, more imaginative details of the millenarian hope.

Origen's opponents continued to object to features of his eschatology, as examples of what was objectionable in his whole system of thought, until shortly before the Council of Nicaea (325). Peter, the anti-Origenist bishop of Alexandria who died a martyr's death in 303, seems, from the few extant fragments of his writings, to have emphasized the identity of every feature of the risen body with the present terrestrial one.[34]

The most insistent anti-Origenist of the period whose works are still extant, however, was Methodius of Olympus, who probably lived in Asia Minor during the last quarter of the third or the first quarter of the fourth century. Methodius professed to be a disillusioned follower of Origen, and although several of his works – especially his treatise *On the Resurrection* – were intended as serious polemics against Origen's position, he retains both an allegorical style of exegesis similar to the Alexandrian master's, and many of Origen's key ideas and attitudes in spirituality and doctrine. In the areas in which he criticizes Origen, Methodius often betrays a glaring lack of understanding of what Origen intended to say. His own main eschatological concern is to underline the participation of the body in future salvation, and the corresponding importance of asceticism and sexual continence in the present life. He also emphasizes the ecclesiological dimension of the salvation to come, and offers, in consequence, an exalted picture of the life and practice of the Church in the present age.

Methodius' dialogue *On the Resurrection* is clearly intended to be an apology for a more "realistic" view of the risen body and its rewards than he understood Origen to have taken. But although the two speakers in book I of the dialogue, Aglaophon and Proclus, are presented as sympathizing with Origen's general approach to eschatology, one could not call their exposi- tions a faithful mirror of Origen's doctrine as it appears in his extant works.[35] The dialogue's anti-Origenist speakers, Eubulius and Memianius, spend book II largely refuting Aglaophon's thesis that the "garments of skin" given to Adam and Eve after the fall (Gen 3.21) imply that the human race was originally created without a material body. Only in book III does Methodius, presumably speaking through his mouthpiece Eubulius, attempt a direct refutation of Origen himself. His attack is aimed mainly against the fragment of Origen's *Commentary on Psalm 1.5* quoted by the speaker Proclus in book I (cf. above, pp. 53f.); much of Eubulius' refutation rests on the mistaken idea that the human "form" ($\epsilon\tilde{\iota}\delta\sigma$), which Origen conceives as the principle of continuity and identity in a body of ever- changing material components, is nothing more than the body's external appearance or $\sigma\chi\tilde{\eta}\mu\alpha$ (so *De Res* 3.7.4). Most of Methodius' criticism, in fact – even his contention that souls are "intellectual bodies" and so need no "vehicles" for their operations in Hades (*De Res* 3.17f.) – Origen would probably have accepted without difficulty.[36]

Methodius' main contention, throughout his criticism of Origen on the resurrection, is that the body that will rise is in every sense the body we now possess.[37] The risen Christ appeared to the disciples in "the body composed of flesh and bones"; for us to hope for a resurrection in "another, spiritual body" is to contradict Christ's teaching (*De Res* 3.12.7). The difference between the earthly body and the glorified body for Methodius, in fact, is simply one of quality. "Now it is a body that has neither self-mastery nor wisdom; in the future, however, it will be characterized by both self-mastery and wisdom" (*ibid.*, 3.16.6).

Methodius occasionally links this material conception of the resurrection with the millenarian hope long cherished in Asia Minor. So the ninth discourse of his *Symposium* is an interpretation of the Jewish Feast of Tabernacles as a type of "the seventh millennium of creation," "the great resurrection day," when the just will celebrate a thousand-year feast for the Lord, and "he shall rejoice in us" (9.1). In "the first day of the resurrection," Methodius asserts, "I stand to be judged on whether I have adorned my tabernacle with the things commanded"; those who have not produced the expected "fruit" in their lives will not be allowed to share in the "first resurrection" (9.3). But those who have purified themselves by "divine discipline" and adorned their tabernacles with a life of chastity (9.4) will be admitted to the feast and "celebrate with Christ the millennium of rest" (9.5). At the end of this "Sabbath" of a thousand years the faithful will undergo another transformation: their bodies will be "changed from a human and corruptible form into angelic size and beauty," and "pass to greater and better things, ascending to the very house of God above the heavens" (9.5). This millennial hope is echoed in the *De Resurrectione* – presumably a later work – by Methodius' explanation that the Paradise where human history began is not some distant heavenly region, but "obviously a chosen spot on this earth, set aside for the painless rest and entertainment of the saints" (1.55.1). So, too, the fiery end (ἐκπύρωσις) expected for this present world will not be destruction so much as restoration, "so that we who are renewed may dwell, without tasting pain, in a renewed world" (1.47.3).

Consistently with his insistence on the continuity between the future, risen body and the present, earthly one, Methodius denies that the saved will in any literal sense "become angels" after death (*De Res* 1.51.2). As a result, human creatures can expect to experience beatitude on this earth. "For each creature must remain in the proper form of its own state, that all places may be filled with all beings: the heavens with angels, the thrones with powers... and the world with human beings" (*De Res* 1.49.4). In that place and state of fulfillment, the saved "will no longer contemplate Being (τὸ ὄν) through [human] knowledge (ἐπιστήμη), but will look on it clearly, having entered in with Christ" (*Symp* 8.11.199). Even before this final state of vision and incorruption, however, "before the resurrection, our souls will have their dwelling with God" (*De Res* 2.15.7f.).

Since its main purpose is to be an encomium of consecrated virginity, Methodius' *Symposium* concentrates its eschatological interest on the reward of virgins in the world to come. Like the martyrs of earlier tradition, virgins are promised immediate entry to "the pastures of immortality" (8.2), where they enjoy "wonderful and glorious and blessed things of beauty, such as cannot be spoken to human beings" (8.3). Indeed, many passages in this work suggest that chastity – at least in its broad sense, as the subjugation of sexual passion to the control of reason and will – is a necessary requirement for admission to the Kingdom of God, and for a share in immortality (1.1,2,5; 4.2; 9.4; 10.6). But Methodius also sees virginity in a more symbolic way, as humanity's anticipation, in this life, of the purity and single-minded fidelity of the eschatological Church, the "Bride of the Word" (8.11) and the persecuted mother of Apocalypse 12. The Church we now know, in fact, is itself a kind of intermediate stage between Old Testament types and eschatological reality, "the image of the heavenly order," whose full truth will only be known and shared after the resurrection (5.7). In his ascetical orientation as in his vision of the Church, Methodius presents us, in effect, with his own form of "realized eschatology."[38]

The dialogue *On Right Faith in God* ($\pi\epsilon\rho\grave{\iota}\ \tau\hat{\eta}\varsigma\ \epsilon\grave{\iota}\varsigma\ \Theta\epsilon\grave{o}\nu\ \check{o}\rho\theta\eta\varsigma\ \pi\acute{\iota}\sigma\tau\epsilon\omega\varsigma$) – attributed by Rufinus, who translated it into Latin, to Origen – probably comes from the same period and the same theological world as did Methodius, and borrows heavily from several of his works. The chief personality in the dialogue is called "Adamantius," a nickname traditionally ascribed to Origen. In the course of the conversation, Adamantius easily overcomes the arguments of his Marcionite and Valentinian opponents; their positions, however, are often suspiciously close to Origen's own, at least as Methodius and other critics supposed them to be, and Adamantius' refutation frequently reproduces Methodius' line of anti-Origenist argument. The work may well be an attempt by a fourth-century Asian admirer of Origen to defend the Alexandrian's reputation by identifying with others the doctrines for which he was being attacked, and by ascribing to him the positions his critics felt were essential to orthodox faith.

So Adamantius defends, with scriptural arguments, the thesis that a single good God is judge of both good and bad alike, and will reward the just and punish the sinner (2.3–6). His opponent here, the Marcionite Marcus, not only advances the Marcionite doctrine of two gods, but insists that "the good God saves all, even murderers and adulterers . . . and does not condemn those who refuse to believe in him" (2.4). The attempt to connect the doctrine of *apokatastasis* with Adamantius' heretical opponents seems to be a clear, if thinly disguised, apology for Origen.

In the final section of the work, which discusses the resurrection (5.15–28), Adamantius also energetically defends the position that "this body, which we now wear, will rise" (5.16), and rejects Marcus' contention – superficially similar to Origen's in the fragment on Ps 1.5 used by Methodius – that "the body is of a fluid substance, constantly slipping away and becoming, from its nourishment, something new" (*ibid.*). Adamantius' response to the familiar question of how a body that has decomposed into its elements can be reassembled is an argument well known from earlier apologetic tradition: "things impossible to humans are possible to God" (5.18). If indeed he is intended by the author to represent Origen, Adamantius is Origen in a highly conventional, and rather unsophisticated, disguise.

6

The dawn of the final conflict: Latin eschatology in the Great Persecution (303–313)

During the last years of the third century, and the decade of violent persecution (303–13) that opened the fourth, Christian interest in apocalyptic speculation seems to have been revived in the Latin Church, just as it had flourished in the turbulent decade of Cyprian's episcopate fifty years earlier. The external circumstances that prompted such hopes were urgent and practically universal: political conflict and social chaos across Roman society, and the renewed attempt by secular authorities to crush the expanding Christian institutions that seemed to them symptomatic of the underlying disorder. The sufferings which the Church underwent seemed, within their own perspective, strikingly like the woes traditionally predicted for God's people at the end of time. Yet the two main exponents of the apocalyptic hope in the West at the beginning of the fourth century – Victorinus, bishop of Poetovium (Pettau or Ptuj in modern Slovenia), and the learned lay convert Lactantius – understood that hope in radically different ways, and propagated it in strikingly different terms.

Victorinus of Pettau

Victorinus, who died a martyr's death early in the persecution of Diocletian (304), was, according to Jerome (*De Vir Ill* 74), a native Greek speaker. He may have been of Asian origin, formed in the same millenarian milieu in which Papias, Irenaeus, and most recently Methodius had absorbed the Church's eschatological hope. As a bishop in Latin-speaking Noricum, however, Victorinus was undoubtedly forced to learn Latin thoroughly, and became the first author to write exegetical tracts in that language. Of his numerous commentaries (see Jerome, *ibid.*), only one on the Apocalypse of John remains: a concise work, interpreting the Apocalypse's vision in a modestly allegorical way that betrays the influence of Origen.[1]

His comments on Apoc 20 and 21 take literally the work's promise of a "first resurrection," in which the just will rise and rule with Christ over all people, and a "second resurrection" a thousand years later, when all the dead will rise to be judged. The "second death," for condemned sinners, which follows that judgment, is, for Victorinus, eternal punishment in hell (20.2). The colors of Victorinus' millenarian vision are subdued, however, especially when compared with the vivid imaginings of Papias and Irenaeus (see, for instance, 21.5). He draws on a number of other biblical texts to support his apocalyptic promises, and interprets allegorically several of the details of the "new Jerusalem" in Apoc 21 (21.6).

Victorinus' short treatise on the days of creation, *De Fabrica Mundi*, also interprets the seventh "day," of Gen 2.2, as a type of "the seventh millennium, in which Christ will rule with his elect"; but Victorinus does not elaborate the theme further. Like his Apocalypse Commentary, this work reveals above all the mutually tempering influence of Asiatic concreteness and Alexandrian spiritual exegesis.[2]

The short Latin *Commentary on Matthew 24*, contained in a manuscript in the Ambrosian library in Milan and published independently by G. Mercati (1903)[3] and C. H. Turner (1904),[4] may well be part of Victorinus' lost commentary on Matthew's gospel (cf. Jerome, *Comm in Matt, praef.*; *Homiliae Origenis in Lucam, praef.*). Although it is essentially a terse paraphrase of the Matthaean Apocalypse, the author argues at some length against an overly materialistic interpretation of the millennial hope (11–13). The millennium, he insists, is a fulfillment of the biblical Sabbath, and will primarily offer to the just a time of rest and freedom from corruption (12). They will not spend their time eating and drinking, since resurrection confers immortality on the body and so frees it from both the appetite and the need for nourishment (11). At the end of the millennial Kingdom, the devil and his followers will be released from prison, and will be defeated by Christ. They and the material world will then be destroyed by fire; as for the creatures that remain, "all will return to God, and will be changed into something better." So the "eighth day" or *ogdoad* will begin (13). The author also discusses the contention of some that the "first resurrection" in Apoc 20 refers to baptism. We know this "by faith, not by sight (*per fidem, non per speciem*) [cf. II Cor 5.7]," he replies; the baptized still look forward to the full realization of the life they have received, and the "first resurrection" of the saints, at the start of the millennium, will be "real not merely in word but in fact" (15).

Lactantius

Lactantius (d. after 317), an African by birth, was a professional rhetorician who eventually became the court-appointed professor of Latin eloquence in Diocletian's Asian capital, Nicomedia. As a Christian convert, Lactantius was forced to resign his position when persecution began in 303, and wrote his large apologetic work, *The Divine Teachings* (*Divinae Institutiones*), between 304 and 313, during his enforced retirement. The seventh and final book of this work – later summarized in chapters 64–68 of his *Epitome* – is Lactantius' vivid and detailed presentation of Christian apocalyptic expectations: a systematic synthesis of earlier Latin eschatological speculation, the Asian millenarian tradition, and a wide range of ancient philosophical and literary speculations on the afterlife. Written for a cultured audience by an author who remained more at home in classical literature than in the Bible, book 7 of the *Institutiones* is a powerful invitation to its readers to enter now into the struggle for future immortality and beatitude, both of which can only be won with great labor (5). Its chief effect on later Latin eschatology, however, was to provide the Christian mind with a program for the great spectacle that was to come.[5]

Lactantius' account of the apocalyptic drama in *Institutiones* 7.14–27 begins with the familiar observation that the ills of contemporary society are the signs of "the extreme old age of a tired and crumbling world" (14). The end of history must come when the world has completed six thousand years (*ibid.*), a date that he calculated to be still some two hundred years away (25).[6] After a period of worldwide injustice and violence, during which "evil will grow strong," the stabilizing rule of Rome will come to an end and "once again the East will rule and the West will serve" (15). This will mean a succession of tyrants: first ten competing kings will try simultaneously to dominate the world; then a "mighty enemy will come from the far North," in whose time the human race's natural environment will come to ruin (16); finally, a Syrian king, a son of the devil, will appear as the "subverter and destroyer of the human race" (17). This king will be the true Antichrist (19), demanding worship, performing astonishing miracles, and killing the prophet whom God will send to rally his people (17). After three and a half years of his persecution, however, "God will send the Great King from heaven" to save the faithful and destroy the Antichrist with all his forces (17–19).

This victory of the triumphant Christ will usher in an age of peace for God's people. First, the living will burn the idols and temples of pagan religion (19). Then all the dead who have "walked in God's religion" – but only such true believers – will rise for judgment; those who have not recognized God are "already judged and condemned" (20), and so must wait in death until the second and final resurrection. The sinners among "those who have known God," whose evil deeds – despite their faith – outweigh their good ones (20), will then be sentenced to punishment in everlasting fire, a "divine" fire that "lives by itself" and restores what it consumes (21).[7] In fact, in Lactantius' scheme all those who rise must pass through this fire as part of their judgment: those who are innocent of sin will not be harmed by it, "because they will have in them something of God, which repels and rejects the power of the flame" (21).

After this judgment of believers – which Lactantius insists does not happen immediately after death, but only at the time of Christ's coming (21) – the just will rule with Christ over the remnants of the nations on earth, for a thousand years of peace and marvelous prosperity (24). Lactantius models his lyrical description of the millennial Kingdom as much on Vergil's *Fourth Eclogue* as he does on *Sibylline Oracles VIII* and other Christian sources. The coming world will be a world of miraculous natural beauty and abundance, in which the saints will be gathered together in God's holy city and "propagate an infinite multitude" of holy offspring to share in their rule (24).[8] During the millennium, the "Prince of Demons" will be chained in prison, but he will be freed at its end to lead a final, fruitless assault against God's people (26). This, too, will fail, as God again devastates the world and its rebellious inhabitants. Satan's defeat will be followed by seven more years of peace for the saints, and then by the total transformation of this natural order. At that point, the living just will become like angels, and "the second, public resurrection of all will take place," in which even unbelievers "will rise to eternal punishment" (26).

Lactantius presents his description of the end of history as "the teaching of the holy prophets," a secret tradition carefully guarded by Christians alone (26). Its contents, however, are a curious hybrid of Christian apocalypticism and the speculations of late pagan "prophetic" literature – of works like the non-Christian *Sibylline Oracles*, the Hermetic tract *Asclepius*, and the Hellenized Zoroastrian work known as the *Oracles of Hystaspes*.[9] This eclecticism is undoubtedly due in part to Lactantius' apologetic and popularizing intentions in writing the work, but it also represents the farthest development hitherto of what would become a much more widespread phenomenon: the blending of biblical eschatology with elements of folk religion, occult speculation and late antique literary traditions, in a vividly concrete picture of our individual and collective destinies. From now on, the apocalyptic myth Lactantius portrays, with both its Christian and its non-Christian elements, was to have a life of its own.

7

Facing death in freedom: Eastern eschatology in the age of Nicaea (325–400)

The sixty years that followed the Council of Nicaea (325) were, in both the Eastern and Western Churches, dominated by controversy over the Trinitarian conception of God. They were also years of rapidly growing prosperity and power for Christian leaders and institutions, as the freedom of worship granted the Church by Constantine in 313 developed into the virtual establishment of Christianity as the Empire's official religion during the reign of Theodosius I (378–95). This new opportunity for Christian thought and action, however, brought with it new questions about the legitimate limits of theological speculation, as well as new demands for discipline and sacrifice in a Church that seemed to be losing its spiritual vigor. All of these changes left their mark – if sometimes only a marginal notation – on the Church's formulation of its eschatological hope.

Ascetical eschatology

Not by accident, the end of persecutions ushered in the beginning of institutionalized asceticism in the Greek- and Latin-speaking Churches. Ascetical practice had been cultivated by various Christian groups since the second century – by the "sons of the covenant" in Syria, for example, by "encratite" or "self-mastering" Judaeo-Christian groups, and by the Montanists. However, it was only when the practice of Christian faith became easy and respectable, during Constantine's reign, that Christian men and women were moved in great numbers to "withdraw" from a now-friendly civilized world and to purify their commitment to Christ by "voluntary martyrdom" in the desert. Traditional expectations of judgment, reward and punishment after this life, as well as a vivid conception of the spiritual drama of death itself, played an important part in the articulation of the driving motives of fourth-century desert spirituality.

This eschatological horizon is evident in the main documents of early Egyptian monastic life: in Anthanasius' monumentally influential *Life of*

Antony (written soon after Antony's death in 356), in the contemporary ascetical letters attributed to Antony and his disciple Ammonas, in the earliest Bohairic and Greek lives of Pachomius (probably composed in the late fourth or early fifth century), and in the fifth-century collection of sayings of the early desert monks, the *Apophthegmata Patrum*.

One of the recurring themes in the spiritual teaching of these Egyptian ascetics was the importance of frequently meditating on death and judgment, heaven and hell, in the most vivid images one could muster, as a way of confirming one's motivation to follow the ascetic life (*Apophth Patr*: Evagrius 1; Theophilos 4,5). The first letter attributed to Antony considers a fear of the "pains and torments prepared for the wicked," and a hope for "the promises prepared for those who walk worthily in the fear of God," to be legitimate sources of a monastic vocation, second in value only to the spontaneous readiness to do God's will (*PG* 40.977C7–10; cf. B7–10). "Let this message be clear to you," we read in a later letter in the collection, "that unless one undertakes his own correction and puts all his strength into the effort, the coming of the Savior will be a judgment . . . Behold, the time is now drawing near when the works of each of you will be put to the test" (*Ep.* 4.4 [*PG* 40.994A2–5, 13f.]).

All the elements in the traditional eschatological hope seem to have been conceived of very concretely by the desert monks, as part of the constant warfare between God and the devil, good angels and bad, with which their own life was surrounded. At the moment of death, especially, angels and demons struggled to claim the departing soul. So both Athanasius' *Life of Antony* and the early lives of Pachomius relate those patriarchs' visions of the passage of souls from this world. In one passage, Antony sees a huge, ugly figure towering against the sky, snatching at souls as they try to fly past him to heaven (66); in another, demonic "customs officers" ($\tau\epsilon\lambda\hat{\omega}\nu\epsilon\varsigma$) demand a reckoning of the life of each departing soul, while angelic escorts act as their advocates (65; cf. *Apophth Patr*: Theophilos 4; *Life of Pachomius* G 93; Bo 83).[1]

The early Egyptian ascetics imagined both the joys of heaven and the punishments of hell in highly personal, often communitarian terms. The "state of souls" in Gehenna, according to a saying ascribed to Evagrius Ponticus, is not merely physical suffering, but "painful silence," "bitter groanings," "fear," "strife" and "waiting." "Shame before the face of God and the angels and archangels and all people" is as terrible a prospect as eternal fire and the "worm that rests not" (*Apophth Patr*: Evagrius 1). Another anecdote from the collection tells of Macarius the Great finding a skull in the desert, which speaks to him of the torments of pagans in hell. They not only stand immersed in fire, but they are unable to see the faces of any of the other damned around them; the prayers of the monks, however, alleviate their sufferings, at least to the extent of letting them get a glimpse of each other's faces (*ibid.*, Macarius 38). The Bohairic life of Pachomius also describes the sufferings of the damned in a world of fire and darkness; here punishments are made to fit each crime, and are administered by angels who have been "created pitiless" by God, and are actually "filled with joy and gladness" by their grim work (Bo 88).

Paradise, on the other hand, where those who have purified themselves in this life will be rewarded, is a place "above this earth and outside the firmament," full of fragrant fruit trees and radiant with light. It is separated from this world "by a great and thick darkness full of tiny insects, so that no one can enter there unless he is led there by an angel of God" (*ibid.*, 114). The warmth of one's reception in Paradise, and the degree to which one actually sees the glory of God there, depend on one's merits (*ibid.*, 82). Still, the desert monks seem also to have conceived the salvation of all the just in essentially social terms, as deliverance from the fear and loneliness inherent in human life. It is "confidence in the face of God the Father and his Son, the angels and archangels and all the people of the saints, the Kingdom of heaven, and the gifts of that realm – joy and beatitude" (*Apophth Patr*: Evagrius 1).

In the eyes of the Egyptian ascetics, Christians prepare for beatitude chiefly by a life of fidelity to the gospel's commands and by purgative suffering. Martyrdom is clearly a principal means of such purification, and the sufferings of one's deathbed another (*Life of Pachomius*: Bo 82). So Pachomius is happy at the end of his vision of Paradise, when he hears the words: "Go, my son, return to your body, for you still have to suffer a small martyrdom in the world" (*ibid.*, 114) – the "bloodless martyrdom" of monastic life.[2] In those who have faithfully practiced prayer and self-denial in the desert, the beginnings of the radiant life of Paradise are already evident, at times, in their own bodies (*ibid.*). As Abba Joseph of Panephysis observed suggestively to Abba Lot, the monk who wishes it can, even during this life, "become all flame" (*Apophth Patr*: Joseph of Panephysis 7; cf. Arsenius 27).

The writings of the desert tradition, in fact, contain a strong element of "realized eschatology" in their attempts to convey the value and hope of an ascetic life to the wider Church. By forming his disciples into a community, "Antony" writes to his brethren, Christ has accomplished already "the resurrection of our minds from the earth" (*Ep.* 5.2 [PG 40.995c4–7]). Not only is Jesus' resurrection a guarantee that we shall rise in the future, Pachomius teaches his monks; "we have already risen with him" by the "spiritual resurrection" of a lived faith (*Life of Pachomius* G 56; cf. 57). Ascetics who yearn for the Holy Spirit, who welcome his charisms and heed his revelations, "will be as people already translated to the Kingdom while

[they] are still in the body" (Ammonas, Letter 8 [*PO* 10.587.13–588.1]). Athanasius' Antony, in fact, appealing to Lk 17.21 ("the Kingdom of God is within you"), boldly identifies that Kingdom with the order and discipline of a life freely and relentlessly committed to the monastic pursuit of human perfection or ἀρετή (*Life of Antony* 20). It was the sight of Antony, healthy in body and mind and radiating love for Christ after twenty years of sleepless fasting and solitary combat with the demons, Athanasius relates, that finally persuaded his contemporaries of the value of the ascetical way, and turned the desert into a "city of monks" (*ibid.*, 14). The categories and the rhetoric of this passage are classically Greek, and so perhaps foreign to the way of thought of Antony and his Coptic friends; but the sense that God's Kingdom had already begun in the life of the monk was to become a common element in the monastic theology of every culture.

Fourth-century Syriac writers

This same period saw the first flowering of orthodox theology in the Syriac language, in the works of "the Persian sage" Aphrahat (d. after 345) and in the verse homilies and hymns of Ephrem (*c.* 306–73), the outstanding poet and exegete of Syrian Christianity. Both writers were deeply influenced by the Syrian Church's long ascetical tradition, and were especially enthusiastic in commending the life of virginity; both drew their theological inspiration, as well as their literary images and forms, more from Judaeo-Christian than from Hellenistic sources. As a result, their eschatological expectations show important differences from those of the Greek and Latin authors we have so far studied. Neither Aphrahat nor Ephrem pays any attention, in his extant works, to Christian apocalyptic traditions on the end of history or the material universe. Both, however, are deeply preoccupied with death, and their vivid depictions of the realm of the dead reflect some of the conceptions of the afterlife found in the Old Testament and Jewish apocalyptic. Their style of thought, as well as the character of the Syriac language, leads them to express their eschatological hopes in dramatic images and personifications, rather than in the analytical categories of scientific cosmology and psychology, so that it is difficult and perhaps misleading to attempt to force their thought into a consistent system. I shall attempt, none the less, at least a preliminary survey.

Of Aphrahat's twenty-three extant *Demonstrations* or tracts, Numbers 8 (*On the Resurrection*) and 22 (*On Death and the Last Things*) present most of his eschatological thinking. For him – as also for Ephrem – death is an active, personal force, a tyrant who seeks to subjugate the human race and who has only been defeated by Christ (22.1–5). Jesus' descent into Hades, the Kingdom of Death (cf. I Pet 3.18–4.6), marked the beginning of the end of

Death's reign; Jesus then gave Death the "poison" that is gradually paralyzing him, and that will soon bring about his end (22.4f.). Nevertheless, Aphrahat reminds his readers, Death still takes every human being captive, whatever his or her possessions and worldly prospects may be (22.6–8); so he urges them, as "children of peace," to set their hearts on the world to come rather than on this world (22.9–11).

On the subject of the fate of souls after death, Aphrahat insists – as does Ephrem – "that as yet no one has received his reward. For the righteous have not inherited the Kingdom, nor have the wicked gone into torment" (8.22; cf. 20). At present, the dead simply "sleep" in their graves, which are collectively referred to as Sheol, or the underworld. Their capabilities for activity and experience are, apparently, almost non-existent, "for when people die, the animal spirit is buried with the body and sense is taken away from it, but the heavenly spirit they receive [i.e., the Holy Spirit, given in baptism] goes, according to its nature, to Christ" (6.14). Aphrahat, however, seems to ascribe to the dead a kind of anticipatory consciousness of their own future which is akin to dreaming in earthly sleep. So "the servant, for whom his Lord is preparing scourging and bondage, while he is sleeping does not desire to awake, for he knows that when the dawn comes and he awakes, the Lord will scourge and bind him. But the good servant, to whom his Lord has promised gifts, looks expectantly for the time when dawn shall come and he shall receive presents from his Lord" (8.19).[3]

The moment of judgment and retribution, then, will be the moment of resurrection, when the human person is reconstituted in his or her full natural integrity. Aphrahat does not reflect at any length on the anthropological implications of this belief, but he repeats many of the arguments for the credibility of resurrection already familiar from the apologetic tradition, drawing on the analogy of seeds in the ground (8.2f.) and on other scriptural testimonies (8.4–16). The judgment of Christ that will be executed at the resurrection will be a judgment of justice untempered by mercy, for the time of grace will then be over (8.20). The just will be led, after judgment, to a place blessed beyond conception or name, where they will be free from all passion and desire, delivered from sexual differences and the process of ageing, and enabled to live forever, united by love in full equality, in an environment of beauty and light (22.12f.). The wicked will be sent back to Sheol, the realm of Death under the world (22.17,24; cf. 6.6), where they will be punished in the measure and the way that their sins deserve – some in "outer darkness," others in unquenchable fire, others by simple exclusion from the presence of God (22.18–22). Finally, this earth, with its firmament, will pass away, and "God will make a new thing for the children of Adam" (22.24). Aphrahat seems unsure whether this promise implies a recreation of this world as the "inheritance" of the saved, in addition to their life with God, or whether the Kingdom of the just is identical with the rewards described before (22.24). Whatever its concrete form, he is certain that their joy will be complete.

Ephrem reflects many of the same conceptions of the life to come, but gives them a fuller and more vividly imaginative treatment in some of his long theological poems: especially in his *Hymns on Paradise* (HP), which may well be an early work;[4] in several passages of the *Memre* (= metrical discourses) *on Nicomedia* (MN), commemorating the disastrous earthquake that destroyed the former imperial capital in 358; and in the latter half of his *Poems on Nisibis* (*Carmina Nisibena*: CN), written after the Persian conquest of Ephrem's home city in 363.

Like Aphrahat, Ephrem personifies Death as a pitiless enemy of humanity, vying with Satan for mastery over the human race (see especially the "Dialogues between Death and Satan": CN 52–60, and the addresses of Death to his human victims: *ibid.*, 61–68). Death, like Satan, is "greedy" to catch and hold people (MN 8.88; CN 38.1), to deprive them of freedom, their most precious possession (CN 52.10; 55.22–29; 56.1; etc.). Yet Death also acknowledges that he is simply the "guardian of the King's treasure, until he comes" (*ibid.*, 56.6), and that Jesus, who has conquered him, has opened Sheol by his own death (*ibid.*, 36.13–17; 38.1–6). So even Death must cry, however grudgingly, "I am your servant now, O Jesus" (*ibid.*, 38.6).

Ephrem, too, conceives of the time between our death and the second coming of Jesus as a "sleep," a period of inactivity in virtually every aspect of human existence. Because his anthropology is more highly developed than Aphrahat's, and because he is so insistent – in contrast to Bardaisan and other earlier, more dualistic Syriac writers – that the human person needs both body and soul to be functional, Ephrem seems to imagine this sleep as deprived even of the "dreaming" Aphrahat mentions. For Ephrem, the soul without the body is "bound," "paralyzed" (CN 47.6); it is like an embryo in its mother's womb or like a blind or deaf person: "living, but deprived of word and thought" (HP 8.4–6). So there is complete equality in Sheol: the equality of indifference, in which no shade is distinguishable from any other, because the human relationships that demand recognition are no longer possible (MN 8.35–58). There is no sin among the dead (CN 38.4) and no remorse (CN 52.22), or at least no profit in it (*ibid.*, 64.8). Ephrem generally seems, in fact, to leave no room for the purification of sinners after death, although he hints at it in one passage of the *Hymns on Paradise* (10.14), and urges his hearers to pray for their dead, "that they may be worthy of the road to Eden" (CN 73.4). Despite this gloomy picture, Ephrem observes that such a sleep is refreshing for those dead who have "fasted and watched" in this life (CN 43.15), and that they are sure to wake at the dawn of resurrection (*ibid.*, 70.18).

The place where the dead sleep is normally called Sheol in Ehprem's poems, and is conceived, in biblical fashion, as a dark, airless collective grave under the earth (e.g., *CN* 36.11–14; 37.9–11; 50.10ff.; 63.20f.). In some passages, however, Ephrem seems to imagine two distinct places where the souls of the dead await resurrection and judgment: those of sinners wait in Sheol, along with the decomposing bodies of all the dead, but those of the just share "coveted lodgings within the area of heaven" – a kind of margin of Paradise (*HP* 8.11; cf. *CN* 38.4).[5]

Because of his insistence on the positive role of the body in human life and its necessity for a full human existence (e.g., *CN* 47.4), Ephrem sees eschatological reward and punishment as delayed until the resurrection of the dead. Resurrection will begin when souls are "awakened" from their sleep by the angel's trumpet and the commanding voice of God (*CN* 49.16f.). The soul will then be led joyfully back to its "house," and will let its light shine once again through its body's eyes. Color will come back to its skin, and the marks of age and illness will vanish. Together, body and soul will again live; the soul, which is the body's "pillar of support" (*HP* 9.16), will give life to the body and use it as its musical instrument (*HP* 8.2,8).

In addition to imagining the process with a poet's concrete vigor, Ephrem echoes much of the earlier apologetic discussion of the resurrection in these works. He not only argues that it is possible for God to find and reassemble the material components of the decomposed body – like a smelter, separating gold from dross (*CN* 43.18ff.) – since God created the body out of dust at the beginning (*CN* 45.13–15); he also insists that justice demands the body should share in the soul's recompense, as it shared the soul's moral struggle during life (*ibid.*, 1–6; 47.2f.).

Ephrem's poetic imagination reaches even beyond the promised resurrection. In his *Hymns on Paradise*, he describes the joys of heaven in carefully crafted scenes of rich and delicate beauty. Though it surrounds this present world like a golden crown, or like the halo around the moon (*HP* 1.8f.), Paradise itself is an enclosed garden, whose gates open only for the just, after they have risen from the dead (2.1; 8.11). Inside, there are various "storeys" or levels of glory, corresponding to the deserts of each inhabitant (2.10f.). The "tents" where the just will dwell are the trees of the garden, each offering shelter, fruit, perfume and a dewy bath for the one who lives in its branches (9.3–6; cf. 7.16,18). At the center of the garden, Christ stands as the tree of life, illuminating Paradise with his radiance; all the other trees bow towards him in homage (3.2,15). In this environment the round of seasons will disappear (10.2–4, 6–9), and the whole year will be blessed with flowers and fruit (*ibid.*), refreshing breezes (9.7–16) and delicious fragrances (9.17; 11.9–15).[6]

Ephrem points out, however, that all these images are but "the words of your [earthly] homeland," (*HP* 11.7.4) clothing a reality which escapes description because "it is, in its essence, pure and spiritual" (*ibid.*, 4.7f.). Ultimately, the only hunger the citizens of heaven will feel is the hunger of their souls for God (*ibid.*, 9.18). And God will satisfy them with his own glory (*ibid.*); the human spirit will "put on the image of the divine majesty" and "clothe" the soul with its beauty, which will in turn clothe the body (*ibid.*, 9.20), until the human person is transformed and totally "nourished" by the glory of God (*ibid.*, 9.28).

Ephrem's picture of Gehenna is less detailed and more traditional than his picture of heaven. The damned there seem to suffer most from their awareness that they have lost all hope of sharing in beauty and happiness (*HP* 2.3f.; 7.29). A "great gulf" separates them from Paradise, as in the parable of Dives and Lazarus (Lk 16.19–31), but because they can see the joys of their loved ones there, "their torments are redoubled" (*HP* 1.17; cf. 1.13).

Although he presents no developed doctrine of universal salvation, Ephrem does allow for the possibility that God will mitigate the exercise of his justice against condemned sinners. So he says the sufferings of the damned will last "without end" in *HP* 2.4, but suggests elsewhere that the Lord, in his mercy, may allow some "drops of water" to fall into Gehenna occasionally to refresh them (*HP* 10.15). In *CN* 59.8 he is still more hopeful, allowing Death to say tauntingly to Satan: "Perhaps some day Gehenna will be emptied by God's mercy, and only you and your servants will remain behind." He also speaks several times in the *Hymns on Paradise* of a kind of grassy border, just outside the walls of Paradise, where those who have sinned without full knowledge – "simpletons and fools" – will be allowed to settle, after they have "expiated their debt," and where they will feed on the "crumbs" of the blessed (1.16f.; 5.15; 10.14). Several times in these poems, Ephrem humbly prays that he, a sinner, may be allowed to participate in at least this marginal beatitude (5.15; 7.26).

Mid-fourth-century Greek writers

Greek theology of the mid fourth century showed little direct interest in eschatological themes. One reason for this, surely, was the new security in which the Church found itself after Constantine's accession, and the consequent receding of the apocalyptic horizon. The end of persecution and the sudden availability of imperial patronage for the Christian community suddenly made the "signs of the times" seem far less threatening, and invited Christian thinkers to take a more immanent view of God's salvation in human history. Another reason for the de-emphasis of eschatology was probably the Arian controversy, which focused the attention of both the

Greek and the Latin Churches, from the early 320s until after the Council of Constantinople in 381, almost exclusively on the formulation of Jesus' relationship to God, and left little theological energy available for other questions.

(a) Some assumptions about Christian expectations for the future are revealed by theologians of this period, however, in the course of arguments about seemingly unrelated issues. Athanasius (c. 295–373), for instance, argues for the immortality of the soul as part of his larger demonstration that humanity needs to know the Word of God for the sake of its own self-fulfillment (Ctr Gentes 33). He also draws on Daniel's prophecies of eschatological conflict to support his identification of the Emperor Constantius II, patron of the anti-Nicene party, as the Antichrist (Hist Arian 74, 78). Eustathius of Antioch (d. before 337), Athanasius' enthusiastic supporter in the early years of the struggle against the Arians, reveals in passing something of his own conception of the afterlife in his anti-Origenist tract on the Witch of Endor (De Engastrimytho: ed. A. Jahn: TU 2.1 [Leipzig 1886]; cf. I Sam 28), where he several times repeats the axiom that only God can truly bring the souls of the dead out of Hades (3[25.17ff.]; 16[52.21ff.]; 23[63.8ff.]; 30[75.19ff.]).

(b) In the works of Eusebius of Caesaraea (d. 339), the new, historically oriented attitude of mid-fourth-century Christians towards the Church's hope is most clearly apparent. A learned and careful defender of Origen, Eusebius synthesizes Origenist exegesis and doctrine in his theological works with a thoroughness of detail that matches their doctrinal moderation. So he refers in a number of passages – especially in his exegetical works – to various features of both an Origenist and a more traditional eschatological hope, without offering much thematic comment on them.[7]

Eusebius' own theological interest is clearly much more directed to the present, where he sees God's saving work throughout history as culminated in the Church's new-found freedom. After the cleansing chastisement of the Great Persecution (HE 8.1), God's Church has now finally been established in peace, through the instrumentality of Constantine, God's chosen servant (Vita Const 1.24). In Constantine's rule, Eusebius finds a new kind of "realized eschatology," a foretaste of the eternal Kingdom: "God – that God, I say, who is the common Savior of all – having treasured up with himself, for those who love godliness, greater blessings than human thought has conceived, gives the pledge and first-fruits of future rewards even here, assuring in some sense immortal hopes to mortal eyes" (Vita Const 1.33; cf. Laus Const 3.5).

This strong sense of the present reality of salvation within the political and historical order makes Eusebius noticeably suspicious of the apocalyptic side of earlier eschatology. His contempt for millenarians like Papias or Nepos of Arsinoe is apparent (*HE* 3.39.13; 7.24.1), and he is himself noncommittal about the authenticity and canonicity of the Apocalypse of John (*HE* 3.24.18–25.4).

God's retribution, both positive and negative, takes place, in Eusebius' eyes, within history as well as after it. For Herod's terrible crime of slaughtering the innocents, for instance, "divine justice overtook him while still alive, giving him a foretaste of what awaited him in the next world" (*HE* 1.8.4). As the earthly kingdom takes on, for Eusebius, more and more characteristics of the Kingdom of promise, the future hopes of the Church become simply a two-dimensional backdrop for the theatre of human history, where human actors corrupt or realize God's gift of salvation, build Christ's ideal society or hinder its coming. For his de-emphasis of eschatology as well as for his reading of the past, Eusebius has been called with some justice "the first political theologian in the Christian Church."[8]

(c) In the writings of Marcellus of Ancyra (d. *c.* 374), whom Eusebius considered his chief theological opponent, even Christology and Trinitarian theology are shaped by the dynamic lines of what Martin Tetz has called Marcellus' "eschatologically determined concept of history."[9] A strong defender of the Nicene teaching that the Son is "of the same substance" (*homoousios*) as the Father, and so a determined ally of Athanasius, Marcellus conceived the relationship of the Logos and the Spirit to God the Father in essentially "economic" or historically developing terms, not unlike those suggested by Hippolytus in his *Contra Noetum* more than a century earlier. Although radically and ultimately one, God has involved himself in human history according to a gradually unfolding plan that is divided into several stages: a "first economy," apparently from the creation of the world to the Incarnation; a "second economy," the "fresh and new economy according to the flesh," which is the age of Christ (frr. 4, 9, 17, 19, 43, 70, 100, 117);[10] and perhaps also a "third economy" of the Holy Spirit, which is the age of the Church.[11] Just as the "second economy," that of the enfleshed Logos, had a beginning in time, it will also have a historical end, when the Logos is fully reunited with the Father and "God is all in all" (frr. 111–2).

At that termination of salvation-history, the flesh which the Logos assumed will no longer remain united with him, "as though it were useful" (fr. 117); it will have accomplished its purpose of being the vehicle for communicating to the Church, which is now his body, the gift of immortality, and both Christ and his body will be absorbed into the divine mystery. "Thus his human economy and reign seem to have an end," Marcellus continues (fr. 117). "For the saying of the apostle, 'until he makes his enemies the footstool of his feet' [I Cor 15.25] seems to mean nothing else but this. So when he 'makes his enemies the footstool of his feet,' he no longer will exercise this partial rule, but will be king of all things that are. For he will rule along with God the Father, whose Word he was and is . . . Therefore also the Acts of the Apostles teaches concerning this man, whom the Word of God assumed and later seated at the right hand of the Father, that 'heaven must receive him until the time of the restoration' [ἀποκατά-στασις: Acts 3.21]. This passage defines a certain limit or fixed period, in which the text says it is right that the human economy is thus united to the Word. For what else does 'until the time of restoration' mean, except to indicate to us a coming age, in which all things will share in perfect restoration (ἀποκατάστασις)? . . . Clearly and explicitly, then, the divine Paul says that in the short time of the ages that have passed and are yet to come, the fleshly economy of the Word has come into being for our sakes, and that it will have an end corresponding to its beginning. So he says, 'Then is the end, when he hands over the Kingdom to God the Father'" (I Cor 15.24).

Marcellus later professed, under pressure from his critics, that there would be *no* end to the Kingdom of Christ (so Marcellus' profession of faith at a Roman synod of 340: Epiphanius, *Pan* 72.2.6f.), and suggested, in the work called *De Incarnatione et Contra Arianos* 20f.,[12] that what *will* come to an end in the divine economy is the separateness of humanity from God and the conflict between the Church and its "enemies": death and the forces of evil. "For so long as his members have not yet all been subjected, he, as their head, has not yet been subjected to the Father, but awaits his own members . . . For we are those who are subjected in him to the Father, and we are those who rule in him until he has set our enemies under our feet. Because of our enemies, the ruler of the heavens became like us and received the human throne of David, his father according to the flesh, in order to rebuild it and restore it, so that when it is restored we might all rule in him and he might hand over this restored human rule to the Father, so that God might be all in all . . ." (*PG* 26.1020C5–1021A8; cf. frr. 110, 121, 127).

In these and similar passages, Marcellus transforms the earlier tradition of a final *apokatastasis* of creation into a grand integration of economic Trinitarianism, a Body-of-Christ ecclesiology, and an apocalyptic vision of cosmic transformation. Despite its obvious resemblance to Origen's eschatological hope, this synthesis seemed to the Origenist Eusebius of Caesaraea a contradiction of the Church's Trinitarian faith – ultimately, perhaps, because it was the antithesis of Eusebius' conception of how God has chosen to save the inhabitants of time and space. Whether eschatological salvation implies the end of all history, or simply the final revelation of God's saving action within it, is, as the controversy over Marcellus reveals, a question of decisive importance for one's understanding of God, as well as for one's politics and one's expectations of the future.

(d) In the eighteenth and last of his *Catechetical Lectures*, Cyril of Jerusalem (d. 386) offers his candidates for baptism a traditional, scripturally founded exposition of the Christian hope for resurrection and eternal life, as it is expressed in the baptismal creeds. Stressing the importance of this hope in motivating the Christian's moral behavior (*Cat* 18.1), Cyril gives an apology for the resurrection (*ibid.*, 2–13), against the criticisms of "Greeks and Samaritans," that incorporates many of the standard arguments we have met before: the creative power of God (*ibid.*, 3, 9), analogies in nature (*ibid.*, 6–8, 10), and the requirement of justice that all the deeds of a human life receive their retribution (4). After providing proofs for the resurrection from the Old Testament, calculated to meet Jewish objections (11–13), Cyril adds further scriptural testimonies to underline the specifically Christian hope for resurrection with Christ (14–18). He concludes his exposition with shattering simplicity: "We shall be raised, therefore, all with our bodies eternal ...," the just in order to "hold converse with the angels" and the sinner in order to "burn eternally in fire" (19).[13]

(e) Apollinarius of Laodicaea (*c.* 310–*c.* 390), known chiefly for his conception of Christ as an organic hybrid of Word and flesh, was accused by a number of his contemporary critics of also being a millenarian, and of reintroducing "a second Judaism" with his expectations of the Kingdom of the just (so Basil, *Ep* 263.4; 265.2; Gregory Nazianzen, *Ep* 102.14; cf. 101.63). Jerome includes Apollinarius among the later followers of Papias, in the tradition of Irenaeus, Tertullian, Victorinus of Pettau and Lactantius (*De Vir Ill* 18; cf. Ps.-Maximus Confessor, *Scholia in De Eccl Hier* 7.2: PG 4.176C10–15). Jerome also quotes a sizeable passage from Apollinarius in his own commentary on Daniel 9.24 (PL 25.548B7–549A5), in which Apollinarius predicts that the coming of the Antichrist, the conversion of Israel by Elijah and the restoration of Jerusalem will all occur in the "seventieth week of years" after the birth of Jesus (i.e., 483–90). Jerome quotes Apollinarius as saying he borrowed this calculation from the works of Sextus Julius Africanus (*ibid.*, 548D10–549A3). Epiphanius (*Pan* 77.36.5), on the other hand, denies that Apollinarius was a millenarian; and the few allusions in Apollinarius' extant writings to the second coming of Christ (κατὰ μέρος πίστις 12) or to eternal life (*De Fide et Incarnatione* 1) suggest nothing unusual about his eschatology. His followers seem to have indulged in a wide range of theological speculations, however, so that millenarian expectations may have been characteristic of at least some in his school.

Basil of Caesaraea

Of the three great Cappadocian Fathers, Basil of Caesaraea (*c.* 330–79) exhibits the widest range in his eschatological thought. An admirer of Origen in his younger days, and the compiler – along with Gregory of Nazianzus – of the anthology of passages from Origen known as the *Philokalia*, Basil shows in many of his works an Origenistic tendency to interpret the traditional images of the Christian hope in psychological or spiritual terms. As a preacher and pastor, however, Basil was also keenly aware of the importance of the prospects of judgment and retribution in the moral life of Christians; as he grew older, he seems to have become more critical of Origenism, in this as in other respects,[14] and more severe in his own expectations for the future.

So in the prologue to his *Moralia* entitled "On the Judgment of God" (*PG* 31.653–76), probably a work of his last years,[15] Basil stresses the serious-ness of God's demands in a way that seems to rule out a doctrine of universal salvation. Observing that Scripture teaches that any sin, however great or small in itself, will be judged and punished with the same severity, because it is disobedience towards God (c. 4:661A15–B6; c. 7: 669B6f.), and that sins of omission will be regarded by God in the same way as sins of commission (c. 8:673B5–C14), Basil states baldly: "I see no forgiveness left at all, in connection with any of [God's] commands, for those who have not been converted from their infidelity, unless one dares to think some other position – one that contradicts such bare, clear and absolute statements – accords with the meaning [of Scripture]" (c. 8:672C12–D1).[16] In the *Regulae Brevius Tractatae* (Resp. 267), Basil replies with a decisive "no" to the question of whether there will someday be an end to all punishment. To imagine that the fires of hell will ever go out, he insists, is a deceit of the devil (*PG* 31.1265A1–6): eternal punishment can no more come to an end than can eternal life (*ibid.*, A6–9).

Basil uses the traditional images of the coming judgment and of eternal punishment to great advantage in homilies and letters, especially those intended for a monastic audience. So in his "Letter to a Fallen Virgin" (*Ep* 46.5), he urges a woman who has abandoned the ascetical life to think both of her own last day, with its prospect of an immediate divine judgment of her deeds, and of "the final end of our common life." When that end arrives, Christ will come again "to judge living and dead, and to repay each person according to his or her actions." Then the sinner faces endless punishment in hell, with no prospect of escape. "This [i.e., the prospect of judgment] is not a myth," he warns at the end of his *Homily in Time of Famine*; "it is a teaching proclaimed by a voice that cannot deceive" (*PG* 31.328C1–3).

Basil paints the punishments of hell with unprecedented vividness in his

Homily on Psalm 33.8, as a way of fulfilling the Psalmist's promise to "teach" his children – presumably the ascetics in his community – "the fear of the Lord" (Ps 33.12). "The one who has done much evil in his life," he preaches, "will be confronted by frightening, sinister-looking angels, emitting fire in their breath and their glances because of the harshness of their character; their gloomy and threatening demeanor will be like the night. See the deep pit, impenetrable darkness; fire without brightness, which has the power to burn but is deprived of light. Then imagine a kind of worm that is venomous and carnivorous, that can eat ravenously without ever being filled, and that causes unbearable pain with its bites. Then think of the worst punishment of all: eternal reproach and shame. Fear these things; and trained by this fear, rein in your soul from its desire for evil" (*PG* 29.372A7–B6). In another passage in the same group of homilies, Basil portrays Satan, "the prince of this world," as examining the "athletes of God" after their death, to see if they have come through life's contest unmarked (*Hom. in Ps.* 7.2: *PG* 29.232C8–D2).[17]

In other passages of his homilies on the Psalms, however, Basil still draws on the gentler, more allegorizing interpretations of the Origenist tradition to articulate the Christian hope. So he suggests, in his *Homily on Psalm* 48.2, that our own conscience is really our only accuser in God's judgment (*PG* 437A5–14). The "burning arrows" God aims at sinners, according to Ps 7.13, are "fleshly loves [that] burn the soul: the desire of money, flaming wrath, the smouldering grief that wastes the soul, and fears alien to God" (*Hom in Ps* 7.7: *PG* 29.248B3–6).[18]

The fulfillment of human desires after death, as Basil often describes it, also owes much to Origen's spiritualizing style of thought. Our "blessed end," towards which we strain during this life in slow, laborious steps, is "the knowledge of God," according to his treatise *On the Holy Spirit* 8.18; it is "to become like God, as far as this is possible for human nature," through the transforming effect of knowledge (*ibid.*, 1.2). This knowledge, which makes the human knower like God, is the work of the Holy Spirit, who purifies and heals those who receive him and "makes them spiritual people through fellowship with himself" (*ibid.*, 9.23; cf. 26.61). The final realization of this fellowship and vision is only possible after the resurrection, when human beings will be freed of the "veil" imposed on their sight by the present weakness of the flesh, and will share the qualities of the angels (*Hom in Ps* 33.11: *PG* 29.377B10–C10). Basil makes no attempt to depict this state of beatitude in earthly images, but contents himself with describing it as a "place" free from all the cares and limitations of earthly existence. "It is the place of the living, in which there is no night, or sleep, the imitator of death; in which there is no food or drink, the supports of our weakness; in which there is no illness, no suffering, no medicine, no lawcourts, no marketplaces, no crafts, no money – the origin of evil, the cause of war, the root of hatred. No, it is the place of those who live, not of those who are dying through sin – the place of those who live the true life, which is in Christ Jesus" (*Hom in Ps* 114.5: *PG* 29.493c5–12).

Gregory of Nazianzus

Gregory of Nazianzus (329/30–*c.* 390), Basil's lifelong friend and somewhat reluctant supporter, was a man of more retiring temperament, and involved himself much less willingly than his friend did in the pastoral and administrative duties of being a bishop. Known as "the Theologian" by the later Greek tradition, Gregory joined wholeheartedly in the defense of Nicene Trinitarianism against the arguments of the later Arians or "Eunomians," and contributed some of the most precise and subtly nuanced formulations of the orthodox doctrine of God in Greek theological literature. At heart, however, Gregory remained an impassioned Christian rhetor, rather than an original or deeply speculative thinker: his gifts and interests were religious and literary rather than dialectical or analytical, and his works, as a result, do not usually offer either new lines of theological development or a comprehensive articulation of earlier tradition.

This lack of systematic development is noticeable in Gregory's treatment of eschatology.[19] A number of his orations and poems contain allusions to traditional Christian conceptions of the end of life and of human history. These are often passages of great power, in which the mode of discourse is clearly meant to be poetic rather than literal or prophetic. In the *Moral Poems*, for instance, he describes existence after death with a gloomy picture of Hades (2.141–44), and later predicts that the "last day" will bring, for the wicked, eternal fire, darkness, and the worm (15.98–100). Other passages offer a more sophisticated theological interpretation of these expectations. So in *Oration 16*, "On his Father's Silence because of the Hailstorm," Gregory develops at some length a picture of "the judgments to come" (cc. 7–9). Making use of traditional apocalyptic imagery to paint the details of the scene (especially c. 9), he nevertheless makes it clear that the heart of the drama will be interior and spiritual. It is our sins that will be our accusers before God (c. 8); union of the soul with God is the essence of the Kingdom; and the chief torment of the damned is "being outcast from God and the shame of conscience which has no limits" (c. 9). His panegyric on his brother Caesarius (*Or 7*) contains, too, in its depictions of the joys of heaven, a number of references to light and the company of angels and saints (e.g., cc. 17 and 21; cf. *Or* 8.23; 40.46). Yet the core of Christian fulfillment, here and elsewhere in Gregory's works, is "the more perfect possession and vision of the good on high (*Or* 7.17), the yet-undreamed-of "teachings" that the eternal Bridegroom will communicate to "the souls that have come in with him" (*Or* 40.46).

At heart, Gregory is always the cautious Origenist, sympathizing with the Alexandrian's spiritual interpretation of Christian images, yet tending to revel still in those images' pictorial power, rather than to explain them away by allegory. Gregory regularly emphasizes – as a shocking yet true paradox – that the goal of the divine economy is our participation, as human creatures, in the Godhead. The divine Logos "assumes the poverty of my flesh, that I may assume the riches of his Godhead. He that is full empties himself, that I may have a share in his fullness" (*Or* 38.13). The Holy Spirit can be proven equal to the Father and the Son by the fact that he "makes me God, joins me to the Godhead" in baptism (*Or* 31.4,28; cf. *Or* 7.23; 11.5; 14.23; 34.12; *Poem Mor* 10.140–43). The longed-for fullness of this union with God, for Gregory, will be above all else a fullness of knowledge: specifically, our understanding of the Triune nature of God which we now only know as mystery (*Or* 23.11).

On two key issues of Origenist eschatology, the purgative nature of all punishment and the hope for universal salvation, Gregory offers a cautious, undogmatic support of the Origenist position. So in *Oration* 39.19 ("On the Holy Lights"), after taking issue with the rigorist position of the Novatianists on baptism, Gregory says he is content to let them go their way, recognizing that, as resisters of "Christ's way," they may have to undergo a painful "baptism of fire" themselves later on. Here and in *Oration* 3.7, he alludes to I Cor 3.12–15 as grounds for expecting that "the stubble of evil" that remains among human works will ultimately be consumed by God's purifying fire. In a famous passage in the oration "On Holy Baptism" (40.36), Gregory briefly discusses the cleansing fire that Christ came to "cast on earth" (Lk 12.49), and adds: "I know also a fire that is not cleansing, but avenging, . . . the unquenchable fire that is associated with the worm that does not die, eternal fire for the wicked. For they all belong to the destroying power – though some may prefer, even on this point, to take a more merciful view of this fire, one more worthy of the one who chastises."

Although he does not speculate about the beginning of created history, Gregory does refer to its ultimate goal, in an important passage of his fourth "Theological Oration" (*Or* 30.6), in unmistakably Origenist terms, as the union of all rational creatures with God. "God will be all in all," he writes, "in the time of restoration (ἀποκατάστασις). I do not mean the Father, as if the Son were to be dissolved in him, like a torch that has been separated for a time from a great fire and is then rejoined to it – nor should the Sabellians be corrupted by this passage [i.e., I Cor 15.28]. I mean God as a whole, at the time when we are no longer many, as we now are in our movements and passivities, bearing in ourselves nothing at all of God, or only a little; we shall then be wholly like God, receptive of God as a whole and of God alone. This, after all, is the perfection ($\tau\epsilon\lambda\epsilon\acute{\iota}\omega\sigma\iota\varsigma$) towards which we strive."

Gregory does not speculate on the physical details of the resurrection, or offer any apologetic for its plausibility, but he does reflect in a more general way, in his panegyric on his brother Caesarius (*Or* 7.21), both on the share of the body in final fulfillment and on the "interim state" between death and resurrection. Here he displays again his characteristic blend of traditionalism and enlightened interpretation: "I believe the words of the wise, that every good soul, whom God loves, departs from here when it is set free from the bonds of the body and immediately begins to sense and perceive the blessings that await it, inasmuch as that which darkened it has been purged away or laid aside – I do not know how else to express it – and it feels a wondrous pleasure and exultation, and goes rejoicing to meet its Lord . . . Then, a little later, it receives its kindred flesh, which once shared in its pursuits of things above, from the earth which both gave and had been entrusted with it; in some way known to God, who knit them together and dissolved them, it enters with [its flesh] upon the inheritance of the glory there. And as it [the soul] shared, through their close union, in its [the body's] hardships, so also it [the soul] bestows upon it [the body] a portion of its joys, gathering it up entirely into itself and becoming with it one in spirit and in mind and in God, the mortal and mutable being swallowed up in life." It is the unitive, spiritualizing hope of Origen and his followers, expressed with the balance and the pathos of the classical artist.

Gregory of Nyssa

Gregory of Nyssa (*c.* 335–94), the younger brother of Basil of Caesaraea, was himself an accomplished and impassioned rhetorician; he was also, however, a more original theological thinker than either Basil or Gregory Nazianzen, and carried on Origen's spiritual and intellectual tradition with unequaled subtlety and depth. Gregory's reformulation of Origen's eschatological perspectives, especially, were to have a lasting if controversial influence on later Greek Patristic and Byzantine theology.

One subject on which Gregory both reaffirms and refines Origen's eschatology is his hope for universal salvation or *apokatastasis*, the restoration of intellectual creation to an "original" unity with God in contemplative beatitude.[20] For the human creature, Gregory frequently identifies the promised resurrection with the first stage of this *apokatastasis*: for "the resurrection promises us nothing else than the restoration of the fallen to their ancient state" (*De Hom Opif* 17.2; cf. *Hom in Eccl* 1.9; *De An et Res: PG* 46.148 A1f., 153C1–3; *Funeral Oration for Pulcheria: GNO* 9.472.7–10; *De Orat Dom* 4; *Or Catechet* 26; *In Beat* 8). "The aim and limit of our journey through this world," he writes in his sermon *On the Dead*, "is our restoration (ἀποκατάστασις) to the ancient state, which was nothing else than likeness to the divine reality" (*GNO* 9.51.16ff.). However, Gregory clearly rejects Origen's notion that this "original state" was a prehistorical existence of unembodied souls, and that our present corporeal existence is the result of a "fall." Such a theory, he points out, actually lessens our hope of ultimate salvation, since it suggests human beings are now in a weaker state than they were when they first fell (*De Hom Opif* 28.4f.). Furthermore, it implies that even a life of heavenly contemplation is not secure from sin, so that the prospect of an endless cycle of falls and restorations cannot be ruled out (*De An et Res*: PG 113B1–D2; cf. 125A1–C2).

What is "restored" or recaptured in the resurrection, in Gregory's view, is first of all the actual perfection or "fullness" of the rational creature's possible reality that is eternally present to the mind of God, a σκόπος or goal that preexists the human race's historical journey and is realized by creatures gradually in time (*De An et Res*: PG 46.152A1–11). This goal, expressed in biblical language, is the "image of God," created as the final reality of human existence by the same divine act that created them "male and female," but now marred by the tensions and ambiguities of fleshly existence (*De Hom Opif* 16). Secondly, *apokatastasis* is for Gregory of Nyssa the realization in the "full number" (πλήρωμα) of human individuals of the bodily and spiritual characteristics their ancestor Adam possessed before his sin. It is a process that must follow the laws and undergo the vicissitudes of gradual, organic growth; but in the end it will see fulfilled in every member of the race – like the grains of wheat in a ripe cornfield – what belonged originally to the one seed from which all have sprung (*De An et Res*: PG 46.156B12–157B5).[21]

In any case, Gregory clearly shares Origen's hope for universal salvation.[22] Although a few passages in his works allude to the exclusion of sinners from God's city (e.g., *In Inscr Psal* 2.16 [*GNO* 5.175.15–19]) or to eternal punishment (e.g., *De Paup Amand* [*GNO* 9.99.12–100.5]), Gregory makes it plain in many other places that he believes God's plan will ultimately be realized in every creature.

Commenting on the common desire of all creatures not only to be rescued from destruction but to be united in the love of God, Gregory observes, at the end of his *Homilies on the Song of Songs*: "There is a common movement in all souls, of every rank, towards such blessedness . . . It is the nature of every creature to strain, in its yearning, towards what is blessed and praised . . . until all become one, gazing at the same goal of their desire, and no evil is left in anyone, and 'God becomes all in all,' while they are joined to each other in unity by sharing in the good" (*In Cant Hom* 15 [*GNO* 6.468.15–469.9]). This restoration to unity will touch "those now lying in sin" (*Or Catech* 26), and will include even those previously condemned to hell, according to *Life of Moses* 2.82.²³

The main reason Gregory gives for adopting this position is that evil, being the corruption or disfigurement of what is good rather than a substance in its own right, must eventually come to an end. Only the good, as genuine being, has the positive characteristic of permanence (*De An et Res* [PG 46.69C1–72B10; 101A2–8; 104B13–105A2]; *De Hom Opif* 21.1; *De Tridui Spatio* [GNO 9.285.14–23]).²⁴ Evil and death are the "creation" of the human race, not of God (*De Virg* 12). Human nature, by its natural dynamism, always moves onward towards the good (*De Hom Opif* 21.2); so the finitude of evil means that the journey of every soul, however perverted its direction may be at the start, will end in the possession of the good. The ability of the human soul to perceive the goodness of the divine nature means both that it will always long for God as its ultimate good, and that it possesses already a likeness to God and the capacity to share in his life (*Or Catech* 5). Gregory takes it as axiomatic that this capacity cannot be permanently frustrated.

The resurrection of the body is a key element in Gregory's conception of final human fulfillment, an event that he often presents as the first stage of the *apokatastasis* or restoration of humanity to its original and ideal form.²⁵ The reason for this lies not only in the Church's traditional stress on the hope of resurrection, which Gregory accepts as a part of orthodox faith (*De An et Res* [PG 46.108C10–109A5; 129B13–132B14]), but also in Gregory's anthropology: for him, the human person is not a soul that later acquired a material body as chastisement, but a true composite of spiritual and material dimensions which were created together, and which depend on each other for their full existence (e.g., *De An et Res* [PG 46.28C1–29B4; 128A14–B3]). Only when this composite recaptures its pristine perfection will the human creature again fully realize the image of God, as Adam and Eve did at their creation.

Gregory develops from this anthropology, in fact, a new apologetic for the intelligibility of the resurrection. Because of the internal coherence of the human person, the soul – which preserves most fully in itself the form (εἶδος) that is the person's principle of continuity in change – "recognizes" that form as it is stamped on every particle of its body's matter, even after death and decomposition. So the soul is capable, at the resurrection, of "attracting again to itself that which is its own" (*De Hom Opif* 27.5,2; *De An et Res*: PG 46.77B8–80A12; *In Sanctum Pascha*: GNO 9.247.2–10; 252.9–24). The soul, in fact, as an uncircumscribed spiritual substance, remains present with all the atoms of the decaying body as they are scattered through the universe, "and there is no force to tear her away from her cohesion with them" (*De An et Res* [PG 46.48 A10–B10; 76A13–B6; 85A1–14]).

From this anthropology, too, emerge the characteristics of the risen body, as Gregory understands them. It will indeed be identical with the present body, and recognizable as such (so *De Mortuis* [*GNO* 9.64.20ff.]), yet it will be "subtle and ethereal" in texture, "with a brighter and more entrancing beauty" (*De An et Res* [*PG* 46.108A2–8]; *De Mortuis* [*GNO* 9.62.18–63.3]).[26] Correspondingly, it will have "deposited in death" all the characteristics that now result from sin and disorder in our natures: "dishonor, I mean, and corruption and weakness and the characteristics of age" (*De An et Res* [*PG* 46.156A6–10]). Nor will it possess the sexual differences now required for procreation (*De Mortuis* [*GNO* 9.63.3–22; cf. *ibid.*, 59.23–60.6]). Freed from the process of ageing and decay, the risen person will be consumed by an ever-increasing desire for God, transcending his or her own limitations constantly in "the beautiful passion of insatiability" (*De Mort* [*GNO* 9.61.19–24]; cf. *In Cant* 11 [*GNO* 6.321.5–25]). "This is really what seeing God is," Gregory remarks in the *Life of Moses*: "never to reach satiety in one's desire; one must look always through what it is possible to see towards the desire of seeing more, and be inflamed" (2.239).

In most of his works, Gregory's reflection on Christian fulfillment is centered on its spiritual character, as eternal contemplation, and on the collective salvation of the whole human race at the end of history. He does, however, occasionally speak in more concrete and traditional terms of the reward of individuals immediately after death, especially in his funeral orations. So he assures his hearers that Meletius, the deceased bishop of Antioch, has already entered into the heavenly sanctuary, where he intercedes for his friends on earth (*In Meletium* [*GNO* 9.454.4–12]). The forty martyrs of Sebaste, too, as "athletes of God," have been allowed to pass by the cherub with the flaming sword and to enter Paradise, where they pray that we may follow them (*PG* 46.772B10–C6). The Empress Flacilla has been received into the bosom of Abraham, "by the spring of Paradise . . . under the shadow of the tree of life" (*In Flacillam* [*GNO* 9.489.16–19]).[27]

In order to participate in the eternal movement of endlessly knowing and loving God, every human being needs to be purified in both these capacities. For Gregory of Nyssa, this need is the fundamental reason both for Christian asceticism and for the punishments traditionally awaited by Christians after death. As we have mentioned, he understands the fall of the human race as the voluntary choice of evil by our ancestors, a choice that established in their descendants "the habit of sinning" (*De Virg* 12). The effect of this epidemic of evil choices has been to disfigure the beauty of the divine image in which the human person was created. To restore that beauty, to reveal the authentic image in the human ability to know and love God, a difficult and painful process of "cleansing" is required, which Gregory describes by a number of vivid similes (*De Virg* 12; *De An et Res* [*PG* 46.97B1–101A8]), including that of purgative fire (*De An et Res* [*PG* 46.152A14–B8; 157C12–

15]; *Or Catech* 8; *De Infantibus* [*PG* 46.168ʙ11–c1]). If such purgation is not realized before death, it must take place after the resurrection, in order to prepare the reconstituted human being to participate in the life of God (*Or Catech* 35).

At the end of the *Catechetical Oration* (40), Gregory reminds his readers that the "fire" and the "worm" traditionally associated with this purgative punishment are very different from those we know on earth; the fact that they are described as "eternal" should be enough to suggest their other-worldly character. Although *they* are eternal, however, Gregory nowhere asserts that sinners will be punished eternally. Such punishment could only be conceived of as vindictive, and Gregory makes it clear that God does not punish in this sense at all, but only "to separate the good from evil and to draw it into the communion of blessedness" (*De An et Res* [*PG* 46.100ʙ13–15]).[28]

Christians who recognize their need for purification can begin it in this life through the practice of voluntary penance and asceticism – especially through celibacy – and through a life given to contemplating the truth and beauty of God (*De Virg* 12). The result of such self-imposed discipline is freedom (*De An et Res* [*PG* 46.101c6–13]), and a deeper insight into the true values of human existence (*De Mort* [*GNO* 9.54.11–17]). It is the start of a necessary educational process, Gregory observes in Origenistic fashion, a process in which one is "either purified in the present life through diligence and 'philosophy' [i.e., asceticism], or after one leaves this world through being melted in the purifying fire" (*ibid.*, 54.17–20). Purgation, for Gregory, is simply the painful, strenuous side of the return journey to God, on which all rational creatures are already embarked. However laborious the journey may be, Gregory is convinced that all of us will someday reach its goal.

The Origenist controversy

At the time that the Cappadocian Fathers were combining traditional eschatological themes, each in his own fashion, with the allegorical exegesis and spiritualized anthropology of the Origenist school, opposition to Origenist theology – and especially to its eschatology – reached a new peak in Egypt and Palestine. A synod held in Alexandria in 400, under its bishop Theophilus, condemned as heretical a number of doctrines the participants in the synod claimed to find in Origen's works.[29] Apparently Origen's writings were being carefully studied in the final decades of the fourth century, and his tradition of theological speculation was being enthusiastically carried on by a small but influential group of contemplative ascetics in the Egyptian desert – particularly at the monastic centers of Nitria and "the Cells."[30]

The outraged reaction against these Origenists in Egypt seems to have been inflamed, if not begun, by Epiphanius (*c.* 315–403), bishop of Salamis in Cyprus, whose *Panarion* or handbook of heresies, written between 374 and 377, devotes a long chapter to an attack on Origen. Besides criticizing Origen's Christology and his theory of the pre-existence and fall of souls, Epiphanius accuses Origen of conceiving of the resurrection in an exclusively spiritual sense, and so of denying that the present body will share in eternal life (*Pan* 64.63–71).[31] Epiphanius' own position, developed more fully in his catechetical handbook, the *Ancoratus* (written in 374), resembles that of Methodius seventy years earlier: this present flesh will rise again, and the risen body will be identical in every important respect with the body of our earthly struggle (87). Arguing both from biblical texts (94, 99) and from analogies in nature (83–90), Epiphanius draws on the classical apologetic, available since Athenagoras, to defend his literal understanding of the Christian hope of resurrection. It is this hope, in his view, that above all distinguishes orthodox Christians from heretics and pagans. "The message of our salvation," he concludes, "is brief and constant in every respect, since a single hope of resurrection has been proclaimed to us" (101).[32]

The main representatives of the fourth-century Egyptian Origenist school whose work survives, however fragmentarily, are Didymus the Blind (313–98), the scholarly ascetic of Alexandria, and Evagrius of Pontus (346–99), a learned civil servant from the imperial court who spent the last fifteen years of his life as a hermit in the Nitrian desert. Although some of his works have only recently been rediscovered, and his theology has not yet been thoroughly studied as a whole, Didymus does seem to have held a number of the positions Epiphanius associated with Origen. He seems, for instance, to have taken it for granted that souls were first created in a purely immaterial state, and to have left their first "fatherland" for this material universe only after they came under the power of Satan (*Comm in Zach* 3.288; *Tura Commentary on Ps* 34.17 [ed. M. Gronewald 3.370]). Gen 3.21 refers to this second stage of creation, according to Didymus, when it tells of God's clothing Adam and Eve in "coats of skin" (*Comm on Gen* 3.21). Since one cannot live in Paradise with a material body (*ibid.*), it follows that "the rebirth (παλιγγενεσία) that will follow the resurrection of the dead" (*Comm in Zach* 1.246) will be the restoration of our original bodiless existence. Didymus thus seems to have taught a doctrine of *apokatastasis* in a strictly cyclic or retrospective sense, and to have understood resurrection only spiritually. Further, he believed that I Cor 15.28 ("God will be all in all") holds out the prospect of a universal salvation in which all enmity to God will cease, and all rational substances – by their nature indestructible – will be perfectly united with each other and with God, beyond all multiplicity, and "will receive the fullness of divinity" (*Comm in Zach* 3.307f.).[33]

Evagrius, too, seems to have developed the Origenist approach to eschatology in ways that appeared dangerously unorthodox to his contemporaries – ways that were probably alien to Origen's own intentions. In his *Kephalaia Gnostica* ("Theses on Knowledge"), where he elaborates his theological system in the puzzlingly terse form of six "centuries" of aphorisms,[34] Evagrius hints at the possibility that souls will undergo new incarnations in future worlds (2.85). He also suggests that the suffering souls will undergo in "fire" after death will be simply a purification of their "passible part" (3.18).

A number of Evagrius' aphorisms express clearly his expectation that "the last judgment will not reveal the transformation of bodies, but their destruction" (2.77; cf. 3.40, 66, 68). In one saying (3.68), in fact, Evagrius speaks of this destruction of materiality in two stages, which he equates with a "first" and a "second" period of rest – a distant echo, perhaps, of the Asiatic millenarian tradition. At the same time, he seems to envisage the development of new "spiritual" or "gnostic members" (ὄργανα) as part of the soul's final transformation (3.51; 6.58). While none of his extant sayings unequivocally teaches universal salvation, Evagrius suggests this when he predicts that "the whole nature of rational beings will bow before the name of the Lord, who reveals the Father who is in him" (6.27; cf. 2.84; 5.20). So, too, in his *Epistle* 59, Evagrius echoes Gregory of Nyssa's conviction of the essential finitude and temporality of evil, when he writes: "There was a time when evil was not, and there will be a time when it will not be; but there was no time when virtue was not, nor will there be a time when it will not be."[35]

Synesius of Cyrene

Sympathetic to the Origenists in many respects, although he began from a quite different starting point, was the enigmatic Synesius of Cyrene (c. 370–413/14), a Neoplatonic philosopher and wealthy man of letters who was elected bishop of Ptolemais in Libya (Cyrenaica), while yet unbaptized, in 410. In his rambling treatise entitled *Egyptian Tales*, or *On Providence*, written before his episcopal election, Synesius endorsed the Stoic theory that history repeats itself in endless cycles, just as the stars and planets return, after long intervals, to the same configurations (2.7). It was understandable, then, that he felt some reservations about classical Christian expectations for the future, when faced with the invitation to become a Christian bishop. In a letter written to his brother at that time, Synesius frankly admits that he cannot accept the Christian belief "that the world, with all its parts, must perish" (*Ep* 105 [PG 66.1485B5f.]). "As for the resurrection, such as common belief accepts it," he continues, "I see here an ineffable mystery, and I am far from sharing the views of the vulgar crowd on the subject" (*ibid.*

[1485B6–9]). It is not clear just how Synesius did understand all the features of the Christian eschatological tradition, in a way that could justify his accepting his bishopric; but these two points of doctrine – the Church's traditional denial of the eternity of the created order, and its affirmation of the corporeality of the risen body – were to trouble Christian Platonists, particularly in the Alexandrian intellectual world, for the next century and a half, just as they troubled the scholarly bishop of Ptolemais.[36]

Like any good Platonist, however, Synesius apparently found it less difficult to accept the Christian expectation of the judgment and punishment of souls after death. In a letter (*Ep* 4) probably written shortly after his election to the episcopate,[37] addressed to a certain John, who had been accused of planning his own brother's murder, Synesius urged his addressee to accept the sentence of his civil judges, if he was guilty of the crime, and to undergo whatever punishment was assigned him, while he was still in this life; "for it will go better for you before the judges of the underworld, John my friend, if you are already purified before you depart from this life" (*PG* 66.1368B11ff.). Drawing on his own "sacred philosophy" as a Christian Platonist, Synesius explains that "it is not the same thing to undergo punishment in this heavy body, and as a phantom (εἰδῶλον)" (*ibid.*, C9f.). Human justice is but a shadow of divine justice, which is administered by punishing spirits "who exercise the same skills on souls that cleaners use on soiled garments" (*ibid.*, D1f.). Such cleaning is always a strenuous and painful process; but while those garments that are indelibly stained are simply worn out by the washing and disintegrate, "the soul, being immortal, suffers immortal punishment, when its sins are so deeply dyed that they cannot be washed away" (*ibid.*, 1369A11f.). However, if one pays the penalty "during the same life in which one has sinned," the stain of sin can be removed more easily by expiatory suffering, because it has not yet had the chance to become deeply ingrained (*ibid.*, A12–16). "Therefore," Synesius concludes, "we must accept punishment as quickly as possible, from human rather than from angelic judges!" (*ibid.*, B1f.). Synesius here combines Christian Platonist conceptions of purgative punishment and the immortality of the soul with picturesque images of the afterlife not unlike those used by the desert monks. The result is a mixture of biblical and Hellenistic hopes, of philosophical speculation and Christian pastoral concern, that is typically Alexandrian, but very much Synesius' own.

8

Redemptio Totius Corporis: Latin eschatology in the fourth century

The second half of the fourth century saw the rise of a Latin theological literature that met the central issues of Christian faith and controversy with a sophistication unknown in the West since Tertullian. However, although the language and the rhetorical style of this literature were Roman, its intellectual impetus still came largely from the East: from the Arian controversy, whose bitter political and theological tensions had spread to the West by the mid 340s, and from the revived influence of Origen. This latter factor, especially, was the central issue in Latin as well as Greek eschatology by the end of the fourth century.

Firmicus Maternus

The earliest fourth-century Latin writer to take an interest in the eschatological tradition of the Church, the Sicilian convert Julius Firmicus Maternus, was less a theologian than a propagandist: an enthusiastic promoter of the new demand of post-Constantinian Christianity to be not merely an accepted religion within the Empire, but the only religion allowed to exist. His tract *De Errore Profanarum Religionum*, written around 346, is a passionate appeal to the sons of Constantine, Constantius II and Constans, to repress all pagan institutions once and for all.

Firmicus adds urgency to this appeal by occasional allusions to the impending end of history. The Incarnation occurred, he says, "almost at the end of the week of the centuries" (25.3) – a phrase that suggests he accepted the tradition of seeing history as a "week" of six thousand years, and perhaps that he knew of the millenarian hope as well. More important for Firmicus, however, is the fiery judgment that inescapably awaits pagan temples and their frequenters: "already the heavenly fire is giving birth, already the approach of divine punishment is manifest, already the doom of coming disaster is heralded" (15.4). The language and images are familiar, reminiscent especially of Cyprian's *Ad Demetrianum* 22;[1] but the recipients of God's punishing wrath, the chaff to be burned in his eternal fire (cf. 15.5), are now not the Roman Empire or the sinful world at large, but false religions – "whatever vain delusions have caused the downfall of erring human beings" (15.4). Indeed, Firmicus' use of the traditional images of eschatological judgment has become here an instrument for exhorting the Christian emperors to reverse the tide of persecution and to begin a destructive campaign of their own against the monuments of pagan religion. In a way quite different from his contemporary, Eusebius, Firmicus too has converted eschatology into imperial politics.

Hilary of Poitiers

Hilary of Poitiers (c. 315–67) combined a wide knowledge of the Bible and a serious concern for the orthodox tradition with a refined sense of classical Latin style. Although the influence of the Alexandrian exegetical tradition is apparent in his moderately allegorical approach to textual interpretation, the main theological influences in Hilary's thought seem to have been Tertullian and Cyprian,[2] a fact that gives his works a curiously archaic flavor at times. As the reviver of serious Latin theology after Nicaea, however, Hilary is also capable of great freedom and originality. Throughout his writings, he shows a strong interest in the eschatological fulfillment of the present realities of Christian life, seeing in the Christian hope the hermeneutical key to understanding the riddles of Scripture (see *In Matt* 19.3).

Hilary, too, alludes in several passages to the conception of the world's history as a "week" of six thousand years, a scheme in which the birth of Jesus is set midway through the final "day" (*In Matt* 17.1; 20.6; *Tract Myst* 1.41; 2.10); however, Hilary is not a millenarian, and stresses with even greater weight the uncertainty of the time of the end. Jesus' avowal that he himself is unaware of its date is, for Hilary, a proof of the divine goodness; God "offers us" in this very uncertainty "a wide space of time for repentance, yet keeps us always concerned by our fear of the unknown" (*In Matt* 26.4).

Hilary conceives of the end of history in the classical terms of Christian apocalyptic. After the Antichrist, the "son of the devil," has set up his kingdom in Jerusalem and confused God's people (*In Matt* 25.3, 8; 26.2; 33.2),[3] Christ will come to Jerusalem, the "place of his Passion" (*ibid.*, 25.8), in a triumphant procession that will recall his entry there just before his death (*ibid.*, 21.2). Then the judgment will take place, revealing all the deepest secrets of human hearts (*ibid.*, 10.16). Despite its universality, however, this revelation will only be a genuine trial for those whose deeds have not already saved or condemned them, only a real "judgment" on "those who are midway between the faithful and the unfaithful" (*In Ps 1.17*; cf. *ibid.*, 15–18; *In Ps 57.7*). Until that day, the souls and bodies of all are "asleep" in what Hilary calls a "temporary death" (*In Matt 27.4*). The freedom of the human will ends with death, and only its self-determined choice remains, fixed in its lifelong orientation and incapable of change (*In Ps 51.23*). It is for this reason, perhaps, that Hilary cautiously suggests the punishment of sinners will begin even before the resurrection (*In Ps 2.48*; *In Ps 57.5*).

The time of Christ's second coming is, for Hilary, also the beginning of "the age of resurrection (*resurrectionis saeculum*)" (*In Ps 118.11.5*).[4] All the dead will rise, both the just and the unjust: "for since all flesh has been redeemed in Christ, so, in order to rise, all must appear before his judgment-seat; the glory and honor of rising is not, however, awaiting all indifferently" (*In Ps 55.7*). Unbelievers will rise "so that there may be eternal material in them for eternal fire" (*In Matt 5.12*; *In Ps 52.17*); their bodies will be of a dry, dusty texture, "in order to be tossed about by the playful movements of their punishments" (*In Ps 1.14*). The just, on the other hand, will rise "like the angels" in heavenly glory (*In Matt 5.11*), sharing in the incorruptible "substance of heaven" (*ibid.*, 5.12). Just as the soul – which for Hilary, as for Tertullian, is a refined form of corporeal substance (*In Matt 5.8*) – will become heavy and more material in risen sinners, so the risen body of a just person will "pass over into the nature of the soul, and the heaviness of its earthly material will be abolished to make way for the substance of soul and will become, instead, a spiritual body" (*In Matt 10.19*; cf. *In Ps 118.3.3*).

Hilary is cautious in explaining the content of the resurrection hope; he takes Jesus' admonition not "to be anxious about what you are to eat, or what you are to put on," but to "consider the lilies of the field" (Matt 6.25–31), as the occasion to criticize those who spend time speculating on the appearance and physical qualities of the risen body (*In Matt 5.8*). He insists that God will "raise up the diverse range of bodies, which will share in life, into a single, perfectly achieved human type, in order to make everyone equal and uniform" (*ibid.*, 5.10), but he refuses to speculate further on the characteristics of this ideal form. Jesus' simile of growing plants suggests to Hilary, however, that the dynamic principles of this future form are already present within each of us (*ibid.*, 5.11). So the identity of the present body with the risen body will be preserved. As Hilary remarks in his *Commentary on Psalm 55.12*, "The bodies of all who will rise will not be formed from extraneous material, nor will natural qualities of strange origin and extrinsic sources be used; it will emerge the same, fit now for eternal beauty, and what is new in it will come about by change, not by creation" (cf. *In Ps 2.41*).

For Hilary, most importantly, the resurrection of the just is the beginning of the final achievement of their salvation: the construction of the "heavenly Sion," whose coming we can already glimpse in the glorious risen body of the Lord (*In Ps* 68.31),[5] the "marriage" of human flesh with its eternal spouse, the Holy Spirit (*In Matt* 27.4). The resurrection will mean the realization of the Kingdom of God in each of us, a Kingdom that will begin at the Parousia as the reign of Christ, and that will only be realized more fully, not ended, when Christ "hands over his Kingdom to the Father" (*In Ps* 9.4; *In Ps* 148.8).

At the end of book 11 of his *De Trinitate*, Hilary develops at some length this eschatological perspective of the relation of Christ to the Father (29–49), using as a vehicle for his reflections Paul's famous passage on Christ's "subjection" in I Cor 15.24–28 – the passage that had occasioned so much controversy, two decades earlier, between Eusebius and Marcellus. Hilary begins by observing that we can only approach the Father, in knowledge or in prayer, through Christ his Son (33). This holds true in the eschatological order, too: we will only become "subject" to the Father, experience his rule in us, by becoming "subjected to the glory of the rule of [Christ's] body" (36) – a subjection that is, presumably, realized by our undergoing the same transformation in our bodies that the risen Christ has undergone in his (38f.). Thus "he shall deliver the Kingdom of God to the Father, not in the sense that he resigns his power by the delivering, but that we, being conformed to the glory of his body, shall form the Kingdom of God" (39). And as Christ "subjects" himself to the Father, the Godhead that is his by right will be communicated to his *whole* Body, to the whole nature of humanity, which he has already assumed in becoming human. "The end of the subjection, then, is simply that 'God may be all in all,' that no trace of the nature of his earthly body may remain in him. Although before this time the two were combined within him, he must now become God only – not, however, by casting off the body, but by translating it through subjection; not by losing it through dissolution, but by transfiguring it in glory" (40). This very transformation of Christ, to become "once again wholly God" (43), will result in the transformation of "us, the assumed humanity," into "the perfect image of God" (49) (cf. *In Ps* 118.10.7).[6] It is the first appearance in a Latin writer's works of the emerging Greek soteriology and eschatology of "divinization."

Zeno of Verona

The *Tractatus* or discourses of Bishop Zeno of Verona (d. 371/72) reflect, on a popular level, some of Hilary's eschatological perspectives, but without Hilary's subtlety or completeness of vision. Zeno's discourse on the resurrection (1.16), for instance, begins with a simple defense of the Christian belief in survival after death, drawing on the parallel of pagan theories of immortality (1–2), on the experience of ghosts (3), and on incidents in the Old and New Testaments (4–5). The heart of the Christian hope, says Zeno, is "that the dead will be raised to their pristine state" (7). He defends this with arguments long familiar from the apologetic tradition, notably with appeals to God's creative power and parallels in nature (7–10).

The details of the resurrection are presented here only sketchily. First the saints will rise, says Zeno, then sinners (11); the bodies of the risen will be restored to the original, "angelic" state in which Adam and Eve lived before the fall (12); they will still be recognizable, since their substance will not be changed, or their perceptible form, "but only that which is useless" (14). This change will be but the conclusion of a process of transformation which the Holy Spirit began in us all at baptism (12).

Zeno's little treatise on the last judgment (2.21) echoes Hilary's theory that the judgment will not involve either the saints or hardened sinners, since both of those groups will have been judged already by their acts (1, 3). Judgment, which "comes into existence in situations of ambiguity" (1), will be exercised on "those who stand between the faithful and the faithless." There are, after all, people who remain members of the Church out of fear, but who are none the less immersed in the pleasures of the world: "They pray because they fear," Zeno observes, "but they sin because they will" (2). It is such people – including, no doubt, many of his hearers – who must face judgment, and those who are judged by the triumphant Christ to be sinners must face eternal punishment (3).

Ambrose

Apart from Augustine of Hippo, surely the two most influential personalities in the Latin Church during the second half of the fourth century were Ambrose and Jerome. Of these, Ambrose (c. 334–97) provided both intellectual and institutional leadership for the growing Christian body, as bishop of Milan from 374, and made both Neoplatonic philosophy and Origenist exegesis respectable in Western Christian thought.[7] Widely learned in both fields of study, Ambrose still remained, in his writing, primarily the Christian rhetor, who adapted the ideas he had assimilated from many sources to the pastoral and persuasive ends his office required. Thus his thought – on the "last things" as well as on other subjects – may lack systematic cohesion, but presents an intelligent and often eloquent distillation of older traditions in a predominately homiletic context.[8]

Although he expressly disagrees, in one passage, with the familiar conception of the world's history as limited to six thousand years (*Exp in Luc* 7.7), Ambrose sees in the wars and disasters of his own day clear signs that the end is near (*ibid.*, 10.10, 14). He echoes the traditional Roman sentiment that the world has "grown old" and lost its vital energy (*De Bono Mortis* 10.46). At the end of history stands, for the Christian, the certainty of God's judgment, in which our deeds will be "weighed" on God's "scales"; "all things are manifest to the Lord, and before his judgment-seat neither can good things be hidden, nor those that are full of offense be covered" (*Ep* 2.14; cf. *Hom in Ps* 118.7.15). Ambrose occasionally warns against taking this courtroom image too literally: "Christ judges by knowing our hearts, not by questioning us about our deeds" (*In Luc* 10.46), and in fact our deeds judge us as we perform them (*Ep* 77.10. 14). So in his homilies on Ps 51, Ambrose echoes Hilary's theory that it is only the "sinful believer," the person who is neither a committed disciple nor a hardened reprobate, who will actually need to be judged at Christ's second coming (51, 56; cf. *In Ps* 1.51). But in his long series of homilies on Psalm 118, he repeatedly stresses that *all* who wish to enter Paradise must pass by the cherub's flaming sword, which – for him as for Origen – is the "fire" of a painful personal judgment (3.16; cf. 3.14–17; 20.12–15).

Ambrose's own position on the nature, purpose and duration of punishment after death varies considerably. In a number of passages he echoes the traditional teaching that God's most incorrigible enemies – the demons, infidels, apostates, the sacrilegious, those generally classed as *impii* – will be consigned to "the place of fire and brimstone, where the fire is not quenched, lest the punishment ever end" (*De Fide* 2.119; cf. *In Ps* 118.3.17; 7.17; 20.11; 21.8; *De Poen* 1.22; *De Nabuthe* 52). In other passages he speaks of eternal punishment in terms of separation from one's loved ones who are with God (*De Exc Frat* 2.11), or interprets the biblical images of fire, the worm and the gnashing of teeth as moral allegories (*In Luc* 7.204ff.).

A long passage in his homily on Psalm 1, however, describes such punishment as a totally medicinal process, in an interpretation similar to that of Origen and Gregory of Nyssa. No real substance can perish, Ambrose argues here; it is simply transformed (*In Ps* 1.47). But since evil is not itself a substance, it must pass away (*ibid.*), and those substances which have been disfigured by evil can only be changed for the better (48). For the sinful human being, this means conversion through purification; "God constrains [us] to repentance through suffering," he writes, "so that the evil accident we know as wickedness is burned and consumed by repentance, and disappears. Then that region of the soul, which was possessed by the accident of wickedness, will be laid open to receive virtue and grace" (*ibid.*). Like Gregory of Nyssa, Ambrose sees this purifying process as having to take place after death, if it has not taken place in life. It is to such purgation after death, and to the freedom from it that the saints will enjoy, he suggests, that Apocalypse 20 refers in speaking of a "first" and "second" resurrection.

Those who "share in the first resurrection" (Apoc 20.6) are those who "will come to grace without needing to be judged. Those, however, who do not come to the first resurrection but are reserved for the second will be burned, until the time between the first and second resurrections has passed – or if they have not fulfilled [their purification], they will remain in punishment longer" (54). So Ambrose transforms the millennial tradition, expressed in this passage, into an allegory of the "interim" state between death and the general resurrection.[9]

In his homily on Ps 36, Ambrose tries to reconcile these varying interpretations of fiery judgment and punishment after death by suggesting that everyone must experience this fire to some degree. "If the Lord is going to save his servants, we will be saved by faith, but nevertheless saved through fire; even if we are not burned up, still we shall be burned." Those who do not deserve salvation, however, will remain in the fire, as Scripture teaches – possibly forever (In Ps 36.26).

In general, Ambrose seems to sympathize with the Origenist doctrine of universal salvation, although he never makes it entirely clear how strictly universal he expects it to be. In the treatise on the resurrection that forms the second book On the Death of his Brother (De Excessu Fratris), he asserts that "all who are considered to be joined to the holy Church, by being called by the divine name, shall obtain the privilege of the resurrection and the grace of eternal bliss" (116). Other passages extend the certainty of salvation to all human beings. The salvation of the Good Thief proves that "no one can be excluded" from God's forgiveness (In Ps 39.17). "Therefore let no one despair, for the mercies of the Lord are many . . . The mercy of a human being is towards his neighbor, but the mercy of God is towards all flesh, that all flesh may ascend to the Lord" (In Ps 118.20.29). Ambrose never suggests, however, that the devils will also be included in that ultimate reconciliation.

Ambrose's apologetic treatment of the Christian hope for resurrection, in De Excessu Fratris II, follows lines long familiar from the works of earlier writers, from Athenagoras and Tertullian to Gregory of Nyssa. After a reflection on the benefit death brings to those weighed down by life (3–50), he argues to the plausibility of the Christian hope from the moral fittingness of resurrection (52), from analogies in nature (53–59) and from God's creative power (60–64); he then offers an array of biblical proof-texts to support these apologetic topoi (66–85).

Despite this lengthy argument for the credibility of resurrection, however, Ambrose's discussion of eternal beatitude generally concentrates on its spiritual and personal aspects, rather than on the participation of the body in its joys. So in his Homilies on Luke 10.49, Ambrose insists that "food and drink are not promised to us as our reward and honor, but a share in heavenly grace and life," nor are the "twelve thrones" promised to the Apostles to be understood as actual chairs, but as their share in the mind and in the universal rule of Christ. In fact, for the just who have left all to find God, "God is their portion" (*In Ps* 118.8.11). So he describes the *redemptio totius corporis*, which the believer awaits as the realization of his baptism, as the opportunity to "see God face to face, as a child by adoption" (*Ep* 35.13). The "good repose" promised the just, he remarks in his funeral oration for the Emperor Theodosius, "is to pass beyond what belongs to this world and to rest in those things that are above the world, to share in the heavenly mysteries" (*De Ob Theod* 29; cf. 30–32).

Ambrose seems to conceive of the beatitude of the saved as admitting both of different degrees of bliss and of the possibility of growth. The dead will not rise all at once, he suggests in his treatise on the resurrection, but in the order in which they came to believe (*De Exc Frat* 2.116). Even in the Kingdom of heaven, there will be a "progression in dwelling-places" (*processus mansionum*) adapted to the merits of each person – a growth from *consolatio* to *delectatio*, to the grateful awareness of being called by God's mercy, and finally to the vision of God that conveys a share in his riches (*In Luc* 5.61).[10] The sources of this scheme probably lie both in the apocalyptic tradition and in the Neoplatonic idea of the homeward journey of the soul, but it also suggests that Ambrose shared the same conception of a dynamic, ceaselessly growing eschatological fulfillment which Origen and Gregory of Nyssa proposed in less mythological terms.

Ambrose's conception of the eschatological fulfillment of the individual, in fact, is more centered on the fate of the soul after death than on resurrection and judgment in an apocalyptic, universal context. Repeatedly he urges his hearers not to fear death or to grieve over the departed, since death is actually a release from the cares of this fleshly life (e.g., *De Bono Mort* 4.14; 5.16; 8.31ff.; *De Exc Frat* 2.3–7, 20ff.). Following Origen and anticipating Augustine, he distinguishes physical death from the "death of sin" (*De Exc Frat* 2.35–38; cf. *De Bono Mort* 1.3); yet even physical death, which is a result of sin, is a providential release from a world loaded with guilt (*De Bono Mort* 4.15; cf. *De Exc Frat* 2.47).

Ambrose has no consistent theory, however, about what the Christian may expect at death. In one passage, he puts forward the theory that after death souls remain in "storehouses" (*animarum promptuaria*) until the resurrection (*De Bono Mort* 10.45–48).[11] Yet even there, they anticipate psychologically the suffering or glory that awaits them, in their recognition of what surely lies ahead (*ibid.*, 10.47). Other passages suggest that the soul remains in suspense after death, unaware of the outcome of the judgment until the resurrection (*De Cain et Abel* 2.2.9), or that the punishment experienced before the judgment is simply the lack of positive consolation (*In*

Luc 8.18).[12] Whatever the fate of the ordinary person, Ambrose follows the old tradition of foreseeing an immediate entry into beatitude for outstanding saints: not only for martyrs, but for patriarchs, prophets and apostles (*In Luc* 7.4f.; cf. *In Ps* 118.20.12). Even a devout Christian emperor will share, after death, the peace of God's eternal Sabbath "in the land of the living" (*De Ob Theod* 29f.). The lack of a consistent eschatological theory does not prevent Ambrose the preacher from holding out to the faithful powerful images of Christian hope.

Jerome

The eschatology of Jerome (331–420), like all of his theology, is inextricably tied in with his knowledge of the Bible, with his intense personal relationships, and with the turbulent external circumstances of his long life of study and asceticism. A biblical scholar of prodigious industry, Jerome took Origen as his model and inspiration during his early years; despite his violent attacks on Origen and the Origenists after 394, he remained an admirer of the Alexandrian's exegetical achievement, and continued quietly to espouse a number of his positions, even on eschatological subjects. Jerome was also an apostle of the flourishing new monastic movement, a spiritual director of many devout Roman women, a controversialist and a tireless ecclesiastical politician – all of which strongly influenced his theology. A compiler and a publicist rather than an original theological thinker or a metaphysician, Jerome made it his main concern to defend what he understood to be the Church's traditional teaching on all points, against all dissenters. So J. N. D. Kelly has remarked that his claim to be called a "Doctor of the Church" rests first of all on his role "as the articulate spokesman and pugnacious defender of popular Catholicism."[13] This holds true, to a great extent, of Jerome's eschatology.

Throughout his life, Jerome favored the "tropological," or spiritual and personal style of allegorical exegesis as a means of unlocking the inner meaning of Scripture. So he repeatedly takes apocalyptic predictions of the end of history as referring primarily to the individual's confrontation with death (*In Soph* 1.14), or even to his freely chosen anticipation of death in the ascetic life (*In Is* 6.14.1). In his later works, however – particularly in his letters and commentaries after the late 390s – a sense of despair over the vulnerability of Roman civilization led Jerome to take the apocalyptic tradition more and more literally, and to feel that the world was indeed near its end. So his *Commentary on Daniel* (written in 399, to refute Porphyry's historicizing explanation of that book) interprets the Antichrist as a human figure, a Jew of humble origin, who will soon overthrow the Roman Empire and rule the world (2.7.7f.; 2.7.11; 4.11.21).[14] "The Roman world is falling," he writes to Heliodorus in 396 (*Ep* 60.16), and he assures the widow Ageruchia, in the midst of worldwide barbarian invasions in 409, that "the Antichrist is near" (*Ep* 123.16). Within the Church, too, heretics like the Arians and the Origenists seemed to Jerome to be fulfilling biblical prophecies for the end-time (*In Is* 6.14.1; *In Ezek* 11.38: his "ecclesiastical explanation" of the assault of Gog and Magog). Yet even if these dangers and threats were signs that "the world was growing old" (*In Is* 14.51.6), Jerome was not willing to accept the conclusion of the Evagrian Origenists that material creation was destined soon to disappear altogether; the "end" of this world can only mean the transformation of it into something better, so that we can look "not for [the world's] destruction, but for the abolition of its former lowliness and for the beginning of the glory that is to come" (*ibid.*). "We shall not see another heaven and another earth," he later adds, "but only the old, former ones, changed for the better" (*In Is* 18.65.17f.).

Jerome's interpretation of the details of the coming age was cautious and traditional. He rejected millenarian literalism as a *fabula* (*In Dan* 2.7.17f.; *In Is* 16.59.14), and preferred, in his *Commentary on Ezekiel* (after 411), to take the details of the new Jerusalem in Apoc 21 as allegorical references to the historical Church (*In Ezek* 11.36). Yet he is careful, in that same passage, to report the millenarian interpretation of Tertullian and Victorinus, Irenaeus and Apollinarius as a venerable tradition, not at all identical with "materialistic" Jewish hopes.[15]

In his interpretation of the hope of resurrection after his "conversion" from Origenism in 394, Jerome abandoned his earlier stress on the asexuality of the risen body (as in *In Eph* 5.29; *Adv Jovinianum* 1.36); he insists, in his mature writings, that the risen body will be the same as the present one in all its organs and members (*Ep* 108.23f.). Nevertheless, Jerome continued to maintain in his later writings that we will be able to act in a radically different, "angelic" way after the resurrection, enjoying a kind of freedom and integrity already anticipated in the practices of virginity, charity and the ascetic life (*In Is* 16.58.14).

Jerome's most detailed discussion of the qualities of the risen body is in a long section of his treatise *To Pammachius, against John of Jerusalem* (written in 397). Here, as part of a ferocious attack on the Origenist bishop of Jerusalem, Jerome gives a detailed refutation of what he presents as the Origenist conception of the resurrection (23–36). After quoting passages, purportedly from Origen himself, which assert the transfigured, thoroughly spiritual character of the risen body (25–26), Jerome criticizes the Origenists for distinguishing between the "body" and the "flesh" (27–28). "The true confession of the resurrection," he insists, "declares that the flesh will be glorious, but without destroying its reality" (29). Jerome then discusses scriptural passages affirming the hope that "this flesh" will rise from the dead, including all its parts and even preserving the differences of the sexes (29–35). The difference of the risen life from the present one will thus be in the use we make of our bodies, not in their material composition. "Likeness to the angels is promised us: that is, the blessedness of their angelic existence without flesh and sex will be bestowed on us in our flesh and with our sex" (31). The remarkable behavior of Jesus' risen body was due to God's power, not to a radical change in its material substance (35). The heart of the Christian hope of salvation, Jerome concludes, is that both our souls and our flesh, born anew in Christ through baptism, will "put on incorruption" and "fly with fresh glory to heaven" (36).[16]

Jerome's discussions of the fulfillment of the saints stress the personal and social, rather than the material, aspects of heavenly joy. He consoles bereaved friends by assuring them that their loved ones who have died now enjoy the company of Jesus and the angels and saints (*Ep* 39.2, 7; cf. *Ep* 23.3), even while they remain concerned about us on earth and continue to intercede for us (*Ep* 39.7; *In II Cor* 5.6). Unlike Ambrose, Jerome is clear and consistent in his belief that both reward and punishment are experienced immediately after death. "After the resurrection of the Lord," he observes in his *Commentary on Ecclesiastes*, "the saints are not detained in the under-world at all," as they were under the old covenant; "whoever is with Christ surely does not remain in the underworld" (*In Eccl* 9.10). So Lea, the recently deceased Roman matron, "now follows Christ," while the aggressively pagan consul-designate Vettius Agorius Praetextatus, who has also died, is now "desolate and naked, a prisoner in the foulest darkness," like the rich man in the parable of Lazarus (*Ep* 23.3).

In explaining the punishment of sinners after death, it is not clear that Jerome shows more decidedly Origenist, universalist traits in his works written before 394 than he does in later works. His early *Commentary on Ephesians*, for instance, which apparently draws on Origen *verbatim* in many passages, confidently predicts that "all rational creatures" will "see the glory of God in ages to come" (*In Eph* 1.2.7); each will be restored to its original place and role in God's creation, even the "renegade angels" (*ibid.*, 2.4.13ff.; cf. *In Eccl* 1.6). The central reality of punishment, Jerome also suggests in some passages of these early writings, is the anguish of a guilty conscience rather than any externally applied castigation (so *In Hab* 2.3.2). Other passages in these same early works, however, attack the idea that the punishment of sin is a purely internal matter (*In Eph* 3.5.6), and insist that serious sinners will be condemned to "endless misfortune," without a chance for repentance or purification (*In Eccl* 7.16; cf. 2.16; 9.3–6; 11.3).[17] On the other hand, while his later works more frequently stress the eternal punishments that await the devil and the enemies of Christ (e.g., *In Matt* 1.10.28; 3.22.11f.; 4.25.46; *In Is* 2.5.14f.; *In Jonam* 3.6), Jerome continued to affirm, throughout his life, that at least all those who believe in Christ will ultimately be received, by God's mercy, into heaven.

In the *Commentary on Amos* 3.7.4ff., for instance, written in 406, Jerome insists: "Even though we shall all have been in sin, and shall have lain under the justice of his sentence, the Lord will have mercy on us, and will raise us up at the time of the resurrection, because we are 'little ones.'" In his *Dialogue against the Pelagians*, composed in 415, Jerome distinguishes between the *impii* or incorrigible sinners (including heretics, apostates and unbelievers), who will be "destroyed in everlasting fire" along with the demons, and believing sinners, on whom God will eventually have mercy (1.28). The basis of this hope, which modern writers sometimes refer to as "misericordism," is for Jerome Jesus' assurance that "everyone who lives and believes in me will not die forever" (Jo 11.26). "So death is a common thing, owing equally to believers and unbelievers," he writes to Minervius and Alexander in 406; "all will rise equally, some for eternal confusion, and others – because they have believed – for eternal life" (*Ep* 119.7).

Perhaps Jerome's most frank statement of his own position on the reality of eternal punishment – as well as his most tolerant reporting of alternative interpretations – occurs at the end of his *Commentary on Isaiah*, written between 408 and 410. After presenting once again, as the plausible positions of "some people," the theory that the traditional images of hell are really metaphors for the sufferings of the human conscience, and after giving the scriptural underpinnings for the hope of "some" that all punishment for sin will eventually end, Jerome himself concludes: "We should leave this to the knowledge of God alone, who holds in his scales not only mercy but punishments, and who knows whom he should judge, and in what way, and for how long. Let us only say, as befits our human fragility, 'Lord, do not reproach me in your anger; do not destroy me in your rage' [Ps 6.1]. And as we believe that the devil and all apostates and impious sinners, who say in their heart, 'There is no God,' will undergo eternal punishments, so we think that those who are sinners – even impious ones – and yet Christians will have their works tried and purged in fire, but will receive from the judge a moderate sentence, mingled with mercy" (*In Is* 18.66.24). It is Jerome at his most generous, and perhaps at his most profound.

9

Grace present and future: Greek eschatology in the fifth century

Just as theology in the fourth century had been dominated by bitter debates over the Nicene definition of Jesus' consubstantiality with the Father, the period that followed the Council of Constantinople in 381 rapidly became, above all else, a period of Christological controversy: controversy about the relationship of divinity and humanity in Jesus, which would preoccupy the intellectual and political energies of Eastern Christianity until the end of the seventh century. In the early decades of the fifth century, especially, Greek theological thought was dominated by the contrast between the methods of exegesis and the types of Christological formulation identified with the Church's two chief intellectual centers, at Antioch and Alexandria. In grappling for the right way to formulate the full paradox of the reality of Jesus, Christological writers in this period allowed their technique of controversy to became steadily more technical, more "scholastic," more dominated by the dialectical methods already long in use in the philosophical lecture-hall. Eschatological questions were generally not prominent in such disputation, except in so far as they were included in large miscellanies of questions and answers concerning difficult points of faith. The Christian hope, in this period, became more and more a preoccupation of homilists and spiritual writers eager to motivate their hearers, or else was subsumed into Christology and soteriology, as a corollary of the theologian's way of conceiving God's relationship to the world. Eschatological doctrine, as such, withdraws in this period from the center of the Greek theological stage.

John Chrysostom

John Chrysostom (344/54–407), bishop of Constantinople, the most famous preacher of Greek Christian antiquity and the Greek Father whose works have survived in greatest abundance, was intensely concerned to focus his hearers' attention on what awaited them at the end of their histories. Eschatological themes recur constantly in his sermons: not with a consistency of detail that can be easily systematized, but with an urgency and a pattern of emphasis none the less characteristic of their author.[1]

In a number of passages, Chrysostom repeats the traditional conviction that the end of the world is near, pointing out, as a sign of this, that the Gospel is now being preached throughout the world (*In Matt. Hom.* 10.5f.; *In Hebr. Hom.* 21.3). If this nearness of the end is a cause of concern for Christians – and he concedes that it should be – he reminds them that the death of each of us is nearer still, and this has "the same meaning" for us as a call to do penance (*ibid.*). Each of us, he concedes, is naturally eager to know the time when the end of history will come; yet much of this is idle curiosity. "Is not the consummation of the world, for each of us, the end of his own life? Why are you concerned and worried about the common end? . . . The time of consummation took its beginning with Adam, and the end of each of our lives is an image of the consummation. One would not be wrong, then, in calling it the end of the world" (*In Ep 1 ad Thes* 9.1).

Chrysostom's teaching on the resurrection of the body is solidly traditional. To the "Greeks" who require argument to establish the credibility of this Christian hope, he offers, in summary style, some familiar apologetic *topoi*, including the power of God to create from nothing and analogies from the world of nature (*In I Cor Hom* 17.1). But Chrysostom insists that no argument should be necessary for the believing Christian: "first, because the one who has revealed it is worthy of belief; second, because the matter itself does not admit of intellectual scrutiny" (*ibid.*, 3). This common faith assumes, however, that the *same* body will rise that we now use in this mortal life; "it is not one substance that is sown and another that rises up, but the same one, grown better' (*In I Cor* 41.2). The heart of the mystery of the salvation of our present nature, in fact, is contained in Paul's teaching that "this corruptible body must put on incorruption" (I Cor 15.53; cf. *In II Cor Hom* 10.3). Along with that transformation of our material nature, the whole material world must be transformed, too, to an incorruptible state, "because it was made for me" (*In Rom Hom* 14.5).

The prospect of judgment and retribution is of central importance, in Chrysostom's eyes, for the Christian moral life; if goodness is not rewarded and evil punished after this life – particularly since the good so often suffer, and the wicked prosper, in the present world – then our most basic sense of justice will be rendered absurd, and our faith in God's provident care of the world contradicted (*In Matt Hom* 13.5). So Chrysostom paints the scene of Christ's judgment with obvious relish; indeed, the evaluation of moral worth is so important to him, and the prospect of a full revelation of our moral worthlessness so terrible, that "even if there were no Gehenna, what a punishment it would be to be rejected in the midst of such splendor and to go away dishonored!" (*In II Cor Hom* 10.3; cf. *In Rom Hom* 5.6; *Ad Theod Laps* 1.12).

Although he is not willing to speculate on *where* Gehenna is, except to say it is "out of this world" (*In Rom Hom* 31.4), Chrysostom does spend a great deal of time discussing the prospect of damnation in vivid detail. So in one of his *Homilies on Matthew* (43[44].4), he offers the following picture of Gehenna: "It is a sea of fire – not a sea of the kind or dimensions we know here, but much larger and fiercer, with waves made of fire, fire of a strange and fearsome kind. There is a great abyss there, in fact, of terrible flames, and one can see fire rushing about on all sides like some wild animal . . . There will be no one who can resist, no one who can escape; Christ's gentle, peaceful face will be nowhere to be seen. But as those sentenced to work in the mines are given over to rough men and see no more of their families, but only their taskmasters, so it will be there – or not simply so, but much worse. For here one can appeal to the Emperor for clemency, and have the prisoner released – but there, never! They will not be released, but will remain, roasting and in such agony as cannot be expressed" (cf. *In Hebr Hom* 31.4). The fire of hell is of such a sort, Chrysostom explains, that it neither consumes nor gives light, but burns perpetually (*Ad Theod Laps* 1.10; *In Hebr Hom* 1.4). And the risen bodies of the damned, being incorruptible, will also be able to endure such punishment eternally (*Ad Theod Laps* 1.10). Despite all this punishment of the senses, however, the principal suffering of the damned will be their exclusion from the presence of the Lord and the company of the saints in heaven (*In Phil Hom* 13.4; *In Matt Hom* 23 [24].8; *In Eph Hom* 3.3).

Although the degrees of punishment in hell will vary, depending on the extent of one's sins and the degree to which one has already suffered for them on earth (*In Matt Hom* 75 [76].5), Chrysostom insists the condemned must remain there forever (*In I Cor* 23.4; *In II Cor* 10.4; *In II Thes* 3.1). God's threats of eternal punishment are not empty, nor are they simply stories told for pedagogical effect; "it is impossible," he asserts, "that punishment and Gehenna should not exist" (*In I Thes* 8.4; cf. *In Rom Hom* 25.4–6). The reason is not simply God's justice, although that would be sufficient (*In Matt Hom* 36 [37].4); it is also proof of God's providential care for us that he has appointed punishments terrible enough to deter any reasonable person from sin (*In I Tim* 15.3). "If God takes such care that we should not sin, and goes to such trouble to correct us, it is clear that he punishes sinners and crowns the upright" (*In Rom Hom* 31.4). "He says that he has prepared Gehenna," Chrysostom remarks in another place, "that he might not cast into Gehenna" (*In Ps* 7.12). More importantly, the very fact that God holds us responsible for our deeds with the prospect of just sanctions is a sign of human dignity; otherwise, we would be no different from the other animals, which injure and tear each other with impunity (*In Philemon* 3.2). Punishment, for Chrysostom, is God's way of upholding the noblest human instincts, and so is a proof of his goodness, "because he does not let good people become evil" (*ibid.*).

In his reflections on the punishment of sinners, Chrysostom often shows a self-consciously anti-Origenist bias.[2] He rejects, for instance, the notion that God's punishment is always medicinal. The punishments we undergo in this life, he observes in one of his *Homilies on Romans*, "are for our correction, but later they will be for vindication" (3.1; cf. *In Joan Hom* 38 [39].1; *In Ps* 49.6). So, too, he makes clear his belief that the devils have no hope of ultimate redemption (*In Col* 6.4; *De Poen Hom* 1.2). For human beings, the reason for the finality of damnation is the fact – which Chrysostom assumes but never explains further, in terms of a philosophical anthropology – that repentance and grace are possible in this life only. After the soul is separated from the body, we are no longer "masters of our own conversion" because we lack the freedom to change our fundamental orientation (*De Lazaro Conc* 2.3; cf. *De Poen Hom* 9). Certainly the damned will experience intense sorrow over their past lives; but like shipwrecked sailors, or doctors whose patients have died, all their regrets will be in vain (*In II Cor* 9.4; cf. *In I Cor* 23.5).

In spite of the finality of damnation, however, Chrysostom does seem to envisage some possibility of spiritual growth in the damned. The rich man of the parable, he suggests, grows more benevolent towards his family in the midst of his sufferings, even though his compunction is too late to be of profit for himself (*Non esse ad gratiam concionandum* 3). So, in a few passages, he urges his hearers to continue the traditional practice of praying for the dead, of offering alms in their name and commemorating them at the liturgy. Even if the dead person whom we mourn is damned, he observes, "it is possible – it *is*, if we wish it – that his punishment will be lightened. If we make constant prayer for him, if we give alms, then even if he is unworthy, God will listen to us" (*In Act Hom* 21.4; cf. *In Phil Hom* 3.3f.; *In I Cor* 31.4f.).

Chrysostom spends far less time reflecting on the beatitude of the saved then he does describing the damnation of the sinner, and he does so in far less picturesque terms. The "City of God" keeps an eternal festival, he remarks, but not one like our own celebrations, full of noise and tumult; "it is a great ordering of all things in fitting harmony, as on a lyre . . . and the soul is initiated there into the divine mysteries, as if it were learning religious secrets in some temple" (*De Beato Philogonio* 6.1). The heart of the joy of heaven is the nearness of the just to God, and their ability to see God "not through a mirror or through faith, but face to face" (*In Phil Hom* 3.3; cf. *In I Cor Hom* 34.2). God's revelation of himself, his gift of light, enables the soul to "run" towards him in knowledge; "and we shall know much that is now hidden, and enjoy there a blessed familiarity and wisdom" (*In I Cor Hom* 34.2). True, our knowledge of God will always be limited by our own natures; we will never know God's essence, as the Son knows it (*In Joan Hom* 15 [14].2). But it will nevertheless be a knowledge that confers a glory beyond description, and that fulfills the most elementary need of our existence. "For why do we live," he asks, "why do we breathe, what *are* we, if we do not receive a share in that vision?" (*In Joan Hom* 12.3). So the vision of God is the heart of beatitude: "O blessed, thrice blessed, many times blessed are those who will be worthy to look on that glory!" (*ibid.*).

Chrysostom does not seem to have had any conception of an "interim" state between death and resurrection, different in kind or degree from a person's ultimate fulfillment. The punishments of the damned begin, in his view, immediately after their death – a point he, too, finds illustrated by the parable of Dives and Lazarus (*In Cap 6 Epist ad Gal* 3; cf. *De Lazaro Conc* 7.3). The souls of the just, on the other hand, go directly to Christ (*De Ss Bernice et Prosdoce* 3; *In Act Hom* 21.4), or enter the "City of God" (*De Beato Philogonio* 1). One passage, however, suggests that the joy of the blessed will not be complete until they are joined by the whole company of the saved, at the end of human history: even Abraham and Paul, he tells his hearers, "are waiting until you have reached fulfillment, that they then may receive their reward. For unless we too are present, the Savior has said that he will not give it to them, just as a kind father might tell his children, who have worked hard and deserved well, that he will not give them anything to eat until their brothers and sisters come" (*In Hebr Hom* 28.1). However much Chrysostom may dwell on the prospect of individual reward or punishment, salvation in its fullness, for him, is a share in the salvation of all God's people.

Cyril of Alexandria

Although he is best remembered for his leading role in the Christological controversies surrounding the Council of Ephesus, Cyril of Alexandria (d. 444) gives glimpses, in a number of his exegetical and dogmatic works, of a conception of eschatological judgment and fulfillment that forms a continuous whole with the doctrine of salvation underlying his Christology. Cyril's soteriology was conceived according to the same "physical" model used by Athanasius and other Greek theologians before him: just as our participation in the flesh and blood of Adam's descendants has communicated to us a share in the corruption and death resulting from Adam's sin, so the sharing of the Logos in our nature, and our individual, deeper contact with him in baptism and the Eucharist communicate to us life and incorruptibility (see, e.g., *Ad Reginas* 2.9).[3] The full realization of this salvation achieved for us by Christ will include the resurrection of our bodies, free from corruption and death and conformed to the glory of the risen Lord (*Hom Pasch* 10.4; cf. *In I Cor* 6.15), an event that remains in the uncertain future for the individual believer (*De Dogm Sol* 7 [= *Adv Anthrop* 9]). So a fragmentary passage on the last judgment, which may be part of Cyril's lost commentary on Matthew (*PG* 72.441–44), emphasizes Jesus' reminder that no disciple can know the time of his second coming.

Cyril stresses, especially in his *Commentary on I Cor* 15, that the foundation of all Christian eschatological hope is the gospel of Jesus' resurrection. "For human nature experienced, in Adam, the aversion of the face of God because of sin; in fact, it was almost confused and shaken into disintegration, and almost returned to its original earth, brought down to death and decay. But when the only-begotten Word of God became one of us, and enriched us with a share in the Holy Spirit, we were formed again into what we originally were, and were, in a sense, created anew; for we have been called to new life, and have escaped the power of death" (*In I Cor* 15.20).

Despite this strong Christological emphasis, however, Cyril does not restrict the promise of resurrection to believers in Christ. All human beings will rise, he explains in the *Commentary on John*, because "the grace of resurrection has been given to the whole of [human] nature" (*In Joan* 6: on Jo 10.10), but unbelievers will rise to a life of punishment that will be worse than death (*ibid.*, 2: on Jo 3.36). The first to rise, after Jesus himself, will be "those who are joined to him by faith" (*In I Cor* 15.20; *In Joan* 4 [*PG* 73.696c]). Only they will be "transformed into the gift of incorruptibility, richly wrapped in the robe of divine glory" (*In I Cor* 15.51). Sinners, on the other hand, will rise unchanged, and "will remain in their dishonorable form, simply in order to be punished" (*ibid.*).

For Cyril, as for so many of his Greek forbears, the heart of eschatological beatitude is direct knowledge of God. Eternal life, he insists, is "not simply to rise, but is, more properly, a life of rest and glory and delight – spiritual delight, of course, and no other. The key to spiritual delight is perfect knowledge of God, and an accurate revelation of the mysteries of Christ; this revelation will no longer be 'in a mirror' or 'through riddles,' as now, giving us merely vague hints of what we seek, but it will shine brilliantly and clearly in us, and implant in us perfect knowledge" (*In Joan* 10: on Jo 14.21).[4] St. Paul writes that "knowledge will cease" (I Cor 13.8) in the life to come, only because our knowledge of God then will make our present knowledge seem non-existent in comparison (*In Mal* 44). And the center of this knowledge will be the vision of the Word as he truly is: no longer veiled by the humanity he has taken on "in the time of the economy of the flesh," but radiant in the glory of God which is his by nature (*In Joan* 11: on Jo 16.25).

In a homily on death attributed to Cyril (*PG* 77.1072–89), at least parts of which seem to be genuine, we read a frightening description of death as a moment of cosmic as well as personal struggle. While evil spirits, dark as Ethiopians, hover near the dying person, ready to exact a reckoning from all his or her five senses for sins committed in the flesh, angels hasten to offer comfort and hope of salvation (*ibid.*, 1072ff.). Here the fears of popular Egyptian Christianity find their echo in Cyril's own theological foreboding.

Cyril is less clear about the state of souls between death and the resurrection. In one of the replies to questions in *De Dogmatum Solutione*, he rejects as absurd the notion that the reward or punishment for human works has already been assigned, because Christ has not yet returned in judgment and the dead are not yet raised (14 [= *Adv Anthrop* 16]). In his *Commentary on John*, however, he insists that the souls of the just go immediately "into the hands of God," while sinners are "sent to the place of limitless punishment" (12: on 19.30). Eustratius of Constantinople has preserved some fragments of a work in which Cyril defends the practice of praying for the dead at the Eucharistic liturgy, in order to move God to be merciful to them. Cyril's underlying supposition here seems to be that "even if the souls of the dead have gone out of their bodies, they still are considered to be alive with God" (*PG* 76.1424f. [= Pusey 3.541ff.]). Here, as elsewhere, Cyril's eschatology is determined more by his sense of the Church's traditional belief and practice than by a well-developed theological anthropology.

Theodore of Mopsuestia

The writings of Theodore of Mopsuestia (*c.* 352–428), the most influential representative of the Antiochene school of biblical exegesis and theology, offer an eschatological doctrine that differs in some important respects from that of most of the other Greek Fathers. Theodore is concerned in all of his theological writing to underline the transcendence of God and to preserve a clear, irreducible distinction between God and his creation. Just as this leads him to seek other conceptual models for the union of the Word with the man Jesus than those of organic or even hypostatic unity, it also imparts to his theology of grace and of history a strong sense of the tension between the divine and the human: between the present world of sin, mortality and change and the future world of God-given freedom, immortality and immutability.[5]

So Theodore develops, in many passages, a scheme of two "states" (καταστάσεις) or "aeons" in which humanity exists: the present state, caused and dominated by Adam – a state of slavery to sin, corruption and death – and the state inaugurated by Christ, the "new Adam," which still lies ahead of us – a state of moral and physical freedom and integrity, of immortality and incorruption (e.g. *In Ep ad Gal* 2.15f. [ed. H. B. Swete, 1.29f.]). In a fragment of his *Commentary on Genesis*, Theodore presents this division of history into stages as God's providential way of teaching humanity the richness of the blessings conferred in the second καταστασις as a gift (Conc Const II, 4.66 [*ACO* 4.1.64f.]). The "hope to come," to which Christians are now called in God's grace, is the prospect of "becoming completely other" than one can be in this present state of existence. "They will become immortal rather than mortal, incorruptible rather than corruptible, impassible rather than passible, unchangeable rather than changeable, free instead of slaves, friends instead of enemies . . . They will no longer cultivate an earth that produces brambles and thorns, but they will live in heaven, far removed from all sadness and sighing" (*Hom Cat* 1.4).[6]

One result of Theodore's division of salvation-history into two clearly marked periods is the clear identification of redemption as a future, strictly eschatological reality. True, in a number of passages, he speaks of the present situation of the Christian believer as occupying a "middle" position between these two καταστάσεις (*In Ep ad Gal* 2.15f. [Swete 1.30]; *ibid.*, 3.20 [Swete 1.49]). The sacraments of the Church, which inaugurate and support this life of faith on earth, are the "type" (τύπος, *forma*) of the new birth and the immortal nourishment that we hope for after the resurrection (*In Ep ad Gal* 3.27f. [Swete 1.56]; *In Ep ad Eph* 4.22ff. [Swete 1.73]; *Hom Cat* 15.18). For this reason, the baptized can already speak of themselves as adopted children of God, and they already possess the Holy Spirit as the "first-fruits" of the transforming presence of God that they will enjoy in the next age (*ibid.*; see also *Hom Cat* 9.17; *In Joan* 3.29 [ed. & tr. J. Vosté: CSCO Syr 62.80; (tr.) 63.57]). But the full realization of these blessings, by the gift of the same Holy Spirit, is reserved for the life to come (*In Ep ad Gal* 3.4 [Swete 1.38]; *ibid.*, 4.29 [Swete 1.85]; *Hom Cat* 16.25); "then these things will be fulfilled actually in us, when the grace of the Holy Spirit irrevocably preserves us forever in those good things, which we have begun to long for in this present life, along with our hatred of sin" (*In Ep ad Gal* 2.15f. [Swete 1.29]). Our present "share" in these eschatological gifts of the Spirit seems to be, for Theodore, more a God-given perception of and longing for the blessings yet to be ours, than the actual enjoyment of them as realities (e.g., *Hom Cat* 12.21). As Joanne McWilliams Dewart has put it, Theodore understands "present grace" essentially as "certain hope of immortality."[7]

Parallel to this "eschatologizing" of salvation is Theodore's reluctance to speak of it, as so many other Greek theologians do, in terms of divinization or any other strong form of identification of the believer with God.[8] In one passage in his *Catechetical Homilies*, Theodore does speak of the union of the Church with Christ, its head, in the Eucharist as a "sharing in the divine nature" (16.13), but this is clearly only a passing allusion to II Pet 1.4, and is not developed further. Elsewhere, he makes it clear that creatures "bear the name of divinity" only by usurpation, or as a simple title of honor (*Hom Cat* 4.10: cf. *In Joan* 10.34ff. [Vosté 217; tr. 154]). On the other hand, it is an exaggeration of his position to suggest, as Wilhelm de Vries does by implication, that Theodore conceives of eschatological salvation as simply the bestowal of extrinsic gifts on an unchanged human nature.[9] For Theodore, the fulfillment of the Christian hope is the gift by the Holy Spirit to human beings of immortality, incorruptibility and immutability (*In Ep ad Gal* 3.2 [Swete 1.37]), qualities that are naturally characteristic of God alone (*Hom Cat* 1.8; 9.16; 16.23f.). Because it is changeable, human nature has been corrupted by sin, and sin has left it subject to death; the final transformation effected in us by the Spirit will be the destruction of sin, even as a possibility (*In Ep ad Col* 1.14 [Swete 1.261]), and the gift of the holiness that, in its fullness, is also peculiar to God (*Hom Cat* 10.21; 16.6; *In Ep ad Eph* 1.7f. [Swete 1.126]; *In Joan* 1.29 [Vosté 42; tr. 29]). So while Theodore prefers to speak of the Christian's eschatological change of state in terms of new friendship and intimacy with God, rather than as a transformation of human nature (e.g., *In Joan* 14.6 [Vosté 267; tr. 191]), the qualities bestowed in this renewal are, in fact, qualities characteristic of God rather than of creatures (so *Hom Cat* 12.12).[10]

Theodore emphasizes that this hoped-for transformation is promised to the whole Church, because it is the body of Christ, united to him in a single human nature; it will be given to individuals only as members of the Church, through their sharing in the Holy Spirit. An important passage for understanding this pneumatological connection of Christology, soteriology, ecclesiology and eschatology in Theodore's thought is his exegesis of Jo 17.11 in the *Commentary on John*. There, after asserting that the man Jesus "received immortality" and "was made Lord of all, in conjunction with God the Word," after his resurrection, Theodore reminds the reader of humanity's hope to share in that same risen life with him, as creatures made in his image. Just as Christ received this gift through the Holy Spirit, it will be the Spirit who will bring about in us what has been achieved in him, "through what one might call our natural conjunction with Christ." "For God the Word is joined by nature to the Father. By being joined with him [the Word], the assumed man was joined with the Father also. So we will receive, as far as possible, along with the natural conjunction with Christ that we have in the flesh, a participation also in the Spirit with him; for we are one body with him, and each of us is a member" (Vosté 314f.; tr. 224ff.).

For the Church as for Christ, the start of the transformation that we call salvation will be the resurrection of the dead. Just as our natural unity with Adam has made us all subject to the domination and destructive results of sin, so our union with Christ, as a new race marked by faith and born anew in baptism, guarantees that his present state of glory, his life with God, will be communicated to us. "As, in the present life, all of us human beings are one body, because we are of one nature, taking Adam as our head, from whom the entire cause of our being seems to have been operative in us, so in the state to come, in which we will rise immortal, we will be one body, because we will receive a common resurrection, and that immortality which will come through resurrection" (*In Ep ad Eph* 1.22f. [Swete 1.140]; cf. *In Ep ad Gal* 3.27f. [Swete 1.57]; *In Joan* 17.11 [Vosté 314; tr. 225]).

Theodore occasionally refers to other aspects of the Church's eschatological hope – to its expectation of the Antichrist, the Parousia and judgment, and to the possibility of damnation, for instance – and does so in unexceptionably traditional terms.[11] Although he was occasionally accused by later Greek theologians of sharing Origen's theory of an ultimate universal salvation,[12] there is no clear evidence in his extant works that Theodore took such a position. In his *Commentary on II Thessalonians* 1.7–9, he even speaks of an eternal, fiery punishment for sinners (Swete 2.45f.). Two passages in the *Catechetical Homilies* refer to death as a "sleep," in which the dead "abide in the hope for which our Lord Christ accepted death" (15.43; cf. 14.5); this may hint at a conception of an interval between death and resurrection similar to the notion of a "sleep of souls" that we have already found in his fellow Syrians, Aphrahat and Ephrem, but Theodore does not develop it further.

Theodore's main eschatological concern, in fact, is not with the prospect of damnation, but with the promise of fulfillment offered to those whom faith and the Church's sacramental life unite to the risen Christ. Life in the "heavenly city" will be a life free from the material needs and concerns of this world (*Hom Cat* 11.14), a life led in the company of "countless angels and innumerable human beings, all of them immortal and unchangeable" (*ibid.*, 12.12). There, "having become immortal and incorruptible, we shall look on Christ alone, whose Kingdom we shall share" (*ibid.*, 1.3). Unlike most Greek writers, Theodore never suggests that the saints will enjoy the direct vision of God, as God, in the life to come, and he stresses a number of times that creatures can only "see" God through faith (*ibid.*, 1.9). Nevertheless, the union with God that is promised to the Church will be a union of knowledge, however that knowledge is to be mediated, and also a union of love. "It is the custom of the divine Scripture," writes Theodore in his *Commentary on Psalm* 44.7, "to call the assembly of those who belong forever to God by knowledge (γνῶσις) his Bride, in order to show the depth of their appropriation to him and their union with him" (ed. R. Devreesse, 287). Here, as elsewhere, Theodore's sober reflections on the Christian hope find their source as well as their limits in the words of Scripture. Speculation beyond those limits is foreign to his theological style.

Theodoret of Cyrus

The leading spokesman of the Antiochene school after Theodore's death, Theodoret of Cyrus (c. 393–466), understandably reflects the same eschatological hope, limited and shaped by the same theological concerns, that we find in the writings of Theodore. For Theodoret, too, the center of that hope is the expectation that at the resurrection we will all share, body and soul, in the immortality and incorruptibility, the stability and changelessness, which are God's natural characteristics (e.g., *In Hebr* 2.9). The result of this transformation will be freedom from the vulnerability and weakness (πάθη) that characterize our present life (*In I Cor* 15.26). "The culmination of these blessings," he explains in another place, "is that the promised life will be free from sin. For when bodies rise incorruptible, and souls receive unchangeability, sin will have no place left for itself . . . A delightful life, free from sorrow, will be granted to the worthy ones, and they will share in divine, intelligible light – or rather, they will themselves become luminous" (*Haer Fab Comp* 5.21). Made possible for the human race through the death and resurrection of Christ (*In Hebr* 2.9), this transformation will be achieved in us by the activity of the Holy Spirit, whom we now possess as a "foretaste" of the salvation yet to come (*In II Cor* 5.14f.; *In Rom* 8.23). It will begin in its fullness at our resurrection, when all believers will be united to the glorified humanity of Christ and will share in his life (*In Rom* 5.17; *In Eph* 2.4; *In Hebr* 1.7–9).

In this last-mentioned passage, Theodoret emphasizes that "we will be sharers and participants not in his divinity, but in his humanity." This accords with the fact that he, like Theodore of Mopsuestia, does not speak of salvation in terms of divinization or of the creature's participation in God's nature, except when he is quoting earlier authors.[13] Theodoret also points out, in one passage, that resurrection and salvation are not the same thing: "for all people will put on the garment of incorruption, but not all will share in divine glory" (*In II Cor* 5.3). The damned, too, will presumably rise, but only to experience punishment in their flesh.

The main difference of Theodoret's eschatological hope from that of Theodore of Mopsuestia lies in his greater openness to the classical Greek theological tradition, and his greater willingness to speak positively of a real union between God and the believer as the goal of human existence. So, in his *Commentary on Ephesians*, Theodoret speaks of the eschatological hope of the whole Church in the language of I Cor 15.28: "In the present life," he writes, "God is in all things, for he has an uncircumscribed nature, but he is not all in all . . . But in the life to come, when death shall cease and immortality is bestowed on us, and when sin no longer has a place, he will be all in all" (*In Eph* 1.23). In his *Commentary on I Corinthians*, Theodoret repeats the same point, adding the nuance that God's future presence "in all things" will be a presence "by good pleasure" ($\kappa\alpha\tau'\epsilon\dot{\nu}\delta\omicron\kappa\acute{\iota}\alpha\nu$): a mutual presence of God and all rational creatures to each other, in harmony and benevolent love, modeled on God's union now with Christ and the saints – a mutual, personal presence that will banish corruption, vulnerability ($\pi\acute{\alpha}\theta\eta$) and sin from the human heart (*In I Cor* 15.28). In some passages, too, Theodoret echoes earlier Greek tradition in seeing this future reception of "the glory of the intelligible light" as the original purpose of our creation (*In Rom, praef.*) and "the vision of the invisible, ineffable beauty of God" as the legitimate goal of Christian yearning (*Graec Aff Cur* 3.92). Elsewhere, however, he agrees with Theodore in affirming that God remains eternally unknowable, and in suggesting that the object of our contemplation in heaven will be the risen humanity of Christ (*Ep* 147 [*SC* 111.228.2ff.]; *In Rom* 8.29; *In I Cor* 13.12).

Like Theodore, too, Theodoret emphasizes that human salvation, in its full sense, implies the resurrection and transformation of the body. Arguing that the participation of the body in a human person's final reward or punishment is required by justice (*Haer Fab Comp* 5.20), he suggests, in several places, that even the martyrs have not yet received their crowns (*Graec Aff Cur* 8.41; *In Ep ad Hebr* 11.39f.). He makes it clear, too, in one strongly anti-millenarian passage, that the good things promised the heirs of God's Kingdom will not be things "of a perishable or temporary kind, but the enjoyment of eternal blessings" (*Haer Fab Comp* 5.21). What these blessings will be, in positive terms, Theodoret is reluctant to say, preferring to restrict his eschatological hope to the promises of Scripture, interpreted soberly and simply (see, e.g., his exposition in *Haer Fab Comp* 5.19–23).

Some manuscripts attribute to Theodoret the *Quaestiones et Responsiones ad Orthodoxos* published among the works of Justin Martyr (*PG* 6.1249–1400). Although this collection of brief responses to assorted theological questions seems to come from the fifth century and may be Antiochene in origin, its ascription to Theodoret seems unlikely, especially since its positions on eschatological issues differ from what we have seen of his in a number of respects. The author of this compendium stresses, like Theodore and Theodoret, the centrality of resurrection in the eschatological fulfill-ment of all, saints as well as sinners (13, 56, 75, 76, 120), and asserts the unchangeability of bodies and souls after the resurrection (6, 7); he argues, however, that the risen will need at least some other creatures from the present world to make their continued bodily existence possible (95). The risen body will be the same in form ($\mu o \rho \phi \acute{\eta}$) as the present one, and will include even the sexual organs, although these will not be used for procreation (60, 53). The author also endorses the tradition that the end of the world will come six thousand years after its creation (71). Between death and resurrection, souls are already judged and divided according to their merits, but they have not yet received their reward or punishment; they can perceive each other, as the parable of Dives and Lazarus illustrates, even though spiritual beings as such are imperceptible to the organs of sense (76, 77). In its eschatology as in other respects, the work is a curious mixture of popular Christianity and classical Eastern theology, in a form characteristic of the new "scholastic" style of the fifth century.

Hesychius of Jerusalem

The presbyter Hesychius of Jerusalem (d. after 450), who is said to have composed many commentaries on Scripture, also left a number of occasional homilies, works which are only now being identified and published. These works seem to have been aimed at a popular audience, and are biblical but non-technical in content. So Hesychius' theological positions reflect traditional doctrine and popular beliefs, rather than the controversies of the age, and underscore his spiritual and ascetical orientation.[14]

One sermon of Hesychius, preserved only in Georgian translation,[15] offers a conventional exposition of the Christian hope of resurrection and judgment; in this context, Hesychius emphasizes above all the necessity for moral vigilance, because the end is, for each of us, utterly uncertain (43). Hesychius also stresses here – perhaps in response to contemporary echoes of the Origenist tradition – that the devil has no chance to be saved, but will reign forever over the damned on a throne of inextinguishable fire (2–4). The just, on the other hand, will be taken up into the sky, radiant with a beauty that will outshine the stars (5). There angels will receive them with joy and adorn them with crowns (6). Like Methodius a century and a half earlier, Hesychius emphasizes the special honor that will be given to virgins in heaven (12), a point that fits well with the ascetical tone of the rest of his homilies.

Ascetical writers

Eschatological themes appear in the writings of several authors in this period whose explicit concern is prayer and the ascetical life.

(a) The corpus of brief spiritual homilies attributed to the desert monk Macarius the Egyptian is now thought by many scholars to have its origin in the "Messalian" sect, which flourished in upper Mesopotamia and parts of Asia Minor in the late fourth and early fifth centuries. The teachings and practices of these wandering, mendicant ascetics, whose name means in Syriac "those who pray," were centered on the conviction that an acquired habit of constant prayer was the only means to human salvation. Thought to be fanatical and anti-social by their Christian contemporaries, the Messalians were condemned by various local synods in Syria, and finally by the Alexandrian party at the Council of Ephesus in 431. The fifty-seven extant Pseudo-Macarian homilies were probably revised, in the interests of orthodoxy, after that condemnation; in their present form, they belong among the classics of Greek monastic literature.[16]

The homilies reflect many of the same imaginative conceptions of life after death that we have encountered in earlier monastic literature. One passage, for instance, speaks of two opposed "worlds," invisible to corporeal eyes but known to the spiritually enlightened, both of which exercise their influence on us in the present life and seek to claim us for the future: the "homeland of Satan," where evil spirits dwell, and "the land, luminous with the Godhead, where the hosts of angels and holy spirits walk about and find their rest" (14.6). At death, our loyalty to one or the other of these hidden worlds is revealed and confirmed. Bands of demons come and drag the sinful soul to their region, while bands of angels receive the just "and carry them at their side into the pure eternity, and so lead them to the Lord" (22).

Resurrection, in the Pseudo-Macarian homilies, is really the actualization, in a reconstituted body, of a transformation in holiness that has already taken place in the just and prayerful soul at death. So several passages speak of a "double resurrection": one of the soul immediately after death, and a second of the body, when the soul's illumination is communicated to its material companion (36.1; 34.2). Because of the Incarnation of the Word, the human soul has received even now the power to be "clothed" with a "heavenly nature" (32.6). At the final resurrection, those souls that have been so transformed, by the practice of prayer and asceticism in this life, will, in turn, clothe their bodies in the same "heavenly raiment" they have begun to wear on earth, and in which they have been clothed more fully after death (32.2). The homilies stress, however, that the glory of the saints does not mean uniformity. Just as the variety of living creatures in this world is almost incomprehensible, so human perfection in the world to come will display a variety of beauties and virtues that will still not conflict with their mutual harmony, because it will reflect the manifold goodness of God (36; 34.2–3).

For the author(s) of the Pseudo-Macarian homilies, the hope for such a fulfillment of our nature is essential for motivating us in our "labors and struggles" to love the Lord in this life (5.6). Yet it is possible, even in this life, to obtain a foretaste of this full inheritance by giving oneself wholly to contemplative prayer. "As at the end of the world," one homily declares, "when the firmament will pass away, the just will thereafter live in the Kingdom and the light and the glory, and see nothing but how Christ is perpetually in glory at the right hand of the Father, so also even now those who are caught up into that other age, and are taken captive [by it], contemplate the beautiful and wonderful things that take place there" (17.4). The "true and eternal Sabbath," which is "the eternal rest and joy of the Lord," is in these writings a blissful state that the faithful disciple can enter even now, provided he or she can be, by the grace of God, "freed from shameful and evil and vain thoughts" (35.3). It is in the practice of ceaseless prayer that the believer begins, in this life, to taste the glory of the life to come.

(b) Diadochus of Photike (d. before 486), a Greek bishop who had studied the works of Evagrius carefully and had spent some time as a captive of the Vandals in Carthage, exercised an important influence on the later ascetical tradition of both the Eastern and Western Churches.[17] One of Diadochus' concerns seems to have been to resist the excesses of Messalian spiritual teaching, in favor of more traditional doctrines.[18] In spite of this, his writings show a good deal of similarity to the Pseudo-Macarian corpus, especially in their emphasis on the continuity of the life of ascetical withdrawal and contemplative prayer on earth with the life of the Kingdom of heaven.

Ultimately, for Diadochus, the needs and desires of the human creature are fulfilled only by union with God in love (*Cap* 12–14, 90–91), a union which is of its nature eschatological. The Holy Spirit often allows beginners in the spiritual life a strong taste of the "sweetness of God, so that the mind might be able to know precisely what the full prize of its labors for God's sake is" (*Cap* 90). Except for a few rare saints, however, this taste remains partial and fleeting in this life; "no one can receive it fully, until mortality is swallowed up by life" (*ibid.*). Our task, in the meantime, is to purify ourselves in preparation for God's gift of perfect love (*Cap* 17), and to endure the "fire of testing," which Diadochus seems to place before death rather than after it (*Cap* 76).

In the *Vision*, a treatise on various subjects of the spiritual life cast in the form of a dream-dialogue between himself and John the Baptist, Diadochus discusses several puzzling aspects of Christian fulfillment. The scriptural promise of the "vision of God," he explains, does not imply that God will take on a perceptible form, but that the human soul and body, endowed with incorruptibility, will live "near God." Simply by being in God's presence, which Diadochus describes as glory and light, they will experience God's love and goodness, and so "know" God truly, without ever being able to comprehend what his nature is (*Vis* 13f.). In the time before the resurrection, the souls of the just will enjoy this divine presence in only a limited way, since they will be deprived of a part of their natural constitution. Unlike the angels, they will not know what is happening in the material world (*Vis* 29), nor will they be able to praise God with their full powers, but will only "sing his praises by interior words" (*Vis* 26). At the resurrection, Diadochus implies, all the powers of human nature will be restored, enabling the saved to enjoy the loving presence of God and to respond with the full range of their transformed affections.

(c) Mark the Monk is another Greek ascetical writer from the fifth or early sixth century, about whose life almost nothing is known; he presents, in his tract on penance, a kind of "realized eschatology" as the basis of his call to conversion and an ascetical life. Although our hope is ultimately for a Kingdom yet to come, Mark concedes, a Kingdom whose arrival-date is uncertain, still the Word of the Lord in this world "has the same meaning (δύναμις) as the Kingdom, becoming for the faithful 'the substance of things hoped for' [Hebr 11.1], the 'foretaste (ἀρραβών) of the inheritance' to come [Eph 1.14], the first-fruits of eternal blessings; but for the faithless and corrupt, it is the concrete proof of their atheism" (*De Poen* 2; cf. 1). Mark's emphasis on the present reality of God's transforming presence shows us another side of the eschatological hope of early Greek monasticism, a hope that grows out of the ascetic's actual experience of grace, and that supports his urgent invitation to others to join him in his "philosophical" quest.

Fourth- and fifth-century Greek apocalyptic

The end of the fourth and the beginning of the fifth century witnessed also a revival of the apocalyptic genre among Eastern Christian writers. This seems to have been rooted in an increased sense of social instability due to the barbarian invasions of these decades, and in a growing disillusionment with politically established Christianity. The anonymous authors of these works remained within the literary and symbolic conventions of earlier Jewish and Christian apocalyptic; except for the *Apocalypse of Thomas*, however, their main interest was now in the fate of the individual at death and afterwards, rather than in the end of the cosmos as a whole.[19]

(a) The largest, and perhaps the most influential, of these later Christian apocalypses is the *Apocalypse of Paul* (*Visio Sancti Pauli*), a work that has come down in a number of early translations, but which was probably composed in Greek shortly before 400. Claiming to record Paul's description of his experiences, when he was "caught up to the third heaven" and "heard things that no one may utter" (II Cor 12.2f.), the work is a detailed, repetitive account of the apostle's supposed tour through the regions of eternal reward and punishment, guided by an angel who explains what Paul sees and answers his questions.

Paul's tour begins with a panoramic view, from the heights of heaven, of the death of his fellow mortals. Good and evil angels take an active role in each person's end, the good angels trying to help and protect the soul, as it passes from the earth, the evil ones challenging it and claiming it as their own (11–14). Despite these competing efforts, every soul is led at death before God, "the righteous judge"; two guardian spirits remind God that they have reported to him each day on the deeds of each soul, and God now makes a final decision on the soul's eternal deserts (16–17). Most souls, apparently, are judged immediately; victims of violence or murder, however, must wait until the death of their tormentors, in order to appear with them before God's tribunal (18).

The joys of the blessed are described in this apocalypse in lyrical terms. The entrance to Paradise is a golden gate, with the names of the righteous who are still on earth inscribed on golden tablets on either side (19). On entering, Paul first is shown the "land of promise": a miraculously transformed version of the present earth that stands ready inside heaven, and which will descend "like dew" on the earth at Christ's second coming. This is the renewed earth of the millenarian tradition, and the author asserts that the Lord will reign over it for a thousand years (21–22). It is destined mainly for those who have lived chastely in marriage, he adds; virgins will receive rewards seven times greater (22). The author then goes on to describe "the city of Christ" itself, a place of fairy-tale-like beauty, to which souls come after being purified by the archangel Michael in the white waters of the Acherusian Lake (22).[20] Saints who were proud of their behavior on earth must do penance in a kind of forecourt of the city, and the just within are arranged according to their deserts in different "places," corresponding to different degrees of happiness (24–29).

Paul is then led down to the region of the damned, and there witnesses the fate of sinners after death in equally vivid detail. Immersed in rivers of fire, assailed by angels with various instruments of torture, weighed down with chains or relegated to regions of ice or stifling darkness, the damned undergo horrifying punishments that correspond to their sins on earth (31–42). Special attention is given to the punishment of sinful clerics (34–36), and to those who committed sins while participating fully in the life of the Church (31, 37). Yet there are rays of hope even here: infants killed by their parents at birth are led by "the angels of Tartarus" to "a spacious place of mercy" (40), and all the damned, because of the intercession of the angels and saints in heaven, are granted by Christ "a day and a night of ease, forever," on "the day I rose from the dead" (43–44). This Easter respite is a

Christian adaptation of the Jewish tradition of a "Sabbath rest" for the damned, here granted as a mitigation of the punishment of sinners by the risen Lord.[21] In this notion, as well as in its sweeping vision of heaven and hell, the *Apocalypse of Paul* left a vivid mark on the later Christian imagination, especially in the Latin West.

(b) The *Apocalypse of Thomas* has survived in two versions, both in Latin, although the shorter, apparently older form may depend on a lost Greek original.[22] This shorter version, which seems to have been composed in the third or fourth century, describes in lurid detail "the signs which will be at the end of the world." Cast in the form of a revelatory speech of Christ to the apostle Thomas, it resembles the *Apocalypse of John* in general style and content. The work divides the events of the end into seven days. On the sixth day the heavens will be rent open; as the angels look down through the cracks, Christ himself will come in the glory of his Father, and the fire that surrounds Paradise will be let loose on the earth, devouring "the earthly globe and all the elements of the world."[23] Then the souls of the saints will come down from Paradise and receive their bodies again, after an earthquake shatters their tombs. These risen bodies will be "changed into the image and likeness and honor of the holy angels," and will "put on the garment of eternal life" that will be given them out of a cloud of light. The just will then be led off by the angels into the realm of light, where the Father lives. The *Apocalypse of Thomas* does not mention the resurrection or the punishment of sinners, but describes, after the passage of the just into glory, the victory of the holy angels over the wicked and the final destruction of the world.

In the longer version of this apocalypse, the narrative of the final seven days of the world is prefaced by a description of the time of conflict and tribulation that will precede them. Here, as in the Book of Daniel, thinly veiled references to contemporary events and personalities taper off into vaguer predictions of rulers and wars yet to come. Allusion to the Emperors Arcadius (d. 408) and Honorius (d. 423), of whom the first is said to have died before the second, date this version to the first quarter of the fifth century at the earliest. These two emperors will be followed by six others, according to this later version of the work, under whom times of peace and prosperity will alternate with times of disaster and the persecution of the saints. Finally, amid signs of cosmic dissolution, the Antichrist will appear, and the drama of the seven final days will begin. The implication in this longer version of the *Apocalypse of Thomas* is that the end of history will come soon – perhaps even at the year 500 – but not immediately, and that the social and political difficulties of the contemporary Roman world were to be understood as remote signs of its coming.

(c) Another reflection of popular eschatological expectation in the middle or late fifth century can be found in the second part of the *Gospel of Nicodemus*, in a passage describing Christ's descent into hell. This is reported by the two sons of the aged Simeon (cf. Lk 2.25–35), who are here supposed to have been raised with other just men and women by the triumphant Jesus on Easter morning. This part of the *Gospel* – found in the later, Greek version of the work, which seems to have been composed after the Council of Ephesus (431) – describes this first resurrection of the just with Christ as their forcible release from the entrails of an unwilling Hades. Adam, the good thief, and an indeterminate number of "prophets and saints" are led by Christ out of Hades, past the flaming sword at the gates of Paradise, and are handed over to the care of Michael and the angels (24ff.). Those who are not yet baptized – such as the two narrators – are first immersed by Michael in the River Jordan, and then "celebrate the passover of the resurrection" in Jerusalem, before departing to be with Christ in glory (27). In repeating the familiar notion that the Incarnation happened 5,500 years after the creation of the world (19), the work places itself within the "cosmic week" tradition of early Christian chronology, and suggests a possibly millenarian perspective.

10

Signs of a Church triumphant: Latin eschatology in the fifth century

During the last decade of the fourth century, as we have seen, the constant pressure on the Roman Empire of barbarian invasions began to cast a pall of anxiety over many Christian writers, particularly in the Latin West. This dark mood was to continue through most of the fifth century, in sharp contrast to the historical optimism of Eusebius and the political engagement of Ambrose. As the institutions of Roman civilization seemed to verge on extinction, Christians became more and more convinced that the end of human history was at hand. Popular interest in apocalyptic speculation grew, and natural disasters and military defeats came more and more to be taken as signs of the imminent coming of Christ.[1] Millenarian hopes – which, since Origen, had always been entertained more seriously in the West than in the East – again took a prominent place in the works of a number of Latin writers, offering the vision of a transformation of the bleak present world into a world of stability and peace. It was in the midst of this eschatological ferment that Augustine developed his own, relentlessly theological interpretation of the prospects of human history.

Gaudentius of Brescia

In Italy, Bishop Gaudentius of Brescia (d. after 406) reflects, in several of his sermons, the positive side of this mood of eschatological expectation. Christ died, he remarks, "at the evening of this world, . . . in the last times of human history (*novissimis temporibus saeculi*)" (*Tractatus* 3.12). The resurrection of Christ, which his disciples celebrate on the first day of every week, is for Gaudentius the sign of another holy "day" yet to come: the long "Sabbath" of the seventh millennium, "which will come after those six days – six ages, that is, each of a thousand years – after which there will be true rest for the saints and for those who have faithfully believed in the resurrection of Christ" (*Tr* 10.15). In that final age, there will be no need to fight against either the devil or our physical shortcomings. The body will no longer be troubled by its drives, but will rise from the dead in a spiritual, incorruptible state (*ibid.*, 16), free from the "sting of death" which is sin (*ibid.*, 17). The saints will then have no other concern but to "do that alone which every holy soul ought to do: join with the ranks of angels in offering to our God eternal hymns and everlasting thanks" (*ibid.*, 22). Gaudentius does not develop his notion of the millennial Kingdom further, in this passage or elsewhere, and it is not clear whether he understands it literally or simply as a figure of eternal beatitude. He does, in any case, promise his hearers a transformation of the present material world, and of their own bodies, at the end of history (*Tr* 3.1–2), and alludes several times to the prospect of eternal punishment, along with the devils, for unrepentant sinners (*praef.* 32; *Tr* 4.16; 17.21; 18.20, 27).[2]

Maximus of Turin

Another Italian bishop at the turn of the fifth century, Maximus of Turin (d. between 408 and 423), gives voice to this same sense of impending judgment in his somewhat simpler, more popular homilies. For Maximus, the perils of contemporary life in northern Italy had the salutary effect of reminding Christians that the end of the world was near; "it is a kind of warning," he writes, "to see a judgment of God which you fear, that you may realize there is still more to fear. For while we are cautious with regard to what we see, we are made still more cautious with respect to what we hope for" (*Serm* 85.2). So Maximus urges the rich to fear the divine judge, rather than the probate judge who determines their patrimony. "Think of the imminent day of judgment and the inextinguishable fires of Gehenna, the terrible gnashing of teeth and the final torture of darkness, and then, if you can, leave the Church and involve yourself in worldly cares!" (*Serm* 32.2). Indeed, as with John Chrysostom, it is the moral effect of the prospect of judgment and retribution that most concerns Maximus the preacher. "It should be emphasized especially to those who do not bear fruit [i.e., by good works]," he insists, "that the end of history is at hand, that the day of judgment confronts us, that the fires of Gehenna are burning and that each of us must give account of his acts and his life" (*Serm* 91.2).

Nevertheless, Maximus finds cause for comfort in the very perils that show the approaching end. "The reason for this," he explains, "is that the nearer we are to the end of the world, so much the nearer are we to the reign of the Savior. So the prospect of war proves that Christ is ever closer to us" (*Serm* 85.1). Like David preparing to confront Goliath, the Christian who awaits God's judgment should arm himself or herself with the weapons of faith and await the threats of the future with confidence and hope (*Serm* 85.3).

Maximus' understanding of the fate of individuals after death follows traditional lines in most respects, but shows some traces of local or peculiarly Latin expectations. So he explains the custom of burying the dead near the tombs of martyrs as a way of insuring that the martyrs will "receive us when we depart from the body . . . lest the fear of hell overwhelm us then" (*Serm* 12.2). He also seems to echo the "misericordism" espoused by Jerome – the doctrine that all the baptized will be saved – in a long passage developing the idea that "the water of baptism puts out the fire of Gehenna" (*Serm* 22a.3). Interpreting, in another sermon, the text, "In that night there will be two in one bed; one will be taken, the other left" (Lk 17.34), Maximus suggests that while all the dead will ultimately be wakened from their sleep in the "bed" of the earth, only those will be "taken" to heaven whose lives have been healed by the grace of Christ (*Serm* 19.3). This exegesis seems to imply, for Maximus, the salvation of all Christians, and of no one else: for while both Jews and Christians look forward to the same resurrection, "the blessed Christian people will be taken up in glory, while the detestable community of Jews will be left in Tartarus" (*ibid.*). Demanding as Christian living appears to be in his sermons, Maximus seems to be confident that the members of his flock will ultimately realize its promise.

Sulpicius Severus

In Gaul, this same conviction that the world was rapidly approaching its end is reflected in the writings of Sulpicius Severus (d. *c.* 420), the disciple and biographer of Martin of Tours. Severus and the speakers in his dialogues simply assume that "the day of judgment is near" (*Vita Martini* 22.3). Reports of false prophets in Spain or the East, of men who claim to be Elijah or Christ or John the Baptist, confirm for him the popular suspicion "that the coming of the Antichrist is imminent" (*ibid.*, 24.3). In one passage of Severus' *Dialogues*, the character Gallus tells of Bishop Martin's conviction – expressed, apparently, about the year 396 – that Nero and the Antichrist were soon to subdue the world, in preparation for history's final struggle; the Antichrist had, in fact, already been born and was "in his boyhood years, ready to assume power when he came of age" (*Dial* 2.14.4). In this time before the end, with discord and confusion being experienced everywhere and with nine of the ten prophesied persecutions already past, Severus finds it "remarkable how strongly the Christian religion is flourishing" (*Chron* 2.33.4).[3]

Although not a millenarian in the strict sense,[4] Severus accepted the common view that the world of his time was "almost six thousand years" old (*Chron* 1.2.1). Christ's second coming, which seemed so imminent, would "return this world, in which earthly kingdoms exist, to nothing," and would "establish another Kingdom, incorruptible and everlasting: namely, the age to come, which has been prepared for the saints" (*Chron* 2.3.7). Severus' hesitancy to describe the qualities of this Kingdom more fully, or to speculate on the punishments in store for the opponents of Christ, demonstrates the sobriety of his eschatological doctrine. His hope is given immediacy and pathos by his sense of the darkness of his own time, yet it remains remarkably free of speculation or of triumphalistic thoughts of vengeance.

Hilarianus

A clearly millenarian reading of history, from the same period, is the brief chronological treatise *De Cursu Temporum*, written in 397 by Quintus Julius Hilarianus, who is thought to have been bishop of Timida Regia, near Hippo, in Proconsular Africa.[5] Attempting to reconstruct the dates of world history from a careful study of Scripture, Hilarianus concludes, conventionally enough, that Jesus died 5,530 years after the origin of the world, and that history's end is therefore to be expected in the year 500, on the same month and day (25 March: the Passover, widely believed by Christians to be the date of Jesus' conception and crucifixion)[6] on which it was created and redeemed (16f.).[7]

Hilarianus' description of the end of history, which concludes his little tract, follows closely the details of the Apocalypse of John. A period of persecution, led by the Antichrist and inspired by the "dragon" Satan (17), will be followed by the "first resurrection" of the saints, after which they will rest for a "Sabbath" of a thousand years (18). This will be followed by a final conflict, in which Satan will be released from prison and will try again to lead the nations astray (19). Finally, fire will come down from heaven and consume all human beings who are still alive. Then there will be a "second resurrection," followed by a "new heaven and a new earth" for the just, and by eternal fire for sinners (*ibid.*).

Tyconius

A very different interpretation of the Johannine Apocalypse and of the dramatic, earthly hopes of the millenarian tradition, emerges in the influential Apocalypse-commentary of the African Donatist Tyconius, who seems to have died during the 380s.[8] Tyconius' other extant work, his *Rules* (*Libri Regularum Tres*) for the interpretation of Scripture, carefully spells out a method of "unlocking" the riddles of the sacred texts that finds the main meaning of almost every obscure biblical passage in its application to the contemporary situation of the Church. This holds true even for the unambiguously futuristic threats and promises of biblical apocalyptic: by applying a "spiritual" interpretation to the text, Tyconius repeatedly discovers that the Johannine Apocalypse, too, refers above all to the Church, both in its ideal form and as it has already begun to be. In Scripture, present and future are always mysteriously intermingled (see Turin fr. 382: Lo Bue 158.3f.) and salvation is, first and last, the salvation of the whole community of believers.[9] It is the Church, in fact, in both its threatened, morally ambiguous present condition and in the transfigured form Christians hope for, that occupies virtually the whole of Tyconius' theological energies. His ability to distinguish the eschatological perfection of the Church from its present, historically limited institutions enables Tyconius to escape his Donatist confrères' narrow and polemical sectarianism and to lay the groundwork for the more spiritualized, universal ecclesiology of Augustine.

Like Augustine some forty years later, Tyconius sees all humanity as divided into two opposed societies or *civitates*. These are represented in the imagery of the Johannine Apocalypse by the "great harlot" of chapter 17 and the "bride of the Lamb" of 21.7, by the "great city which has dominion over the kings of the earth" (17.18) and "the holy city Jerusalem, coming down from heaven out of God" (21.10). "The bride of the Lamb, and the city and kings of the earth," Tyconius concludes, "are [each] one church (*ecclesia*), one body. So then, there are two cities, one of God and one of the devil" (Beatus 9.3.12: Sanders 574). Throughout Scripture, he finds references to these two opposed "bodies," the *corpus Christi* and the *corpus diaboli* (*Lib Reg* 1 and 7: Burkitt 1–8, 70–85); "Christ is the head of his own members, and the devil of his own," and each "body" is subject to the will of its head (Beatus 6.4.75f.: Sanders 494).

To take account of the complexity of the world as it is, and of the relationship of his own Donatist Church to the wider Christian community, Tyconius often distinguishes further groups within these two bodies. What seems to be the one "body of Christ" is actually a *corpus bipartitum* (*Lib Reg* 2: Burkitt 8–11). Even among baptized Christians, who adhere to Christian institutions, there are many who belong to the *corpus diaboli*. "There are two parties in the world," he writes, "the people of God and the people of the devil. But the people of the devil is itself divided into two parties: [false] Christians and pagans. So these two parties fight against one – the Church. For this reason, the Church is called one-third [of the world], and the false brethren within the Church another third, and the pagans outside another third" (Beatus 4.1.25f.: Sanders 338f.; cf. Beatus 8.8.3f.: Sanders 552, where Tyconius uses the same scheme to explain Apoc 16.19: "the great city was split into three parts").

Tyconius' expectation of the end of history grows from this conception of the Church, and of its relationship to the social forces that oppose it. The final days of the world will be days of struggle and persecution for God's people all over the earth, similar to the struggles the Donatist faithful have already heroically endured. "For as has happened in Africa, so it must be that the Antichrist is revealed throughout the world, as he has partly been revealed to us . . . Nothing else will take place but oppression, such as has not been since the nations began to exist; and the Antichrist will be overcome by the Church everywhere, in the same way that he has already been partly overcome by her, to show what the lines of that final struggle will be" (Beatus 2.6.82: Sanders 243; cf. *Lib Reg* 6: Burkitt 67.10–15).[10] Until Tyconius' own time, the Antichrist has been persecuting the true Church of Christ in an oblique way: "not with open mouth, but under the guise of sanctity, in the hidden mystery of evil" (Beatus 6.3.38: Sanders 478).[11] When his "time" comes, however, the Antichrist's true identity and all his hypocritical adherents will be revealed; "then the fact will be stripped bare and laid open, recognized and known, that he has until now been speaking blasphemies to God in a hidden way, under the guise of religion – for now and then he speaks Catholic words!" (Beatus 6.3.39: Sanders 478f.). That same moment of revelation, however, will include the full revelation of Christ, whose body, the Church, has also been growing constantly, in "invisible glory," during its time of hidden struggle (*Lib Reg* 1: Burkitt 4.21–23).

When this period of growth and ambiguity is over, and the "full number of the saints" has been reached, Satan will be released from the spiritual "abyss" where he is now confined – "the secret depths of the human heart" – and his people will sin so openly that they will "obscure the preaching of the Church" (Beatus 5.6.6ff.: Sanders 423f.). The Church's teaching role in the world will then cease, fulfilling the prophecy that "heaven will vanish like a rolled-up scroll" (Apoc 6.14), and "the saints will have no power except for shedding their blood" (Beatus *praef.* 4.12: Sanders 8; *ibid.*, 4.3.11ff.: Sanders 353f.). Christ's faithful will then be forbidden even to honor their own martyrs (Beatus 5.12.12: Sanders 450f.), yet their witness to the gospel will continue throughout the earth, just as it has continued in (Donatist) Africa despite oppression and contradiction (Beatus 5.10.36ff.: Sanders 443).

The coming end will be, in Tyconius' view, a time not only of revelation but of purification for the Church. Angels will be sent to "harvest the grapes" in the Lord's vineyard, and "a winepress will be built outside the city" (Apoc 14.18ff.). These images clearly refer to the future exclusion of sinners from the community of Christ (Beatus 7.2.21: Sanders 522; *ibid.*, 7.4.17f.: Sanders 530). "Those who are not tortured now by penance," he adds, "will undoubtedly be tortured then in Gehenna" (Beatus 7.2.15: Sanders 522).

Tyconius was apparently convinced that this apocalyptic program was soon to begin; the prophecies of Scripture were already being realized in Africa, in the persecution his own Church had undergone, and they would soon be realized throughout the world (*Lib Reg* 6: Burkitt 67.10–15; Beatus 4.1.41: Sanders 341f.). According to his calculation, the "three and one-half days" mentioned in Apoc 11.9, in which the pagans will triumph over the dead bodies of the saints, refer to the three hundred and fifty years of oppression and subtle blasphemy that must elapse between Christ's passion and the revelation of the Antichrist (Beatus 5.6.6: Sanders 450; *ibid.*, 6.3.38: Sanders 478): a period just coming to a close, presumably, at the time Tyconius was writing. This sense of the immediacy of the end allows Tyconius to translate the promise of the apocalyptic tradition into a form of "realized" eschatology peculiarly his own; the final trials of the Christian people, with all their paradoxical consolations and their promise of immi-nent reward, were already a part of the Donatist experience. "The present time is never separate from that last time, when the 'spiritual hosts of wickedness' (Eph 6.12) will be revealed," he writes, "because [Satan] never ceases now to urge wicked deeds on human beings, nor shall he then cease to do these things" (Turin fr. 382f.: Lo Bue 158.3–6).

So Tyconius interprets the millenarian promise of Apoc 20.3–6 as referring to the time of the Church, "from the passion of the Lord until his second coming" (Beatus 11.5.9: Sanders 604).[12] The "first resurrection," which inaugurates the Church's thousand years of rule with the trium-phant Christ, is the rebirth of baptism, which brings release from the death of sin (Beatus 11.5.15f.: Sanders 605); it is "the promise, available in the present age through penance . . . the beginning of the eternal day" (Beatus 1.5.91: Sanders 99). In the present age the saints are already enthroned with the triumphant Christ, judging the world (Apoc 20.4). For the throne of the Lord's glory is his glorified humanity; "and the whole generation of the saints is continuously being added to his body, and sits, through its head, at the right hand of the Power, judging through its priests and all its servants. He judges now in the Church, because each [Christian] occupies himself with penance, and one rouses the other to the love that is charity" (Beatus 11.5.3: Sanders 603). All the blessings promised to the faithful for the future life – health, youth, nourishment in plenty – are already available *spiritualiter* in the Church, because "we have put on Christ and are filled with the joy of the Spirit" (Beatus 4.6.75–78: Sanders 404f.). The "servants of God, who give up all activity in the world," already anticipate in their withdrawal the Church's translation to the beatific vision of God, "and in

their contemplation here they begin to enjoy eternal life" (Beatus *praef.*
4.22: Sanders 9; cf. Beatus 6.2.34: Sanders 465).

In many respects, Tyconius anticipates both the ecclesiology and the
eschatology of Augustine, who acknowledged his debt and his somewhat
grudging admiration for the Donatist writer.[13] Yet Tyconius' theological
vision also recalls the Church-centered eschatological urgency that characterized the *Shepherd* of Hermas more than two centuries earlier: the sense
that the very immediacy of crisis and reward had given the internal
discipline and faith of the Church new seriousness and meaning. The time in
which Tyconius writes is still an age for preaching and controversy and
conversion, an age when there is time for schismatics to return to the unity
of faith (Beatus 2.6.101: Sanders 246f.), and for unbelievers to "flee . . . to
the doctrine of the apostles, begging the Lord's mercy" (Beatus 4.3.37:
Sanders 358). It is a time when many sinners may still return to God, "some
through a long penance, others through a brief one" (Beatus 6.2.67:
Sanders 470). "But after [Satan] enters into his 'vessel' [= the Antichrist],
then no one will be converted, because he will lead off under the yoke of his
authority all whom he finds to be fleshly in the concerns of their lives" (*ibid.*).
In the eyes of Tyconius and his beleaguered Donatist community, the need
to purify and extend the institutional Church is all the more vital, because
the time left for doing it is so short.

Augustine

Without a doubt the theologian who has most influenced the development
of Latin eschatology, as indeed all Latin theology, was Augustine of Hippo
(354–430). Augustine's eschatological doctrine is, in most of its details,
thoroughly traditional, based on the accumulated theological resources of
the Eastern Church since Origen and the Western Church since Tertullian
and Hippolytus, as well as on the practices and the cherished hopes of
African Christians in his own day. What is new in Augustine's eschatology
is its systematic cohesion, its integration into a broad theological synthesis
that is both philosophical and scriptural, speculative and pastorally practical, subtly consistent in theory yet passionately personal and experiential in
its source and expression. In Augustine's reinterpretation of early Christian
hope for the world and the individual, the Western Church found a
balanced, sober, yet profoundly inviting theological structure for articulat-
ing its own expectations.

The key to understanding Augustine's eschatological hope is to understand the sharp, metaphysically grounded distinction he draws between
time and eternity – between human existence now in history, with all the

ambiguity of value and relationship that comes from our life as changeable spirits embodied in a finite, material universe, and the final existence we long for, released from the "distention" of space and time and united in stable knowledge and love with God, our source and our goal.[14] Eternity, in Augustine's brand of Christian Neoplatonism, is no longer the endless duration of Origen's "aeons," but a total freedom from duration, extension or sequence; it is the utterly simple, unchanging present of God's being. The dividing line between temporal and eternal existence is, for the creature, nothing less than total transformation: the transformation of our material reality, and that of our world, which God will work at the moment of resurrection. Without destroying human identity as flesh and spirit, without annihilating the world in which that identity has been realized, the resurrection will mean, in Augustine's view, the end of our existence in time as changeable, restless "fallen souls," and the confirmation of the present, historically conditioned order of loves in the changelessness of eternal beatitude or eternal self-destruction.

One result of this distinction between time and eternity is a transformation, in Augustine's thought, of traditional apocalyptic conceptions of the "end of the world." For Augustine, the eschaton is not simply the end of this present age and the beginning of a new one, but the end of history itself and the beginning of the "eternal Sabbath," when God, who is beyond all time and all temporal succession, will "rest in us" (*Conf* 13.37). Throughout his life, however, Augustine was prepared to take seriously the details predicted in Scripture for the end of the world. So, in his correspondence on this subject with the Sicilian bishop, Hesychius of Salonae, Augustine insists on the literal fulfillment of Matt 24.14 ("The Gospel of the Kingdom shall be preached in the whole world") as a condition for recognizing the end (*Ep* 197.4; 199.46–51 [dating from 418/19]). In *De Civitate Dei* 20.30 [425/ 26], he lists the following events as belonging to the final drama, though not necessarily as coming in the following order: the return of Elijah, the conversion of the Jewish people to faith in Jesus, the persecution of the Antichrist, the coming of Christ as judge, the resurrection of the dead, the separation of the good from the wicked, and the burning and renewal of the material world. But he is hesitant to be more specific about the details of this *consummatio saeculi*, careful not to speculate further on the identity and career of the Antichrist, and especially reluctant to identify any of the traditional apocalyptic signs of the end with the disasters of contemporary life (*Ep* 199.34f.).[15]

Faced with the threats experienced by Roman society during his episcopate, and challenged by the widespread recriminations and fears that followed the sack of Rome by the Western Goths in 410, Augustine willingly made use of the old rhetorical *topos* that the world was in a state of senility. Like an old man racked with the "complaints of age – coughing, phlegm, inflamed eyes, anxiety, lack of energy," Augustine preached in that year, so "the world has grown old, and is full of oppression." But just as Abraham had a son in his old age, so Christ, the "seed of Abraham, . . . came when all had grown old, and made you anew." Augustine urges his hearers to "become youthful in Christ, who says to you: The world is dying, the world has grown old, the world is running down and struggles with the breathlessness of age. Do not fear; your youth will be renewed like the eagle's!" (*Serm* 81.8 [410]).

Augustine seems, in fact, like many of his contemporaries, to have been fascinated by the old Roman fashion of conceiving history as a "cosmic week" of six periods or "ages," to be followed by a final "Golden Age" of peace and cosmic renewal.[16] In a few early works he compares these historical periods to the six "ages" of a human life: infancy (*infantia*), childhood (*pueritia*), youth (*adulescentia*), young adulthood (*juventus*), mature adulthood (*gravitas*), and old age (*senectus*) (*De Genesi contra Manichaeos* 1.35–41 [388/89]; *De Diversis Quaestionibus* 58.2 [391–95]). More often, he connects them with the account of the six "days" of creation in Gen 1, and superimposes on that narrative a schematized summary of sacred history in six successive periods of renewal and fall, "morning" and "evening," to be followed by a "day of rest" that will have no end (*ibid.*; see also *Serm* 259.2 [before 394]; *De Catechizandis Rudibus* 22.39 [400]; *Ctr Faustum* 12.8 [c. 400]; *In Jo Ev Tr* 9.6 [407[17]]; *De Trinitate* 4.4.7 [401/407?]; *Enarr in Ps* 92.1 [412]; *De Civ Dei* 22.30 [426]). Although in a few early works (*Serm* 259.2; *Serm Mai* 94.4f. [393–95]; *Ctr Adim* 2.2 [394]) Augustine took the further step of identifying the "Sabbath" yet to come with the millennial Kingdom promised in Apoc 20, he soon abandoned this exegesis of the Apocalypse passage in favor of a "realized," ecclesiological interpretation similar to that of Tyconius.[18]

Even in these early allusions to the millennium, Augustine is careful to avoid emphasizing its literal duration of one thousand years, or the details of its earthly delights. He understands it simply as "the future rest of the saints on earth," when the Church will be purged of all the wicked elements now mixed among its members and Christ will rule peacefully in its midst (*Serm* 259.2). The millennium, for the early Augustine, is still not eternity but a part of history, "the seventh and last period of this age" (*Ctr Adim* 2.2). "It is one thing to rest in the Lord within this present time," he observes in *Serm Mai* 94.4, "and another thing to pass beyond all time and be united with time's maker without any end." The purpose of this "spiritual Sabbath" at the end of history, which the *amici huius mundi* fail to understand, will be to direct the gaze of the faithful beyond this world to the incorruption and immortality of the eternal "eighth day" that will follow the "second" resurrection.

In *De Civ Dei* 20.7 [425/26], four years before his death, Augustine still acknowledges that such a moderate, "spiritual" millenarianism is a tenable Catholic position, and admits that he once held it himself. He goes on, however, to sketch out in detail an ecclesiological interpretation of Apoc 20.1–6, which he now prefers (*ibid.*, 7–9). In this version, the "thousand years" of the earthly Kingdom stand in a symbolic way for "all the years of the Christian era" (7). Augustine readily identifies this Kingdom with the present Church: "his saints reign now with [Christ], although certainly in a different way from how they shall reign hereafter" (9). The Church in time is a *regnum militiae*, a Church struggling against the forces of evil both outside and inside her own ranks (*ibid.*). Satan is now "chained in the abyss," according to Apoc 20.2f.: shut up in the hearts of the wicked (7) and restrained by God from exercising his full powers against the faithful, although he is certainly active (8). The "first resurrection," which stands at the start of this temporal Kingdom of Christ, is for each member of that Kingdom his or her resurrection from sin in baptism (9). The "thrones of judgment" mentioned in Apoc 20.4 are positions of authority in the Church (9), and the souls of martyrs, which the writer also saw (Apoc 20.4), are a reminder that the faithful dead belong, too, to the temporal Church (9).

In thus translating the millenarian vision of Apoc 20 into ecclesiological terms, Augustine undoubtedly laid the foundation for the widespread tendency of later Latin theology to identify the Kingdom of God, at least in its first stage of existence, with the institutional Catholic Church. In the context of *De Civ Dei* 20, however, his purpose is more to clarify his theology of Christian hope than to reinforce a vision of the Church: to sharpen the distinction between the temporal working of God's saving grace, in any age of human history, and its eschatological fullness in a "Sabbath" that is utterly beyond time and the world as we know them.[19]

Throughout his career, Augustine remained steadfastly agnostic about the time of the world's end, and skeptical about even the most respectable Christian attempts to calculate it from Scripture and contemporary events. Two favorite texts he used to support this position were Acts 1.7 ("It is not for you to know the times or seasons that the Father has fixed by his own authority") and Matt 24.36 ("But of that day and hour no one knows, not even the angels of heaven nor the Son, but the Father only"), texts from which he concluded that it is not God's will that humans should ever know when the end is coming. "So we are gladly ignorant," he adds in an early homily, "because God wants us to be ignorant" (*Enarr in Ps* 6.2 [*c.* 392]; cf. *Serm* 93.8 [411/12]; *Ep* 197; 199.1 [418/19]). Since the first Christian

Pentecost, Jesus' followers have spoken of themselves as living in the "last times," he writes to Bishop Hesychius (*Ep* 199.23); and "if there were 'last days' then, how much more now – even if there remained as many days until the end as have already passed from the Lord's Ascension until today" (*ibid.*, 24). Apocalyptic signs of the end seem always to be appearing, and those who try to compute from them the exact time of the cataclysm are always disappointed (*ibid.*, 34f.; *Serm* 93.7). Christian watchfulness, for Augustine, is simply to wait for the Lord, persevering in Christian love until the "sleep" of death overtakes us (*Serm* 93.7, commenting on Matt 25.5). To insist that the Lord is coming soon and to be wrong, Augustine cautions Hesychius, can be damaging both to one's own and one's neighbors' faith; on the other hand, to long for the Lord's coming but to believe it will be long delayed gives one grounds for both patience, if one is right, and for a happy surprise, if he *does* come soon. And there is also a third possibility: "The one who admits that he does not know which of these views is true hopes for the one, is resigned to the other, and is wrong in neither of them" (*Ep* 199.54). Augustine confesses, here and elsewhere, that he belongs to this third category.

This agnostic attitude towards the time and details of the end does not mean Augustine is uninterested in the apocalyptic tradition, or considers it unimportant for faith. Only those who now weaken their faith by "yielding to the devil" will have doubts about Christ's second coming, he writes in *Quaestiones Evangeliorum* 1.15 [399–400]. That coming will allow those who now follow Christ in faith to see his glory directly (*per speciem: ibid.*), and will fill the "house" of his followers – the Church – with glory, as well (*Serm* 50.7.10 [394/95]). Hope in the return of Christ, and in the resurrection that is to follow, is, in fact, the main legitimate source of consolation for Christians who rightly mourn the death of their loved ones (*Serm* 173.3). But the second coming of Christ will also mean judgment: the purifying process of final revelation that will cleanse the Church and its members of the remains of sin, as fire burns away stubble (*Quaest Evang* 1.15 [399/400]; *Serm* 362.9.9 [410/11]; *Enarr in Ps 103, Serm* 3.5 [415] – all referring to I Cor 3.13ff.). This unmasking of human history will inaugurate the eternal, irreversible distinction between the saved and the damned, between lovers of God and lovers of self (*Enarr in Ps 6.2* [c. 392]; cf. *De Civ Dei* 15.1–6 [419/20]).

Augustine's last and fullest treatment of the end of the world and the final judgment, in *De Civ Dei* 20 [426], is almost entirely a collection, and a sober exposition, of the passages in the Bible that refer to these events. He emphasizes the need for a judgment to reveal the justice and goodness of God's providence, which are often concealed in the present life (2). He also stresses again the importance of the cosmic conflagration that will accompany God's judgment, "burning away the corruptible characteristics proper to corruptible bodies," and so preparing the way for the transformation of material nature that is to follow (16; 25). It is in this context that he presents the ecclesiological interpretation of the millennial kingdom, Apoc 20.1–6, that I have mentioned already.

Augustine's restraint in interpreting the apocalyptic tradition, like his studied agnosticism on the time of the end, comes undoubtedly from his concern to stress the purely eschatological character of these events, and of the rewards and punishments to follow. Although prophesied in our present history and foreshadowed in our present experience, they escape our powers of prediction precisely because they form the frontier between time and eternity. Augustine occasionally underlines this eschatological "distance" of the last things by contrasting them with their temporal foreshadowings in the present life of the Church. So he contrasts God's final judgment on all his creatures with the constant process of judgment and punishment that he exercises towards sinful individuals within history (*De Civ Dei* 20.1 [425/26]). Following the language of Apoc 20.5f. and 14, Augustine also distinguishes between the "first death" of human beings, in time, which is their separation from God in sin and their consequent liability to the violent separation of soul from body in physical death (*De Civ Dei* 13.3 [417/18]; *Serm* 65.4.5; *De Trin* 4.3.5 [401/407?]; *Enarr in Ps 70, Serm* 2.3 [414/15]), and the "second death" of eternal damnation, to be experienced by sinners in a reunited soul and body that will never be annihilated (*De Civ Dei* 13.2). Correspondingly, he speaks in these same passages of both a "first" and a "second" resurrection: the raising of "dead souls" from sin in this life, through conversion and the acceptance of divine grace, and the final raising of reanimated bodies from death, when Christ will come again as judge (*Enarr in Ps 70, Serm* 2.3; *De Trin* 4.3.5; *In Jo Ev Tr* 23.13ff. [413]; *De Civ Dei* 20.5 [425/26]).

Augustine draws the parallel between these two deaths and two resurrections mainly in terms of *life*. "There are two kinds of life," he writes in *Enarr in Ps 70, Serm* 2.3 [414/15], "one of the body, the other of the soul. As the soul is the life of the body, so God is the life of the soul. So just as the body would die if the soul should depart from it, the soul dies if it departs from God." The point is made still more clearly in *De Trin* 4.3.5 [401/407?]: "The death of the soul is impiety, and the death of the body corruptibility, because of which the soul is separated from the body. Just as the soul dies when God departs from it, so the body dies when the soul departs from it; the soul becomes foolish, the body lifeless. The soul is raised through penance, and in the mortal body this renewal of life begins in the faith by which one 'believes in him who justifies the sinner' (Rom 4.5) . . . The resurrection of [the body] is put off until the end, when our very justification is made perfect in an unspeakable way." In *Tractatus in Johannis Evangelium* 23.13ff. [419/21], Augustine makes the further, perhaps over-subtle distinction that the "first resurrection" of forgiveness is the work of the whole divine substance, willed by Father and Son and achieved through the Spirit; the "second resurrection," on the other hand, will be the proper work of the incarnate Word (achieved *per dispensationem humanitatis Filii temporalem*), presumably because it has already begun in his own flesh.

One result of Augustine's double use of all these terms is to defer the truly eschatological fate of the individual – be it judgment, life, death or resurrection – until the end of time itself, and to make it simultaneous with the collective judgment and transformation of the whole community of rational creatures. Consequently, he distinguishes clearly between the fate of those now dead, who still belong to the realm of time and are subject to its limitations, and the finality of eternal reward or punishment. True, Augustine confidently asserts, in his later writings, that the souls of the dead are immediately judged at the end of their lives (e.g., *De Natura et Origine Animae* 2.4.8 [419]), and holds that "the separated souls of the saints are now in peace, while those of the wicked are in pain" (*De Civ Dei* 13.8 [417/18]; cf. *De Praedestinatione Sanctorum* 12.24 [429]). Souls enter this place of reward or punishment without the body, but with "some sort of likeness of the body," a phantom that makes possible, in this world, visions of the underworld and apparitions of the dead (*De Gen ad Litt* 12.32.60–33.62 [401/15]). He holds, too, that the time for meriting reward or punishment from God is "here and now," not in the time after death (*Enchiridion* 29.110 [423/24]), and that even the ability of the dead to profit from the prayers and good works offered for them by the living depends on their having come to deserve that ability during their lifetime (*ibid.*). Nevertheless, Augustine insists that the rewards and punishments experienced now by the souls of the dead are only a hint of their full eternal destinies, a dream of the reality that will come when their bodies have been raised (*Serm* 328.6.5 [405/11]; cf. *Ep* 159.4 [*c.* 414]). Even the martyrs now in glory, though incomparably happier than we are, possess only "a small part of the promise, a consolation as they wait" (*Serm* 280.5). "But when the resurrection occurs," Augustine promises, "then the joy of the good will be greater, and the torments of the wicked worse, as they are tortured [or rewarded] along with their bodies" (*In Jo Ev Tr* 49.10 [413]).

In a few passages, Augustine suggests that the souls of all the just immediately experience the transforming joy of God's presence. So he speaks of his departed friend Nebridius, in *Conf* 9.3.6, as already "happy without end," already "drinking from the fount of the divine wisdom." Arguing from Jesus' words on the cross to the good thief, "This day you shall be with me in Paradise" (Lk 23.43), Augustine concludes that those saved by God's grace immediately enjoy the "beatific presence of his divinity" after death (*Ep* 164.8 [*c*. 414]; cf. *Ep* 187.3, 7 [417]). However, Augustine never speaks of this beatitude before the resurrection in terms of vision, or of the "angelic" activity of intuitive contemplation and ceaseless praise – the terms in which he describes the eternal state of the risen saints.[20] Usually, he is content to employ vaguer metaphors taken from the Bible and the earlier Latin tradition: the souls of the just are in "the bosom of Abraham," about whose location Augustine confesses his ignorance (*Conf* 9.3.6 [397/400]; *Ep* 187.6; *De Gen ad Litt* 8.5; 12.33.63 [401/15]), but which is at least "the distant, hidden place of rest, where Abraham is" (*De Natura et Origine Animae* 4.16.24 [419]; cf. *Ep* 164.3.7 [*c*. 414]; *De Gen ad Litt* 12.33.63); they are in Paradise, "a general term meaning a happy state of living" (*Ep* 187.2.6 [417]); they are enjoying "rest" (*requies*: e.g., *Quaest Evang* 2.38.1 [399]; *Ep* 55.9.17 [*c*. 400]; *De Civ Dei* 13.8 [417/18]), "refreshment" (*refrigerium*: e.g., *De Gen ad Litt* 8.5 [401/15]), "the reward that fulfills" (*merces perficiens*: *De Perfectione Justitiae Hominis* 8.17 [415/16]). Augustine is equally vague about the place of this "interim" fulfillment of souls. They are "reserved in secret storerooms (*abditis receptaculis*)," he asserts in *Enchiridion* 29.109 [423/24], "at rest or in tribulation according as each has deserved for its situation while it lived in the flesh" (cf. *De Civ Dei* 12.9 [417/18]). For the just, at least, this place of waiting is not a part of hell, but a "dwelling of some hidden kind of repose (*secretae cuiusdam quietis habitatio*)," far removed from hell's sorrows (*Ep* 164.5.7; *De Gen ad Litt* 12.33.63).

Throughout his life, Augustine remained convinced that the souls of some of the dead, who are condemned to punishment immediately after death because of their sins, will be released from that punishment before God's sentence of judgment is passed, either because, in their suffering, they have been "purged" of their attachment to self, or because they have been helped to win God's forgiveness by the prayers of their fellow Christians. In the moving conclusion to book 9 of the *Confessions*, for instance, he asks his fellow Christians to join him in "remembering" his parents "at God's altar," because he is confident God will forgive them, in death, whatever "debts" they may still owe him (*Conf* 9.35ff.). The underlying reason for this certainty is, first of all, the Latin Church's long tradition of intercession for the dead. "There is no doubt," he asserts in a sermon of uncertain date, "that the dead are helped by the prayers of the holy Church, by the saving sacrifice [i.e., the Eucharist], and by alms given for their souls, in order that God may deal more mercifully with them than their sins have deserved." It is the tradition of our ancestors, he continues, to pray by name, during the celebration of the Eucharist, for "those who have died in the communion of the body and blood of Christ . . . And when works of mercy are done in order to commend them [to God], who doubts that they are helped, since prayers for them are not offered to God in vain?" (*Serm* 172.2). In his tract *De Cura pro Mortuis Gerenda* 1.3 [424/25], Augustine adds to the weight of this Christian tradition the scriptural evidence of II Macc 12.43 as justification for these practices.

Behind Augustine's understanding of Christian prayer for the dead is undoubtedly, once again, his strong sense of the difference between time – to which even the dead still belong – and eternity. "The souls of the holy dead are not separated from the Church, which is now Christ's Kingdom," he observes in *De Civ Dei* 20.9 [425/26]; "otherwise they would not be commemorated at the altar of God in our communion in the body of Christ." They are *membra Christi* (*De Nat et Orig An* 1.9.10 [419]), and so participate still in the struggle and growth of the Church towards its eschatological goal. And since the dead still belong to time, it is perfectly understandable that some of them should still be undergoing the "temporal," limited and often beneficial experience of punishment that sinful members of Christ also undergo during their life on earth (*De Civ Dei* 21.13 [425/26]). "Some people suffer temporal punishments (*temporarias poenas*) in this life only, others after death, others both now and then, but they suffer them before that most severe and final judgment.[21] Not all, however, who undergo temporal (*temporales*) punishments after death will come to everlasting punishments (*sempiternas poenas*), which will take place after that judgment. For some, as we have said above, will be forgiven in the age still ahead (*in futuro saeculo*) for what has not been forgiven in this age, so that they will not be subjected to the eternal punishments of the coming age" (*ibid.*).

In most of his works, Augustine makes no distinction between the kind of punishment after death designated for those who will ultimately be saved and that meant for the damned. As J. Ntedika has observed, Augustine conceives of this "temporal" punishment of the dead as "une condamnation provisoire": a condamnation that does not anticipate God's final, eternal verdict on them at the end of time.[22] Against this background, Augustine's explanation of Jesus' *descensus ad inferos* after his death, mentioned in I Pet 3.19f., is more readily understandable: he insists that Jesus visited not the just, who were in the "bosom of Abraham," but sinners in the hell of the damned, and that he released at least some of them from their "sorrows" (*dolores*) (*Ep* 164.7f. [414]; *De Gen ad Litt* 12.33.63 [401/14]). Apparently hell is not a permanent state, for Augustine, until the common passage of all creatures from time into eternity.

Augustine frequently insists, however, that not all the dead are capable of receiving God's mercy through the prayers and meritorious actions of the Church done in their name. "These things clearly profit the dead," he observes in *Serm* 172.2, "but only those who so lived before their death that these things could be useful to them after death. For those who have left their bodies without 'the faith that works through love' (Gal 5.6), and without its sacraments, receive acts of such piety from their relatives in vain ... No new merits are won for the dead, when their relatives do some good work for them, but only complementary merits are added to what they have previously achieved. And nothing is achieved unless they so lived while on earth that these works should be of help to them when they had ceased to live here." Augustine makes this point still more clearly in *Enchiridion* 29.110 [423/24]: "Such acts are of advantage to those who during their life have deserved that such acts should be of advantage to them. For there is a certain manner of living, neither good enough to dispense with the need for these acts after death, nor bad enough to preclude their being of advantage to it after death; and there is a manner of living which is so established in goodness as to dispense with the need for them, as again there is one so established in evil as to be incapable of benefiting even from these when it has passed on from this life."[23] Clearly, neither proven saints nor hardened criminals are in a position to be helped by prayers or to receive God's forgiveness after death. And it is only because she is ignorant of any particular person's true standing before God that the Church prays for all the dead, just as she prays for all the living (cf. *De Civ Dei* 21.24 [425/26]).

It has long been debated, then, whether Augustine presents, in his writings, a doctrine of temporary, remedial suffering after death substantially corresponding to the later Latin doctrine of purgatory.[24] Although, as we have seen, he often affirms that some sinners are only punished within history, not eternally, and that the prayers of their fellow Christians are effective in moving God to pardon their offenses, Augustine never presents this temporal punishment as being carried out in a distinctive "place," or as having, of itself, a healing or cleansing effect on the sinner. In fact, Augustine always seems hesitant to speak of punishment for sin as purgative or medicinal, presumably because he is contemptuous of the attempts of other "tender-hearted" Christians to see all punishment as purgative and therefore temporary (see below, and esp. *De Civ Dei* 21.17–27). Augustine's understanding of punishment is, in fact, wholly vindictive: God's truth and justice require that the creature who turns away from him, the one authentic source of its being, should suffer as a result (*Enarr in Ps* 44.18 [403]; *Serm* 19.2[419]). Punishment is simply the natural, painful effect of sin (*Enarr in Ps* 7.16 [392]); "when God punishes sinners, he does not inflict an evil of his own on them, but sets them loose amid their own evils" (*Enarr in Ps* 5.10 [392]; cf. *Ctr Julianum* 5.16 [423]).[25] In *De Civ Dei* 21.13, however, he concedes that the suffering that results from sin may be called "purgative" if it leads the sinner to a change of heart: "We profess that in this mortal life punishments are not purgative, if they are inflicted on those whose life does not improve or even grows worse as a result, but they are purgative for those who are corrected by their discipline. But all other punishments," he continues, "whether temporal or eternal, as each person is treated by divine providence, are inflicted either for past sins or for sins in which the person being afflicted still lives . . ."

Augustine is even reluctant to apply I Cor 3.10–15, the biblical *locus classicus* for belief in a temporary, purgative "fire of judgment," to the punishment of sinners after death. In at least two **passages**, he identifies the "fire" Paul refers to here as the pain and sadness involved in detaching ourselves from the "love of temporal things," in order to make Christ our true "foundation" (*Enarr in Ps 80.21* [403]; *De Fide et Operibus* 16.28 [413]).[26] In a few later works, however, Augustine is willing at least to allow the legitimacy of speaking of some kinds of punishment for sin after death as expiatory and purgative, and for that reason as aptly represented by the image of fire (see, for instance, *Quaest in Heptateuchum* 6 [Joshua] 9.2 [420]; *Enchir* 18.69 [423/24]). *In De Civ Dei* 21.26 [426], Augustine uses the language of I Cor 3.10–15 to present the theory some earlier writers (doubtless including Ambrose) have espoused, of a "fire of transitory suffering" through which all the dead must pass, between death and the moment of resurrection. The just, according to this theory, will not feel any burning from the fire, but those whose life and loves in this world were made from a mixture of base "straw" and more precious materials will have their "worldliness, which may be pardonable if damnation is at stake," burned away. Augustine's judgment on such an hypothesis is cautiously affirmative: "I do not reject it, because perhaps it is true." But where and how this "fire of judgment" is to be experienced is, in Augustine's eyes, less clear: "whether there only [i.e., between death and resurrection] or here as well as there, or here and not there." It may, he suggests, include the very experience of "the death of the flesh," which is itself a punishment resulting from original sin; and it seems appropriate, too, to apply it to the persecutions that every Christian, in one way or another, experiences. Surely it will include the tribulations the Church will suffer at the end of the world.

Because it stands as the dividing-line between time and eternity, between humanity's age of growth and change and its age of fulfillment, the resurrection of the dead is, for Augustine, the one genuinely eschatological event. Expectation of a resurrection is "the distinctive faith of Christians" (*Serm* 241.1 [405–10]; cf. *Serm* 214.12 [391]), the hope that marks off the followers of Christ from "the wise among the pagans" (*ibid.*). "Our hope is the resurrection of the dead," he insists; "our faith is the resurrection of the dead. It is also our love, which the preaching of 'things not yet seen' (Hebr 11.1) inflames and arouses by longing . . . If faith in the resurrection of the dead is taken away, all Christian doctrine perishes . . . If the dead do not rise, we have no hope of a future life; but if the dead do rise, there *will* be a future life" (*Serm* 361.2 [410/11]). If we ask ourselves what Christ has promised us, he remarks in a sermon on the Psalms, and find that it is only the "happiness of this age," we have every right to grumble, since this age is a time of endless change and disappointment. "What happiness did he promise you? What but in the resurrection of the dead?" (*Enarr in Ps* 36.1.9 [403]).

Although he continued, through his life, to accept the indestructibility of the human soul as a philosophically evident truth, Augustine laid less and less stress on the theological importance of this immortality as his thought matured. So in his early treatise *De Immortalitate Animae* [387], Augustine borrowed heavily from Neoplatonic psychological theories[27] to prove that the soul is immortal. His argument follows two lines: that the soul, unlike the body, has experience of eternal and immutable truth, and therefore, by the principle that like can only be known be like, must be eternal and immutable in its own essence (1–6.11); and that the soul, which gives being to the body (7.12–10.17), must have the source of its being either in itself or in the supreme, self-existent Good, neither of which will allow it to cease to be (11.18–15.24). In subsequent works, Augustine took a more explicitly Christian approach, arguing to the soul's immortality either from its being made in the image of its creator (*De Quantitate Animae* 2.3 [387/88]) or from the natural desire for beatitude that the creator has implanted in it, a yearning which requires unending existence if it is not to end in frustration (*De Trinitate* 14.8.11 [417/18]). In *De Civ Dei* 13.2 [417/18], however, Augustine points out that this natural immortality is itself of rather limited value, since the soul still experiences a kind of death if it is abandoned by God because of its sin.

Augustine was convinced, as I have already said, that the rewards of the good and the punishments of the wicked after death are only a partial anticipation of what they will be when body and soul are eternally reunited at the end of history (cf. *De Civ Dei* 13.19 [417/18]). So the souls of the departed just "look forward with patient longing for the resurrection of their bodies" (*De Civ Dei* 13.20), and are hindered from enjoying the full vision of God by their "natural appetite for managing the body" (*De Gen ad Litt* 12.35.68 [c. 414]).

The starting-point of Augustine's hope for the resurrection of the dead is unquestionably not philosophical speculation, but the news of the resurrection of Jesus. It is only in their own rising from the dead that humans will be, in the fullest sense, "conformed to the image of the Son" of God (*De Trin* 14.18.24 [417/18]; cf. Rom 8.29). So the whole aim of Jesus' post-resurrection appearances was "that we might believe in the resurrection of the dead" (*Serm* 243.3 [408/409]). Christ's "Pasch," his "passage" (*transit-*

us) to the Father, had as its purpose to prepare for his disciples "dwelling-places in the Kingdom of heaven, which he will give them in the resurrection of the dead" (*Quaest in Hept* 2 [Exodus] 154.1). And just as the gospel accounts stress the corporeality of Jesus' risen body, and its identity with the body in which he preached and underwent death, so Augustine is at pains to oppose any interpretation of the Christian hope that would turn to allegory the promise that our bodies will rise again (see, e.g., *Ep* 147.22.51 [413]).

Christian teaching, he insists, is that "the saints, in the resurrection, will possess the identical bodies in which they labored here on earth" (*De Civ Dei* 13.19 [417/18]; cf. *Serm* 256.2 [418]); as God is the creator of both our souls and our bodies, so he will be the restorer of both (*Serm* 277.3 [413]). It is an essential part of Christian faith that "this visible flesh will rise again" (*De Fide et Symbolo* 10.23 [393]). The contempt for the body that leads to a denial of the resurrection is either Manichean dualism (so *De Agone Christiano* 32.34 [397]) or the "worldly philosophy" of the Platonists and their over-enthusiastic Christian supporters (*Serm* 277.3; cf. the anti-Platonist apologetic in *De Civ Dei* 13.16ff. [417/18]; 21.2f.; 22.26 [425/26]; *Serm* 241 [405/10]). Responding to the ascetic pagan, Manichee or Christian who proclaims, in late classical style, "I am not flesh but spirit; I groan in my prison, and when these bonds and fetters have been dissolved I depart in freedom," Augustine cites I Cor 15, and proclaims as the Christian answer: "I do not put off the flesh forever; I put it aside for a time" (*Serm* 256.2 [418]).

Following this same chapter of Paul, however, Augustine repeatedly emphasizes that the risen body will be a "spiritual body." In a few early works, alluding to I Cor 15.50 ("Flesh and blood will not inherit the Kingdom of God"), he explains that "at the moment of its spiritual transformation [the body] will no longer be flesh and blood, but simply a body" (*De Fide et Symbolo* 10.24 [393]; cf. *De Agone Christiano* 32.34 [397]). In *Retractationes* 1.16 and 2.29 [426/27], however, Augustine modifies this interpretation, taking "flesh and blood" in the Pauline passage to mean either an immoderate love of the "works" of the flesh, or the flesh's present corruptibility. So, in his mature works, he interprets the term "spiritual body" as referring first to the incorruptibility of the risen body (*Enchir* 23.91 [423/24]; *De Civ Dei* 22.21 [426]), and secondly to its perfect subjection to the human spirit (*ibid.*; also *Serm* 242.8.11 [405/10]; *De Civ Dei* 13.20 [417/18]). The conflict between the inner and outer person, between the ideals of the "spirit" and the desires of the "flesh," which characterize the human situation in this present age, will be overcome in the resurrection; "we shall have a body, but it will no longer be a burden since it will no longer be corruptible" (*De Civ Dei* 14.3 [418/19]). Reunited with the bodies for which they have longed since death, and perfectly integrated with them in desire and in action, souls will then be perfectly content (*De Civ Dei* 22.26 [426]).

In a number of his mature works, Augustine also deals with the objections raised by opponents of the Christian hope for resurrection to what seem to be the absurd implications of the doctrine; in the process, he sketches out a concrete picture of how he imagines the resurrected body, which was to exercise great influence on Thomas Aquinas and later Latin scholasticism (see especially *Serm* 242–43 [408/409]; *Enchir* 23.84–93 [423/24]; *De Civ Dei* 22.12–21 [426]). Following the tradition of most of his Patristic forbears, both Eastern and Western, Augustine clearly understands the process of resurrection quite literally as a reassembling of all the particles of matter that originally belonged to each individual. Appealing, like all apologists for the resurrection since Athenagoras and Tertullian, to the omnipotence of God, Augustine also argues from analogies in everyday experience that heavy, earthy bodies can be suspended in a lighter, airy medium, such as heaven must be (*Serm* 242.5ff.). Those who have died as infants or small children will receive additional matter, in order to rise in the size which they would have reached, had they lived to maturity (*Serm* 242.3; *Enchir* 23.85; *De Civ Dei* 22.14f.).[28] Parts of the body that have been discarded during life in the interest of appearance, such as hair or nails, will not necessarily be reclaimed in the same form (*Enchir* 23.89; *De Civ Dei* 22.19), nor will present disfigurements of size and shape be restored as they now exist (*Enchir* 23.87, 90; *De Civ Dei* 22.19); harmony and proportion will determine the reshaping of our present, distinctive form (*ibid.*). Matter that has been shared, in the course of time, by more than one person – human flesh eaten by cannibals, for instance, or by animals that are then eaten by other humans – will be restored to its original owner (*Enchir* 23.88; *De Civ Dei* 22.20). All the organs of the present body will be restored in ideal form, even though many of them will not be used (*Serm* 243.4, 7f.). Even the sexual identity of men and women will be preserved, free from its present connection with shame and passion (*De Civ Dei* 22.17). Infused with the quickness and universal intentionality of the mind, the risen body will possess "a wondrous ease of movement, a wondrous lightness" (*Serm* 242.8.11; cf. *Serm* 277.12.12 [413]), and the "inner" life of the mind will be so fully integrated with the body that each person will know everyone else thoroughly, even his or her inmost thoughts (*Serm* 243.5f.).

Augustine's insistence on the material reality of the risen body is undoubtedly derived, in large part, from his understanding of the resurrection as utter transformation: the beginning of a new phase for created existence in all its aspects, the threshold between time and eternity. The blessed existence promised us is existence in the "land of the living. Nothing begins and grows there; whatever is there, is in the same way and is so forever" (*Serm* 45.4 [408/11]). To pass into this new, changeless mode of life presupposes death in this historical order, the complete end of this temporal existence and the inauguration of a new, incorruptible mode of being.[29] The present form of the material world will also "pass away in a conflagration of earthly fire," and so will be purged of its "corruptible qualities"; in the end, "the world, remade into something better, will be rightly adapted to human beings who also have been remade, in their flesh, into something better" (*De Civ Dei* 20.16 [425/26]).[30] The new cosmos will not simply be a repetition of the old, a setting in which spirits may once again fall and be purged of their sin, he insists against the reported theories of the Origenists (*Ad Orosium contra Priscillianistas et Origenistas* 8.10 [415]). Rather, both we and our world will be so changed that "wherever we turn our eyes we shall, with the clearest accuracy, see God present everywhere and controlling all, even material, things, through the bodies we shall have and through those we shall see" (*De Civ Dei* 22.29 [426]).

In many passages throughout his works, in fact, Augustine stresses the direct contemplative vision of God as the very heart of the eternal beatitude of the saints (e.g., *Enarr in Ps* 26.2.9 [411/12]; *Enarr in Ps* 43.5 [412]; *Serm* 362.29.30–30.31 [410/11]; *Ep* 130.14.27 (c. 412]).[31] A question that long exercised him, however, was whether after the resurrection the blessed will "see God face to face" with the eyes of their transformed bodies, or will still see him only in the internal, metaphorical sense of "seeing with the heart." In *Ep* 92 [408], Augustine scornfully rejects as *dementia* the notion that human beings will ever be able to see the essence of God with their bodily eyes, in this world or in eternity, since that would imply God is localized and corporeal. In several later treatises on the same subject (*Epp* 147 [413], 148 [413] and 162 [414]; *Serm* 277.13–19 [413]), his tone is more conciliatory, but his conclusions are much the same: it has been promised that "the clean of heart shall see God," but the safest interpretation of this promise is to take it as referring to the kind of spiritual "vision" by which we now "see" invisible realities (*Ep* 147.37; 148.3.11). In these works, Augustine does not openly reject the hypothesis that the transformed, spiritual body of the resurrection may also be able to see God in some way, but feels it is, at best, an unresolved question (*Ep* 147.48f.; 148.5.18; *Serm* 277.19). In the final book of *De Civitate Dei* [426], however, while still conceding that philosophical considerations weigh against the possibility of a corporeal vision of God, Augustine suggests that Scripture encourages the believer to take a more daring view, and to hope that as our eyes now "see" life in other bodies, simply by looking at them, so the eyes of the spiritual body will be able to "see" God directly, in their own way: as present in all the material elements of the transformed universe, and as enlivening them by his rule (*De Civ Dei* 22.29). Whether sensory in any corporeal way, or simply an intuition of the spirit, the vision of God will be the basis for union with him (*Ep* 147.37 [413]), the cause of the "unspeakable joy" in which, "in a certain way, the human mind dies and becomes divine, and is inebriated with the riches of God's house" (*Enarr in Ps* 35.14 [412]).[32]

Augustine does not suggest, however, that the blessed will simply contemplate God passively for all eternity. Heaven will have a kind of activity all its own, perfectly compatible with eternal rest: the activity of praise (e.g., *Enarr in Ps* 85.24 [412]). "Then we shall see best," he insists in *Serm* 362.30.31 [410/11], "because we shall be supremely at leisure. When, after all, are we fully at leisure, except when these times of labor, these times of the hardships in which we are now ensnared, have passed? . . . We will be at leisure, then, and we will see God as he is, and when we see him we shall praise him. And this will be the life of the saints, the activity of those at rest: we shall praise without ceasing." In a body reconstituted in perfect harmony and grace, "every fiber and organ will play its part in praising God" (*De Civ Dei* 22.30 [426]). So Augustine often speaks of the joys of eternity in liturgical terms: "all our activity will be 'Amen' and 'Alleluia'" (*Serm* 362.28.29 [410/11]; cf. *Serm* 243.9 [408/409]; *Enarr in Ps* 85.11 [412]), as we celebrate the consecration of God's everlasting temple (*De Civ Dei* 15.19 [418/19]; cf. *Serm* 337.2 [412]). Heaven will also mean the gift of new qualities and characteristics to the human frame: a share in the eternity of God's own substance (*Enarr in Ps* 101, *Serm* 2.10f. [395]);[33] a freedom that is beyond the power of human nature alone but given to those who are *participes Dei*, freedom so great as to exclude even the possibility of sin (*De Civ Dei* 22.30 [426]); a healing of our corrupted human natures so that they will be fully integrated and fully subject to God (*De Civ Dei* 19.21 [425/26]); a peace that is the "tranquillity of order," reigning within each individual and marking all our relationships (*De Civ Dei* 19.13), a peace that is both our ultimate happiness and our highest good (*De Civ Dei* 19.27).

In many passages, Augustine summarizes his hope for eternal beatitude by affirming that those humans who are saved will be "the equals of the angels," with whom they will comprise a single heavenly community (e.g., *Serm* 303.2 [425/30]; *Ep* 148.2.8 [413]; *Ep* 187.5.16 [417]; *Enchir* 9.29 [423/24]).[34] The *societas angelorum*, in fact, is one of the "eternal rewards" he frequently lists when depicting the details of Christian fulfillment (*Serm* 19.5 [419]; *Serm* 80.7 [c. 410]; *Serm* 252.6 [396]; *Serm* 337.4; *Enarr in Ps* 119.6 [412]; *De Gen ad Litt* 7.25.36; 11.18.24 [401/15]; *Hom in I Jo* 9.10 [414?]; *De Adulterinis Coniugiis* 2.8.7 [419/20]; *Ep* 102.2.15 [c. 409]). In a few late passages, Augustine even speculates that God has determined to save some members of the fallen human race in order to make up the original number of the angels, which had been depleted by their own "revolt from God" (*Enchir* 9.29 [423/24]; *De Civ Dei* 22.1 [426]). Together, the faithful angels and those humans who have been transformed by the grace of Christ will form an eternal community, "one common City of God" (*De Civ Dei* 22.29; cf. 12.9).

This emphasis on eternal fellowship with the angels as a central feature of human beatitude reveals the essentially ecclesial, social character of salvation as Augustine conceives it. So he speaks at length of those who adhere to their creator as the "City of God," an image that would have no meaning "if the life of the saints were not social" (*De Civ Dei* 19.5 [425/26]). The resurrection of human bodies will mean that "the Church will be perfected in its angelic fullness" (*De Consensu Evangelistarum* 2.75.145 [400]). Even though there will be many different levels of happiness and glory in the eternal city, there will be no envy or discontent among its citizens (*De Civ Dei* 22.30 [426]); all will be joined in the peace that is the heavenly city's most basic structural characteristic, a peace that Augustine twice defines as "the perfectly ordered and harmonious common life (*societas*) of those who enjoy God and one another in God" (*De Civ Dei* 19.13, 17). "Who does not long for that city," he asks in *Enarr in Ps 84*.10 [after 410], "where no friend leaves and no enemy enters, where no one tries or disturbs us, no one divides the people of God, no one wearies God's Church in the service of the devil? . . . We will have God as our common sight (*spectaculum*), we will have God as our common possession, we will have God as our common peace." The fulfillment of the present life of Christian faith and struggle is not simply the salvation of individuals, but the unity in everlasting love of the body of Christ, "and the end will be the one Christ, loving himself" (*Hom in I Jo* 10.3 [414?]).[35]

Corresponding to this emphasis on the social nature of salvation is Augustine's insistence that damnation, too, is meted out justly by God to the human race as a whole, because the whole race is "rooted" in Adam, who freely turned away from God (see, e.g., *De Civ Dei* 21.12 [425/26]; *De Correptione et Gratia* 10.28 [426]). If some individuals are chosen out of this condemned "clay," this *massa perditionis*, and formed into "chosen vessels" for salvation – a pottery-metaphor drawn from Rom 9.21ff. – such an act of election reveals God's gratuitous mercy, over and above his justice, with a clarity that would not be achieved if he had simply decided to save the whole condemned race together (see, e.g., *Ep* 186.4.12 [417]; *Ep* 190.3.9–12 [418]; *Ep* 194.2.4f. [418]; *Serm* 26.12.13 [418]; *Ctr Duas Epistulas Pelagianorum* 2.7.13 [422/23]; *Enchir* 25.99 [423/24]; *De Praedestinatione Sanctorum* 8.16 [429]; *De Dono Perseverantiae* 14.35 [429]). So Augustine occasionally applies to human society Tyconius' metaphor of the *corpus diaboli*, whose head is Satan, as the foil against which the much smaller community of grace, the *corpus Christi*, can more clearly be seen (*De Gen ad Litt* 11.24.31 [401/15]; *Enarr in Ps* 139.7 [414]).

Augustine is characteristically cautious, however, in attempting to describe the punishments of the damned, generally refusing to go beyond what he takes to be the clear statements of Scripture. He does, it is true, make some conjectures about the nature of damnation. In his early treatise *De Vera Religione* (391), he speculates that the "severe penalties" that await sinners after this life consist mainly in their being deprived of the light of reason and so of their being unable to confess God (52.101). In several passages, too, he advances the opinion that there will be various types and degrees of punishment in Gehenna, suited to the particular crimes of the damned (*De Vera Religione* 54.104f.; *De baptismo* 4.19 [401]; *Ep* 102.4 [*c*. 409]; *De Civ Dei* 21.16 [425/26]; *Enchir* 23.93 [423/24]). In most of his works, however, Augustine is content simply to use scriptural images for eternal punishment, and to interpret them literally. Relying especially on Is 66.24 and its dependent passage in the New Testament, Mark 9.42–48, he insists that the "fire" of Gehenna, and probably also its "worm that never dies," are material realities that will torture the risen bodies of the damned (*De Civ Dei* 21.9 [425/26]). The misery and pain experienced in Gehenna, both corporeal and psychological, will continue without end.[36] Augustine recognizes that to speak of this pain as eternal will appear self-contradictory to his pagan contemporaries, since classical anthropology generally identified suffering with corruption, and thus assumed that both must end in the destruction of the subject (*De Civ Dei* 21.2). So he develops an elaborate apologetic for the paradox of eternal suffering, arguing from parallel phenomena in nature (*ibid.*, 4–7) and appealing to the unknown properties of the risen body (*ibid.* 3, 8) to support the credibility of the "miracle" of eternal punishment (*ibid.*, 9). Like the physical sufferings we undergo in this life, the "fire" and "worm" of Gehenna will also afflict the souls of the damned, who will be "tortured by fruitless repentance" (*ibid.*). Although it is not clear how they will be affected, Scripture (Matt 25.41) assures us that "the devil and his angels" will also suffer from these same material torments (*ibid.*, 10). In his mature works, Augustine is, understandably, hesitant to hazard a guess as to "what kind of fire this is and in what part of the world or of creation it will be" (*De Civ Dei* 20.16 [425/26]), though he had earlier accepted the traditional belief that the place of torment is under the earth (*De Gen ad Litt* 12.33.62, 12.34.66 [401/15]). He also refuses to speculate on what the damned will look like (*Enchir* 23.92 [423/24]). The most that can be said is that their existence will more truly be termed death than life: "for to be continually in torment is eternal death, not any kind of life . . . It is called 'second death' (Apoc 20.6, 14) and 'death,' and no one there dies. I should say, more adequately and better, no one there lives. For to live in sorrows is not to live at all" (*Serm* 306.5.5; cf. *De Civ Dei* 6.12 [416]; 19.28 [425/26]).

For Augustine, in fact, the aspect of damnation that needed the most elaborate defense was not its materiality but its eternity: not only before skeptical pagans but also before some of "our tender-hearted [fellow Christians]" (*De Civ Dei* 21.17 [425/26]), who refused to believe that a merciful God could punish anyone without end (cf. *Enchir* 29.112 [423/ 24]). Augustine devotes some ten chapters (17–27) in *De Civitate Dei* 21 to refuting the various forms of this misplaced trust in God's mercy. Some Christians, like Origen, genuinely hope in universal salvation, believing that all rational creatures, including the devils, will ultimately "be associated with the holy angels" (17). Others believe God will at least pardon every human sinner (18), and still others see his mercy as assured at least to all the baptized (19), or to all Catholics (20), or to Catholics who persevere in the Church until death (21), or to Catholics who have been generous and forgiving towards their neighbors (22). To each of these groups, Augustine offers the same response: "Scripture, infallible Scripture" makes it clear that all sinners, angelic or human, when they have missed the opportunity for conversion, are to be consigned to a punishment that is literally everlasting (23). Thus the Church has never prayed for those whom it knows to be condemned (24). Even if they have been baptized or have shared in the Catholic communion (25), even if they have been merciful to others (27), sinners will be condemned "unless they cease from these actions and have charity, 'which does no wrong' (I Cor 13.4)" (27; cf. *Enarr in Ps* 80.20 [403]). The only concession Augustine is willing to make to those who argue that God's mercy extends even to the most hardened sinners is to allow "that he will let them suffer less horrible punishments than what they deserve" (*De Civ Dei* 21.24), and to conjecture that he may, from time to time, "give some ease or intermission to their torments" (*Enchir* 29.112 [423/24]).

Both the tragic agony of damnation and the blessedness of eternal reward are, for Augustine, far more than simply expressions of God's just response to the value of human action. They represent, respectively, the failure and the success of the rational creature's long quest in time for his true and stable "homeland," for the blessedness of finding his own true identity in "adhering to God" and loving all other creatures in God. The human creature who has found the "way" to his homeland in Jesus Christ and in his Church will rejoice, on arrival there, like the Prodigal Son when he returns to his Father (e.g., *Ep* 55.17f. [400]; *Serm Mai* 94.5; *Conf* 1.18; 2.2; 3.6; 4.15f.; 8.3 [397–400]), or like the pilgrim who discovers that his journey through distant lands has only shown him how much better his homeland is (*Enarr in Ps* 119.6 [412]; cf. *Conf* 5.8). For the "place" of beatitude – eternity in God's presence – is truly the "home" of the human creature, in Augustine's view; the Sabbath of rest and the "eighth day" of our new creation are but the restoration of our creaturely existence before the fall, the origin that we dimly remember, and whose lingering presence in our memories gives us hope (*Enarr in Ps* 37.9–12 [395]; *Conf* 12.10.10; 12.11.13; 12.15.21; 12.16.23 [397/400]; *Ep* 55.17f. [400]).[37] "Then we shall return to the beginning," Augustine says of the eschaton in an early sermon for the octave day of Easter. "Just as when these seven days are over, the eighth is like the first, so after the seven periods of this passing age are finished and all is accomplished, we will return to that immortality and that blessedness from which humanity fell" (*Serm* 259.2 [393]). In later works he would be less outspokenly cyclic in his conception of the progress of time, but his underlying conviction remained the same: that human salvation is the achievement, by God's gracious gift, of the union with God for which alone humanity was made, and that the only genuine meaning of human history is to be found in God's eternity.

Contemporaries of Augustine

The distinctive character of Augustine's eschatological hopes can be seen all the more clearly when they are contrasted with the speculations of some of his friends.

(a) One document that seems to come from contemporary Africa, and that may have been written by Augustine's fellow bishop and correspondent Evodius of Uzala, about 412, is the *Consultationes Zacchaei et Apollonii*, an apologetic exposition of Christian faith composed in the long-familiar form of a dialogue between a pagan and a Christian.[38] The document seems to reflect questions raised by educated Roman pagans about the plausibility of Christian faith in the aftermath of the sack of Rome in 410 (cf. Augustine, *Ep* 135 and 137).

Unlike Augustine, the author is convinced by the violence and disasters of his time that the end of the world is very near. Christ came, the Christian Zacchaeus assures his friend, not in the middle of human history but near its end, lest abuses and forgetfulness corrupt, through long ages of further waiting, the faith he left with his followers (1.21). Although the exact time of Christ's return is known only to God, the signs predicted in the gospels are clearly being fulfilled in contemporary history: wars and violence are everywhere, and the gospel is indeed being preached throughout the world (3.8). With the coming of Elijah, all will be accomplished (*ibid.*). Then the Antichrist will appear, "the devil raging about in a human person" (3.7); he will try to reestablish the Jewish law and will lead many pagans to pay him divine honors (*ibid.*). After three and one-half years of great turmoil and suffering for the Church, Christ will come as judge and put an end to the confusion. The period left before the end, therefore, is short, but Zacchaeus asks pointedly: "Consider, I beg you, whether the age can bear this for long?"

Zacchaeus strongly denies his pagan friend's suggestion that souls, after death, are "purged in ethereal fire" and so return, free of all corrupt materiality, to the divine substance out of which they were formed (1.22). Human souls and bodies are alike created by God, whose substance is in no need of purgation; when the end of the world comes, the bodies of the dead will be raised and reunited to their souls, in order to be judged and to receive the reward or punishment their deeds deserve (*ibid.*; cf. 3.9). To the familiar question of how consumed and dissipated particles of matter can be reassembled after so many years, the author gives the familiar answer that God, who has created all things, can certainly recreate them as well (1.23). And since matter never perishes completely, it will be possible for God to reconstitute the very same bodies human beings now possess (1.24).

After the resurrection and judgment, "a new heaven and a fresh earth will be revealed," where the just will "dwell in the splendor of the sun" and be rewarded with the continual vision of God (1.26). The author's description of this new world seems to be drawn from the millenarian tradition, although he does not mention the millennial Kingdom explicitly. It will be a land of eternal spring, enriched with every kind of fragrance and visual beauty (1.26), a world that will put to shame all the most precious luxuries of this present age (3.9). Armed both with this promise of reward and with his apocalyptic interpretation of the calamities of his age, Zacchaeus urges his pagan friend to accept the Christian message while there is still time. "We are forced now by the nearness of the end and the terror of the judgment ahead of us to abandon our idols and worship the true deity; in this short space between the first coming of Christ, which we know, and the second coming, which we look forward to, we should not let his commandments be forgotten, or despair that the happiness promised us will come" (1.21).

(b) Another friend and contemporary of Augustine, who also offered an apologetic response to the challenges of contemporary paganism, was the Spanish presbyter Paulus Orosius. Orosius is chiefly known to posterity for his *Historia adversus Paganos*, a chronicle in seven books whose express purpose was to provide, at Augustine's suggestion, further documentation for the argument in the third book of *De Civitate Dei* that the lot of humanity has improved rather than declined since the advent of the Christian faith.

Although Augustine's original request may simply have been for a brief dossier of historical examples, Orosius' work is a full-scale, if sketchy, history of the world. His thesis is stated clearly in the preface to the work: "I found the days of the past not just equally oppressive as these, but all the more wretched, the more distant they are from the solace of true religion; it has, in fact, become clear from this examination that bloodthirsty death reigned as long as the religion which forbids bloodshed was unknown; that, as that religion dawned, bloodshed and death grew fainter; that they have come to an end, now that it has prevailed . . ." (prologue to book 1). In fact, Orosius' history of human society thoroughly adulterates Augustine's argument in *De Civitate Dei* by historicizing the "City of God" and identifying it openly with historical Christian institutions.[39]

Understandably, then, Orosius avoids millenarian speculations and shows little interest in the eschatological dimension of Christian faith, despite his apologetic purpose. He does, to be sure, hold loyally to the positive details of traditional eschatological doctrines. Thus he sent Augustine a list of the errors of the Priscillianists and Origenists (the *Commonitorium*) in 414, in which he included prominently among the latter the moral or psychological interpretation of the fire of Gehenna and the hope for universal salvation that one finds in the Origenist tradition (*CSEL* 18, 155.19–156.20).[40] In his history, Orosius accepts the disasters predicted for the end of time, and the coming persecution of Christians by the Antichrist, as the only exceptions to his thesis that things are steadily getting better for the world (prologue to *Hist*; *ibid.*, 7.27.16). The end, he occasionally suggests, may even not be far off; Roman civilization is now suffering from "the infirmity of old age" (*Hist* 2.6.14), and he characterizes himself as "placed at the end of time" (*ibid.*, 4.5.12). But these are, by now, simply accepted turns of phrase, rhetorical concessions to an established apocalyptic tradition; they have little effect on Orosius' interpretation of history or of Christian institutions. In its theological content, Orosius' reassuring message stands in the tradition of Eusebius and is the diametrical opposite of the dire warnings of the *Consultationes Zacchaei et Apollonii*, just as it runs counter to Augustine's critical reading of secular history and culture. Whatever eternity may bring, salvation, in Orosius' view, has already begun in the events of human history.

Liber de Promissionibus

A work almost certainly from Augustine's milieu, which reflects many of the details of his eschatological system, is the *Liber de Promissionibus et Praedictionibus Dei*, attributed in the Middle Ages to Prosper of Aquitaine, secretary to Pope Leo I, but now generally recognized as the work of

Augustine's friend and correspondent, the bishop Quodvultdeus of Carthage (d. 453, in exile in Campania).[41] This curious work, probably composed between 445 and 449,[42] is a catalogue of 153 "promises"[43] of the saving acts of God and "predictions" of the sinful acts of human and diabolical forces, all culled from the Old and New Testaments. The first 80 of these are a selection of Old Testament texts whose meaning the author sees as "fulfilled" in the life of Jesus; reversing the perspective, he takes as his next 40 "promises" incidents in the gospels, which he shows to be fulfillments of Old Testament texts. As an appendix to this typological collection, the author adds 33 scriptural "promises" and "predictions" for the end of time: 20 concerning the "half-time" (*dimidium temporis*),[44] a providentially shortened period of conflict and diabolical persecution culminating in the second coming of Christ, resurrection and judgment; and a final thirteen chapters summarizing the biblical hope for the "glory and the kingdom of the saints."

These final 33 chapters, like the rest of the work, are little more than a florilegium of scriptural texts with brief commentary, arranged according to a schematic conception of the eschatological events that seems to be largely inspired by the last three books of *De Civitate Dei*.[45] The only non-scriptural authority cited here, in confirmation of the biblical scenario, is book VIII of the *Oracula Sibyllina* (*Dim Temp* 17.27; 18.29; 19.31; 20.32). After six introductory chapters on the origin and fall of the devil and his present, "restrained" activity in the world, the section on the end of the world assembles passages that describe the person, characteristics, and influence of the Antichrist (cc. 7–12), the return of the prophets Elijah and Henoch (cc. 13–16), the second coming of Christ (c. 17), the resurrection of all people (c. 18), the judgment of Christ (c. 19), and the "purifying fire" that will accompany it (c. 20). The chapter on the resurrection contains the now-familiar appeal to the creative power of God as the explanation of how bodies consumed by other animals can be reassembled. The final section of the work, entitled *de gloria regnoque sanctorum capitula*, assembles, in thirteen still briefer chapters, what the author sees as the main scriptural promises for the reward of the risen just. These promises include: (1) "a new heaven and a new earth," where the saved will dwell; (2) an ideal age of about thirty years for all the risen; (3) a new Jerusalem free from pain, where (4) the just will shine like the sun, although (5) with varying degrees of brightness; (6) a special place in this city for virgins; (7) rewards for each individual beyond all imagining, centered on (8) the face-to-face vision of God; (9) a transformation of the human person to conform more fully to the image of God; (10) the handing-over of royal power by the Son to the Father; (11) the perpetual singing of *Alleluia* by the saints; (12) the renewal of the whole universe so that it will last eternally, and the constant sustenance of the saints by Christ;

and (13) a final state when "God will be all in all." Each of these promises ends with the added observation: "This the wicked (*impii*) will not see." It is a kind of Augustinian catechism, based on biblical sources, of the Church's eschatological hope.

Salvian of Marseilles

A contemporary of Quodvultdeus, whose works apparently had great influence on the life of the Church in southern Gaul during the mid fifth century and whose theology of human perfection stands in sharp contrast to Augustine's, was the presbyter Salvian of Marseilles (d. after 470). Aside from nine letters, Salvian's extant works are two substantial treatises, both probably written in Marseilles during the 440s: four books *Ad Ecclesiam*, written under the pseudonym of "Timothy" and known, apparently, in the ancient world also as *Adversus Avaritiam*; and eight books *De Gubernatione Dei*.[46] Both are eloquent appeals to Salvian's fellow Christians to be converted to deeper social concern, austerity and moral uprightness. A skilled rhetorician and a powerful moral preacher, Salvian uses all the devices of irony, invective and exhortation to move his readers to reform their lives. However, the specific aim and arguments of each work are different. In *Ad Ecclesiam*, Salvian's purpose is to preach against greed, which he sees as the principal vice opposed to the moral teaching of Christ; he urges his hearers to donate their goods to the Church, so that their wealth might be used for the poor. In *De Gubernatione Dei*, he reflects at length on the violence and misery rampant in Gaul during the barbarian invasions, and depicts the apparent collapse of Roman institutions there as a providential divine judgment on a sinful society.

Both these works occasionally suggest that with the decay of Roman civilization the world is nearing its end (*Ad Eccl* 1.7.35f.; *De Gub* 4.6.30). But it is an essential part of Christian faith, Salvian reminds his readers, to believe in the rewards and punishments that will follow this life; in fact, he writes, "it seems inconsistent with the Christian name if one says he does not believe in the things to come" (*Ad Eccl* 3.15.62). For Salvian, the Church's eschatological hope is centered on God's judgment and retribution. So he speaks of the resurrection as part of the larger process of judgment (*Ad Eccl* 3.14.61; 3.18.79), and of judgment, in turn, as part of God's constant, providential "government" of creation (*De Gub* 1.4.18). Corresponding to this emphasis on God's role as judge is Salvian's strong and clearly enunciated doctrine of human merit and self-determination: although salvation is clearly "a gift (*munus*) and a mercy of God" (*Ad Eccl* 4.2.10), it is a gift for which one infallibly prepares oneself, or of which one finally deprives oneself, by one's actions in life. After death, both moral action and change of will are impossible. "Necessarily, each person possesses in eternity what he has won for himself here with his own hands; bound to his own will and opinions, he will cling, in the future, with his whole state of being to what he clings to here in his affections" (*Ad Eccl* 1.1.7).

The logic of human action, then, ought to move everyone to a life of virtue on earth, in order to obtain virtue's eternal rewards. Enumerating the traditional images of eternal punishment and eternal bliss in some detail (*Ad Eccl* 2.10.48f.; cf. 3.18.78), Salvian observes ironically: "We think of these things, we contemplate them, we rush to the cult and practice of holy religion and take it up as if it would support us in obtaining these goods and be an effective advocate to intercede for us; with ambitious humility, we make it our protector and patron" (*Ad Eccl* 2.10.49). Yet the one really necessary moral condition for eternal reward – freedom from greed, generosity to the poor with our material goods – is precisely what most Christians hesitate to fulfill (*ibid.*, 11.50–56). So the real threats of Christ in the gospels are aimed, Salvian insists, not against adulterers or murderers, but against the rich (*ibid.*, 1.7.34f.). Before Christ's judgment seat, the only real consolation will be "a good conscience, an innocent life, or – what is the nearest thing to a good life – compassion (*misericordia*); there will be no help for the guilty man or woman except a generous heart, fruitful penance, and ample gifts of alms . . ." (*Ad Eccl* 3.3.13). If we really did believe that we will rise and be judged by God, we would expend all our efforts to "obtain permanent goods by our good works," and to avoid "suffering eternal evils for our evil deeds" (*Ad Eccl* 3.14.61). So as we prepare to leave this life, "the only refuge that remains for us in our extremity, the only chance for escaping eternal fire, is to offer up whatever property [we] have, for [our] salvation" (*Ad Eccl* 3.18.81). The fact that so many Christians are more concerned to preserve their wealth for their heirs than to care for the poor is, in Salvian's view, simply a proof of the weakness of their eschatological faith (*Ad Eccl* 3.15.62ff.).

Pope Leo the Great

Although his sermons and letters contain surprisingly few references to eschatological themes, Pope Leo the Great (bishop of Rome 440–61) echoes Salvian's social message in his fourth sermon *On the Collections* (*Serm* 9.2). As part of his exhortation to contribute to the Church's collection for the Roman poor, Leo here depicts the coming judgment in terms taken directly from Matt 24–25. "But since this severity is only proclaimed that we might seek mercy," he continues, "we too must live in this present life with such generous mercy that, returning to the works of piety after dangerous neglect, we may be freed from this sentence . . . Let those who wish Christ to spare them have mercy on the poor; let them be free in caring for the wretched, if they long to reach the companionship of the blessed." Leo repeats this appeal for active charity in an Epiphany sermon, adding that God's judgment of our works has been deferred in order that we might repent, not in order that we might grow morally sluggish (*Serm* 35.3f.). So he warns against taking the prospect of eternal punishment lightly, or thinking that Gehenna is simply a metaphor for a guilty conscience, which is brought to an end by conversion. "In the underworld there is no correction," he warns, "nor is any substitute for vindictive suffering (*satisfactio*) possible when the activity of the will no longer remains" (*ibid.*, 4). Thus Leo echoes Augustine's rejection of the Origenist doctrine of purgative punishment, as he exhorts the faithful to works of charity.

Christian Latin poetry

Besides the homiletic, exegetical and controversial literature in which the period abounded, the end of the fourth century and the first half of the fifth witnessed the first flowering of genuinely Christian poetry in the Latin West. A product of the often uneasy marriage between Christian faith and classical culture that followed the tensions of Julian's reign (361–63) in both East and West, this poetry reflected the desire of a new, classically educated class of Christians to be both uncompromising in their commitment to their faith and eloquent in the traditional medium of their highly verbal culture. As a result, the Christian Latin poetry of the period is a good mirror of the faith and hopes of educated believers; while one cannot expect to find theological originality there, one does find much from the common fund of contemporary doctrine and devotion, touched with the studied timelessness of classical art.

(a) The earliest Christian poet whose works deal to any extent with eschatological themes is Aurelius Prudentius Clemens (348–after 405). Born in Calaharra in northern Spain and thoroughly trained in rhetoric and the law, Prudentius held high positions in the imperial bureaucracy until he retired, near the end of the fourth century, to devote himself completely to the service of God. Shaped, undoubtedly, by the literary and artistic revival in the Latin West during the 380s and 390s that is known today as the "Theodosian renaissance," Prudentius clearly stands out among ancient Christian poets both for the quality and originality of his poetic craft and for the balanced, sincere Christian faith that his works express. His vision of life after death, and of humanity's ultimate reward and punishment in the judgment of God, seems deeply to have influenced the eschatological imagination of the ancient and medieval Latin world.

Although Prudentius gives no hint of millenarian expectations or of a sense that the world was about to end, he occasionally draws on the apocalyptic tradition for vivid pictures of history's final crisis.

> One day the heavens will be rolled up as a book,
> The sun's revolving orb will fall upon the earth,
> The sphere that regulates the months will crash in ruin,

the martyr Romanus proclaims in *Peristephanon* 10.536ff.[47] The Lamb of God will come again, a triumphant hero, as the seer of the Apocalypse reveals, defeating the Antichrist and banishing the "beast" to Gehenna (*Cathemerinon* 5.81–112). Central to Prudentius' faith in Christ, in fact, is the certainty that he will come again as *iudex mortuorum*, to mete out just retribution for the good and evil deeds of the human race (*Cath* 9.106ff.; 11.101–12). Prudentius is confident that the martyrs whose praise he sings in the hymns of his *Peristephanon* will intercede, in that hour of judgment, as powerful patrons for their native cities and their devoted earthly clients (*Perist* 4.9–60; 6.157–62; 10.1131–40).

Central to Prudentius' faith, too, is the conviction that he and all human beings will rise from the dead, just as Christ has risen (e.g., *Apotheosis* 1046f.; 1062–84; *Perist* 4.199f.). In some passages he suggests that soul and body are allowed by God to be immortal in order to make retribution for their deeds possible (*Ctr Symmachum* 2.182–93); in others, he hints that immortality is a natural quality of the soul to be communicated to the body at the resurrection (*Cath* 3.186–90; 10.37–44), or that the resurrection of the body is a gratuitous gift, a particular proof of God's love (*Hamartigenia* 656–61). Whatever the reason for personal immortality, Prudentius echoes in several passages the old apologetic tradition of explaining the seeming impossibility of resurrection by appealing to the creative power of God, who brings living plants from apparently dead seeds (*Ctr Symmachum* 2.191–211; *Cath* 10.121–28, 136–48). When the time of resurrection comes, our bodies will rise, whole in their members and free from the marks of age or sickness (*Apoth* 1065–79; *Cath* 10.97–108), as physically real as the body of the risen Christ is real (*ibid.*, 1046–51). Then those whose wills have been weighed down by earthly loves will "sink," body and soul, into the underworld, while those who have "avoided sin's contagion" will rise and "wing their way to the heavens" (*Cath* 10.25–32, 41–44).[48]

Prudentius gives no detailed description of the future punishment of the damned; "Gehenna" and "Tartarus" are, for him, the abode of the evil spirits (*Cath* 11.112; *Perist* 1.111), the place to which the apocalyptic beast will be banished (*Cath* 6.112). In one passage in his "Hymn for the Lighting of the Lamp," he reflects the popular tradition that even the souls of the damned enjoy a respite from their pains during each Easter night (*Cath* 5.125–36). Prudentius also shows a curious similarity to Ephrem's *Hymns on Paradise* (see above, p. 76) in suggesting that lesser sinners, like himself, who do not dare hope for "a home in the region of the blest" as their immediate destiny after death, may at least be allowed to escape Gehenna and to undergo the "gentler flames" of Avernus, a "lesser punishment" (*poena levis*) that will purify them of "fleshly stains" and eventually die away (*Hamart* 953–66).[49]

Prudentius devotes much more of his poetic attention to describing the joys of Paradise, combining biblical garden images with others taken from the Bucolic tradition of classical poetry. With a lavish delight that also reminds the reader of Ephrem's *Hymns on Paradise*, he depicts the garden of the blessed as a place of eternal spring, watered with clear streams and strewn with flowers of every description (*Cath* 3.101–106; 5.112–20; *Hamart* 855ff.), the "green pasture" where the Good Shepherd brings his flock (*Cath* 8.41–49). There, in their "ancestral home" (*Cath* 10.167), the saved will "drink ambrosial dew from roses" (*Hamart* 858), breathe exotic perfumes and fill the air with their hymns (*Cath* 5.117–24).[50]

In his "Hymn for the Burial of the Dead" (*Cath* 10), Prudentius asks directly the question about the "interim" state of the dead that had long vexed Latin minds:

> But until the perishable body
> Thou shalt raise up, O God, and refashion,
> What mansion of rest is made ready
> For the soul that is pure and unsullied? (149–52)

His answer is given in biblical terms, yet touched with classical associations:

> It shall rest in the Patriarch's bosom,
> As did Lazarus, hedged round with flowers . . . (153f.)

The dead Christian will follow down "the bright road to Paradise," along with the Good Thief (157–62), while we on earth reverently honor his tomb "with violets and garlands" (170). In the company of Vergil and Horace, Prudentius has turned the biblical hope of Christians into a literary monument of their own.

(b) Of lesser stature as a poet, but probably of greater importance in his own time as a churchman and worldwide correspondent, was Augustine's exact contemporary, Paulinus of Nola (Pontius Meropius Paulinus; 353–431). Paulinus was born of a wealthy and important Christian Roman family in

Bordeaux, received a distinguished education and rose quickly in the imperial civil service to be proconsular governor of Campania by about the age of twenty-five. In the early 390s, he and his wife Therasia were baptized and underwent a conversion to deeper Christian commitment similar to that of Augustine and many of their aristocratic contemporaries; by 395, they had established a kind of monastic community at Nola in Campania, near the grave of Paulinus' patron, St. Felix. After being made bishop of Nola himself in 409, Paulinus continued to carry on a rich literary activity there, as a poet and letter-writer, until his death.[51]

Like many Western Christians of the late fourth century, Paulinus has a strong sense of the imminence of the end of the world, and admits that fear of the coming judgment played a large role in his own conversion. Signs and wonders are taking place all over the world, indicating that the end is near and that the Lord is busy to save, Paulinus writes about the year 400 (Ep 38.7). "All creation now waits in suspense for his arrival; faith and hope train their gaze totally on this king. The world, which must be transformed anew, is already pregnant with the end that is to come on the final day" (Carmen 31.401–404; cf. Carm 8.28–33; 19.285–88). Following the Latin tradition of Zeno and Hilary, Paulinus sees the scope of the coming judgment as confined to that "great crowd" of sinners who can still not be classed as impii, because they have not totally rejected God (Carm 7.24ff.). Only their actions need to be examined by the "fire of judgment" (ignis arbiter), a fire that will "run through all their works" and burn away the traces of worldliness and sin (ibid., 32–36); "those impious ones," however, "who have refused God the worship due him, will rise not to be judged but to be punished" (ibid., 18ff.). To his friend and mentor Ausonius, Paulinus confesses, in a verse letter from the time of his conversion, that his own "believing heart, with inner apprehension, tremblingly awaits [Christ's] coming" (Carm 10.304f.); his fear is that his soul may be found to be too much "bound by the weight of material things" to fly up "with thousands of honored saints to meet the king" (ibid., 306f., 309f.).[52]

Paulinus is not given to lyrical speculation about the details of heaven or hell. Asked by Augustine for his opinion on "what the activity of the blessed will be in the next age, after the resurrection of the flesh," Paulinus first replies that he is more interested to receive Augustine's advice on how to live in the present world (Ep 45.4 [from 408]).[53] He suggests, however, like Augustine, that the norm for conceiving the state of the blessed in heaven must be the risen Christ, and that their activity will be to praise God, in harmony with each other and with the angels, using the tongues of their transformed bodies as well as their minds (ibid., 6).

Paulinus' most detailed discussion of the resurrection is found in Carmen 31: a long consolatio, in elegiac distichs, addressed to Pneumatius and his wife Fidelis, on the death of their seven-year-old son, Celsus. After encouraging the grieving parents not to mourn excessively, because of the good news of salvation in Christ, Paulinus elaborates a poetic treatise on the Christian hope of resurrection (231–406). He points to a whole variety of analogies for rebirth in nature (231–50) and then argues that God, who created such a world, can certainly make our bodies capable of rising from the dead (251–70). The old conundrum about the fate of bodies eaten by beasts is pointless, Paulinus insists, because the "seed" of eternal life, planted in the flesh by the rational soul, always remains with it; "only that flesh which was the vessel of the rational soul will experience the power of resurrection" (271–302, esp. 295f.). Paulinus then paraphrases the main scriptural passages promising the resurrection (303–406). Towards the end of the poem, he returns to the resurrection theme, pointing out the difference between those who will rise to glory with Christ and those who will rise to damnation. After the just are raised, "the bodies of the ungodly will also rise from their tombs uncorrupted, but to become the food of long punishment. Their life will be unending death, and their death a life of punishment, for their flesh will survive to nourish their tortures. The sinner will himself bring forth his executioners (carnifices) from his own body, and he will be food for the worms within him. But those whom a life of devotion in saintly behavior has borne upwards will wear garlands in common with God their king, and they will live forever in the image of Christ the Lord, their bodies clothed in divine light" (557–78, esp. 569–78).

Like his Latin contemporaries, Paulinus was convinced that the souls of the dead remain fully conscious in the period between their death and the resurrection, and he suggests in one place that the joy or pain they experience comes from their recognition of what their fate will be after the resurrection (*Carm* 18.75–81). In some passages, he speaks of the souls of sinners as already in the "infernal prison" with Satan (*Carm* 19.241–48), or of innocent souls like that of the young Celsus as already "in the chaste land of the blest" (*Carm* 31.591); in others, he prefers to use the images of the parable of Dives and Lazarus (*Ep* 23.1; 25.2f.; 34.6), and interprets the "bosom of Abraham" as meaning God himself, in whom the just find rest (*Ep* 23.1). In any case, Paulinus is convinced that all the saints – the martyrs as well as the souls of the less illustrious just – continue to intercede for us on earth, and that their blood, which they originally received from us, may be a "light" and a source of refreshment for us in the fire of judgment (*Carm* 31.609–12).[54]

(c) Another Latin Christian poet from Southern Gaul in the same period, who was still more deeply preoccupied with the prospect of death, was Orientius, the author of a moralizing poem in two books that has been referred to since the Middle Ages as the *Commonitorium*. Orientius is generally identified with the Orientius or Orens who was bishop of Auch, near Toulouse, in the 430s.[55] The *Commonitorium* gives a vivid picture, in one celebrated passage (2.165–84), of the violence and social instability that characterized Roman provincial society during the Gothic and Vandal invasions, a tableau that complements well the impression given by Augustine, Salvian and their contemporaries of the dangers of the times.[56]

The aim of Orientius' strict moral and ascetical exhortation is eschatological from the start: "Whoever is urgently seeking the rewards of eternal life, whoever desires things that will endure rather than perish, whoever would enter heaven, flee death and avoid bitter suffering – let him run on the path to happiness, let him learn the way" (1.1–4). Public dangers have convinced him that he is witnessing "the funeral rites of a collapsing world" (2.185; cf. 2.210); and death is the sure fate of everyone, whether it arrives late or soon – "even now, as we are speaking, we anticipate death (*praemorimur*)" (2.196; see 195–262). Against this dark background of social and individual fragility, Orientius emphasizes the natural immortality of the soul (1.45–48) and the freedom of each person to determine his or her eternal fate by present deeds (1.51–58). Our reward or punishment will begin immediately after death: the adulterer, the drunkard, the murderer and the conspirator "will pay the price before the day of judgment, so that the delay of the judgment will not give the smallest respite from punishment" (2.303f.).

Orientius also presents, however, a detailed and dramatic, if thoroughly traditional, picture of the final transformation of the world and its inhabitants. In book 1 of the *Commonitorium* he describes the resurrection of the dead as a return of the soul to "the same limbs" it had once had (259), including its bones, hair and nails (261f.). No matter how widely scattered they are after death, the parts of our bodies will be reassembled by the same divine power that makes seeds grow and brings spring from winter (265–94). The purpose of resurrection is justice: that the guilty may be punished and the virtuous rewarded in the same body in which they have merited their fate (273–76). So Orientius goes on to describe the punishment of sinners in eternal fire (311), and returns to this theme at length in book 2 (263–318). The particulars are familiar: fire, cold, terror and tears, worms living in the body (284, 307f., 317f.), but Orientius emphasizes that every sin will be punished in its own fitting way, and not simply be subsumed under a common sentence of eternal death (285–98). The picture he paints of beatitude is less explicit, and is drawn mainly from the gospel account of the transfiguration of Jesus and from Apoc 14.4: shining like the sun, in garments white as snow, the saved shall "follow the Lamb wherever he goes," bathed in the "light of God" (323f., 343f.).

Orientius' description of the Parousia and judgment (2.347–92) is the most vivid and impressive section of his work, embellishing the scene of Matt 24 with dramatic apocalyptic touches. Summoned by earthquakes and lightning (349ff.), the whole human race will rise from the earth, led by their *progenitor*, Adam, and will be gathered from every corner of the world (353–67). Christ will then mount the judgment seat in his glorified flesh, "holy in appearance, high on his throne, so terrible to see that though he is in full view, no one will be able to look at him" (373f.). Surrounded by flames and the sounds of angelic music, he will examine the deeds of everyone – to the joy of some and the anguish of others (375–78; cf. 367f.). For both sinner and saved, his sentence will be everlasting: "The glory which will surround the just will take away death; so, too, the one condemned to punishment will never die" (391f.).

(d) A fourth Latin poet, whose date, place and message are all much less certain, is the mysterious Commodian, author of two books of *Instructiones* and a long anti-Jewish poem called, in its most recent edition, the *Carmen de Duobus Populis*.[57] Although a number of scholars have offered strong arguments for identifying Commodian as a Roman, perhaps of Syrian origin, writing in the second half of the third century,[58] the few scraps of ancient external evidence we possess, as well as historical allusions in the poems and literary parallels to Orosius and Salvian, still seem to justify our placing their author in Africa or Southern Gaul, shortly after 450.[59] Jean-Paul Brisson, in fact, has made the interesting suggestion that the moral rigorism of the poems, their strong criticism of the social "Establishment" and their emphasis on the constant persecution of God's elect all converge to identify Commodian as a late fifth-century Donatist.[60] Although the hypothesis of such a late date has not been established with certainty, the eschatology of Commodian's works seems to fit most easily against the background of historical pessimism, apocalyptic speculation and sporadic millenarianism that we have seen as characteristic of the fifth-century West.

Written in a lumbering, semi-accentual meter and a homely, vulgar Latin,[61] Commodian's poems are difficult to understand on the purely linguistic level; their literary form adds considerably to this obscurity, since they imitate the esoteric style of apocalyptic documents.[62] Commodian's purpose in the *Instructiones* is, above all, to call his readers to religious and moral conversion, in the face of the world's imminent end. So he writes, at the beginning of the work, "Our first preface shows the way to the wanderer and [tells him how to obtain] a good report, when the goal of history comes" (*Instr* 1.1.1f.; cf. 2.35.1–7). Unlike Salvian, however, Commodian is not content simply to point to the miseries of his own times to reinforce his moral message, but cloaks his judgment of history in the cryptic epithets, symbolic events and visionary narrative style familiar from apocalyptic literature.

Although Commodian's two works differ in some of the details of the eschatological events they foretell, their overall scenario for the end is the same. After six thousand years of history (*Instr* 2.35.8; *Carm* 791), a great struggle will break out between God's people and the forces of darkness led by the Antichrist. Amidst such traditional apocalyptic signs as the sound of a heavenly trumpet, earthquakes, fire and universal darkness (*Instr* 1.43.1ff.; *Carm* 901–904), the "seventh persecution" of God's "hidden, final, holy people" will begin with great savagery (*Carm* 808, 942; *Instr* 1.42.1f.). According to the *Carmen*, an additional sign of the end will be an invasion of Roman territory and an attack on Rome itself by an army of Goths, who will, however, treat the Christians there as brothers (*Carm* 809–22).[63] After the Roman forces have been led to recovery by a "Syrian king," Nero will be raised from hell as the Antichrist, to take charge of the war against the Church; the prophet Elijah will also return and prophesy against him (*Carm* 825–36; *Instr* 1.41.5–20). The *Carmen* then predicts the coming of a second Antichrist in the East, a false Messiah who will outlive Nero and perform deceptive miracles in Judaea (*Carm* 837–41; 891–926). The *Instructiones*, on the other hand, foresee only one Antichrist: Nero, who, as *victor Latinus*, will "go to Jerusalem" after reconquering the West and deceive the Jews into accepting him as the Messiah (*Instr* 1.41.13–20).[64] After indescribable bloodshed and the loss of countless lives (*Carm* 880–90; *Instr* 1.42.39–46), God will "cast down his eyes" and cry out, "Behold, I have put up with your crimes in silence long enough!" (*Instr* 1.43.5; cf. *Carm* 1004, God's cry at the start of the "second judgment"). The Lord will then judge the earth by fire, according to the *Instructiones*,[65] a fire that will "lick round" the just but not touch them (1.43.9–19; 2.35.10f.).

Commodian also offers his own version of the millenarian tradition, foreseeing a "first resurrection," in which those dead who have been faithful to Christ will rise and enjoy peace and security in the "heavenly Jerusalem" that will come down from heaven (*Instr* 1.44.1–5).[66] There they will again marry and beget children for a thousand years (*Instr* 1.44.9), enjoying an abundance of the fruits of the earth in continuous health and in an atmosphere of unvarying warmth and light (*ibid.*, 10–15; cf. 1.42.25f.; *Carm* 947–78). In this kingdom of peace, the nobles of this present age will become the slaves of God's blessed poor (*Instr* 2.35.12–16; *Carm* 987f.). Meanwhile, the damned will continue to burn in the fire of judgment (*Instr* 1.43.16f.; cf. 2.35.19).

At the end of this period of temporary punishment and reward, according to Commodian, a new and more terrible period of judgment will begin (*Carm* 993–96; *Instr* 2.35.17). Fire will again rain down from heaven, the earth will be racked by lightning and earthquakes and the stars will fall from their places (*Carm* 999–1012; *Instr* 1.45.9ff.; 2.35.19). No human being will then be able to hide from these trials (*Carm* 1013–16), but those "known to Christ" will come through them unharmed (*ibid.*, 1017f.). The purpose of this heavenly fire will be to "cleanse the earth" (*ibid.*, 1041); the wicked will be burned up completely (*Instr* 2.35.10), but "a portion of the unbelievers" – those, perhaps, with some redeeming moral qualities – "will be saved, being only gently burned" (*Carm* 1018). At the end of seven months, "he who was humble will appear, coming from heaven" (*Carm* 1042). Then a "second resurrection" of all the dead will take place (*Instr* 2.35.20; *Carm* 1044); the just will rise to meet Christ in the air (*Carm* 1045; cf. I Thes 4.17), and the wicked, with all their sins revealed, will be plunged into hell (*Instr* 2.35.21f.; *Carm* 1049–55). The narrative is a familiar one, drawn from apocalyptic sources, but Commodian retells it with a grim conviction that seems to show personal experience of a dangerous and threatening age.

Peter Chrysologus

A witness of a different kind to popular eschatological hopes in the Latin Church of the mid fifth century is offered by the 179 extant sermons of Peter Chrysologus (*c.* 380–*c.* 450), bishop of Ravenna.[67] Although composed in a powerful, lively style and reflecting a good deal of exegetical sophistication, these biblical and liturgical homilies make no pretense of complicated theological reflection. They show us, rather, the everyday doctrine of an effective and admired preacher.

Peter's eschatology is traditional and classically balanced;[68] although he frequently urges his hearers to think about judgment and reward, about the certainty of death and the promise of resurrection, his sermons are free of the brooding pessimism we have found in Salvian, Commodian or even Paulinus of Nola. Death, for Peter, is the result of sin, the work of Satan, with whom Christ came to do battle (*Serm* 17.1; 101.5f.). Although death serves the useful and salutary purpose of reminding us of our dependence on God, and allows us to give thanks to our creator when we rise again (*Serm* 101.8), it is, in itself, simply ugliness and evil: decay and hideous corruption for the body (*Serm* 19.5; 118.5), "the mistress of despair, the mother of disbelief, the sister of decay, the parent of hell, the spouse of the devil, the queen of all evils" (*Serm* 118.3).

This last-mentioned sermon, Peter's eleventh dealing with St. Paul, is essentially a homily on I Cor 15.1f. Observing that the Christian preacher is always glad to speak about the resurrection, "because death is never welcome but life always delights us" (*Serm* 118.2), he readily concedes that the prospect of death can lead us towards despair, unbelief and self-indulgence (*ibid.*, 3f.). All of this is part of death's "war" on humanity, a campaign of violence and deception that has wrongly led some philosophers, and even some Christians, to speak of death as a "good," a release from the troubles of life (*ibid.*, 6).[69] Peter rejects such an interpretation outright: "They are wrong, brothers and sisters, who try to write about 'death as a good.' It is nothing strange: the wise ones of our world think they are great and distinguished if they can persuade simple folk that the greatest evil is really the greatest good . . . But truth removes these notions, brothers and sisters, the Scripture puts them to flight, faith challenges them, the apostle marks them down and Christ destroys them, who, while he restores the good that life is, unmasks and condemns the evil that death is, and banishes it from the world" (*ibid.*).

Peter refers in many homilies to the importance of hope in the resurrection for Christian faith and practice. "The whole hope of Christian faith is built upon the resurrection of the dead," he asserts at the start of Sermon 118. "Hear the voice of the shepherd: 'My sheep hear my voice, and follow me.' It is necessary that the sheep who have followed [him] to death should follow [him] to life . . ." (*Serm* 40.5). The purpose of the resurrection, Peter implies in a few homilies, is to allow God to fulfill his justice by rewarding the just and punishing sinners in the flesh that they now possess (*Serm* 57.11; 59.12; 83.4). More frequently, however, he emphasizes that the resurrection is a proof of God's creative power and a sign of his loving compassion.[70] If God can make living plants grow from dried and decaying seeds, and can bring day from night and spring from winter, he can certainly bring the bodies of the dead to life again (*Serm* 57.15; 59.16; 103.2ff.; 118.8f.; 176.4). "If you do not believe God," he remarks, "or accept the Scripture, if you do not assent to what you hear, at least believe your eyes, at least assent to the elements as they constantly preach to you your resurrection!" (*Serm* 118.8). Likewise, if the tears of a widowed mother were enough to move Christ to raise her dead son from his bier, how much more will the tearful prayers of the Church, and the bloody sweat of her martyrs, move him to raise "the Christian people . . . from its bier of death and restore it to eternal life, to the everlasting joy of its heavenly mother" (*Serm* 103.5).

Following tradition, Peter occasionally alludes to the everlasting joys of Paradise or to the flames of Gehenna (e.g., *Serm* 47.5; 122.5; 123.6), but he makes little effort to elaborate on their details. More important is his insistence that although the souls of all the dead were confined to two separate regions of the underworld – one for the just, the other for sinners – before the death of Christ, Christ's *descensus ad inferos* meant the release of the just from this "detention (*custodiam*)," the extinguishing of the "fiery sword" at the gate of Paradise and the admission of the saved to beatitude within (*Serm* 66.5; 123.6f.). Although he makes it clear that the martyrs already enjoy "delights that are not passing, but strong and stable and everlasting" (*Serm* 129.1), Peter suggests, with Augustine, that the present state of the dead is, in a sense, provisional. "The death of the saints is only a sleep," he observes (*Serm* 96.6), and Christ can raise them more easily than we can wake a sleeper (*Serm* 34.5). Even though the souls of sinners "live" only for the punishment of eternal death (*Serm* 96.6), still the pain they now experience is but "the heat of conscience, not that ultimate burning" that awaits them after the resurrection and final judgment (*Serm* 122.5).

Only in one passage does Peter allude to the possibility of a temporary, purgative suffering for some sinners after death. In his third homily on the parable of Dives and Lazarus, he makes the following comment on the "great chasm" that prevents souls in Abraham's bosom from crossing over to help those suffering in Hades (Lk 16.26): "The sound of this phrase is frightening, very frightening for us, brothers and sisters. It shows that those who have once been consigned, after death, to penal detention in the underworld cannot be transferred to the peace of the saints, unless they are redeemed by the grace of Christ and released from this despair by the intercession of the holy Church. What their sentence denies them, the Church wins for them and grace gives to them" (*Serm* 123.8). Like Augustine, he seems to be thinking of the possibility of a temporary experience of hell for some souls, before the final transition of resurrection, rather than of a distinct state of purgatorial punishment; like Augustine, too, his main concern seems to be to explain the Church's ancient custom of praying for the dead.

Although he is not a prophet of doom, Peter occasionally echoes the conventional Latin belief that his own age was "the end of time" (*Serm* 36.3), and that the world had grown weak and weary with age (*Serm* 167.3). While this recognition that "the Kingdom of God is near" must lead us, first of all, to see the urgency of conversion and repentance (*Serm* 167.4f.), it ought also to give the conscientious Christian cause for confidence and joy. "Brothers and sisters, the world takes its beginning from its end; creation is renewed, not depleted by its end; history fails for the criminal, not the creator, and the elements are not depleted for the just, but for sinners . . . You, who are faithful, 'rejoice in the Lord always!'" (*Serm* 47.5).

Opus Imperfectum in Matthaeum

One other work deserves to be mentioned among the documents of fifth-century Latin eschatology, even though its precise date, its author and its geographical home remain uncertain: a fragmentary Latin commentary on the Gospel of Matthew, Arian in origin but attributed by ancient and medieval readers to John Chrysostom, and known since Erasmus' time simply as the *Opus Imperfectum in Matthaeum*.[71] The author's exegesis of Matthew 24 (homilies 48–54) reflects the self-understanding of a small, beleaguered Christian sect looking forward to vindication in the day of judgment. Although the dire events predicted in Matt 24.5–28 refer, on the historical level, first of all to the destruction of Jerusalem, according to the commentary, they refer "spiritually" to the present and future devastation of the Church, the "heavenly Jerusalem," by heresy and schism (*Hom* 48: *PL* 56.902ff.). So when the "abomination of desolation," false belief, is installed in God's "temple" by the armies of heretics under their leader, Satan or Antichrist, all that remains for Christ's faithful is to "flee to the mountains" of Scripture and apostolic tradition (*Hom* 49; *ibid.*, 906–909). Only those "signed" by right faith and good works can hope to be spared in the "great tribulation" to come (*ibid.*, 913).

In a way curiously characteristic of the Western Arian provenance of this work, its picture of the second coming of Christ – creature though he is – particularly stresses his transcendent, superhuman majesty. When Christ comes, his radiant presence will fill the whole universe, yet will not be contained by it (*Hom* 49: *PL* 56.917). As the sun allows all objects to be seen in its light, "so all the more when Christ, our spiritual sun, comes, he will be seen in all the world – or rather all the world will be seen in him" (*ibid.*). Led by a majestic procession of angels, "with lightning bolts for torches," he will arrive as heavenly king (*ibid.*, 919); to the sound of dreadful thundering, he will raise the dead from their tombs (*ibid.*) and then sit down at his tribunal to hold judgment, surrounded with all the panoply of a royal court (*Hom* 54: *PL* 56.941). There he will mete out rewards and punishments far greater than we can presently imagine; "as far as God differs from humans, so the heavenly judgment will differ from earthly judgments" (*ibid.*). The disparity between saints and sinners may not be apparent in our present world, but when the gospel is finally known to all and Christ comes in glory as judge, the very light of his presence will reveal everything that is hidden in human hearts (*ibid.*, 942).

Apokatastasis and apocalyptic: Eastern eschatology after Chalcedon

The two centuries after the Council of Chalcedon (451) were, for the Eastern Churches, a time of almost continual dispute. Most of this period's theological energies were occupied with Christology· with the controversy over the relationship of divinity to humanity in Christ that broke out with renewed force after the Council of Chalcedon. The "last things" remained, for the most part, a marginal theme, touched on especially in homiletic or ascetical works and couched in the traditional terms of the Bible and the creeds. There were, however, some distinctive new developments. Although the sense that the world was nearing its end had never been as strong in Eastern Christianity as it was in the Latin West, the beginning of the sixth century witnessed a limited revival of the apocalyptic genre in the Byzantine world, as well as the first Greek commentaries on the Apocalypse of John. And the controversial spirit of the age turned to eschatological themes in the debates over the Platonist theory of the eternity of the world, and over the Origenist hope for universal salvation. So, through the scholastic literary forms in which theology was now almost exclusively done, the Christian hope came gradually to be incorporated, in the Eastern world, into a wider systematic synthesis of accepted "orthodoxy" that would reach its final form by the end of the seventh century, notably in the works of John of Damascus.

Non-Hellenic works

The late fifth and early sixth centuries were a time of new theological productivity in several languages and cultures of the Christian East, not simply in the Greek-speaking world. Several of these non-Hellenic works were centrally concerned with the Christian eschatological hope.

(a) One of the earliest theological works in the Armenian language is the so-called *Teaching of St. Gregory*, a catechetical treatise included in the *History of the Armenians* that comes to us under the pseudonym of "Agathangelos."[1]

Written probably between 430 and 460 by one of the disciples of the Catholicos Mashtotz (= Mesrop, d. 440), the father of Armenian Christian literature, Agathangelos' *History* tells the legend of the conversion of Trdat (= Tiridates), king of the Armenians, by Gregory the Illuminator at the beginning of the fourth century. More than half the work is made up of the *Teaching*, a systematic tract on Christian doctrine presented as Gregory's instruction to Trdat and his court, and probably representing the mid-fifth-century theological synthesis of Mashtotz and his school. Strongly biblical in content, and influenced by the *Catecheses* of Cyril of Jerusalem, as well as by Irenaeus and John Chrysostom,[2] the *Teaching* presents classical Greek Patristic theology in a concise and often original way.

Adopting the familiar scheme of a "week" of six thousand years for the duration of human history (366; 667–71), Agathangelos asserts that the sixth and final age of the world began with the coming of Christ, is now characterized by the gifts of the Holy Spirit (671), and will end with Christ's return (670). Without indicating how soon he expects the end to come, he characterizes the seventh age, which is to follow it, as "a long year without limit," a time of "rest and gifts without number and without measure" for all who have labored "in the six ages of their time" (670). The author gives no hint that this eschatological "Sabbath" will itself come to an end, or that it is simply a provisional reward for the saints; he seems rather to be using the traditional symbol of a cosmic Sabbath to represent eternal beatitude.

Following the Synoptic Apocalypses, especially Matt 24, the *Teaching* conceives of the coming end of this present age as a time of conflict and persecution (471). Suddenly Christ will appear, heralded by a cross of light shining in the heavens, and he will "judge all races with fire in his anger" (*ibid.*; cf. 502, 676). Although this will be a terrible moment for the enemies of God, it will be a time of joy and new life for the saints, as they emerge from their graves to meet their Savior. "Rising from heaven in the glory of the Father, he will come, and before all the host of his angels, take by hand each of his beloved and bring them to himself, and give them the enjoyment of eternal life in his divine dwelling" (713).

In several passages, the *Teaching* describes the resurrection of the dead in extended poetic detail. It will be an organic process of fulfillment, similar to the ripening of grain or to the coming of spring (528ff., 646–51); just as the returning birds herald the arrival of spring, "the blessed apostles became heralding trumpets to prepare all hearers to be ready to wait on the divine trumpet of the [Lord's] coming" (659). The bodies that will rise are "the same bodies with the same spirit" that we now possess, unchanged in nature (529; 646). But their form will be as different from its present state as ripe fruit is from seed; "as they rise, they will put on glory, as the grain when it shows maturity in itself . . ." (529). Having stripped off "the impurities of the body" during this life, like a maturing snake sloughing off its skin (602f.), they will then "take the form of a dove with rapid wings, and will fly on the wings of the Holy Spirit to attain the Kingdom of heaven" (605f.). And as their bodies are reconstructed, member for member, the risen just "will carry the appearance of each one's works on their heads," like crowns of flowers (648, 650), while sinners will rise enveloped in thorns that will ignite and burn (530f.).

Following orthodox tradition, the *Teaching* makes it clear that the reward of the just and the punishment of sinners will both be eternal (535, 713). For sinners, there waits "the burning fire of evil which consumes in Gehenna and in darkness" (511; cf. 524, 528), where repentance is useless (526, 535). On the other hand, God "arranges his Kingdom for his beloved as a region of Paradise, a wonderful dwelling near to God, there to settle and install near himself, for their delight, all worthy rational creatures" (714). The *Teaching* offers no further speculations on the details of heaven and hell, but remains – like Cyril of Jerusalem's *Catecheses* – securely within the limits of the biblical promise. Nevertheless, the emphasis that this instructional handbook gives to the traditional elements of the Christian eschatological hope suggests that the author – like Mashtotz himself[3] – was well aware of their theological and pastoral importance.

(b) In the Coptic literature of the fifth century, the most interesting evidence of growing eschatological concern is found in the works attributed to Schenute (*c.* 348–466), who ruled for many decades over the Pachomian "White Monastery" of Atripe.[4] Following in the tradition of the earlier desert monks, but adding a new note of urgency and warning, Schenute holds out to his monastic hearers the vivid prospect of judgment, and the danger of condemnation to eternal fire if they do not repent of their sins and give themselves to the works of asceticism and charity (*Opus* 42, *De Judicio Dei: CSCO* 42.189; tr. 96.110f.; *Op* 47, *De Judicio Dei* [= *Serm* 8]: *CSCO* 42.222; tr. 96.129). The punishments of the next life will simply be the consequences of our present sinful acts, which will "follow" us on the day of judgment (*Opus* 81, *De Discrimine Temporum*, 17f.: *CSCO* 73.181f.; tr. 108.109f.). Avenging spirits will be sent by God as the agents of his wrath (*Op* 42: *CSCO* 42.189; tr. 96.111);[5] so the fragmentary *Apocalypse of Schenute* depicts "pitiless angels, different in face and terrible, spitting smoke and fire from their mouths," carrying off a sinful priest "to the regions of the West" and eating him (*Op* 82.1: *CSCO* 73.199–202; tr. 108.121f.). Christ's final judgment, separating sheep from goats, will touch every class of humanity, clergy and monks included, with equal rigor, and will not be deflected by social or ecclesiastical connections (*Op* 47: *CSCO* 42.219–22; tr. 96.127ff.). "It is right, it is necessary," Schenute insists, "that all these holy ones" – i.e., the apostles and martyrs, who have announced God's judgment to us – "and Jesus, their king, should require of us works [worthy] of their labor and their blood" (*Op* 81.22: *CSCO* 73.184; tr. 108.111).

One striking passage in Schenute's "Apocalypse" describes a vision which the abbot once had of the saints entering heaven in a great procession: "Light had dawned, and I saw the saints going in as people do when a [liturgical] gathering is over, with rosy faces shining like the light ... emitting rays from themselves; and their garments shone like snow" (*Op* 82.3; *CSCO* 73.202; tr. 108.122). Otherwise, however, his allusions to the reward of the just seem chiefly to be a foil to emphasize the loss suffered by the damned.

Schenute also puts little emphasis on the cosmic or ecclesial aspects of judgment and retribution. His "Apocalypse," surprisingly, lacks any detailed description of the coming end of the world; seeing an angel pouring water and hot steam on the earth, the seer asks, "What is this fire?" and hears simply, "This is destruction and death" (*Op* 82.1: *CSCO* 73.199, tr. 108.121). He also has little to say about the hope of resurrection, except for one passage in a homily for the fourth day of Easter week, where he balances the Christian's present experience of rejection and persecution with the assurance that we, like Jesus, will rise again (*Op* 35, *De Passione et Resurrectione*: *CSCO* 42.105f.; tr. 96.60f.). Emphasizing the physical integrity of the risen body in a way that recalls pre-Christian hopes and practices, Schenute also echoes, at the end of the passage, Paul's doctrine of spiritual transformation: "Even if individual members are cut off from you, you will not only rise without lacking even your little finger or little toe, but you will also rise a spiritual body."[6] The day of this transformation, however, remains distant and mysterious; it is the certainty of individual judgment, in all its severity, that dominates the abba's thoughts of the future.

(c) The late fifth and early sixth centuries were a time of vigorous literary activity among Syriac-speaking Christians, among whom the debate over the natures and person of Christ that reached its critical point at Chalcedon in 451 had a particularly divisive effect. Although much of the Syriac theological literature of this period was occupied with Christological controversy, many works – especially the verse homilies or *memrē* in which it abounds – were also devoted to themes of wider pastoral and devotional concern, including the Christian eschatological hope.

(i) The first Syriac theologian of the fifth century whose works survive in abundance is Narsai (399–503), head of the strongly diphysite theological school at Edessa; he oversaw its transfer to Nisibis, in Persian territory, during the anti-"Nestorian" persecution that broke out in eastern Syria after the death of his patron, Bishop Ibas of Edessa, in 457. A number of Narsai's eighty-one surviving *memrē* include powerful reflections on the Christian hope for eternal life and for the transformation of the cosmos – an emphasis probably due not only to the influence of the diphysite master, Theodore of Mopsuestia, but also to the need felt by Persian Christians to define their hope over against the Mazdean eschatology of the state religion.[7]

Like Theodore, Narsai stresses in many of his works that the future for which Christians hope is a new state (κατάστασις) of creation, related to the present world yet more sublime, because it will be eternal (*Hom.* 44: Mingana 2.56.1.17–24, 57.1.1f.).[8] By a simple "sign" or "wink" (*remzā*) of the creator, all nature will be transformed from its present round of laborious activity to its primordial state of rest (*ibid.*: Mingana 2.57.1.13–16). The struggle of humanity against nature, and the enslavement of lower creatures to serve human purposes, will come to an end; even the succession of day and night and the order of the seasons will cease, because humanity will no longer need such services (*Hom.* 18: Gignoux 475f.; cf. *Hom.* 44: *ibid.*, 477–81). Creatures will no longer reproduce themselves, because they will no longer die; the earth "will remain in the order in which it was at the beginning of its existence, and it will neither be dissolved nor corrupted in its composite state" (*Hom.* 44: *ibid.*, 480).

Before this cosmic transformation occurs, however, Narsai foresees a time of crisis and conflict. Drawing on the apocalyptic predictions of Matt 24, he speaks of a period of wars and paralyzing natural catastrophes (*Hom* 34: Mingana 1.318.1.17–319.1.3), during which human beings and angels will long for Christ's return like athletes waiting for the contest to begin, filled with both desire and fear (*Hom.* 18: Gignoux 335f.). The Antichrist will then appear: a human being, but so fully possessed by Satan that he will perform dazzling miracles, establish a deceptive peace, and begin a cult of himself (*Hom.* 34: Mingana 1.315.1.2–317.1.15). Elijah will also return to the earth to confront the Antichrist, in the name of faithful humanity, and will ultimately defeat him in single combat, empowered by the Holy Spirit and armed with the Word of God (*Hom.* 51: Gignoux 339f.; *Hom.* 52: *ibid.*, 341f.).

At the end of their struggle, Christ himself will appear and will crown Elijah's victory by annihilating the Antichrist in both body and soul.[9] Christ's coming will be bathed in a radiance eclipsing all created light. In a glorious procession of chanting spirits, led by an angel bearing a cross on his head, the Lord will descend to earth in his transfigured humanity (*Hom.* 34: Mingana 1.321.2–322.19). By a simple "sign," once again, he will raise the dead from the earth, and will transform all those still living, clothing them with immortality (*Hom.* 52: Mingana 2.5.19–63; 9.16–10.8; cf. *Hom.* 18:

Gignoux 483f., 485f.).[10] By another sign, Christ will separate the good from the evil in a great act of judgment, "leading all rational creatures into the furnace of judgment and melting them down, that he might choose the true gold and reject the false" (*Hom.* 18: Gignoux 23f.).

With this judgment of Christ, the reward of the just and the punishment of the wicked will begin. Narsai describes both of these final states almost exclusively in psychological and relational terms, couched curiously in spatial metaphors. The heart of eternal punishment will be the "stupefied" realization by the damned that they are, through their own fault, forever separated from Christ and the saints, whose company they long to share (*Hom.* 52: Mingana 2.12.14–13.9); the saints, on the other hand, will be forever at peace in God's presence, spiritually nourished at his banquet table and happy in the realization that conflict and division are permanently at an end (*ibid.*, 10.23–11.8; cf. *Hom.* 34: Mingana 1.325.13–326.3). Narsai emphasizes, in *Hom.* 52, that both the saints and the damned will possess the same knowledge of God and God's goodness; the difference in their lot will simply be that the saints will be allowed to associate with God and enjoy his presence, while the damned will not. "They will be equal in their knowledge because their resurrection, too, is equal, and there will be no difference in the love of the good that their spirits possess . . . It is only in *place* that the groups will be separated from each other, and the wicked will not have the power to mingle with the good" (Mingana 2.8.24–29). The "place" of the damned – Gehenna – will in fact be the earth itself, since "they have loved the things of earth" (*ibid.*, 9.6f.), while the saints will be empowered by their good works to fly to a new dwelling-place, between the firmament and the "higher heaven" (*ibid.*; cf. *Hom.* 34: Mingana 1.323.23–324.8, 325.6f.; *Hom.* 52: Mingana 2.13.16–14.4).[11]

Both saints and damned "will know with exactitude all things in heaven and on earth" – the details of every creature's existence, the causes of all things, even the secrets of human hearts – with the penetrating knowledge of Christ the judge (*Hom.* 52: Mingana 2.18.21–19.12). The only being whose essence they will not know is God, who remains beyond all knowledge; but they will see the humanity of Christ, the temple in which God's invisible reality dwells (*Hom.* 52: Mingana 2.20.9–21; cf. *Hom.* 18: Gignoux 36ff.). In this state of knowledge and vision, all beings will be preoccupied solely with the goodness of God, and overpowered with love for him. "Love alone will remain in this new creation; to love our soul's instincts will attach themselves, and it will never grow slack . . . This thought that the good will possess in the Kingdom on high will be equally possessed by the sinners in Gehenna; just and sinners will have one single thought, and there will be no difference between them. By one single thought they will glorify the name of the one Creator; they will love him and honor him constantly" (*Hom.* 52: Mingana 2.18.9–15). In other words, it is this single-minded recognition of the all-embracing goodness of God that will be, in Narsai's view, both the heart of beatitude for those united with God, and the heart of torture for those who have condemned themselves to eternal separation.

Following in the tradition of Ephrem and Aphrahat, as well as that of Theodore of Mopsuestia, Narsai assumes that the souls of the dead do not receive the reward or punishment for their deeds before they are reunited with their bodies in the resurrection; until then, they must all wait in Sheol, the earthly place of the dead, in a state of conscious but powerless inactivity that Narsai refers to as a "sleep."[12] In *Hom.* 39, "On the Value of the Soul and on How it Controls the Body, its Dwelling" (Mingana 2.249–54), Narsai explains that guardian angels lead each soul, at death, to its designated place: the souls of the just to a "part of the earth" called Eden, where Adam and Eve first lived, and the souls of sinners to another place. There both groups will await resurrection and retribution, alive and conscious, but unable to receive new knowledge or to communicate with others because they lack the bodily means of sensation and action. Aware only of themselves and unable to change their moral attitudes, they will also be aware of the reward or punishment that awaits them, with the dim consciousness of a dreamer or a child in the womb. Parallel, in some respects, to the Aristotelian view of the dependence of the human mind on the body for knowledge and action, this conception of the "interim" state of the dead – shared by most early Syriac writers – is not fully consistent with the tradition (expressed, for instance, in Narsai's *Hom.* 25) that the martyrs are crowned with glory immediately after death and assist the Church with their prayers.[13] But it would be artificial to attempt to reconcile these two convictions; they are simply further evidence of the many elements – philosophical, biblical, liturgical and folkloric – that together shape ancient eschatology.

(ii) Much of the theology, as well as the personal identity, of the fifth-century writer Isaac of Antioch (= Isaac the Syrian) remains to be studied. The body of *memrē* published under his name[14] appears to be the work of at least two authors: Isaac of Amida, an orthodox writer from the first half of the fifth century, and Isaac of Antioch, a writer from the second half of the century who sympathized with the growing anti-Chalcedonian or "mono-physite" party in the Syrian Church.[15] While it is impossible, at the present stage of research, to distinguish fully the theologies represented in their joint corpus, it is worth observing that several of the eschatological themes we have observed in Narsai and earlier Syriac writers appear also here.[16]

"Isaac," too, is convinced that the final reward and punishment for human deeds awaits the resurrection (e.g., Bedjan 724.4 from bottom). Then those who died in "peace and quiet" with the Lord will find eternal peace (Bedjan 276.15), while sinners will be banished to a darkness far away from God (Bedjan 117f.). Gehenna, the kingdom of the demons (Bedjan 203.4 from bottom), is a place of fire, and on the day of judgment this fire will burst forth from the bodies of the damned (Bedjan 73.4f.; 118.3–7). Until the resurrection, the dead must wait in Sheol, which the author seems to imagine as a collective grave (Bedjan 366.3 from bottom; 368.5; 369.4). Some passages in the corpus suggest that the dead continue to act, in Sheol, as they have acted during life (e.g., Bedjan 90.13; 366.10–18). Others declare that action for good or ill is no longer possible after death (e.g., Bedjan 392.4 from bottom), and even envisage Sheol, before the judgment, as a place of fire ruled over by Satan (Bedjan 93.4f.). In any case, existence in Sheol is a temporary state, from which all the dead will rise to praise the Son at his second coming (Bedjan 71.10–15); it is both the symbol and the end of the mortality that overshadows our present existence (Bedjan 91.1–11; 656.2).

(iii) Another Syriac writer of the period whose works await much further textual and theological study is Jacob of Sarug (c. 450–521), friend of Philoxenus of Mabbug and Severus of Antioch, and eventually bishop of Botnan, in the east Syrian district of Sarug.[17] Trained in the diphysite school of Edessa with Narsai, Jacob nevertheless sympathized with the party that rejected both the Antiochene Christology and the Chalcedonian definition. His many *memrē* and prose sermons are of a pastoral and devotional rather than a polemical character, however, and show a theology that is conservative but essentially orthodox.[18]

Jacob's style of theological thought is less abstract and systematic than that of Narsai, and relies much more on the use of vivid poetic images. His eschatology remains within the Syriac tradition. Thus he speaks often of death in personified terms, as the captor of an enslaved human race or as an insatiable glutton; although Sheol, where the dead now exist, is a dark place of sleep, Jacob also describes the experience of death as a dangerous journey across a sea of fire.

When the time of Christ's second coming arrives, the whole universe will be shaken, and will return to the chaos (*tōhu w*^{*a*} *bōhu*) that existed before God began to create the present world. The earth will then give birth to a new human creation; the dead will rise from Sheol like buried seeds springing to life, and will be formed like the angels, without defect and without sexual differences. Christ will then judge everyone with great exactitude and impartiality, showing special strictness towards Jews and Christians because they have shared the privilege of divine teaching. The wicked will be condemned to the eternal fire of Gehenna, and the just will be taken to Paradise, to join in the marriage feast of the Great King.[19]

In a letter addressed to his younger contemporary, Stephen Bar Sudaili,[20] Jacob strongly opposes the notion, apparently espoused by Stephen, that both reward and punishment after death will be of limited duration, proportionate to the length of time for which one has sinned or practiced justice during life. "It is not so, my friend, it is not so," affirms Jacob; although the brevity of this present life limits the time of our good and evil works, God judges our intentions, according to which we would go on acting justly or unjustly forever if we could. So God is justified in rewarding and punishing eternally.[21] This rejoinder against what Jacob understands as the eschatology of Stephen, a known Evagrian (see below), anticipates one of the principal objections sixth-century theologians would raise to the revived Origenist theology: it did away with the permanence of divine retribution, a permanence that they felt was fundamental to authentic Christian doctrine and practice.

(iv) Although he devoted most of his energies to assailing the two-nature Christological formula of Chalcedon, the Syrian monophysite leader Philoxenus (= Xenaias) of Mabbug (*c.* 440–523) offers, in several passages, a vision of final salvation that closely resembles some aspects of Evagrian Origenism. In several unpublished fragments of his Gospel Commentaries, Philoxenus presents the goal of human salvation as a penetrating knowledge that will totally unite the believer with God. Explaining the baptism of Jesus, in a note on Matt 3.1–16, Philoxenus sees in this event the "type" of the "return of the universe to God" that will be fully achieved at the resurrection of the dead, "when the universe will be submitted to the Son and the Son to the Father, and when God is all in all."[22] At that eschatological moment, the bodiless souls of all the just, united in Christ, will "penetrate all spiritual things . . . while the souls of the wicked will not be able to feel or penetrate [spiritual things]."[23] Error, evil, even the evil spirits will then be annihilated; the materiality of the human body will also disappear, although the true "nature of the body" will be preserved in a spiritualized mode of existence.[24] God will then animate the whole renewed universe as a soul animates the body[25] – although Philoxenus insists elsewhere, in a letter of his own against the doctrines of Stephen Bar Sudaili, that this union of God with creation will never reach the point of complete personal identity.[26]

Philoxenus connects this unitive goal with the whole history of salvation that has gone before it. God first "mixed" his Wisdom with the created world, he observes in a comment on Luke 2.52, and when humanity proved incapable of finding it in creation, God's Wisdom became flesh. "When the time of training and teaching is over, and when the time of inheriting the Kingdom is revealed, Wisdom will gather itself in its own place."[27] The final union of the saved with God, which is included in this "gathering" of Christ,[28] will be the fulfillment of the Church's destiny as well as of the faith of individuals. "When the composite reality, by which [the knowledge of God] is reflected to us as in a mirror, is destroyed," he remarks, "it [i.e., knowledge of God] will gather itself completely in its own place, in Christ; and we in him, as members belonging to his body, will contemplate [this knowledge] face to face."[29] It is a cautiously phrased version of Evagrius' "Gnostic" eschatology, but one that places Philoxenus clearly with the sixth-century Origenist revival.[30]

(v) A much more radical version of this revived Evagrian eschatology, one that shows many similarities to second- and third-century Gnosticism, appears in the writings associated with Stephen Bar Sudaili (c. 480–c. 543). This Syrian monk, originally from Edessa, seems to have been living in the Judaean desert at the time of the outbreak of the controversies over Origenism there in 514.[31] A vigorous proponent of universal salvation, and of the eventual substantial union of all beings with God, Stephen at one time tried to win Philoxenus over to his views, but was sharply attacked as a heretic by both Philoxenus and Jacob of Sarug.[32] According to several eighth- and ninth-century Syriac authors, he is the author of the "Book of the Holy Hierotheos,"[33] a mystical tract on the "ascent" of the soul and on the origin and end of creation that seems to be influenced by both the Neoplatonism of Proclus and the cosmic theology of the Pseudo-Dionysius, as well as by the Evagrian system.[34] None of his other works survive, but the account given by Philoxenus of his doctrines makes this identification probable.

Philoxenus' *Letter to Abraham and Orestes* raises three main criticisms against Stephen's doctrine, all concerned with his eschatology. First he seems to accuse him of a version of "Jewish" millenarianism, according to which the "six days" of the present world – already in their final "day" – will be followed by two distinct periods of retribution: a Sabbath of rest for the saints, when the "movement" of the present age will be at an end, and then a time of "consummation," when "God will be all in all," which Stephen calls "the mystery of the first day of the week."[35] Implied in this understanding of the fulfillment of history are the two other points Philoxenus finds most objectionable: a doctrine of universal salvation, reminiscent of the Origenist theory of *apokatastasis*, and a pantheistic conception of the final union of all creatures with God. In Stephen's eschatology, Philoxenus complains, all will be "the equals of the apostles and are to become consubstantial with God, the Lord of the Universe," whether they are pagans, heretics or faithful Christians[36] – an expectation that makes nonsense of the efforts and institutions of the Church. Worse still, Stephen interprets the promise of I Cor 15.28 ("that God may be all in all") to mean that creatures will eventually be identified in substance with God, "so that there will no longer be He who creates and those who receive his creative action."[37] Even Christ, in Stephen's eschatology, will finally be absorbed into God, and the persons of the Trinity will become "a single nature and a single hypostasis (*qnomā*)."[38] Significantly, according to Philoxenus, Stephen refers to the "seventh day" of his scheme as "rest" or "liberation" and to the "eighth day" as "consummation" and even "divinity"[39]; in the end, all will simply be God.

The *Book of the Holy Hierotheos* traces, in its first four sections, the origin of the mind in primal unity, its fall into multiplicity and its laborious "ascent" to the rediscovery that all is really part of the divine essence (4.17). The ultimate vocation of every mind is a "commingling" (*ḥabhikuthā*) with God and with other minds that goes even beyond unification in the normal sense, because it means the permanent end of all distinction (4.21). So the work's most explicitly eschatological passage, in section 5, describes this final unity in the most radical terms: "Hells shall pass, and torments shall be done away; prisoners shall be released; for even reprobates are absolved, and outcasts return ... and chastisement ceases ... and the judge shall judge no more ...; for demons receive grace and humans receive mercy ... and everything becomes one thing. For even God shall pass, and Christ shall be done away, and the Spirit shall no more be called the Spirit – for names shall pass away and not essence . . . This is the limit of All and the end of Everything" (5.2).[40] Stephen's unitive vision boldly blends Platonism, Gnosticism and Origenist theology in a "commingling" that touches the outer limits of Christianity itself.

Greek apocalyptic works

In the Greek cultural realm, the end of the fifth and the beginning of the sixth centuries witnessed a new current of expectation that the world would soon come to an end, and a new, if brief revival of interest in apocalyptic literature, largely neglected in the Greek Christian world since the mid third century. An apocalyptic work called the *Seventh Vision of Daniel*, now preserved only in an Armenian version, was probably composed at this time.[41] Also from the last years of the fifth century is a curious compilation of pagan oracles and Christian pseudo-oracles called the *Theosophia* – now only extant in various abbreviated forms – which originally concluded with a brief summary of world history, reaching from Adam to the Emperor Zeno (474–91) and prophesying that the world would reach the end of its sixth and final millennium 500 years after the birth of Christ.[42] Although the existence of various chronological systems in the Greek world meant that even the prophets of an immediate world crisis could not compute its date exactly, this expectation – familiar from the time of Hippolytus[43] – made the early years of the Emperor Anastasius' reign (491–518) a time of fervent, if short-lived apocalyptic anxiety in the Byzantine world.

The only full-fledged apocalyptic text from this period that still exists in Greek was published for the first time in 1967 by Paul Alexander, under the title of the *Oracle of Baalbek*.[44] Datable by historical references to the years between 502 and 506, this work is probably a Greek revision of a lost Latin work written in the time of Theodosius I (377–95), the so-called "Tiburtine Sibyl," of which medieval descendants survive. The Greek version may well come from Baalbek (Heliopolis) in Syria.[45]

According to this prophecy, the eschatological "birth pains of the world," including earthquakes, floods and wars, began in the reign of the Emperor Leo I (457–74) (136ff.).[46] The crisis will begin in earnest, however, after the end of Anastasius' reign, which the author fixes in the year 522. People will then "assume the appearance of barbarians" (175) and attack one another with unprecedented savagery (173–78). A series of rulers, all embodying traditional features of the Antichrist, will preside over history's final years of conflict: first four kings, ruling together, two from the East and two from Syria, under whom a mighty Assyrian army will march west and cause much bloodshed (180–86); then a "king from the East" named Olibos who will slay the four kings, grant an exemption from taxes and restore the people of Palestine and the East (186–90); then a "king who has a changing shape," who will rule for thirty years amid still greater violence and revive the pagan religion of Egypt (190–204); then a "king from Heliopolis," renewing the tax-exemption of Olibos, who will be killed by the "king with the changing shape" after three and a half years (205–209). When this "ruler of perdition" alone remains, amid yet greater cosmic catastrophes, Enoch and Elijah will appear to do battle with him (210–16). Crying, "My time has come," the Antichrist-figure will kill the two prophets (216f.), but will himself then be slain, with all his forces, by the triumphant Christ, who will "come from the heavens like a great and flashing star" (217–21). Christ will then judge the whole of humanity, and will "rule with his holy angels" (224–27) – a hint, perhaps, of the millenarian tradition in this otherwise largely political apocalypse.[47]

Oecumenius

The first decade of the sixth century is also the most likely date for the earliest known Greek commentary on the Apocalypse of John, written by Oecumenius, who seems to have been a high military official (*comes*) and a correspondent of Severus of Antioch.[48] Written in the form of twelve discourses, this work interprets the whole text of the Johannine Apocalypse with learning, balance and a strong sense for practical application. Although Oecumenius frequently quotes the great Greek Fathers of the past, he apparently has no earlier model of a full-scale commentary to follow, and shows great originality in his moderately allegorical style of exegesis.

Commenting on Apoc 20:1–7, Oecumenius rejects the idea of a millennium as a notion of "the godless Greeks" that smacks of the Platonist theory of the transmigration of souls (Hoskier 213.16–19). His own interpretation of the passage is Christological. Identifying "a thousand years" with a single day, in classic biblical fashion, and taking that "day" to symbolize the time of Christ's presence on earth, he asserts that "in this day, that of the Lord's Incarnation, the devil was bound, unable to rebel against the divine revelation of the Savior" (Hoskier 215.6ff.; cf. 2–19). During Jesus' lifetime, the apostles were already enthroned "in a modest way" as judges (Hoskier 217.19–24), and some "rose" already to the new life of faith (cf. Hoskier 219.1–15). For the relatively short time between the life of Jesus and the end of the world, the devil has again been released to do his work (Hoskier 216.10–21). During this time, however, new disciples will be "brought to life" by the Holy Spirit, as seed is brought to life by rain and light; this is the "first resurrection" of Apoc 20.5f. (Hoskier 219.13–19; 220.19–27).

Oecumenius does not speculate on the time of the end, and gives no hint that he shares the expectation of some of his contemporaries that it would come soon. His explanation of the final struggle, as the Apocalypse presents it, is straightforward and traditional: "Gog and Magog" (Apoc 20.8) refer to unknown barbarian tribes who will join Satan in persecuting the faithful (Hoskier 225.14–20); the Antichrist will be a human being dominated by Satan; he will become king of the Jews and will kill Elijah and Enoch, the two prophets of the last days (Hoskier 131.3–13; cf. 128ff.; 155.12ff.).[49]

Oecumenius also strongly affirms the physical character of the "general resurrection of bodies," an event that will include all human beings, "even the unwilling" (Hoskier 221.1ff.). To reject the resurrection of the dead as impossible is to "despise us and our teaching, which says that their bodies will rise again" (Hoskier 229.1–4). Some skeptics point to the dissolution of decomposed bodies into the original four elements as proof that our present bodies can never be reconstructed exactly. But if humans can develop a technique to distill the water out of wine, and if the sun can separate the salt from sea-water, he argues, surely God the creator will be able to locate and reassemble the material components of the human body (Hoskier 229.4–230.6).

Along with the resurrection of the body, Christians hope for "a new heaven and a new earth" (Apoc 21.1): not that the present heaven and earth will be annihilated and replaced, but that the corruptible elements in them will be discarded like an old and soiled garment (Hoskier 232.3–9). "Then creation will become pure of all the corruption that has been kneaded into it by human sin" (Hoskier 232.9ff.); the new world, symbolized by the seer's vision of the new Jerusalem, will be the spiritual "lot and abode of the saints" (Hoskier 233.1ff.), where their joy will know no interruption (Hoskier 234.2–11).

Oecumenius takes seriously the traditional expectation of the eternal punishment of sinners, but tries to interpret its images in the Apocalypse in a spiritual and humane way. Just as the "first death," on the sensible level, is the separation of soul from body, so the "second death" promised in Apoc 20.14 is fundamentally a spiritual ($\nu o\eta\tau\acute{o}s$) reality: "punishment and retribution that have sin as their mother" (Hoskier 231.14f.). All sinners will suffer this fate (ibid., 15ff.), but not in the same degree; just as there are different grades of fever, so those condemned to the "lake of fire" will experience its burning in different ways, corresponding to their guilt (ibid., 17–23). Indeed, Oecumenius elaborates in several passages a threefold scheme for the retribution of human acts in the last judgment: the "completely holy and pure" will "be with Christ forever, gazing on the throne of God" (Hoskier 111.9–12), the faithless and the totally reprobate will be "given over to punishment" (ibid., 112.1), but there will also be a third group, of baptized believers who "are, as it were, halfway between virtue and vice" and who will simply remain on earth, without further punishment (ibid., 111.12–17). These will be allowed to rule over lower creatures, and their lot will seem like punishment only because it is unchangeable, forever excluding them from the companionship of Christ (ibid., 17–26). In describing the punishment of the damned, Oecumenius stresses the aspect of deprivation rather than physical pain. Gehenna is a place of real fire, in which "only the power of burning remains, along with darkness" (Hoskier 110.12f.). Even though the damned "seem to exist as far as hypostasis and essence are concerned," their existence is not worthy of the name, since "it does not come to the notice or memory of God" (Hoskier 186.27–187.2; cf. 186.14f.).

Oecumenius' explanation of the punishment of the damned is marked also by the attempt to show how it is compatible with the mercy and saving purpose of God. This suggests his awareness of the Origenist tradition, especially as it was represented by Gregory of Nyssa and Gregory Nazianzen, even though Oecumenius is careful to distance himself from their doctrine of a strictly universal salvation.[50] For instance, Oecumenius emphasizes strongly, in one passage, that "even if some of those who have sinned are given over to punishment, still the purpose of Christ and the intention of his

Incarnation was that all should become heirs of his Kingdom" (Hoskier 103.11–14). To those who ask how one can reconcile the proclamation of a God of "manifold mercy" with the prospect of eternal punishment, Oecumenius suggests that no sinner is punished, even eternally, to the degree he deserves, and probably not as strictly as Scripture threatens. "If one is worthy of fire and darkness, and is condemned to darkness, but is only punished in that one does not share in God's gifts, and only suffers pain in this way, but is not punished in the senses," then God's mercy as well as his justice is preserved (Hoskier 164.14–19). The seer is prevented from interpreting the meaning of the seven peals of thunder in Apoc 10.4, says Oecumenius, because they have revealed to him that the punishment of sinners is less severe than Christians expect (Hoskier 122.13–18) – knowledge that might cause them to think less of God's threats of retribution, if it were widely known.

Explaining Apoc 9.5f., in which an angel is allowed to torment humanity for five months with a sting like that of scorpions, he observes that "some Fathers draw from this [a doctrine of] restoration (ἀποκατάστασις)," according to which all punishment will be medicinal and of limited duration. The more common opinion, however, and the teaching of the Scriptures, is that "the sufferings of those punished are eternal" (Hoskier 112.11–16). Insisting that he adheres to the teaching of the Church, Oecumenius suggests that as an "exercise" (γυμνασία) or theoretical speculation, if not as a categorical statement (κατάφασις), one might "mix both opinions together" (*ibid.*, 16–21) by "taking a middle path" (Hoskier 113.1). It is possible, namely, "that for a certain period, which this passage in the Apocalypse calls 'five months,' using a symbolic number, sinners will be punished very severely, as if a scorpion were stinging them. After that, [we will be punished] more gently, but we will not be totally free from punishment – so much so, that we will seek for death and not find it . . . So it says, 'Death will flee from them': for they will remain forever in punishment" (*ibid.*, 2–10).

When describing the rewards to be given to the saints at Christ's second coming, Oecumenius emphasizes their spiritual and relational character. Those who endure their earthly trials with undiminished love for the Lord will rejoice in the contemplation of God (Hoskier 62.4–9), enjoying his indwelling presence (*ibid.*, 13ff.) and being called by the "new name" of friends, brothers and servants (*ibid.*, 15–18). The "countless throng" of Apoc 7.9, who have "inhabited the place of glory" (Hoskier 100.7), will spend eternity joined with the angels in praising God (*ibid.*, 16–21). The "opening of the seventh seal" (Apoc 8.1), a symbol for "the second coming of the Lord and the reward of the saints" (Hoskier 103.10f.), will mean "perfect glory": no longer simply the limited kind of revelation and reconciliation that we can experience on earth, "but unspeakable blessings:

being called children of God, heirs of God, fellow-heirs with Christ, brothers and sisters, friends and children of Christ, reigning and being glorified with him . . ." (Hoskier 103.2–8).

Oecumenius most often describes eternal beatitude in terms of God's overshadowing presence (κατασκήνωσις: Hoskier 101.15–18), his "dwelling in the saints" (ἐπ' ἀγθοῖς κατοίκησις: Hoskier 62.14). And this eternal indwelling of God he interprets in intentional terms, as "the memory of him, remaining ceaselessly in the souls of the saints" (Hoskier 101.15ff.). Even the Apocalypse's most vivid images of beatitude, such as the vision of the new Jerusalem in chapter 21, become, in Oecumenius' sober exegesis, metaphors for an indescribable union of spiritual beings with God, "so that from what is said in sensible terms we might turn our mind to the spiritual blessedness and condition of the saints" (Hoskier 233.3–6).

Pseudo-Dionysius

One of the most influential figures in sixth-century Greek theology was the highly original writer who styled himself "Dionysius the Areopagite." Although his identity remains a mystery, modern scholarship has reached wide agreement in identifying him as a Syrian, probably a monk, writing in Greek in the first quarter of the sixth century.[51] His works are, for the most part, meditations on the biblical and liturgical traditions of Eastern Christianity, and his Christology shows clear sympathy with the unitive emphasis of the "monophysite" party; nevertheless, the chief intellectual influence on his thought is undoubtedly the Neoplatonism of Proclus.[52] As a result, the world in which he is most interested is the spiritual, highly structured world of intelligences, to which the human person belongs as a fallen and embodied spirit.[53]

Dionysius' philosophical orientation profoundly influences his articulation of the Christian hope. The goal of all created existence, in the Dionysian system, is to regain the lost unity of intelligent creatures with God in contemplative knowledge and love, a unity that forms in the creature the likeness of God (*Div. Nom.* 7.3; *Cael. Hier.* 3.2; *Eccl. Hier.* 2.1). As God reaches out to creatures in the "perpetual circle" of creative gift and unitive attraction (*Div. Nom.* 4.14; cf. 4.17), he awakens in them an experience of his divine reality that leads them towards this union in a constant process of "ascent" (e.g., *Div. Nom.* 4.5), "enlightenment" (e.g., *Eccl. Hier.* 1.1) and "divinization" (e.g., *Eccl. Hier.* 1.3f.).

In addition to this Neoplatonic conception of the movement of creatures towards God, Pseudo-Dionysius also reflects on the more traditional features of Christian eschatological hope in chapter 7 of his *Ecclesiastical Hierarchy*, as part of an interpretation of the Christian funeral liturgy. Here the author identifies the time of eschatological fulfillment as "the regeneration" (παλιγγενεσία: *Eccl. Hier.* 7.1.1, 3; 7.3.1), a biblical term signifying both the transition of the soul "to an immutable state of steadfastness" and the resurrection of the body to share in the soul's incorruption (*Eccl. Hier.* 7.1.1; 7.3.9). Rejecting as equally foolish a totally spiritual conception of fulfillment, the theory of transmigration of souls, and materialistic images of beatitude[54] (*ibid.*, 7.1.2), Pseudo-Dionysius insists that just as our bodies now share in all the struggles of the spirit, so "they will receive a godlike and imperishable immortality as their blessed portion" (*ibid.*, 7.1.1). He does not speculate on the details of the rewards of the just, except to insist that they will correspond to the degree to which one "imitated God" on earth by a "divine and holy life" (*ibid.*, 7.3.1). The biblical metaphors used to describe heaven in the funeral liturgy – phrases like "light," "the land of the living" and "the bosom of Abraham" (*ibid.*, 7.3.4) – simply remind us that the reward promised the just, which surpasses human understanding, will be a share in the "ageless and most blessed fulfillment" to which the saints and patriarchs have already come (*ibid.*, 7.3.5).

Pseudo-Dionysius has even less to say on the punishment of the wicked. He assumes that the possibility of moral change ends with death (*Eccl. Hier.* 7.1.1), and so readily affirms that "the sufferings threatening the unholy will have no end" (*ibid.*, 7.3.3; see also 7.3.6). The heart of this suffering, for Pseudo-Dionysius, seems to be the tragic experience of realizing, as life ends, the goodness of all that is commanded by the Scriptures, and of being no longer able to achieve it; as a result, he observes laconically, sinners "leave this life miserably and unwillingly, not being led off to a holy hope" (*ibid.*, 7.1.2).

Although he speaks of the rewards of the just as coincident with the resurrection (*ibid.*, 7.1.1; 7.3.1), Pseudo-Dionysius suggests that it is legitimate to think of those who died a holy death as already "sharing truly in eternal rewards" (*ibid.*, 7.3.3). Because the dead can no longer change, he recognizes the theological difficulty raised by the practice of praying for them, but seems to interpret such prayer as having a declaratory rather than an intercessory character: above all, as assuring the living that God will surely reward the just with a share in his own life (*ibid.*, 7.3.6f.).[55]

Severus of Antioch

The leader of the anti-Chalcedonian party in the Greek Church of the early sixth century, and the most accomplished and influential theologian of the "monophysite" tradition, was Severus (*c.* 465–538), from 512 until 518 patriarch of Antioch. Although his controversial writings deal almost entirely with various aspects of the Christological debates of his time,

Severus' many pastoral writings – sermons, letters and hymns – present us with a broader glimpse of his theological system, including elements of an eschatological doctrine that is solidly rooted in earlier Greek tradition, and carefully distanced from both Origenistic optimism and darker, popular expectations.[56]

Far from conceiving death, as earlier Syrian writers had done, as a powerful, personal enemy of human nature, Severus refers to it dispassionately as the separation of soul and body (*Ep.* 71: *PO* 14.109; *Ep.* 93: *PO* 14.171), our "common end," which the believer faces willingly, even eagerly (*Ep.* 93: *PO* 14.171). Although death still remains inescapable for each of us, as a result of the sin of Adam that lost for us our natural expectation of immortality (*Ep.* 27: *PO* 12.250; *Ep.* 65: *PO* 14.15f.), Christ's resurrection in our flesh "has broken the reign of death" (*Hom.* 90: *PO* 23.158; cf. *Hymn* 74: *PO* 6.118). Even so, the death of the individual is clearly a violent passage, as angels and demons struggle to gain possession of the soul (*Ep.* 107: *PO* 14.262f.; *Hom.* 86: *PO* 23.71).

Although he occasionally refers to the immediate entry of the martyrs into "the blessed dwellings of the angels and holy Fathers" (*Hom.* 52: *PO* 4.15; cf. *Hom.* 62: *PO* 8.278; *Hom.* 64: *PO* 8.315), Severus seems to assume that the dead must normally wait for the resurrection and judgment before receiving their final punishment or reward (*Ep.* 107: *PO* 14.261). For the souls of the just, the place of waiting is not Sheol – which Christ has broken open – but "a reign of light," to which angels conduct them safely at the moment of death (*Hom.* 49: *PO* 35.352f.; *Hom.* 71: *PO* 23.71).

Severus apparently did not share the expectation of some of his contemporaries that the end of the world was near. "The Lord does not delay his promise," he writes to John of Bostra, "but he is long-suffering towards us, not wishing that any should perish" (*Ep.* 81: *PO* 14.129). Even using the traditional scheme of six thousand years for the world's history, he continues, it is impossible to know how near the end is, since the interpretation of these numbers remains uncertain (*Ep.* 81: *PO* 14.130f.). In some passages, Severus refers to the present time as the seventh "day" of the world, and uses "the eighth day" to refer to the endless age to come (*Ep.* 96: *PO* 14.188; cf. *Ep.* 79: *PO* 14.126; *Ep.* 96: *PO* 14.188). In other places, however, he identifies the time of the Church, "the days of Christ's Kingdom and the evangelic life," as "the beginnings of that eighth day, and of that new life without evening and without end" (*Ep.* 80: *PO* 14.127; *Ep.* 81: *PO* 14.129f.). The reality of the eschatological Kingdom has, in a partial way, already begun.

Like most of his predecessors, Severus insists on the physical reality of the resurrection. Even though the risen body will not be subject to passion or need earthly food, it will still have its teeth, genitals and other organs (*Ep.*

96: *PO* 14.187f.). Severus also takes seriously Paul's promise that the whole of creation will share in the incorruptibility conferred on the human race in the resurrection (Rom 8.21), a promise that he sees as derived from the essential goodness of the cosmos and from its radical identification with the fate of its human inhabitants (*Ep.* 27: *PO* 12.250–58, esp. 250).

In a number of his liturgical and pastoral works, Severus dwells on the details of the coming day of judgment, drawing especially on Matt 24 (see esp. *Hymn* 29: *PO* 6.70; *Hymn* 87: *PO* 6.127f.; *Ep.* 71: *PO* 14.111), and recommends meditation on the judgment and the torments of the damned as a healthy practice for both monks and lay people (*Hom.* 62: *PO* 8.277–80; *Hom.* 86: *PO* 23.66). He describes the punishment of sinners in traditional terms, as "inextinguishable fire and unbearable, endless sufferings," from which no intercession can win release (*Hom.* 80: *PO* 20.334). The fire of Gehenna has no need of fuel, but continues to burn forever (*Hom.* 53: *PO* 4.33). In two homilies, he recounts with great gusto the report that possessed people in Alexandria have recently been seen to spit out nails, broken glass and burning coals; he sees in the incident an example of what sinners will suffer in the eternal company of demons (*Hom.* 53: *PO* 4.34f.; *Hom.* 62: *PO* 8:272ff.). More important, however, will be the psychological aspect of the suffering of the damned, as they see the blessed from afar and come to realize the good they themselves have lost (*Ep.* 117: *PO* 14.285f.). So he interprets the Pauline phrase, "God will be all in all" (I Cor 15.28) as the recognition by all intelligent creatures of the goodness of God: "it is . . . knowledge, on the part of all creatures equally, that he will be the God of those who are subject to him – of some, because they have already recognized him in his perfection and have submitted to him; of others, when finally they recognize him in the endless torment which at that time will burn without giving light" (*Hom.* 49: *PO* 35.357).

Severus stresses that the punishment of sinners will be eternal, because the forgiveness of sin will no longer be possible after death (*Hom.* 98: *PO* 25.161f.). So he devotes an entire letter (*Ep.* 98) to refuting the doctrine of *apokatastasis*, arguing (along with Jacob of Sarug) that sinners are punished according to their evil intention, not in proportion to the amount of time they have lived in sin, and are therefore justly punished for all eternity (*PO* 14:201ff.).

In describing the rewards of the blessed, Severus emphasizes the spiritual content of eternal happiness. Rejecting as foolishness the literal millenarian hopes of Papias, Irenaeus and Apollinarius (*Ep.* 96: *PO* 14.193; cf. *Ep.* 72: *PO* 14.118f.), he insists that "the kingdom of heaven is not sensual, nor does it consist in eating and drinking" (*ibid.*, 182). Although it may include "a fresh return to our primitive state" (*ibid.*, 190), eternal beatitude is not simply the regaining of a lost Paradise (*ibid.*, 183), but "leads those who are formed anew to a higher and more divine condition," "a greater likeness to God" (*ibid.*, 183f.). There will be different degrees of beatitude, corresponding to the love and fidelity of each of the saints (*Ep. 72: PO* 14.118f.; *Ep. 73: PO* 118f.; *Hom.* 86: *PO* 23.71), but all will be "nourished" in their new life by the self-revelatory "teaching" of the Word (*Ep. 87; PO* 14.150). "And this, one might say, is the food of those who are about to live the awaited life," he suggests in another letter: "continual songs of praise and the sublime contemplation on which the angels also feed, and joy and inexplicable exaltation, in a life that does not end" (*Ep. 96: PO* 14.186f.). It is a new version of the spiritual hope sketched out by Origen and Gregory of Nyssa, modified by an anthropology that takes more seriously both the possible finality of sin and the unprecedented newness of the grace of Christ.

John of Caesaraea; Leontius of Byzantium

The works of other controversial theologians of the early sixth century pay less attention to eschatological themes – simply because what remains is almost exclusively concerned with Christological debate. Several of the anti-Manichaean syllogisms that have recently been identified as the probable work of Severus' "neo-Chalcedonian" opponent, John of Caesaraea, base their rejection of the idea that evil is an eternal substance on the argument that the purpose of all punishment is to "transform the wicked" and so bring evil to an end (*Syll.* 1, 3, 5, 10).[57] These syllogisms show the strong influence of the anti-Manichaean work of Didymus of Alexandria,[58] and suggest that their author may have sympathized more generally with Didymus' Origenist eschatology.

The most important Chalcedonian Christological writer of this period, Leontius of Byzantium (d. *c.* 543), refers to eschatological hopes only in passing, but in such a way as to affirm conventional belief in the eternity of punishment and the materiality of the risen body – despite Leontius' apparent reputation for Origenism.[59]

So he refers to the punishment of the demons in the traditional terms of "Gehenna and darkness and the gnashing of teeth" (*PG* 86.1368D9f.), and repeats the traditional theory that the bodies of sinners will be able to suffer eternally there, along with their souls, because their sufferings will replenish rather than consume them (*ibid.*, 1337B12–C11). Though the bodies of all, after the resurrection, will be free from the need of food and sleep (*ibid.*, 1337A15–B2), they will be the same bodies we now possess, reconstituted "just as nature knit them together when it formed them in the womb" (*ibid.*, 1941D6f.).

Sixth-century Origenism

Although the Origenist theological system, especially its eschatology, had always been controversial, it became the focus of particularly bitter debates in the second quarter of the sixth century, between several rival groups of Palestinian monks.[60] Led by a certain Nonnus, four monks of the community of the Nea Lavra, in the Judaean desert, became known as devotees of the speculations of Origen, Didymus and Evagrius, and were expelled from their monastery in 514 for "pretending to profess Christian doctrine and feigning piety, while holding the teachings of the wicked pagans, Jews and Manichees" (Cyril of Skythopolis, *Vita Sabae* 36). Returning to influence in the 530s, apparently under the leadership of Leontius of Byzantium, the "Origenists" took an active part in the defense of Chalcedonian Christology and seem to have become a sizable and important party within Palestinian monasticism, dominating not only the Nea Lavra but also the monasteries of Martyrius and Firminus. To their confrères of more traditional piety and more limited education, they appeared both arrogant and doctrinally dangerous: "intelligentsia" or "Gnostics" who were ready to sacrifice traditional teaching for daring philosophical theories.[61]

A vivid example of the way in which their contemporaries saw the Origenist monks of this period is provided by several of the *Replies of Barsanuphius and John* (nos. 600–607), a collection of answers given to a wide range of theological and spiritual inquiries by two famous recluses of the desert near Gaza (*c.* 520–40).[62] In the first of these, a monk tells of having come across works of Origen and Didymus, along with the *Kephalaia Gnostica* of Evagrius; he is apparently troubled by what he has read, particularly by the Origenist theories of the pre-existence and fall of souls and of universal salvation or *apokatastasis*. Abba Barsanuphius replies with horror, "These are Greek speculations; these are the silly chatterings of people who think they are important" (600). Such doctrines do not lead to repentance but to intellectual pride; a monk would do better to read the words and lives of the Fathers! (*ibid.*). After receiving a similar reply from Abba John (601), the monk returns to Barsanuphius with some confrères and asks how it is that the Cappadocian Fathers seem to support the Origenist position on some points. Barsanuphius answers that even the saints "have not been able to comprehend in reality all the deep mysteries of God," and that as a result they have sometimes espoused traditions that are less than fully orthodox (604). Asked, further on, about the contemporary Origenist theory of the resurrection – that the risen body will be "ethereal and spherical," totally transformed into a non-material state – Barsanuphius insists, with abundant references to Scripture, that "bodies will rise with bones, nerves and hair, and will remain so forever" (607); he also reaffirms that the punishment of the damned, like the beatitude of the just, will be eternal. Any teaching to the contrary is, for Barsanuphius and John, a snare of the devil.

Encouraged by Palestinian leaders opposed to the Origenist party, the Emperor Justinian (Emperor 527–65), in a letter to the patriarch Menas of Constantinople in 543, attacked Origen for a number of theories associated with his name, especially those of the preexistence of all souls (including that of Jesus), the spherical form of the risen body, and the limited duration of all punishment.[63] Justinian contemptuously brands the notion of a spherical risen body to be a "Greek theory" that shows disrespect for the risen Lord and makes a mockery of our own hope of resurrection (ACO 3.204.10–15).[64] Further, he attacks the notion that "the punishment of all wicked men and women, and even of the demons, has a limit and that both sinners and demons will be restored to their original position"; his reason is that such doctrines "make people lazy about keeping the commandments of God" (ibid., 205.9–12). If punishment will come to an end, he adds, so must eternal life – and then "what reason is there for the Incarnation of our Lord Jesus Christ?" (ibid., 23–26). The document includes both the spherical conception of the risen body and the theory of apokatastasis among the objects of its concluding nine anathemas (Anath. 5 and 9: ibid., 213.25f.; 214.4ff.).

During the decade that followed Justinian's letter, the Origenist party seems to have remained active in Palestine, and even to have gained influence at the imperial court through Theodore Askidas, bishop of Caesaraea in Cappadocia, and Domitian, bishop of Ancyra – both former monks of the Nea Lavra. Theodore's followers came to be known as "Isochristoi," apparently because they so emphasized the Evagrian hope for the final unity of all intelligences with Christ that they predicted all, in the end, will be "equal" to him, and will be able to join in creating other worlds.[65] A more moderate group of Origenists, centered at the Judaean monastery of Firminus, who eventually joined forces with the anti-Origenists in condemning the "Isochristoi" as heretics, were known as "Proto-ktistoi" or (abusively) "Tetradites,"[66] presumably because they stressed the distinctive position of Christ, the "first-born of creation," in his relationship both to the Trinity and to other creatures.

In the Life of Cyriacus, Cyril of Skythopolis has his hero summarize the doctrine of the more extreme Origenists of the 540s as follows: "They say Christ is not one of the Trinity; they say that the risen body – first Christ's, then ours – is in the end totally annihilated; they say that the holy Trinity did not create the world, and that in the restoration (apokatastasis) all intelligent beings, even the demons, will be able to create worlds; they say that our bodies will be raised in an ethereal and spherical form, and indeed that the Lord's body has already been raised thus; they say that we will be equal to Christ in the restoration" (*Vita Cyriaci* 12: ed. Schwartz 230.3–10). The source is hostile, and the picture it gives of sixth-century Origenist doctrine doubtless over-simplified; none the less, these were the main points of Origenist doctrine as its enemies perceived it, and indicate that Origenism's speculative, highly unitive and spiritualized eschatology was, for its contemporaries, one of its most scandalous features.

The Fifth Ecumenical Council, which met at Constantinople in the spring of 553, was convoked by Justinian mainly to define an official consensus position in Christology. It now seems certain however, that the assembled bishops also issued fifteen anathemas condemning Origenist theology, probably before the synod's official agenda began on 5 May.[67]

The ninth-century chronographer George Hamartolos preserves a letter sent by the Emperor to the assembled bishops, complaining that "certain monks in Jerusalem are following and teaching the doctrines of Pythagoras, Plato and Origen," notably on the subject of the original unity, fall, and final restoration of souls.[68] After producing quotations from Plato to prove that such doctrines are Greek rather than Christian, Justinian says he is sending the Council Fathers a summary of Origenist teaching, with the instruction to "examine carefully the attached exposition and to judge and condemn each of its propositions." The fifteen propositions condemned by the bishops were probably based on Justinian's dossier. Far more clearly than the nine propositions Justinian had condemned ten years earlier, these theses represent a radicalized Evagrian Christology and cosmology, and a doctrine of *apokatastasis* that went far beyond the hopes of Origen or Gregory of Nyssa. They envisage not only a spherical, ethereal risen body (10), but the complete abolition of material reality in the world to come (11), and the ultimate absorption of all created spirits into an undifferentiated unity with the divine Logos, so that even the humanity and the Kingdom of Christ will come to an end (12). Although no authors are mentioned by name, Greek writers from the sixth century onwards took this conciliar document as a condemnation of Origen, Evagrius and Didymus, as well as their Palestinian disciples.[69] After 553, in fact, Origenism – especially Origenist eschatology – was generally considered heretical in both the Eastern and Western Churches.

Aeneas of Gaza

Many of the anthropological and cosmological issues that exercised both sides in the Origenist controversy prompted another debate, in the first half of the sixth century, between some Christian apologists and the pagan academic philosophers at Athens and Alexandria. The first Christian work to challenge long-accepted Platonic assumptions about the eternal existence of the spiritual and material worlds and the endless cycle of the incarnations of souls is the apologetic dialogue *Theophrastus*, written by the rhetorician Aeneas of Gaza sometime in the last quarter of the fifth or the first quarter of the sixth century.[70] Cast in the form of a conversation, held at Alexandria, between an Athenian Platonist named Theophrastus and a Christian from Gaza named Euxitheus (whose opinions clearly represent those of the author), the work criticizes the accepted Platonic conceptions of the world and the human person, and attempts to defend Christian anthropology and eschatology by philosophical arguments and parallels. Citing Plato and other ancient philosophers as his authorities, rather than the Bible or Church tradition, Aeneas is determined to overthrow Greek philosophy's radically non-eschatological conception of history in its own terms. Yet the content of his arguments is recognizable as Christian doctrine – so much so that at the end of the dialogue the pagan Theophrastus acknowledges in his opponent's arguments "the grace of God," and adds: "Farewell to the Academy – let us go to Him!"

The principal Platonist doctrines attacked in the dialogue are those of reincarnation (ed. Colonna, 4–17), the eternity of creation (*ibid.*, 46f.), and the preexistence of souls before their bodily existence (*ibid.*, 38f.) – all doctrines that had at least been considered favorably as possibilities by Origen and Evagrius. Aeneas argues that the constant creation of new beings in time, whether plants and animals or human souls giving form to material bodies, demonstrates the power and wisdom of the creator, who alone always remains (*ibid.*, 36f.). Yet although every creature has a temporal beginning, all rational substances are naturally immortal, he insists,[71] because they are, in their simplicity and rationality, images of God: "that which is similar to the immortal is also immortal" (*ibid.*, 39.23f.). And although material creation, in virtue of its composite nature, is destined to disintegrate (*ibid.*, 48), the informing of bodies by rational souls is the creator's way of "sowing in mortal things the seed of immortality" (*ibid.*, 49.17; cf. 62.5). As a result, in Aeneas' view, "nothing brought into being by the Creator is completely mortal, nor will it remain mortal" (*ibid.*, 50.2f.).

So Aeneas speaks of the end of history not in biblical or apocalyptic terms, but as the end of the present constant "motion" of generation and death, and as the attainment of the unity and perfection every creature now longs and strives for (ed. Colonna, 43.7ff.). Although this state of fulfillment and rest will be primarily enjoyed by rational creatures – by souls and by bodiless spirits – the material universe will also participate in it, because of its organic relationship to the human person. "After the judgment of souls and the open condemnation of evil," Aeneas writes, "all sensible reality will be transformed into something immortal, in order to be conformed to human immortality and to become the proper place, once again, for the happiness of those who dwell in it. A mortal creature, after all, has to live in a mortal world, but an immortal creature in an immortal one. There will be a single harmony throughout it all, nothing disorderly or unharmonious; each creature will be friendly and useful towards every other, and will naturally do the Creator's will" (*ibid.*, 43.12–19). Aeneas, however, apparently understands this transformation and immortalization of material creation in a global way, not as implying that every aspect of the present world must be preserved for eternity. So he later insists that irrational animals, unlike humans, will not rise again, because their bodies have not received the "seed of immortality" (*ibid.*, 62.2, 11ff.).

Towards the end of the dialogue, Aeneas defends the doctrine of a future resurrection of the body at some length, using arguments long familiar from the Christian apologetic tradition. After making fun of the Platonic notion that the soul may wear many different kinds of body – astral, ethereal or earthly – depending of its environment (ed. Colonna, 52.9–53.5), Aeneas insists that we will rise to be judged in the same bodies that have served our choices for good or ill during life (*ibid.*, 54.15–18). In answer to the difficulties raised by his pagan interrogator, Euxitheus shows the possibility of such a reconstitution by arguing that the soul, as form of the body, is always the principle of the body's continued identity through material change (*ibid.*, 58.9–59.9). Like the vital force preserved in a decaying seed by its generic form, which brings new life out of apparent death if the creator provides the necessary conditions of moisture and light (*ibid.*), the soul will reassemble the scattered elements of its decomposed body when the creator gives the signal – an act no more marvelous than the original production of a human body from a single drop of semen (*ibid.*, 55.16–56.8). Aeneas does not speculate on the appearance or characteristics of the risen body, except to say that its material component will "escape heaviness and distension and mortality, by the ambitious contrivance of the Creator, and will become pure and light and immortal" (*ibid.*, 59.22ff.). A sign of the vital power that inheres even in the present bodies of the dead is the miracles worked by the bones of heroes and saints, and the reverence that we instinctively show to them (*ibid.*, 60.3–61.5).

Although his conception and explanation of the resurrection owes much to Gregory of Nyssa,[72] Aeneas is careful in other ways to distinguish his position from that of the Origenist tradition, especially on the key issues of the finality of our self-determination in this present life and *apokatastasis* or universal salvation. Speaking of life, in one passage, as an athletic contest, Aeneas makes it clear that this is the only test that the human spirit will undergo. After it, "the soul that has distinguished itself in the contest and shown vigor and skill . . . [God] crowns as the victor, and judges it worthy of nectar and glory and a place in the chorus on high, from which it may not fall; while the cowardly and lazy and foolish and talkative soul, which disturbs the spectators and violates the law, he curses and sends first into custody and then to a prison of punishment, from which no one may escape" (ed. Colonna, 35.23–36.3).

In one rather puzzling section (ed. Colonna, 49.7–51.23), Aeneas explains the participation of rational, immortal spirits in the present mortal world of material reality as the result of an act of disobedience. Originally commissioned to care for "lower," material creation and to link it to God by using it in conformity with his will (*ibid.*, 50.13–22), these spirits grew dissatisfied with service and attempted to seize control of the material world for their own purposes (*ibid.*, 22ff.). Such an act of disorder plunged them into the "darkness of mortality" themselves, as in a kind of river that carries them away against their will (*ibid.*, 50.24–51.2). This is a providential plan, however, for the healing of those who have fallen: when the world in which they seek to rule has perished, the rebellion of souls will come to an end, "and after the destruction of their tyranny, he will again make that part immortal which, for their sakes, he first made mortal" (*ibid.*, 51.8f.). "So," he concludes, "that change once and for all will be for the better, and there will be no further change; the human person will come to life, never to die again, for there will no longer be any mortal thing, but all will be new and immortal – both the whole of this world and the human person" (*ibid.*, 20–24). Although this passage seems to suggest a doctrine of a fall and of universal restoration similar to the modified Origenism of Gregory of Nyssa, it seems clear, too, that Aeneas is speaking in global terms, of the broad lines of salvation-history, and does not necessarily mean to rule out the possible damnation of individuals.[73]

Zachary of Mytilene

Another Christian work of this period, similar in both form and content to the *Theophrastus*, is the *Ammonius*, an apologetic dialogue by Zachary of Mytilene (*c.* 465–before 553).[74] Composed probably after Aeneas of Gaza's death (*c.* 518), this work shows unmistakable signs of dependence on the *Theophrastus*, and may well have been intended to repeat its criticism of contemporary Neoplatonist cosmology and anthropology in even more clearly orthodox Christian terms, without the ambiguous traces of Origenist speculation suggested by some passages of Aeneas' treatise.[75] Thus it may come from the 540s, when Zachary's orthodoxy, as bishop of Mytilene, was solidly established and when the Origenist controversy was well underway.

Although Zachary's dialogue devotes less space than Aeneas' to strictly eschatological themes, its concluding section (ed. Colonna, 1163–1501) is an exposition of the Christian hope for immortality, a bodily resurrection and the transformation of the material universe, written in explicit contrast to the Platonist theory that the world is coeternal with its creator. "We understand that the world is by nature corruptible," he writes, "for it has come into being; but we say it will not be completely or eternally dissolved, because of the goodness of its Creator. Rather, it will be transfigured into something more beautiful, and will be made immortal along with our bodies, after the general consummation" (*ibid.*, 1329–33). God allows the present world to undergo corruption and change, according to its natural limitations, because it must share in the inherited corruptibility of a disobedient humanity, as the environment for human life (*ibid.*, 1187–1220). But after death has achieved its purpose of bringing human disobedience to an end (*ibid.*, 1251–59), and of teaching rational creatures that they depend on God's grace for the gift of immortality (*ibid.*, 1337f.), both humanity and the cosmos it inhabits will share in the eternal life that naturally belongs to God alone, "for none of those things that have come to exist on their own, having their origin in the Good, will be committed to lasting corruption" (*ibid.*, 1333f.; cf. 1347–58; 1479–82).

Zachary's discussion of the resurrection follows the classical lines of the Greek tradition, depending especially on Gregory of Nyssa, as well as on his more recent disciple, Aeneas.[76] The "seed of immortality," Zachary observes, was planted in the human body by God when he "bound it up" with the soul, the image of his Word (ed. Colonna, 1233–37). It is only appropriate that the body, which has shared in the soul's struggle to live virtuously, should in the end share in its recompense (*ibid.*, 1482–85). The resurrection will be no trivial event, but a re-creation of the human person's present material component, free from its present marks and habits of weakness (*ibid.*, 1261., 1261–64). In answer to the usual difficulties, raised by the dialogue's pagan interlocutors, Zachary affirms that the God who originally formed the body out of the four elements, beginning with a tiny drop of semen fertilizing a womb, can find and reassemble all its scattered particles without further difficulty (*ibid.*, 1435–79). "The way of immortality for the creature and its leader," he adds, "and its source and explanation, in simple terms," is the risen Christ, whose Incarnation was the beginning of our own renewal (*ibid.*, 1271–76).

Zachary also makes it clear that both the reward of the just and the punishment of sinners will be eternal and irreversible. Those who allow themselves to be refashioned by the saving mercy of God will "look on the Good itself, the One, their first and only source, and will never be satiated with contemplating their Savior, but will love their own creaturehood and will enjoy forever the radiance of the Good . . ." (ed. Colonna, 1339–42). But eternal failure is also possible, despite God's saving love. In language recalling Plato's *Phaedrus*, Zachary insists that those who "fly downwards from virtue" and are brought to earth by the "weight" of evil desires will "be deprived of their intended immortality . . . and go to the sacred prison of punishment . . . which the Holy Scripture calls a river of fire and a worm that never sleeps, and Gehenna and everlasting shame and detention and retribution and the like" (*ibid.*, 1487–97). In terms intelligible to both the pagan and the Christian worlds, and more clearly than either his Cappadocian or Gazaean predecessors, Zachary is here reaffirming the traditional biblical prospect of an irrevocable recompense for our moral behavior.

John "Philoponus"

This same concern to defend the Christian understanding of God's transcendence over creation, by affirming the temporal beginning and end of the world in both its material and formal aspects, characterizes the philosophical and theological work of John "Philoponus" (d. after 565), an Alexandrian academic philosopher and fervent monophysite Christian.[77] A pupil of the pagan philosopher Ammonius Hermeiou, John edited some of his master's lectures on Aristotle for publication; he also wrote a number of commentaries and philosophical treatises himself, including a long refutation of Proclus' arguments for the eternal coexistence of the sensible and intelligible worlds,[78] and a treatise in six books, now lost, refuting Aristotle's hypothesis that the heavenly bodies are made of an incorruptible "fifth element."[79]

John's espousal of Aristotelian anthropology led him to deny any real distinction between an individual human *hypostasis* and human nature in its concrete realization. In his view, any individual can be called an "individual nature" as well as a hypostasis, a position that supported his monophysite Christology but that also led, in its application to Trinitarian theology, to his being called a tritheist. More important for his eschatology, John's Aristotelian anthropology also formed the basis of his insistence that both the form and the matter of material bodies are corruptible and mortal, and that despite the soul's immortality, the resurrection for which Christians hope will be a totally new creation of bodies that had perished completely.

In fragments of his lost treatise *On the Resurrection*, John argues that the resurrection of the body cannot simply be a reassembling of its scattered material elements by an immortal soul. "All sensible and visible bodies were brought by God from non-being into being, in both matter and form," he writes; "they are corruptible, and will be corrupted in both matter and form, and in their place other bodies will be created by God, better than these

195

visible ones, incorruptible and eternal" (*ap.* Nicephorus Kallistos, *Eccl. Hist.* 18.47 [PG 147.424D8–425A2]). In Syriac fragments of the same work, he insists that the risen body of Christ is different in species (εἶδος) from the mortal body that died; his whole earthly being has been transformed into a new state of incorruptibility, the first exemplar of a transformation in which all Christians hope to share.[80] So John criticizes Gregory of Nyssa and Cyril of Alexandria for suggesting that we will become, in the resurrection, simply an incorruptible version of what we already are; in saying this, they fail to recognize that mortality and corruptibility are part of our present essence, and that our eschatological transformation will mean, for us and our universe, the beginning of something essentially as well as qualitatively new.[81]

John Philoponus' conception of the resurrection made his reputation still more controversial, among monophysites and Chalcedonians alike. Later Orthodox writers criticized him for denying the resurrection of the present body, and for abandoning the earlier Patristic tradition.[82] Germanus of Constantinople even identified Philoponus' understanding of the resurrection – erroneously – with that of Origen.[83] Two of his fellow "tritheist" monophysites of the late sixth century, Conon of Tarsus and Eugenius of Seleucia, apparently also rejected John's view of the resurrection, arguing that the body is corrupted, in death, only in its form, and that the same matter presently included in it will receive a new and better form at the moment of resurrection. Similarly, the transformation of the cosmos at the end of time will consist, according to Conon and Eugenius, in the reception by its material substrate of a new, imperishable form (Nicephorus Kallistos, *Eccl. Hist.* 18.47 [PG 147.425A7–B3]). This understanding of the metaphysics of eschatological transformation is a complete reversal of Origen's theory of formal continuity amid constant material change.

Cosmas "Indicopleustes"

A contemporary of John Philoponus, who also held strong theological views on the structure and history of the universe, was the Alexandrian Cosmas, known also since the Middle Ages by the surname of "Indicopleustes" ("the voyager to India"). A former merchant, who had traveled at least as far as southern Ethiopia (*Top. Christ.* 2.54ff.), and a devoted partisan of the Antiochene Christological tradition, Cosmas wrote his curious *Christian Topography* in Alexandria between 547 and 549, as an attempt to advance a literal biblical conception of the universe and to refute the Christian Aristotelianism of his fellow townsman John Philoponus.[84] Cosmas was convinced that the Aristotelian conception of a spherical, eternally rotating universe contradicted the biblical understanding of creation,[85] and saw in

Philoponus' unitary conception of the world a reflection of his monophysite Christology.

Drawing on second-hand geographical and scientific information, as well as on the exegesis, cosmology and anthropology of Theodore of Mopsuestia and his school,[86] Cosmas argued in his elaborate treatise that the universe is a stationary, two-tiered rectangular box with an arched lid, typologically represented by the tabernacle of the Old Testament.[87] In accord with the Antiochene tendency to distinguish sharply between heavenly and earthly realities, and between the present and future "states" ($\kappa\alpha\tau\alpha\sigma\tau\acute{\alpha}\sigma\epsilon\iota\varsigma$) of redeemed humanity, he sees in the image of the divided tabernacle an inspired model of creation holding strong implications both for Christology and eschatology. Like Moses building his tent, "God, from the beginning, divided the single space that reaches from earth to heaven into two regions, by means of the firmament. As in the tabernacle there is an outer and an inner room, so here there is a lower and an upper region. The lower is this world; the upper is the world to come, where the Lord Christ has ascended first of all, having risen from the dead, and where the just will later ascend in turn" (*Top. Christ.*, Hypothesis 6: *SC* 141.267ff.).[88] The whole purpose of his treatise, he insists, is to demonstrate from the Bible that God "has prepared two states of existence, this one and the one to come, while explaining also the shape of the whole universe . . . The belief of the Greeks," he continues, "is without hope, because they do not expect a second state of existence or believe that there will be a resurrection of our bodies" (5.248: *SC* 159.363). Without a two-tiered universe, hope in a real "world to come" seems to Cosmas out of the question.

This spatial transformation of the Christian hope allows Cosmas to insist, against John Philoponus, on the material and substantial identity of the present body and the body of the resurrection; in book 7 of the *Christian Topography*, in fact, he introduces a lengthy exposition of the resurrection hope, drawn largely from I Cor 15, as an argument for the existence of two distinct parts of creation corresponding to the two successive "states" of human existence (7.23–47). After insisting here that our hope for the resurrection is founded on the resurrection of Christ (23–26) and expressed in our baptism (27), Cosmas follows I Cor 15 in arguing that the risen body will be transformed, spiritualized, but not wholly other than the body we now have (30–33). Following Christ, those who are to be saved "will become heavenly in likeness to him" (34), and will "pass from this perishable condition into that which is to come: into that heavenly place, which he calls 'the Kingdom of heaven'. . ." (35).[89]

All will be given the gifts of immortality and incorruptible life in "the condition to come," but each will be rewarded or punished according to his deeds (5.188). The abode of the just will be "a place in the heights of heaven, beyond this visible firmament" (5.184); that of the wicked, on the other hand, will be "below, surrounding the earth, where the devil has been thrown" (*ibid.*). Those who have a sincere and correct faith, but who lack love and the other virtues, will not be admitted to either place, Cosmas adds, but will be "in the middle, condemned to remain outside the bridal chamber – that is to say, [below] the firmament" (5.185). He also cautiously suggests that fetuses who have died with only rudimentary knowledge of God will be consigned, at the judgment, to this "intermediary state" (7.80).

Cosmas stresses that our present knowledge of future reward and punishment is confined to the earthly comparisons that the Lord has revealed to us (5.186); entering into the "condition to come" will bring a transformation of our experience as great as that which took place at our entry into this world from the womb (*ibid.*, 187f.). The time of the end is hidden from everyone but God, although Cosmas finds scriptural evidence for the theory that it will come when the number of humans born equals the number of the angels (5.255). He is certain, however, that the transformation of humanity will bring with it the renewal and perfection of the material universe and of all other rational beings – a renewal "already accomplished in Christ" (7.65f.).

Andrew of Caesaraea

Another sixth-century expositor of the Apocalypse of John was Andrew, metropolitan of Caesaraea in Cappadocia sometime between 563 and 614.[90] A collection of twenty-four of his homilies has survived, commenting on the whole text of the Apocalypse in a theologically moderate and balanced way – a work that became the standard Apocalypse-commentary for the later Byzantine Church.[91] Although he makes use of the commentary of Oecumenius, Andrew never mentions him by name, and seems bent on refuting some of the earlier writer's Origenist speculations. Andrew's own eschatological doctrine, in its cautious Biblicism and its moralistic anchoring in the present world, resembles that of Augustine more closely than it does previous Greek authors.

Andrew presents the Antichrist, for instance, in traditional terms: he will come from the tribe of Dan (Schmid 79.3f.), from Bashan in the region of the Euphrates (35.7, 102.6ff.); he will have a precursor, parallel to John the Baptist, who will make him seem divine (142.5–10); he will pose as a Roman Emperor, and will attempt to reestablish the dominance of Rome (137.1; 189.18–21; 202.5f.). Yet the kingdom that longs for his coming is not simply Rome, but "the earthly kingdom in general," the body of those who, in all times and places, have resisted the Word of God (181.6–9;

202.8–13). Like Augustine, Andrew takes the thousand-year reign of the saints in Apoc 20 to refer to the age of the Church, from the first coming of Christ until the arrival of the Antichrist (216.13–18); the number 1,000 is primarily a symbol of completeness, he argues, and only God knows how many years are needed for the Church's fulfillment (*ibid.*; cf. 221.15–222.6).

Andrew speculates little about the details of the world's end. He stresses the Christian hope that the present material universe will share in the renewal of the resurrection (227.19f.; 229.11ff.; cf. 232.6f.), and considers it at least plausible that the saved will then be cleansed by the purifying fire of judgment, as some have suggested (91.11–13). He rejects emphatically, however, any purely medicinal understanding of the punishment of hell. Assuming that the damned will outnumber the saved (91.14), Andrew insists that their punishment will be eternal, and will not cause their repentance or purification, but will only harden them in their resistance to God's love (171.6–17). The reason for punishment is not the prevention or purification of sin, so much as the working of justice (172.2–6). God's mercy will lead him to mitigate the future sufferings of those who have suffered in this life (87.6f.; 89.4f.; 96.19f.; 163.15ff.), but those who think there will be an end to the punishment of sinners are "fools" (131.10f.).

Andrew is even more reticent in speculating about the rewards of the saints. They will be "like the angels" and join in their praise of the Triune God (203.11f.). However, the precise details of their share in the blessings of the coming age "exceeds all understanding" (205.18), and Andrew prefers to remain within the bounds of biblical imagery. He does, however, insist that the just will not enter the heavenly Jerusalem to enjoy their full reward until the final judgment, when God's anger will also be fully expressed towards sinners (163.7–13). Until then, the just repose in "the bosom of Abraham," a place appropriate to their deeds of virtue (68.1–5; 206.2f.).

Although the *Commentary on the Apocalypse* is Andrew's main extant work, Franz Diekamp also recovered five fragments of his *Therapeutike*: a set of questions and answers on eschatological subjects that further reveal the bishop's moderate, anti-Origenist doctrine.[92] After separation from the body, Andrew here explains, the souls of the dead are confined in "storerooms" (ταμιείοις) corresponding to their merits, where they will receive a foretaste of their future reward or punishment (Q. 1). At the resurrection, the bodies of the dead will be transformed from corruption to incorruption, radiant in the shared glory of God, but they will continue to possess the limbs and features of their present form; they will not be spherical, "as has seemed likely to some erring people" (Q. 2). Those who have been dead the longest will be raised first, to show the power of God more fully (Q. 4). All must then pass through the fire of judgment; but while those adorned with good works will pass over unharmed, "those who have lived in the opposite way will be held there, to be punished forever in proportion to their works" (Q. 5).

Eustratius

An unusual controversial piece on the fate of the soul after death, written at about the same time as Andrew of Caesaraea's commentary, is the work of Eustratius, presbyter of the Hagia Sophia in Constantinople, entitled *A Refutation of those who Say Human Souls, after they are Separated from their Bodies, are not Active and Receive No Benefit from the Prayers and Sacrifices Made for them to God*.[93] Eustratius sets out to refute the "pseudo-philosophers" of his time, who contend that souls can do nothing apart from their bodies, "but rest from all activity" (2). According to such theorists, the apparitions of the dead that are sometimes experienced by the living are really visions of heavenly spirits, who have assumed the shape of former human beings. The souls of the dead, they argue, are in a place where they cannot appear to anyone (*ibid.*).

Comparing the human body to the ant, who lives underground, and the soul to the bee, who lives in the air, Eustratius argues in reply that the soul lives on after death in a place known only to the mind, but that it can be active within the physical world (4). He then amasses a number of scriptural passages to illustrate the continuing activity of the dead (5–12) and adds a collection of excerpts from Patristic authorities and saints' lives (13–24) to show that it is the souls of the dead themselves who appear in visions and dreams, making use of immaterial representations of their former bodies (24). Even the souls of the damned are occasionally permitted by God to appear to the living (25), although their proper place is "in the deepest bowels of the earth" (26). In a final section (26), Eustratius argues that the souls of the dead are indeed helped by the "oblations, prayers and supplications" of their living friends; the practice of offering special prayers for them on the third, ninth and fortieth day after death is grounded in the Scriptures and recommended by earlier Christian writers, and must therefore be of some benefit to the dead as well as to those who pray for them.

Romanos "the Melodist"

Another sixth-century reflection of the Greek and Syriac eschatological tradition, quite different in character from those we have discussed, is *Hymn 50, On the Second Coming of Christ*, by Romanos "the Melodist" (d. *c.* 560).[94] Probably composed before 542,[95] and traditionally sung on the Sunday of

"Farewell to Meat," eight days before the beginning of Lent, this poem depicts, with great dramatic power, the trials of the last days and the Parousia and judgment of Christ.

After an opening strophe stressing the fear that will seize upon all before the throne of the divine judge (Str. 1), Romanos compares the first coming of Christ with his second coming (Str. 2–5). He then describes the tyranny of the Antichrist in some detail (Str. 6–14): he will be the devil incarnate (7), will oppress Christ's faithful greatly (9–10) and will put an end to the Church's worship (13). But Christ will return in majesty, accompanied by "all the armies of angels" (Str. 15–16), and will raise the dead (Str. 17) and lead the just into his "bridal chamber" (Str. 18). The Enemy will be thrown into eternal fire, with his angels and with all the wicked (Str. 19). Both the righteous and the damned will be incorruptible and immortal in body (Str. 21). The hymn ends with an urgent call to repentance (Str. 23) and an earnest prayer for the mercy of Christ (Str. 24).

Maximus the Confessor

The last great original theologian of Greek Patristic literature was undoubtedly Maximus the Confessor (c. 580–662), the Constantinopolitan monk whose life and whose thought united the theological voices of the Eastern and Western Churches, for the last half of the seventh century, as they had not been united since Chalcedon. Like most aspects of his dense and speculative theology, Maximus' eschatology integrates biblical images and Church tradition in a broad yet cohesive view of God's gracious involvement in created history; to a large extent, it is worked out in dialogue with the eschatology of Origen, the Cappadocians and the Pseudo-Dionysius, on whom much of his written work forms a sympathetic but critical commentary.

For Maximus, the goal of history, as far as God's own plan is concerned, is clearly the salvation of the whole human race and the union of all creation with himself (*Quaestiones ad Thalassium* 64: PG 90.700A14–B3; *Ambigua ad Joannem* 10: PG 91.1165D1off.; *Capita Theologica* 47: PG 90.1100B12–C4). For the human person, this union will mean perfection of body, mind and will, a "transformation of the faculties of deliberation and choice," as well as the acquisition of incorruptible life by the bodies of the dead. Their resurrection will be simply part of a wider "resurrection" and transformation of the whole created universe (*Expositio in Ps.* 59: PG 90.857A4–15; *Mystagogia* 7: PG 91.685B12–c6). The heart of this eschatological renewal will be divinization, "in which God is united with those who have become gods, and makes everything (τὸ πᾶν) his by his goodness" (*Amb. Joan.* 7: PG

91.1088C13ff.). God will totally penetrate the reality of his faithful creatures, and there will be in all things only one activity (ἐνέργεια): that of God (*Amb. Joan.* 7: *PG* 91.1076C10–14; *Quaest. ad Thal.* 22: *CCG* 7.136–47).

Yet Maximus is not, as has sometimes been argued, a proponent of the theory of universal salvation or *apokatastasis* in the unqualified form espoused by Origen and Gregory of Nyssa.[96] Although he recognizes Gregory's vision of the restoration of the human soul and body to their original integrity as a legitimate Christian hope (*Quaestiones et Dubia* 19[1, 13]: *CCG* 10.17f.), Maximus makes it clear in a number of passages that the final divinization of rational creatures will only be realized in those who have shown themselves worthy of God's gift (*Amb. Joan.* 7: *PG* 91.1076C10–14; *Quaest. ad Thal.* 22: *CCG* 7.136–47). Each person remains free to frustrate the achievement of God's saving purpose in himself by refusing to follow the way of Christ (*Quaest. ad Thal.* 63: *PG* 90.668C6–9; cf. *Quaest. ad Thal.* 47: *CCG* 7.323.182–88). Although God loves all creatures, is united with all as creator and offers all a share in his own being, this very offer becomes, for those who freely reject it, the cause not of "eternal well-being" but of "eternal ill-being"; in choosing to affirm themselves rather than God, creatures enter into a conflict with ultimate love and grace that leads to the contradiction of their own natural finality (*Amb. Joan.* 42: 91.1329A1–B7; *ibid.*, 65: *PG* 91.1392C9–D13; *Quaest. ad Thal.* 59: *PG* 90.609B14–C12).

So Maximus holds out to his readers not only God's plan of universal salvation and the hope of deification, but the more traditional prospects of judgment and eternal punishment. In a number of passages, he describes the sufferings of hell in vivid physical and psychological terms: as darkness, silence, torture and eternal fire (*Ep.* 1: *PG* 91.381B13, D5; 388A2; *Ep.* 4: *PG* 91.416B11–417A2; *Ep.* 24: *PG* 91.612C7–11), as well as everlasting shame, remorse, hatred, and ignorance of God's love (*Ep.* 1: *PG* 91.389A8–B9; *Ep.* 24: *PG* 91.612B1–4; *Quaest. ad Thal.* 11: *CCG* 7.89.22–91.32). Though he makes no allusions to a special state of temporary, purgative punishment, Maximus asserts that those "who have deeds of both sin and virtue to their name" at the time of final judgment will be purified by the painful process of judgment itself (*Quaest. et Dub.* 1, 10: *CCG* 10.142f.). In other passages, he identifies this purgative experience with the "fire" referred to in I Cor 2.13ff. (*Quaest. et Dub.* 159 [1, 74]: *CCG* 10.110f.), and with the final conflagration expected in apocalyptic literature (*Ep.* 4: *PG* 91.416C7–10). In the Origenist tradition, his instinct is to personalize and spiritualize the eschatological hope wherever possible, yet the very breadth and inclusiveness of his vision draws him beyond Origenism and allows his eschatology to be more broadly representative of biblical and popular expectations.

John of Damascus

If Maximus brought the Greek Patristic tradition of theological speculation to new depth and integration, it was the Syrian monk John of Damascus (*c.* 650–*c.* 750) who organized and synthesized that tradition with unprecedented clarity and consistency, and so truly brought the Patristic age, in the East, to a close. In all his many doctrinal, ascetical and homiletic works, John has surprisingly little to say about the Christian eschatological hope;[97] what he does say forms a terse and classic expression of later Greek eschatology.

In his *Expositio Fidei* (= *De Fide Orthodoxa*), an explanation of basic Christian doctrine that forms the final section of his three-part *Summa* of Christian knowledge, the πηγὴ γνώσεως (*Fount of Knowledge*), John devotes the last two chapters to a thoroughly biblical discussion of the Antichrist and the resurrection of the body (cc. 99–100: ed. B. Kotter [Berlin 1973] 232–39).

Rejecting the notion that the Antichrist will be an incarnation of the devil (Kotter 233.31ff.), John insists he will be an ordinary mortal, born in fornication and possessed by Satanic power. He will be received enthusiastically by the Jews (232.23) and will persecute the Church, deceiving many people with false signs and wonders (233.39–43). To resist him, God will send the prophets Enoch and Elijah again, but both will be put to death (233.44–47); then Christ will come again on the clouds of heaven, just as he once ascended in glory, and will overthrow "the man of lawlessness" (233.47-234.52).

John then turns to the Christian hope of resurrection, asserting that the God who created our bodies from the earth can raise them once again incorruptible, and reunite them to our souls (234.2–11). The first reason for the resurrection, he argues, is that it is required by God's justice: if the soul does not realize vice and virtue apart from the body, the body must share in its punishment or reward (284.12–285.26). After a lengthy discussion of scriptural evidence for a bodily resurrection, John concludes with a brief reference to the judgment of Christ (238.123ff.). The devils, the Antichrist and all sinners will be consigned to eternal fire: "not material fire, as we know it, but a kind of fire that God knows" (238.127f.). The just will share eternal life with Christ, "seeing him and being seen, and enjoying as his gift joy without end" (239.128–31).

Here and in other works, John emphasizes that the soul, after death, is no longer subject to change, and so naturally remains, like the angels and demons, forever in the condition of its final self-determination (*Exp. Fid.* 86:

Kotter 191.15ff.; *Dial. contra Manichaeos* 75: *PG* 94.1573B1–5). For the soul that has been purified of earthly passions during life, this likeness to the angels after death means that it will eternally share in their knowledge of God, illumined by the light of the Trinity (*De Virtutibus et Vitiis*: *PG* 95.93D6–9). Filled with the Holy Spirit in their souls and even in their buried bodies, the saints are united to the divinity of Christ and become like him by participation, so that they can truly be called "gods" (*De Imaginibus* 1: *PG* 94.1249C2–D3; *Exp. Fid.* 88: Kotter 203.8–11). With characteristic lucidity and restraint, John Damascene brings the early Church's hope for human divinization to its final, unmistakable form as a vital part of the Christian tradition.

The end of all flesh: eschatology in the sixth-century West

The final period of Latin Patristic theology can roughly be identified with the sixth century: a time of violence, social turmoil and political unrest, as the Latin world was gradually brought under the control of migrating Germanic peoples. Contact between the Eastern and Western Churches, like the cultural and political relations of Byzantium and the Latin world, became strained in these years and was occasionally marred by hostile controversies. Classical learning continued to be pursued vigorously in the West, by aristocrats such as Boethius and Cassiodorus; sixth-century Latin bishops were often men of letters, like Avitus of Vienne and Ennodius of Pavia, and Christian Latin poetry reached a technical zenith in the biblical paraphrases of Dracontius and the hymns of Venantius Fortunatus. Still, the end of the sixth century undoubtedly witnessed a decline in the availability and quality of education in the West, and in the public promotion of Latin culture. The result for the life of the Church was a temporary end to original Latin theology after the death of Gregory the Great. And the sense of foreboding, the perception of decay and impending disaster, that was already apparent in fifth-century Christian writings came to dominate the Church's preaching by Gregory's pontificate, and to lend it a new apocalyptic tone. Even as eschatology lost much of its intellectual sophistication, it became, by the beginning of the seventh century, the central Christian concern.

Julianus Pomerius

Practically nothing is known about the life of Julianus Pomerius, an African rhetor who emigrated to Arles in southern Gaul late in the fifth century and there became a priest and widely admired teacher and writer. Julianus corresponded with a number of eminent Churchmen of the period, and briefly had Caesarius, later bishop of Arles, as his pupil about 497.[1] Julianus' only extant work, *On the Contemplative Life*, shows the strong influence of

Augustine in thought and in style.[2] Purporting to be a response to ten questions sent to the author by a bishop who is also named Julianus, the work first discusses the relationship between the contemplative and the active life in the episcopal ministry, and then offers a more general treatment of vices and virtues, meant to apply to all Christians. Although it makes no allusions to a sense of approaching crisis or to an imminent end of history, Julianus' treatise frequently refers to future beatitude and punishment as the full, everlasting realities of which earthly bliss and suffering are only a passing shadow. Thus, although it lacks eschatological urgency, Julianus' work reflects a kind of spirituality in which concern for the afterlife has become a main source of pastoral motivation, the test of the seriousness of Christian life and the hallmark of responsible preaching (see, e.g., 1.15; 2.14).

Julianus begins his discussion of the contemplative life with a series of chapters on eternal beatitude and on the risen body (1.1–7), since contemplation, which essentially consists in seeing God, will only be realized fully in eternity as the reward of the just (1.1.1). Although we can now "see" God "in part" (I Cor 13.9) by meditative prayer and by a lived faith (1.6), Scripture makes it clear that the real vision of God is reserved, even for the pure in heart, for "the future life" (1.7). Echoing Augustine's terminology, Julianus presents the life of eternal beatitude as a return of the human person to his "homeland" (1.1.2; 1.4.1; 1.10; 1.12.2; 3.12.3; 3.13; 3.28.2; 3.31.5; etc.), where he will join the angels as his equals in a single, heavenly "city" (1.2; 1.4.1; 1.12.2; etc.). It will be a state of endless joy (1.1.1), a life "happily everlasting and everlastingly happy, where there is true security, secure tranquillity, tranquil happiness, happy eternity, eternal happiness" (1.2). Although everyone will have a different status and glory in heaven, corresponding to his or her merits, all will be completely satisfied (1.4.3). Each person will be completely transparent, in thought and desire, to all the rest, yet completely without embarrassment (1.4.1), for all will be unable to sin (1.9). This mutual openness will lead to a "divine and reciprocal love" that will bind the citizens of heaven to each other eternally, as well as to God (1.4.1; cf. 1.11).

Julianus includes the body in this future state of contemplative bliss, conceiving the resurrection as the recovery of the full image of God, in which the human person was created. So the risen man or woman will essentially be the human person without his or her present, sinful flaws, enjoying "understanding without error, memory without forgetfulness, thought without wanderings . . ." Any damage done to the body in this life will be repaired, and "incorruptible soundness will preserve those bodies which will have been renewed in all their members" (1.4.2). Sexual identity will be preserved in the risen body, but without passion (1.11); both perception and movement will be as swift as willing itself, since none of the conditions that presently slow the body's response to the will shall remain (*ibid.*).

The damned will also be raised incorruptible, Julianus emphasizes (1.3.1), but will be permanently separated from the just "not only in recompense but in location" (*ibid.*). Although he echoes the traditional description of the place of the damned, in order to inspire salutary fear in his readers (3.12.3), Julianus stresses the moral and psychological aspects of damnation rather than its physical tortures. So the "binding" of the condemned is, above all, their eternal inability to do good (3.12.2; cf. 1.3.2, on their loss of all desire to change for the better); the "exterior darkness" is their banishment from God as the light of created minds (3.12.2). The "fire" of hell is also "useless repentance," the "worm" an eternally reproachful conscience (*ibid.*). Although the damned, like the saved, will exist unchanged forever, unconsumed by the flames that attack them, their existence could more properly be called eternal death, "a state of pain rather than of life" (*ibid.*).

In all of his detailed reflections on the eternal rewards and punishments that await us after death, Julianus does little more than repeat the expectations of an individual and ecclesial eschatology that had already had a long history in the Latin Church. His insistence on the continuity of the present life of contemplation and future human fulfillment recalls the more philosophical Christian anthropology of Clement of Alexandria and Origen. In his classical restraint, however, and in his choice of certain Augustinian themes (e.g., the society of angels; the transparency and mobility of risen bodies; the unchangeability of both saved and damned), Julianus' influential treatise moved the Western tradition a step further towards the coherent view of the afterlife that was to prevail in orthodox eschatology from the sixth century onwards.

Caesarius of Arles

Caesarius (*c.* 470–543), bishop of Arles and metropolitan of Southern Gaul during the first four decades of the sixth century, dominated the ecclesiastical and civil life of the region during much of his lifetime and left a theological and spiritual legacy that was to last far longer. Besides his leadership in having a moderate version of the Augustinian doctrine of grace canonized at the Synod of Orange in 529, Caesarius' main contribution to theological literature was the large collection of sermons associated with his name: either his own original homilies or the works of earlier Fathers excerpted and rewritten at his direction, all intended for use in rural churches where local priests felt unable to preach on their own.[3] The content of these sermons is essentially moral, and constantly shows Caesarius' urgent concern to call Gallic Christians away from the remains of paganism and towards a stricter standard of ethical and ascetical practice. Although he is uninterested in apocalyptic detail, and seems to assume that the end of the world lies in the indefinite, even distant future (see *Serm.* 154.5; 157.1), Caesarius – like his countryman Salvian fifty years earlier – constantly alludes to the coming judgment to motivate his hearers to seek a holy way of life, and to expiate past sins by almsgiving (e.g., *Serm.* 157, 158, 224, 227, 228).

In one of his most typical phrases, Caesarius often reminds his hearers that they must expect to appear "before the tribunal of the eternal judge" (e.g., *Serm.* 7.1; 175.5; 220.3; 221.5; 227.3; 230.6). Christ will then appear with great majesty, "surrounded by the light of the heavenly hosts"; and as the human race is raised, trembling with fear, from the depths of the earth, "the Lord, now more just than merciful, will begin to demand an account of each one's life" (*Serm.* 57.4). In that trial, the devil will act as adversary and accuser of each human suspect (*Serm.* 21.5 [possibly from Augustine]; 178.3), but all will be called to give honest account of the use they have made of God's gifts (*Serm.* 89.5; 142.8).

Alluding repeatedly to the picture of the coming judgment in Matt 25.31– 46, Caesarius insists that, provided one avoids very serious and habitual crimes (*Serm.* 32.2f.), Christ's ultimate norm for conviction or acquittal will be how each person has acted towards the poor and weak; "no one can live without sin," he observes, "yet with the Lord's help everyone can redeem his sins by almsgiving" (*Serm.* 158.2; cf. 157.3; 224.4; etc.). For priests and bishops (*Serm.* 2, preface), as for all Christians, nothing is a more effective spur to moral responsibility than "to endeavor always to think of the day of our death and the terrible, dreadful judgment" (*Serm.* 56.1; cf. *Serm.* 17.2f.; 57.2; 157,4; etc.).

Caesarius' allusions to the resurrection, to the beatitude of the just and the punishment of the damned are traditional and surprisingly lacking in graphic details. Heaven, for Caesarius, is the place of eternal joy (e.g., *Serm.* 150.3) and rest (e.g., *Serm.* 151.2), where the just will be "adorned with the garments of [their] own charity" (*ibid.*, 8). Surrounded by angels, who will be their equals and "fellow citizens" (e.g., *Serm.* 19.1; 150.3; 151.2), the saved will find in the heavenly Jerusalem their true homeland (e.g., *Serm.* 7.2; 36.6f.; 150.3; 151.2). In one unusually detailed reflection on heaven, Caesarius predicts that the risen bodies of the saints will shine there as brightly as the sun, and will be free both from physical infirmities and from all conflict between flesh and spirit. There will be no need for food or sleep there, no envy (despite the differing grades of glory) and no further possibility to commit sin. Perfectly happy, the just will "never tire of giving thanks" for their eternal inheritance (*Serm.* 58.4).

Hell, on the other hand, is presented by Caesarius as the state of "eternal death" (e.g., *Serm.* 1.12; 16.4; 100A.6), made painful not simply by the absence of God, but by everlasting fire (e.g., *Serm.* 53.3; 140.6 [largely from Augustine]); 157.3f.; 158.3f.). "The burning pit of hell will be open, and there will be a way down to it but no rising from it . . . There will be a wide path into the abyss, but no breath or free respiration will be left when the doors press down from above" (206.3; cf. 167.5 [both largely Augustinian]). Far more painful than earthly excommunication, the exclusion of the damned from God's presence will mean "night without the light of day, bitterness without pleasure, darkness without light" (*Serm.* 227.4); the fire of hell will torture its victims all the more because it preserves them as it burns (*Serm.* 31.4).

A few homilies in the Caesarian corpus, apparently alluding to I Cor 3:11–15, refer to a "purgative fire" (*purgatorius ignis*), in which less serious sins will be removed in the day of judgment. In *Serm.* 167.6f. (a work identical with Sermon 6 in the collection of "Eusebius Gallicanus"[4]), Caesarius depicts the souls and risen bodies of all as passing through "the reasonable discipline of flames" at the time of judgment. Because it is "wise fire," this ordeal will "punish a person as much as his guilt demands" (167.6), but will spare and even refresh the bodies of the just (*ibid.*, 7; cf. *Serm.* 206.3). In *Serm.* 179, Caesarius warns his hearers against presuming that all sins will be punished in this temporary way; only "slight offenses" will be purged in the day of judgment, and then only if they are not too numerous (*Serm.* 179.1), and if the sinner has not been careless about "redeeming" them by works of mercy in this life (*ibid.*, 8). Since one day with the Lord is as a thousand years, the day of judgment will assuredly seem very long to those who are being purged, and "that fire of purgation will be more difficult than any punishment in this world that can be seen or imagined or felt" (*ibid.*, 5). In all three of these Sermons dealing with purgative punishment, Caesarius emphasizes that it will affect both soul and body, and he identifies it with the process of judgment; there is no trace in his writings of the idea that such purgation will be accomplished in the "interim" between death and resurrection, nor does he show any particular interest in the fate of souls before the final judgment.[5] His eschatology, in this respect as in others, is essentially biblical and traditional, and remains at the service of his homiletic purposes.

The *Carmen ad Flavium Felicem*

The same use of descriptions of the afterlife for the purpose of moral exhortation characterizes a Latin poem written in North Africa in the late fifth or early sixth century, and ascribed in the manuscripts to Cyprian of Carthage: The *Carmen ad Flavium Felicem de Resurrectione Mortuorum et de*

Iudicio Domini.[6] "If anyone wants to avoid the pains of eternal fire . . ." the poet begins, "he must remember God alone, who weighs the whole world in his scales" (40–44). As soon as the soul "lays down the burden of its members" in death, it goes to its proper reward, in darkness or in joy (88–96), to await the resurrection. The resurrection of the body is certain: as creator, God surely has the power to restore dead bodies to their original form (105–10).

The poet then describes, in vivid, often majestic language, the coming of God and his angelic ministers (137–52), the opening of the earth to release the great and varied throng of rising dead (153–75), and the solemn scene of judgment (176–85). The just will be clothed in light and sent "to the blooming kingdom of old, to groves ever pleasant and green, where they will live forever in bodily splendor" (189–92). After a long and sensuous description of the garden of Paradise (193–249), the poet turns to the punishments reserved for sinners, for those who have failed to thank God for his gifts in this life (278–97). They will go "to the dark fires, to the sulphurous depths" (298), and suffer there forever. At the end of history, as the fire of hell surges up to consume the universe (305–32), the damned will cry out in fear "and want now to know the God they have refused to know before" (335). After alluding to the predictions of these things by the prophets, the poet ends with an urgent appeal to his readers: while there is still time, "look out for your own salvation" by turning from sin to prayer, good works and the observance of God's law (380–406).

Primasius; Apringius

A growing interest at this time in interpreting the biblical apocalyptic tradition is suggested by two Latin commentaries on the Johannine Apocalypse, written during the middle decades of the sixth century. Primasius (d. after 553), bishop of Hadrumetum in North Africa and an important Western participant in the Council of Constantinople of 553, composed his full and careful commentary[7] sometime before 543, when it was mentioned by Cassiodorus (*Inst.* 9). Primasius admittedly bases his interpretation on the commentary of Tyconius and on Augustine's *De Civitate Dei* xx–xxii, and so tends to be similarly restrained in his speculations about the end, taking the Apocalypse to refer principally to the time of the Church.

Apringius, bishop of Beja in modern Portugal, composed a briefer commentary shortly after 553, of which large fragments remain.[8] Somewhat more daring than Primasius in his allegorical interpretation, Apringius shows more interest in the Christological and moral implications of the Johannine Apocalypse than in applying it to human history. His commentary was largely incorporated into the eighth-century compilation of the Spanish bishop Beatus of Liebana.[9]

Neither of these sixth-century Latin commentaries on the Apocalypse shows any particular sense that the end of history is near, or makes more than passing and conventional references to the Church's eschatological hope.

Gregory the Great

By the end of the sixth century, however, the atmosphere of Christian expectation had darkened considerably: mainly because of the strong sense of eschatological crisis that penetrated the writings of the Western Church's most prominent and eloquent spokesman of the age, Pope Gregory the Great (c. 540–604). Although a man of considerable learning, Gregory had little interest in the secular sciences and philosophy, and characteristically explained the events of history and the phenomena of the world around him less in terms of natural causes than as signs of God's providential care for creation, and of God's struggle against the forces of evil.[10] As a result, while Augustine remained cautious about reading in the disasters of his day signs that the end was near (see especially *Ep.* 199), Gregory did so without hesitation. Living in an Italy that was economically and socially ravaged by the Lombard invasions, and personally overwhelmed by a sense of Rome's political decline, the former *praefectus urbi* was convinced that the Parousia and judgment were not far off, and considered it one of his chief pastoral responsibilities, as bishop of Rome, to communicate this sense of impending crisis to his hearers and to the wider Christian world.

"In all his words and acts," writes Gregory's ninth-century biographer, John the Deacon, "Gregory considered that the final day and the coming judgment were imminent; the closer he felt the end of the world was coming, with its numerous disasters, the more carefully he pondered all human affairs" (*Vita* 4.65: *PL* 75.214A15–B5). The Lombard invasion of Italy, with all its accompanying devastation of buildings and crops, had convinced Gregory that "the world was not merely announcing its end, but pointing directly to it" (*Dial.* 3.38.3: *SC* 260.430.35f.); as his friend, bishop Redemptus of Ferentino, learned from the martyr Justicus in a dream, "The end of all flesh had come" (*ibid.*, 2:428.18f.). Following a long Latin tradition, Gregory saw in the social ills of his time signs that "the world had grown old" (*Hom. in Ev.* 1.1.1: *PL* 76.1077c7f.), and was showing the symptoms of its final agony (*ibid.*, 5: 1080c2–14; cf. *Hom. in Ezek.* 2.6.22ff. [593]: *CCL* 142.310–13).[11] All the signs predicted by the Bible for the final days of history were now realities: "The very plagues of the earth have now become like the pages of our books" (*Ep.* 3.29 [April 593]: *CCL*

140.175.41f.). "There will be no delay," he writes grimly to the Emperor Maurice; "heaven will burn, earth will burn, the elements will blaze up, and the awful judge will appear with angels and archangels, with thrones and dominations, with principalities and powers" (*Ep* 3.61 [August 593]: *CCL* 140.210.51–54). In the apparent arrogance of his brother bishop, John of Constantinople, Gregory could already see the pride of the Antichrist at work (*Ep.* 5.39 [June 595]: *CCL* 140.316.48f.; 7.30 [June 597]: *ibid.*, 491.31ff.).[12]

Yet the picture Gregory paints is not simply a bleak one. Although the world was at war, the Church was internally at peace – a sign that further tribulations predicted in the gospels were still to come (*Mor. in Job* 19.9.16: *CCL* 143A.968). The preaching of the gospel and the influence throughout the known world of Christian doctrine, the "teaching of the wise" (*doctorum scientia*), meant that faith was on the increase, and "each day the knowledge of God was more widely revealed" (*ibid.*, 9.11.15: 143.467.83–89). Like a nesting bird, the Church was nurturing more and more fledgling Christians in her peaceful bosom (*ibid.*, 19.27.48: 143A.994f.). "The more richly, in fact, that she is enriched by new members," he observes, "the more clearly she reveals that time is moving towards the end of this present age" (*ibid.*, 35.15.35: *PL* 76.769B8ff.), but has not quite reached its goal.

Although the signs of the times show the nearness of the end, he writes to Ethelbert, king of Kent, one can rest assured that "not all these things will happen in our day" (*Ep.* 11.37: *CCL* 140A.931.50f.); there is still time to prepare oneself, and still time to extend the peace of the Church through missionary activity. The main point of Gregory's eschatological urgency, in fact, is not to spread gloom but to move his correspondents and hearers to fear God and his judgments (*Hom. in Ev.* 1.1.1: *PL* 76.1077C9–13), to learn not to love a passing world (*ibid.*, 1.4.2: 1090B5–15), and to "lift up their minds in hope of the glory that is to follow, confident because of the resurrection of their Redeemer" (*Mor. in Job* 13.24.28: *CCL* 143A.684.30f.).[13]

Gregory saw in the disasters of his age a constant reminder not only of the endangered situation of all humanity, but of the death, judgment and retribution that directly challenged each individual. "We must consider carefully," he urges his hearers, "how terrible the hour of our departure will be, what mental terror will be ours, how much we will remember past sufferings and forget past happiness, how great will be our fear and respect for our judge" (*Hom. in Ev.* 2.39.8: *PL* 76.1298C11–15). Death is always a moment of cosmic struggle: demons loom over the dying person, ready to carry him off (*ibid.*, 4: 1294B11–C14; 8: 1298D4–7),[14] but Jesus and Mary also come to receive faithful souls (*Dial.* 4.17f.: *SC* 265.68–72). For many people, Gregory believes, death is a moment of special illumination from

God, above all a time when the mysteries of life after death are revealed (*Dial.* 4.27.1: *SC* 265.86). For others, the pain and terror of death can be a means of expiating minor faults (*ibid.*, 4.24.2–25.1: *SC* 265.82). Yet for the good, death is also a release from the evils of the world's final days, God's means of gathering "living stones" to build the heavenly Jerusalem (*Dial.* 3.37.22: *SC* 260.426).

Gregory's reflections on the details of the afterlife, by contrast, are homely, restrained and traditional. He stresses that the souls of the just go immediately to be with Christ in bliss at their death (*Dial.* 4.26.1f.: *SC* 265.84), even though their happiness will be all the greater when they are reunited with their bodies at the resurrection (*ibid.*, 3:84ff.). The souls of sinners, likewise, go directly to hell (*Dial.* 4.29: *SC* 265.98), where they suffer in a spiritual way from recognizing that they are immersed forever in corporeal fire (*ibid.*, 30.2: 100). Gregory cautiously asserts that hell is a region below the earth (*ibid.*, 44: 156ff.), and that a single fire burns there, in which each sinner suffers according to his or her own deserts (*ibid.*, 45: 160).[15] God's justice requires that the punishments of hell be eternal, even though human sins are of finite malice, because the truly hardened sinner has shown by his or her actions that he or she wishes to remain permanently in a state of sin (*ibid.*, 46.3: 162). Both the just in heaven and the damned in hell are "gathered into bundles" to experience their reward or punishment with those of similar deserts, since both joy and pain are enhanced by companionship (*ibid.*, 36.13f.: 122ff.; cf. 34: 112–16). Although both the just and the damned will be able to see each other, at least in the time before the resurrection, and will experience still greater joy or pain as a result (*Hom. in Ev.* 2.40.8: *PL* 76.1308D3–1309B7), only the inhabitants of heaven know what is happening on earth, because in contemplating God they know all things (*Mor. in Job* 12.21.26: *CCL* 644f.).

In his *Life of Gregory* 1.28–30 (*PL* 75.73ff.), John the Deacon reports a disputation that Gregory had with Eutychius, patriarch of Constantinople, on the nature of the risen body, shortly before the patriarch's death in the spring of 582, while Gregory was still a deacon and the papal representative in the Eastern capital. In a pamphlet he had written, the patriarch apparently defended a moderately Origenistic conception of the resurrection, emphasizing the spiritual and transcendent character of the glorified body; as Gregory understood him, Eutychius was thus arguing that "our body will be impalpable in that glorious risen state, more subtle than the winds and the air" (*Mor. in Job* 14.72: *SC* 212.434). Gregory – in the wake of the condemnation of Origenism in 543 and 553 – considered the patriarch's position heretical, and after a public debate succeeded in persuading the Emperor, Tiberius II Constantine (Emperor 578–82), to have the pamphlet burned (*Life* 29; Gregory, *Mor. in Job* 14.74). In the disputation and in his own homilies on Job, delivered shortly afterwards to his monastic companions, Gregory insists that if the risen body is truly to be in continuity with our present body, it cannot undergo any substantial transformation: "in the glory of the resurrection, our body will surely be subtle, as a result of its spiritual power, but it will be palpable because of its true nature" (*Mor. in Job* 14.72). The transformation our flesh will undergo in being raised from the dead will be, above all, a moral one – a liberation from the tyranny of the passions; but it will not include any change in its fundamental, material character.[16]

On the subject of a "cleansing fire" (*purgatorius ignis*) for lesser sins after death, Gregory exhibits the same caution that Augustine had shown. Scripture tells us, he says, that some sins can be forgiven "in the world to come," so "we must believe in a cleansing fire before the judgment for certain minor faults" – unnecessary talk or laughter, for example, or excessive concern with this world's goods (*Dial.* 4.41.3f.: SC 265.148). But Gregory is uncertain whether this purgation, referred to by Paul in I Cor 3.12–15, is achieved in "the fire of suffering we experience in this life," or "the cleansing fire of the world to come" (*ibid.*, 5:150). He seems hesitant to speak of a third "place" for temporary, purgative suffering after death. Nevertheless, he strenuously defends the usefulness of offering Masses for the souls of the dead, as bringing about pardon of their sins (*Dial.* 4.57: SC 265.184–94), and his anecdote about the dead monk Justus, who is released from "the torments of fire" after the Eucharist has been offered for him for thirty consecutive days (*ibid.*, 57.14f.: 192), suggests he is thinking of this temporary purgation as having a distinctive venue of its own. The later Western notion of Purgatory, as well as the custom of offering "Gregorian Masses" for the recently deceased, drew much of its inspiration from this passage.[17]

With Gregory the Great, Latin Patristic eschatology reached its final form. His intense conviction that the end of history was near – a conviction that seems to have been a peculiar preoccupation of his own, as well as a characteristic notion of his troubled age[18] – reflected a recurrent mood in Western Christianity's reading of human history; it proved, in fact, to be mistaken, as it had been before. Nevertheless, Gregory's concern for dying well, and his clear and concrete conception of the afterlife, woven together out of the biblical and theological tradition of the West and the popular religion of contemporary Italian believers, became a principal source for Latin eschatology in the centuries to come. Drawn upon by Isidore of Seville (c. 580–633) for his own encyclopaedic compilations of Christian thought, excerpted and arranged schematically by Julian of Toledo (c. 652–90) in his eschatological handbook, the *Prognosticon Futuri Saeculi*,[19] and embellished with further folkloric material by the erudite Bede (672–735), Gregory's picturesque understanding of what awaited the human soul at death became the starting-point for much of medieval preaching, ascetical practice and theological speculation. The reason, perhaps, was less its depth than its nearness to home: it was an eloquent distillation of the age-old hopes and fears of Latin Christianity.

Epilogue: a common hope

At the end of this survey of Patristic eschatological thought, one might justly wonder if it is proper at all to speak in the singular of "the hope of the early Church." The range of images and ideas we have seen among early Christian writers, expressing their expectations for the future of planet and individual, saint and sinner, suggests that one might perhaps better speak of many facets of a rapidly developing, increasingly detailed Christian view of human destiny, of many hopes – and many fears – enveloped within a single, growing, ever more complex tradition of early Christian faith and practice.

In the broadest terms, a certain direction in the evolution of early Christian eschatology is evident: from a sense of imminent apocalyptic crisis to a well-developed theology of creation, a future-oriented cosmology and anthropology; from a vivid expectation of the end of this historical order, followed by the raising of the dead and the creation of the wholly new human world, to a systematic doctrine of "the last things" as the final piece in a Christ-centered view of history's whole; from an early focus on the community's hope for survival in the coming cosmic catastrophe, to a later preoccupation with the hope of the individual as he or she faces death. But this pattern, as our study has amply shown, is a general and somewhat superficial one, admitting of many variations of emphasis and detail; philosophers and polemicists, poets and spiritual writers, bishops in times of peace and prophets in times of persecution all had their own ways of assimilating and reshaping the growing eschatological tradition.

Are there, one may ask, any hints of a more profound continuity within this complicated narrative of hope? What discernible shape, if any, had eschatology taken within the emerging consensus of orthodox Christian doctrine in East and West by the end of what is commonly regarded as the Patristic age, the close of the seventh century? What issues remained open, as "disputed questions," for medieval preaching and spiritual theology, and

216

for the Greek and Latin schoolmen who drew on Patristic theology as their normative source for interpreting the biblical tradition?

Hope and faith

One thing is clear from the beginning of Christian literature: hope for the future is an inseparable, integral dimension of Christian faith, and the implied condition of possibility for responsible Christian action in the world. "From the confession of faith," writes St. Augustine (*Enchiridion* 30.114), "is born the good hope of the faithful, with holy charity as its companion." Hope, for the Christian disciple, is the indispensable link between faith and love: the affirmation of real possibilities for the world and oneself, the awareness of a promise for the future, which gives to the person of faith the freedom to give himself or herself away, to God and to his or her neighbor, with liberated imagination and with a generosity unhampered by the anxious need to secure the future on his or her own. And since the heart of the Christian gospel, as Paul reminds his readers, is the proclamation that Jesus is risen from the dead (I Cor 15.1–11), that the crucified Jesus is "Lord" (Rom 10.8f.; II Cor 4.5; Phil 2.11), and that the death and resurrection of Jesus mean the possibility of reconciliation with God and "new creation" for the whole of sinful humanity (II Cor 5.17–19), the hope that springs from Christian faith is clearly a hope centered on the risen Christ, a hope that what faith sees accomplished in him will be accomplished also, through union with him, in those who dare to be his disciples (see I Cor 15.12–23). Christian hope, rooted in faith and empowering the believer to love, is understood by Paul to be a vital part of the graced relationship between the believer and God that is experienced as the work of the Holy Spirit: "Since we are justified by faith, we have peace with God through our Lord Jesus Christ. Through him we have obtained access to this grace in which we stand, and we rejoice in our hope of sharing the glory of God . . . And hope does not disappoint us, because God's love has been poured into our hearts through the Holy Spirit which has been given to us" (Rom 5.1–5).

One finds relatively little direct reflection on this Christocentric and Pneumatic quality of Christian hope in the Patristic literature we have surveyed, yet the starting assumption is always the same: the Christian can look forward to the resurrection of his or her own body, to a merciful judgment and to a lasting, transforming and utterly fulfilling union with God, because he or she is part of a community that believes Jesus is risen, reigns in glory, has sent forth his Spirit and will come again as judge of history. Christ is always the heart and goal of Christian hope, and as such, its source of unity.

Realism

Another key unifying element in early Christian eschatology is what one might call its realism: in a crescendo of consensus, although in a variety of ways, Patristic writers insist that the Christian lives in hope *within history*, and is freed by that hope to take history seriously. Jewish apocalyptic literature held out a hope for new beginnings, beyond the present order of time and space, to a people who had been led by centuries of oppression to doubt the possibility of the fulfillment of its hope within history. Platonic philosophy, supportive though it was of the religious instinct, implicitly discounted the value of the world of concrete, changeable individual things, while Stoicism called on the philosophic mind to resign itself to being consumed in the toils of an endless, cyclic cosmic process. Gnostic religion, in both its non-Christian and Christian forms, held out to its "enlightened" initiates the hope of escaping – in the spiritual, luminous core that was their best self – from the visible world, the body, and the institutions of everyday life, all of which it regarded as the product of a primordial cosmic mistake. Much as it drew on all these traditions for its themes and images, Christian eschatology from the second century onwards insisted on the continuity of its hope with *this* world and its history: on the necessary inclusion of the body in the human person's final salvation, on the relevance of Church, sacraments and doctrine to one's ultimate fate before God, on the necessity of moral goodness within this present life for those who wish to share in a life to come and – perhaps most significantly – on the presence of the *eschaton* already within time in the person of the risen Jesus. The Spirit of Jesus, experienced within the community of faith, was for the early Christians "the guarantee of our inheritance, until we acquire possession of it" (Eph 1.14), the "first-fruits" of "the redemption of our bodies" (Rom 8.23). The finality of God's Kingdom had already begun in this perennially unstable human realm.

Different authors, as we have seen, emphasized the active presence of this promised, future salvation to different degrees. Aside from a few works of a more mystical character, however, like the *Odes of Solomon* or some fourth-century spiritual writings, there are not many clear examples of what New Testament scholars have called "realized eschatology" in the Patristic period; most Patristic authors are, in their own ways, painfully aware of the gulf between the present world and the world of promise. For the Greek tradition, which spoke of salvation in terms of the "divinization" of the believer since the time of Irenaeus and Clement of Alexandria, the Christian eschatological message reflected a tension between hope for the final realization of God's saving plan in Christ, on the universal stage of history, and the believer's hope to be assimilated to that plan in his or her own history. In terms of God's approach to us, writes Maximus the Confessor, the "end of the ages" has come; in terms of our approach to God, it still lies ahead, realized only in the "types and patterns" of the present life of grace (*Quaest ad Thal* 22).

More important for the West, perhaps, is the question of how far the present, historical order can actually be seen to anticipate the Kingdom of God in its social progress and in the external life of the Church. Some more optimistic voices, like that of Augustine's friend Orosius, could speak of the Christian Church and Empire in Eusebian terms, as embodying in a visible way the "first-fruits" of the Kingdom. But it was the Augustinian picture of a heavenly city, making its way as a pilgrim through time and living in only a provisional peace with the earthly city of creaturely self-seeking, that was to become the paradigm, in Latin theology, for conceiving the tension between present and future. Linked with the visible community of faith yet not identical with it, international in composition yet everywhere hidden in its actual dimensions, the City of God now lives, in Augustine's view, a life of hope and longing, rather than one of realization. Only when the restless motion of history comes to an end will the human heart find its rest in the God who "is always at work and always at rest" (*Conf.* 13.37.52). Even more than their Greek contemporaries, Augustine and his Latin followers saw the realization of the gospel's promise as a state literally beyond time, as a share in God's eternity.

Common doctrine

Risky though it always is to speak of a consensus among theologians, one may at least discern the outlines of a common eschatological *doctrine*, as well as these common axioms or presuppositions, emerging in the writings we have studied, despite many variations of interpretation and emphasis on the part of individual writers.

(a) Central, for instance, to the early Christian theological tradition is what has been called a *"linear" view of history*: the conviction that history has an origin and an end, both rooted in the plan and the power of God. So both the Gnostic contempt of the temporal world and Origen's apparent flirtation with the possibility of future cycles of salvation-history were sharply rejected by most Orthodox writers as making the gospel absurd. Sixth-century apologists contested, with equal fervor, Platonic theories on the eternity of the world. In order to be a history of salvation, time must have its limits and must move unrepeatably in a single direction.

219

(b) Equally central to Patristic eschatological thought is the insistence that the fulfillment of human history must include the *resurrection of the body*. From the tracts of the second-century apologists, through Methodius' critique of Origen, to the detailed speculations of Gregory of Nyssa and Augustine's *De Civitate Dei*, Christian writers stressed the need to take the biblical promise of resurrection literally, and went to extraordinary lengths to argue that such a hope is neither impossible nor unworthy of human dignity. Since the body is an integral part of ourselves, and an integral part of God's good creation, the body must share in whatever salvation is promised.

(c) Following the expectations of both the Jewish Scriptures and the New Testament, early Christian writers also agreed on the prospect of God's *universal judgment*. The God who created the human person capable of self-determination stands also in judgment, for the whole Patristic tradition, over each of our histories and all history together; and it is Christ, God's Word made flesh, who will embody and execute that judgment by coming to be visibly present in the world again at the end of its history. It is this sense of ultimate accountability to a God who sees all things, Patristic apologists constantly remind their readers, that is the foundation of Christian moral earnestness.

(d) From the end of the second century (Tertullian), Patristic writers begin also to suggest the prospect of a *judgment* pronounced by God *at the end of each individual's life*. Even before this, the apologists seem to assume that our personal histories each come to final resolution at death, rather than at the end of the world; so they began to hint at the conception of what modern theology calls an "interim state" between death and resurrection, during which the dead in some way begin to experience the fate that will be theirs in fullness when all history reaches its goal. Some early writers, like Justin and Irenaeus, explicitly reject the Greek philosophical notion that the soul is, with all its powers, immortal by nature, and conceive of this interim as a shadowy existence in Hades, the realm of the dead; the Syriac tradition speaks of a "sleep of souls," in a kind of suspended animation, between death and the resurrection. From Tertullian on, however, most Greek and Latin Patristic authors confidently accept Platonic philosophical arguments that the soul, as the conscious and self-determining core of the human person, is indestructible, and so anticipates its eternal fate, through a preliminary personal judgment, from the moment of death.

(e) With judgment comes also *retribution*. Following the Jewish apocalyptic tradition, as reflected in the New Testament, early Christian writers almost universally assumed that the final state of human existence, after God's judgment, will be permanent and perfect happiness for the good, and permanent, all-consuming misery for the wicked. Apocalyptic imagery continued to dominate the conception of both these states throughout the Patristic period, especially in the portraits drawn of the suffering of the damned. But it became commonplace, by the fourth century, to emphasize that the heart of both beatitude and damnation is to be found in the relation of the human creature to God: made for union with God, we find our fulfillment only in a loving adherence to him, and are consumed by self-destructive agony if we choose decisively to turn away from him. The pains of hell and the joys of heaven, in sensible terms, are more and more clearly presented, in later Patristic literature, as simply the effect on the body of one's fundamental relationship with God.

(f) Although few of them reflect much on it directly, early Christian theologians seem to share the general sense of their fellow believers that *the dead are still involved in the life of the Church*, both in praying for the living and in experiencing the benefit of their prayers. This sense of the "communion of saints" is most clearly expressed by Augustine, when he asserts that "the souls of the pious dead are not separated from the Church, which even now is the Kingdom of Christ" (*De Civ. Dei* 20.9). Gregory of Nyssa and later Greek writers drew on reports of ghosts to argue that souls, even when separated by death from their bodies, remain closely bound to the material world and its inhabitants. Salvation and the longing for it, though experienced distinctively by each human individual, are always seen as ecclesial, social and even cosmic events; before the final resolution of all history, every human person remains identified with the process of the world.

Areas of disagreement

If the outlines of a consensus among early Christian writers may be seen, despite the blurring of its edges, on these general points of eschatological hope, other questions remained undecided, even subjects of enduring controversy, at the close of the Patristic age.

(a) Opinions continued to vary widely about the *time and nearness of the world's end*: from the urgently immediate expectations of the Apostolic Fathers and apologists, to the longer horizons of sixth-century commentators on the Johannine Apocalypse, to the studied agnosticism of Augustine. Various writers at every period attempted to read a prediction of the time of the end from the Scriptures, often with the help of pre-Christian traditions about the ages of the world. Millenarian hopes, promising a period of earthly reward for the just before the dramatic dénouement of history, continued to be revived at various times and places, usually by authors who sensed themselves part of a persecuted minority. Though the majority of orthodox Patristic writers rejected millenarianism as an overly literal reading of Apoc 20.1–7 and explicitly discounted the ability of anyone to predict the end of the world, both themes have remained a perennially fascinating prospect for some Christians.

(b) Controversy also continued, throughout the Patristic period, on the *materiality and physical character of the resurrection*. Origen stressed the Pauline teaching that the risen body, although in continuity with its present form, will be "spiritual" and so unimaginably different from any historical, fleshly body; and though reaction against Origen's conception, shaped by Methodius and later by Jerome, was often astonishingly violent, it continued to have its appeal, even after the condemnation of certain "Origenist" propositions at Justinian's Councils of 543 and 553. Discussion of the qualities of the risen body by the Latin scholastics in the high Middle Ages, and even renewed discussion in our own time, point up just how mysterious and unclear in content the notion of bodily resurrection remains, despite its unquestioned acceptance by Christians as an article of faith and hope.

(c) Another disputed point, at the end of the Patristic age and beyond, was the actual *extent of eschatological salvation*. Origen's clear hope for the salvation of all spiritual creatures – the *apokatastasis pantōn* – was shared openly by Gregory of Nyssa and Evagrius, as well as by some sixth-century anti-Chalcedonian writers, but bitterly contested by others from Origen's time onwards. Jerome, even after his repudiation of Origen in 394, continued to argue that at least all Christian believers will experience the final mercy of God. Augustine assumed, on the other side, that the majority of human beings will not be saved and that even the perseverance of believers in the life of grace is far from assured. Both positions have found their passionate defenders throughout Christian history, and continue to be proposed in our own time. Both remain enshrouded in the double, mutually limiting mystery of God's providential love and the genuineness of human freedom.

(d) A less urgent question for the early Church, perhaps, but still a point of varying opinion, was the *possibility of change and progress for those whose final destiny has been determined*. Most ancient writers assume that the end of life in the body is also the end of human change and self-determination. Origen, however, followed by Gregory of Nyssa, suggested that souls after death continue to grow in their knowledge and desire for God; for Gregory, in fact, beatitude consists in continual progress towards deeper union with God, corresponding with a continual expansion of the human person's capacity to know and desire the Good (*Vita Moysis* 162f., 225f., 238f.). This issue must be seen, to a large extent, as an anthropological, even a metaphysical question: is human perfection to be found in continued growth or in the gift of changelessness? But it has wide-ranging implications for the Church's way of imagining the content of the final salvation that is promised.

(e) A related issue to the one we have just mentioned is that of the possibility of *purgation* from sin after death. Both Greeks and Jews, in the pre-Christian era, considered suffering to be, at least potentially, a way to wisdom and a personal means of expiating sin. Origen, who saw human suffering as part of a medicinal process aimed at the restoration of all souls to their original union with God, suggested the possibility of a long period of purgation after death for those who had not been sufficiently schooled during life. This theory, welcomed by later Origenists in East and West, was considered at least plausible by Augustine; Gregory the Great, at the end of the sixth century, speaks vividly of his own conviction that the souls of those who die imperfect in faith and virtue must be purged for a time in fire before being admitted to the presence of God. While it is true that the notion of Purgatory as a separate, interim "state" for some souls is first found, in developed form, in Western medieval theology, its roots clearly lie in both the Greek and the Latin Patristic tradition; yet it is equally clear that many Patristic authors oppose such a notion as compromising the finality of death and the judgment of God. Controversial in the early Church, the notion of purgation after death was to remain controversial in the ecumenical discussions of the Middle Ages and the post-Reformation West, and challenges theological interpretation still.

To return to our starting question: can one legitimately speak of "the hope of the early Church"? If one seeks such a hope in the finished form of conciliar definitions, or of an articulated and widely shared theological system, the answer is clearly no; the eschatological consensus we have sketched out here was far less well formed, far less consciously enunciated, in the Patristic centuries, than was the orthodox Christian doctrine of God or of the person of Christ. Nevertheless, the expectations of early Christians for the future formed, on the whole, a remarkably consistent picture, despite serious areas of unresolved disagreement.

The reason, I suggest, is that beyond the influences of apocalyptic speculation and Platonic philosophy, of classical poetry and of pagan folklore – all of which clearly had their influence on the Church's articulation of its belief – the real basis of Christian hope for the future is the experience of Christians now: the sense that as disciples of Jesus, who is risen, they are already sharers in a larger, richer stream of life, whose full dimensions lie hidden from their minds. Living within history and affirming its lasting value because it has become, in Christ, God's history, the Christian conceives of this history as capable of finally revealing God's "plan for the fullness of time" (Eph 1.10). Christ, who fulfilled that plan in time, is himself the only norm by which the Christian judges history, and so Christ is understood to be God's norm and agent of judgment, too. Christ's resurrection becomes, for his disciples in every age, the promise of resurrection for all humanity; Christ's summons to join in his way becomes an invitation to share in the purification and growth that must precede a share in the Kingdom he reveals.

From the vantage point of faith in the risen Lord, human time is wrapped in eternal love; the many hopes that rise – gropingly, picturesquely – in the heart of the believer are really only attempts to articulate in words the one abiding "mystery, which is Christ in you, your hope of glory" (Col 1.27). It is as an expression of the mystery of Christ that all Christian eschatology finds its unity and its meaning.

NOTES

Introduction

1. See K. Rahner, "The Hermeneutics of Eschatological Assertions," *Theological Investigations* IV (London 1966) 323–46.
2. *Die Entestehung des christlichen Dogmas* (Bern/Tübingen ²1954).
3. See, for example, O. Cullmann's criticism of Werner's thesis: "Das wahre durch die ausgebliebene Parusie gestellte neutestamentliche Problem," *ThZ* 3 (1947) 177–91; also *Christus und die Zeit* (Zurich ²1962; tr. *Christ and Time* [London 1962]). See, more recently, D. Flusser, "Salvation Present and Future," in R. J. Z. Werblowsky and C. J. Bleeker (eds.), *Types of Redemption* (= Supplement to *Numen* 18 [Leiden 1970]) 46–61; D. E. Aune, "The Significance of the Delay of the Parousia for Early Christianity," in G. F. Hawthorne (ed.), *Current Issues in Biblical and Patristic Interpretation* (= Festschr. M. C. Tenney [Grand Rapids 1975]) 87–109.
4. See the dissertation of A. R. Marmorstein, "Marking Well the End: Eschatological Solutions to Dilemmas Faced by the Ante-Nicene Church" (Diss. University of California, Davis 1988), which rightly stresses the consistency and continuity of eschatological hope within the growing pre-Nicene articulation of orthodox faith, and its close link with the ethical message of the early Church.

1 Visions of a new day: early Semitic Christianity and Christian apocalyptic

1. See U. Fischer, *Eschatologie und Jenseitserwartung im hellenistischen Diasporajudentum* (Berlin 1978).
2. See D. S. Russell, *The Method and Message of Jewish Apocalyptic, 200 B.C.–A.D. 100* (Philadelphia 1964); P. Vielhauer, "Apokalyptik des Urchristentums," in E. Hennecke (rev. W. Schneemelcher), *Neutestamentliche Apokryphen* (= NtA; Tübingen 1959–64) II.428–54 (Engl. edn. II.608–42); P. D. Hanson, *The Dawn of Apocalyptic* (Philadelphia 1979); J. J. Collins, *The Apocalyptic Imagination, An Introduction to the Jewish Matrix of Christianity* (New York 1982).
3. For an exposition of the characteristics of this broader kind of "Jewish Christianity," see especially J. Daniélou, *Théologie du judéo-christianisme* (Paris 1958) (Eng. tr.: *The Theology of Jewish Christianity* [tr. and ed. J. A. Baker, London/Chicago 1964]); also R. A. Kraft, "In Search of 'Jewish Christianity'

and its 'Theology.' Problems of Definition and Methodology," *RSR* 60 (1972) 81–92; A. F. J. Klijn, "The Study of Jewish Christianity," *NTS* 20 (1973–74) 419–31.

4. For evidence of the continued existence of such groups, probably in Syria, as late as the seventh or eighth century, see S. Pines, *The Jewish Christians of the Early Centuries of Christianity according to a New Source* (Israel Academy of Sciences and Humanities monograph [Jerusalem 1966]).

5. See Gal 4.1–10. The most comprehensive attempt to describe the theology of these sects – although highly speculative in places – is H. J. Schoeps, *Theologie und Geschichte des Judenchristentums* (Tübingen 1949); see also his shorter account, *Das Judenchristentum* (Bonn 1964), and his collected essays on the subject, *Urgemeinde, Judenchristentum, Gnosis* (Tübingen 1956). Patristic and early medieval references to such groups are collected conveniently in A. F. J. Klijn and G. J. Reinink, *Patristic Evidence for Jewish-Christian Sects* (Leiden 1973).

6. So Schoeps, *Theologie* 78–82.

7. *Ibid.*, 85.

8. For a survey of earlier literary and historical treatments of their origin, see *ibid.*, 37–63; cf. G. Strecker, *Das Judenchristentum in den Pseudo-Klementinen* (= TU 70 [Berlin 1958]); G. Strecker, reconstruction of fragments of the *Kerygmata Petrou* from the Pseudo-Clementine writings, *NtA* II.63–80 (Engl. edn. II.102–27); J. Rius-Camps, "Las Pseudoclementinas. Bases filologicas para una nueva interpretación," *Revista catalana de teologia* 1 (1976) 79–158.

9. *Theologie* 82f.; F. S. Jones, "The Pseudo-Clementines: A History of Research," *The Second Century* 2 (1982) 1–33, 63–96.

10. So Daniélou takes these works as the first documents of his study of "Jewish Christianity": *Theology* 11–28

11. For a translation of the text and introductory notes, see *NtA* II.468–98 (Engl. edn. II.633–83). For an investigation of parallels in Greek and Roman religion, see A. Dieterich, *Nekyia: Beiträge zur Erklärung der neuentdeckten Petrusapokalypse* (Berlin 1913). Cf. A. Ruegg, *Die Jenseitsvorstellungen vor Dante und die übrigen literarischen Voraussetzungen der "Divina Commedia"* (Einsiedeln 1945) I 238–50; M. Himmelfarb, *Tours of Hell. An Apocalyptic Form in Jewish and Christian Literature* (Philadelphia 1983).

12. *NtA* II.454–68 (Engl. edn. II.642–63).

13. *NtA* I.126–55 (Engl. edn 1.189–227). Cf. M. Hornschuh, *Studien zur Epistula Apostolorum* (Berlin 1965).

14. *NtA* II.488–98 (Engl. edn. II.689–703); the more recent English translation of this work, by B. M. Metzger in J. H. Charlesworth (ed.), *The Old Testament Pseudepigrapha* I (New York 1983) 516–59, follows the Latin manuscript tradition in calling the whole work, in sixteen chapters, simply *IV Ezra*.

15. *NtA* II.504–509, 510–25 (Engl. edn. II.712–19, 720–41).

16. So the Ethiopic version of the text; the Coptic version sets the date at 120 years after the resurrection. For an attempt to harmonize these two versions, as both referring to a date about the year 150, see L. Gry, "La Date de la parousie d'après l'Epistula apostolorum," *RB* 49 (1940) 86–97.

17. Already one notes in these two passages an apologetic, presumably anti-Gnostic insistence on the physical reality of the risen body and its continuity with the present body; in *Ep Ap* 19 it is explicitly connected with an insistence on the reality of the flesh of Christ. *Asc Is* 4.16f., on the other hand, makes it clear that the saints in glory wear only their "garments which are stored on high in the seventh heaven" – apparently an angelic body of light – and that they will leave their present bodies on earth (cf. 8.14f.; 26; 9.2, 9–11, 26; 11.40). For the idea that resurrection will be limited to those who have believed in the risen Christ, see the so-called "Third Letter to the Corinthians" in the late second-century *Acts of Paul* 8.3.24–32 (*NtA* II.260; Engl. edn. II.376f.).

18. For the history of this notion, which has its origin in Jewish apocalyptic, see A. Michel, "Feu du jugement," *DThC* 5.2 (1939) 2239–46.

19. This is the effect of M. R. James's emendation of the fragment (*JThS* 32 [1930] 270ff.), but it is not supported by the parallel text in the Ethiopic translation; cf. *NtA* II.480 (Engl. edn. II.679). On the imagery and concepts used here, cf. E. Peterson, "Die 'Taufe' im Acherusischen See," *VigChr* 9 (1955) 1–20 (= *Frühkirche, Judentum und Gnosis* [Rome 1959] 310–32).

20. *Ep Ap* 19, however, denies that there will be eating or drinking in the place of reward.

21. This insistence on the absence of private property, and of the social distinction it begets, is characteristic of the *Sibylline Oracles'* view of life after death, and probably reflects the socio-economic concerns of their authors; cf. VIII 107–21, where this same "classless society" is projected for the existence of the dead in Hades.

22. Cf. O. Knoch, *Eigenart und Bedeutung der Eschatologie im theologischen Aufriss des ersten Clemensbriefes* (Bonn 1964).

23. So B. Weiss, "Amt und Eschatologie im I Clemensbrief," *ThPh* 50 (1975) 70–83.

24. Cf. W. C. Van Unnik, "Le Nombre des élus dans la première Epître de Clément," *RHPhR* 42 (1962) 237–46.

25. The text and punctuation of this passage are somewhat uncertain.

26. See J. Daniélou, "La Typologie millénariste de la semaine," *VigChr* 2 (1948) 1–16; Daniélou, *Theology* 396–401; correcting his view, A. Hermans, *Le Pseudo-Barnabé est-il millénariste?* (Bruges/Paris 1960; summarized in *EThL* 35 [1959] 849–76).

27. For a literary analysis of the text of this chapter and a hypothetical reconstruction of its genesis, see R. Trevijano Etcheverría, "Discurso escatológico y relato apocalíptico en Didakhe 16," *Burg* 17 (1976) 365–94. For the eschatology of the *Didache* in general, see: A. Agnoletto, "Motivi etico-escatologici nella Didachè," in *Convivium Dominicum: Studi sull' Eucaristia nei Padri della Chiesa* (Catania 1959) 259–76; O. Giordano, "La escatologia nella Didachè," *Oikoumene* (Catania 1964) 121–39.

28. For a parallel to this conception of the Parousia, cf. *Ep Ap* 16; *Or Sib* VIII, 68–72.

29. The *Didache* here reflects an older rabbinic and apocalyptic Jewish notion that sinners will be excluded from the coming resurrection; cf. E. Lohse, *Märtyrer und Gottesknecht* (Göttingen 1955) 50f.; H. L. Strack and P. Billerbeck *Kommentar*

zum Neuen Testament aus Talmud und Midrasch (Munich 1922–61) iv.799–976; see also Ignatius, *Trall* 9.2; *Smyrn* 2.1; 5.3; Polycarp, *Phil* 2.2; 5.2.

30. The most debated issue is the relationship of "future" eschatology, or apocalyptic hope, to "realized" eschatology, or the belief in present salvation, in Ignatius' letters. H. Schlier, *Religionsgeschichtliche Untersuchungen zu den Ignatius-Briefen* (Giessen 1928) 180f., sees in the letters signs that the eschatological message of apostolic Christianity was already largely abandoned by the "hellenized" community at Antioch, which Ignatius led. R. Bultmann, "Ignatius und Paulus," in J. N. Sevenster and W. C. Van Unnik (eds.), *Studia Paulina* (= Festschr. J. de Zwaan [Haarlem 1953]) 37–51, and *Theology of the NT* ii (New York 1955), 192f., 198f. (Theologie des Neuen Testamentes [Tübingen ³1953] 541, 547), sees in the letters the same tensions between the "already" and the "not yet" of God's eschatological action that one finds in Paul and John, even though Bultmann, too, asserts that the orientation towards the future which characterized most New Testament eschatology has virtually disappeared. H. Paulsen, *Studien zur Theologie des Ignatius von Antiochien* (Göttingen 1978) 60–78, finds in Ignatius' hope for salvation through and beyond his martyr's death "eine eigentümliche Dialektik von Zukunft und Gegenwart" (76). D. Aune, *The Cultic Setting of Realized Eschatology in Early Christianity* (Leiden 1972) 163, concludes cautiously: "Eschatological salvation is present within the Christian community, but an individual only participates in that salvation conditionally. The full and irreversible possession of the benefits of eschatological salvation are dependent upon final eschatological unity with God in eternity through Jesus Christ." Obviously such assessments depend to a great extent on how one conceives the "eschatological" element in Christian hope.

31. This use of παρουσία to refer to the earthly life of Jesus need not connote any anticipation of his final coming; Paulsen (above, n. 30) 66f. suggests, however, that such a non-eschatological use of the word would be an innovation of Ignatius.

32. An excellent recent study of Ignatius' theology and spirituality, as dominated by this expectation of martyrdom, is K. Bommes, *Weizen Gottes: Untersuchungen zur Theologie des Martyriums bei Ignatius von Antiochien* (Karlsruhe 1976).

33. This characteristic phrase (τυγχάνειν or ἐπιτυγχάνειν τοῦ Θεοῦ) appears in various forms throughout the letters, as a way of referring to the attainment of salvation (*Eph* 10.1; *Magn* 1.2; *Rom* 9.2; *Smyrn* 11.1) and more specifically as a way of referring to the Christian vocation of martyrdom (*Eph* 12.2; *Magn* 14.1; *Trall* 12.2; 13.3; *Rom* 1.2; 2.2; 4.1; *Smyrn* 9.2; *Pol* 2.3; 7.1). Cf. his use of ἐπιτυγχάνειν Ἰησοῦ Χριστοῦ, mentioned above, and ἐπιτυγχάνειν alone, in the same context (*Rom* 8.3; *Phil* 5.1). Such phrases suggest, with blunt simplicity, the immediate finality of eschatological fufillment.

34. It is also possible, as P. N. Harrison (*Polycarp's Two Epistles to the Philippians* [Cambridge 1936]) argued, that chapters 13 and 14 are an early letter of Polycarp, written to accompany the collection of Ignatius' letters which he was forwarding to the community at Philippi, and that chapters 1–12 are a hortatory message written to the same community about the year 135. Only in these first twelve chapters is Polycarp's eschatological hope reflected.

35. On this conception of a "selective" resurrection in Polycarp's letter, see A. Bovon-Thurneysen, "Ethik und Eschatologie im Philipperbrief des Polycarp von Smyrna," *ThZ* 29 (1973) 241–56.
36. On this tension of present and future in the strongly "realized" eschatology of the *Odes*, see Aune, *Cultic Setting* 166–94, esp. 185f.
37. The crown is a standard feature of life in the eschatological paradise, as that is conceived in the writings of Qumran and in Jewish and early Christian apocalyptic; see *ibid.*, 186ff. The image is a frequent one in the *Odes*: e.g., 1.1–4; 5.12; 9.8–11; 20.7f.
38. So 26.3, 8–10, 12; for a discussion of the possibility that this may have been the original title of the collection, see J. H. Charlesworth, *The Odes of Solomon* (Missoula, Mont., 1977) 105 *ad loc.*, and the works cited there.
39. "Apokalyptik des Urchristentums," *NtA* II.445 (Engl. edn. II.630). For a general interpretation of the work, see *ibid.*, II. 444–54 (Engl. edn. II.629–42); R. van Deemter, *Der Hirt des Hermas, Apokalypse oder Allegorie?* (Delft 1929); E. Peterson, "Beiträge zur Interpretation der Visionen im 'Pastor Hermae,'" *Frühkirche, Judentum und Gnosis* 254–70.
40. *Vis* 3.7.6f., possibly representing an earlier stage in the composition of the work, speaks of a painful process of purification for those rejected "stones" that repent. Even after this purification, however, they will not be included in the tower itself, but "in another, much inferior place."
41. Hermas' encounter with the beast in *Vis* 4.1 is a clear use of a traditional apocalyptic image in a thematically adapted way, to underline the work's overall insistence on the need for repentance (cf. 4.2.5). On the possible meaning of "the great tribulation to come" (*ibid.*), see A. P. O'Hagan, "The Great Tribulation to Come in the Pastor of Hermas," *StPatr* 4 (1961) 305–11; R. J. Bauckham, "The Great Tribulation in Hermas," *JThS* 25 (1974) 27–40.
42. For a description of the Phrygian cults of Cybele, Attis and the Great Mother, and their influence on Roman religion, see the old but still useful chapter of F. Cumont, *Oriental Religions in Roman Paganism* (New York 1911) 46–72.
43. So L. Gry, *Le Millénarisme dans ses origines et son développement* (Paris 1914) 65. The evidence for this seems to be Irenaeus, *AH* 1.26 (where Cerinthus is linked with the Ebionites and Nicolaitans), and Eusebius, *HE* 3.27–29, who seems to be following Irenaeus, as well as other sources.
44. So Eusebius, *HE* 3.28, citing the Roman presbyter Gaius and Dionysius of Alexandria; also Victorinus of Pettau, *Comm on Apoc* 21. 3 (in Jerome's edition); Augustine, *De Haeresibus* 8; Theodoret, *Haer Fab Comp* 2.3. For the presence of Cerinthians in the provinces of Asia and Galatia as late as the end of the fourth century, see Epiphanius, *Pan* 28.6.4.
45. For the sources of Papias' millenarianism in apocalyptic Judaeo-Christianity, see L. Gry, "Le Papias des belles promesses messianiques," *RB* 52 (1944) 118–24 (suggesting the millenarian writer may be a Jewish-Christian of the same name); L. Gry, "Henoch 10.19 et les belles promesses de Papias," *RB* 53 (1946) 197–206. Cf. C. Mazzucco and E. Pietrello, "Il rapporto tra la concezione del millennio dei primi autori cristiani e l'Apocalisse di Giovanni," *Aug* 18 (1978) 29–45.

46. See K. Aland, "Bemerkungen zum Montanismus und zur frühchristlichen Eschatologie," *Kirchengeschichtliche Entwürfe* (Gütersloh 1960) 105–48.

2 Making history intelligible: eschatology and the apologists

1. In favor of Justin's authorship are F. Loofs, *Theophilus von Antiochien adversus Marcionem, und die anderen theologischen Quellen bei Irenaeus* (TU 46.2 [Leipzig 1930]) 211–57, 281–99; and more recently, P. Prigent, *Justin et l'Ancien Testament* (Paris 1964) 50–61. Against it are F. R. Montgomery Hitchcock, "Loofs' Asiatic Source (IQA) and the Ps.-Justin De Resurrectione," *ZNW* 36 (1937–38) 35–60; and W. Delius, "Ps.-Justin, Uber die Auferstehung: ein Werk Melitons von Sardes?," *ThViat* 4 (1952) 181–204. Despite Prigent's criticisms, Montgomery Hitchcock's arguments against Justin's authorship seem conclusive.

2. This term is also frequently used in Gnostic sources, to refer to the dissolution of the present world: e.g., *Gospel of Truth* 24.37–25.4; *Pistis Sophia* 86.6ff.; 126.30ff.; *Excerpta ex Theodoto* 62.1; 63.1; cf. Irenaeus, *AH* 1.5.3.

3. For this image of the "garments" of immortality, which has a Jewish apocalyptic origin, see above, chap. 1, n. 17; Justin, *Dial.* 116f.; and *The Concept of our Great Power* (Nag Hammadi VI, 4) 44.25f.; 46.12–18.

4. Against its genuineness are R. M. Grant, "Athenagoras or Ps.-Athenagoras?," *HThR* 47 (1954) 121–29; and W. R. Schoedel, *Athenagoras: Legatio and De Resurrectione* (Oxford 1972). Both of these authors hold it to be an anti-Origenist work of the third century. Its authenticity has been defended vigorously by L. W. Barnard, especially in *Athenagoras. A Study in Second Century Christian Apologetic* (Paris 1972) and "Athenagoras' De Resurrectione. The Background and Theology of a Second-Century Treatise on the Resurrection," *StTh* 30 (1976) 1–42. See also E. Bellini, "Atenagora e il trattato sulla risurrezione dei morti," *ScC* 101 (1973) 511–17; and J.-M. Vermander, "Celse et l'attribution d'un ouvrage sur la résurrection des morts," *MSR* 35 (1978) 125–34 (arguing the work is a response to Celsus). For useful earlier treatments of the contents of this work, see M. Pohlenz, "Die griechische Philosophie im Dienste der christlichen Auferstehungslehre," *ZWTh* 47 (1904) 241–50 (pointing to Peripatetic influence on the treatise); and L. Chaudouard, *La Philosophie du dogme de la résurrection de la chair au IIe siècle: étude sur le Περὶ ἀναστάσεως d'Athénagore* (Lyons 1905).

3 Regaining the light: eschatology in the Gnostic crisis (150–200)

1. J. M. Robinson (ed.), *The Nag Hammadi Library in English* (New York 1977). Unless otherwise stated, my references in this section will be to this edition. Critical editions of all of the Coptic texts of these documents are not yet available but are appearing in the *Coptic Gnostic Library*, published in Leiden. Facsimile editions of all thirteen Nag Hammadi codices are available (Leiden 1972–77). These publications of the Nag Hammadi documents also include the closely related Berlin Gnostic Codex 8502. The *Pistis Sophia*, the only other extant

Coptic Gnostic document of any size, has recently been republished, with a new English translation by Violet MacDermot, as part of the same Coptic Gnostic Library (Leiden 1978).

2. Cf. A. Méhat, "Apocatastasis chez Basilide," *Mélanges H.-C. Puech* (Paris 1974) 365–73. In the Basilidean Gnostic conception of ἀποκατάστασις as the "achievement" of our eschatological goal rather than the "restoration" of an original state, Méhat sees an earlier sense of the term, parallel to its usage in Acts 3.21; cf. his earlier article: "'Apocatastase': Origène, Clément d'Alexandrie, Act 3.21," *VigChr* 10 (1956) 196–214.

3. On this point see G. Filoramo, "Rivelazione ed escatologia nello gnosticismo cristiano del II secolo," *Aug* 18 (1978) 81f., n. 12.

4. For the appearance of this motif among orthodox writers, especially in late Latin Patristic sermons, see J. Rivière, "Le Rôle du démon au jugement particulier chez les Pères," *RevSR* 4 (1924) 43–64.

5. Apparently under the influence of book x of Plato's *Republic*, this document presents reincarnation in a new body as the next step after such purification; the sinless soul, unlike the others, will be given "a body that is not able to sleep or to forget," in which it will be constantly "goaded . . . to seek for the mysteries of the light until it finds them, . . . and inherits the light" (147, end). Cf. H. J. Schoeps, "Bemerkungen zu Reinkarnationsvorstellungen der Gnosis," *Numen* 4 (1957) 228–32. On the notion of such a purifying, rather than simply destructive, fire, which is therefore considered to be "wise," see W. C. Van Unnik, "The 'Wise Fire' in a Gnostic Eschatological Vision," in P. Granfield and J. A. Jungmann (eds.), *Kyriakon* (= Festschr. J. Quasten [Münster 1970]) 1.277–88.

6. On this brief but important Valentinian essay, see W. C. Van Unnik, "The Newly Discovered Gnostic 'Epistle to Rheginos' on the Resurrection," *JEH* 15 (1964) 141–52, 153–67; R. Haardt, "'Die Abhandlung über die Auferstehung' des Codex Jung aus der Bibliothek gnosticher koptischer Schriften von Nag Hammadi: Bemerkungen zu ausgewählten Motiven," *Kairos* 11 (1969) 1–5; M. L. Peel, *The Epistle to Rheginos. A Valentinian Letter on the Resurrection* (London 1969: text, translation, commentary); H.-G. Gaffron, "Eine gnostische Apologie des Auferstehungsglaubens," in G. Bornkamm and K. Rahner (eds.), *Die Zeit Jesu* (= Festschrift H. Schlier [Frankfurt 1970]) 218–27; B. Dehandschutter, "L'Epître a Rhéginos. Quelques problèmes critiques," *OLoP* 4 (1973) 101–11; J.-E. Ménard, "La Notion de 'résurrection' dans l'Epître a Rhéginos," in M. Kraus (ed.), *Essays . . . in Honor of Pahor Labib* (Leiden 1975) 110–24; E. Peretto, "L'Epistola a Rheginos: il posto del corpo nella risurrezione," *Aug* 18 (1978) 63–74.

7. Cf. G. Jossa, "Storia della salvezza ed escatologia nell' *Adversus Haereses* di Ireneo di Lione," *Aug* 18 (1978) 107–25, esp. 117f.

8. Although Irenaeus is cautious about turning apocalyptic symbols into precise calculations (cf. *AH* 5.30, on the interpretation of 666, the "Number of the Beast" in Apoc 13.18), he is convinced that the world will come to an end six thousand years after creation (*AH* 5.28.3). He does not offer any precise reckoning of when this will be, but situates the Incarnation of the Word "in the last times, " at the evening of history (*ibid.*, 5.15.4). Cf. W. C. Van Unnik, "Der

Ausdruck, 'In den letzten Zeiten,' bei Irenäus," in W. C. Van Unnik (ed.), *Neotestmentica et Patristica* (= Festschr. O. Cullman [Leiden 1962]) 293–304.

9. *Dem* 42, however, suggests that resurrection will be granted only to believers, because they have retained the Holy Spirit given them in baptism. On Irenaeus' insistence on the salvation of the flesh, see J. Arroniz, "La salvación de la carne en S. Ireneo," *ScrVict* 12 (1965) 7–29.

10. On Irenaeus' millenarianism, see E. Buonaiuti, "Il millenarismo di Ireneo," *Saggi sul cristianesimo primitivo* (Rome 1923) 79–96; V. Crewers, "Het millenarisme van Irenaeus," *Bijdragen van de philosophische en theologische Faculteiten der Nederlandsche Jezuiten* 1 (1938) 28–80; M. O'Rourke Boyle, "Irenaeus' Millennial Hope. A Polemical Weapon," *RThAM* 36 (1969) 5–16; P. Bissels, "Die frühchristliche Lehre vom Gottesreich auf Erden," *TThZ* 84 (1975) 44–47; C. Mazzucco and E. Pietrella, "Il rapporto tra la concezione del millennio dei primi autori cristiani e l'Apocalisse di Giovanni," *Aug* 18 (1978) 29–45, esp. 44f.; E. Norelli, "Il duplice rinnovamento del mondo nell'escatologia di San Ireneo," *Aug* 18 (1978) 89–106.

11. See Norelli 97–100.

12. Irenaeus makes a point of stressing several times that God himself is not the direct cause of the punishment of the damned, but simply prepares for them the "furnace of fire" into which they banish themselves by "avoiding the light" and "flying from God": *AH* 4.39.4–40.2; 5.27.2.

13. On Irenaeus' idea of companionship with God and participation in his life as the ultimate content of salvation, see M. Aubineau, "Incorruptibilité et divinisation selon Saint Irénée," *RSR* 44 (1956) 25–52; E. Lanne, "La Vision de Dieu dans l'œuvre de saint Irénée," *Irén* 33 (1960) 311–20; J. Arroniz, "La immortalidad como deificación en S. Ireneo," *ScrVict* 8 (1961) 262–87.

4 *Senectus Mundi*: eschatology in the West, 200–250

1. Eusebius, for instance, attributes to the general fear of persecution the predictions of a Jewish Christian named Judah, who wrote in his treatise on Daniel that the world would end in 202/203 (*HE* 6.7). Hippolytus mentions two Eastern bishops in his own time – one in Syria and one in Pontus – who led their people to believe that the Parousia was imminent (*In Dan* 3.18f.); Firmilian of Caesaraea (Cappadocia), writing to Cyprian, tells of a local prophetess in Anatolia who urged the faithful to go immediately to Jerusalem and await the coming of the Lord, during the Eastern persecution under Maximinus Thrax in 236 (Cyprian, *Ep* 75.10.1–4). These instances all come from the Greek-speaking part of the Empire, but probably reflect a mood prevalent everywhere, except in the more sophisticated intellectual world of Alexandria.

2. See R. Frick, *Geschichte des Reich-Gottes-Gedankens in der alten Kirche bis zu Origenes und Augustin* (Giessen 1928) 69f. This tension is nowhere more evident than in Tertullian's *Apologeticum*, where Tertullian assures his readers that Christians pray for the stability of the Empire, in order to put off the *clausulam saeculi*, with its attendant horrors (32; 39), yet insists that "only one thing in

this life greatly concerns us, and that is to get quickly out of it" (*ibid.*, 41; cf. *De Orat Dom* 5).

3. Tertullian uses this same consideration elsewhere to argue that souls themselves have a material, if subtle, bodily substance: cf. *De An* 7; *De Res* 17. He agrees, however, that the capacity of souls to suffer and to act without the body is severely limited: cf. *De Res* 17.

4. On the structure and content of the *De Carnis Resurrectione*, see P. Siniscalco, *Ricerche sul "De Resurrectione" di Tertulliano* (Rome 1968); R. Sider, "Structure and Design in the *De Resurrectione Mortuorum* of Tertullian," *VigChr* 23 (1969) 177–96; F. Cardman, "Tertullian on the Resurrection" (Diss. Yale University 1974). For an analysis of his apologetic arguments for a resurrection, see P. Siniscalco, "Il motivo razionale della risurrezione della carne in due passi di Tertulliano," *AAST* 78 (1960/61), 195–221.

5. Apparently Tertullian treated future beatitude, both material and spiritual, in a now-lost work entitled *De Spe Fidelium*: cf. *Adv Marc* 3.24. *Adv Hermogenem* 11 describes the final state of history, when the devil is cast into fire and there is "an end of evil," in terms both of a restored natural harmony in the universe and of the triumph of Christ; it is not clear how far the millennial hope is still in his mind in this passage.

6. In *De Anima* 55, Tertullian follows an earlier tradition in insisting that the souls of martyrs are admitted to "the region of Paradise," which is apparently distinct from even the more pleasant parts of Hades. In *Apol* 47, he refers to Paradise as "the place of heavenly bliss appointed to receive the spirits of the saints." Unfortunately, his treatise on Paradise, which he mentions in *De Anima* 55, is now lost. On the Latin Patristic conception of a "place of rest" for the just between death and resurrection, and its possible use in ancient Christian funerary art, see A. Stuiber, *Refrigerium Interim. Die Vorstellungen vom Zwischenzustand und die frühchristliche Grabeskunst* (Bonn 1957); cf. the critical response of L. de Bruyne, "Refrigerium interim," *RivAC* 34 (1958) 87–118.

7. For a study of Tertullian's language in speaking of Hades and the afterlife, see H. Finé, *Die Terminologie der Jenseitsvorstellungen bei Tertullian: ein semasiologischer Beitrag zur Dogmengeschichte des Zwischenzustandes* (Bonn 1958).

8. On these visions, see F. Dölger, "Antikeparellelen zum leidenden Dinocrates in der *Passio Perpetuae*," *AuC* 2.1 (1932).

9. This controversy began with the publication of P. Nautin's book, *Hippolyte et Josippe* (Paris 1947), in which he proposed an elaborate argument to distinguish two authors at work in the Hippolytean corpus: a Roman schismatic bishop, for whom he hypothesized the name Josippus, and a Palestinian named Hippolytus – both of whom wrote during the first half of the third century. The argument against Nautin's thesis was carried on vigorously by several French-speaking scholars, notably Marcel Richard, who summarized his position for the unity of authorship of the Hippolytean corpus in his article "Hippolyte de Rome," *DSp* 7 (Paris 1968) 531–71. For a survey of the literature of this controversy see R. Butterworth, *Hippolytus of Rome: Contra Noetum* (London 1977) 21–33. On the question of unity or diversity of authorship of the Hippolytean corpus, see also

V. Loi, "La problema storico-letteraria su Ippolito di Roma," *Ricerche su Ippolito: Studia Ephemeridis 'Augustinianum'* 13 (Rome 1977) 9–16; V. Loi, "L'identità letteraria di Ippolito di Roma," *ibid.*, 67–88; and M. Simonetti, "A modo di conclusione: una ipotesi di lavoro," *ibid.*, 151–56.

10. *PG* 10.796–801. Most of this passage is contained in two fragments preserved under the names of Meletius of Antioch and Josephus respectively, in John Damascene's *Sacra Parallela: Coll. Rupefucaldina* A71 and Ω (*PG* 96.484c2–485A2; 541B10–544D11). It is possible that this is the same anti-Platonic treatise *On the Universe* mentioned by Photius (*Bibliotheca*, Cod 48: ed. R. Henry 1 [Paris 1959] 33ff.), which his manuscript ascribed to Josephus, but which its marginal scholia attributed to the Roman presbyter, Gaius.

11. For an analysis and intepretation of this passage in the *Elenchus*, see D. Ritschl, "Hippolytus' Conception of Deification," *SJTh* 12 (1959) 388–99.

12. On the Stoic background of this idea, see M. Spanneut, *Le Stoïcisme des Pères de l'église* (Paris 1957) 258; on Cyprian's debt to Seneca, in particular, see H. Koch, *Cyprianische Untersuchungen* (Bonn 1926) 286–313. Cf. J. Daniélou, *The Origins of Latin Christianity* 251–58.

13. In *De Hab Virg* 31, Cyprian refers to the reward of martyrs as a "hundred-fold" recompense, and to that of virgins as "sixty-fold." This scheme is carried out in more detail in the Pseudo-Cyprianic sermon *De Centesima, Sexagesima, Tricesima* (*PLS* 1.53–67), which identifies the "thirty-fold" fruit of the sower's seed, in Matt 13.8, as the reward due to married people who practice chastity. J. Daniélou has argued convincingly that this work is a late second-century Latin sermon of Judaeo-Christian origin: "Le Traité De centesima, sexagesima, tricesima et le judéo-christianisme Latin avant Tertullien," *VigChr* 25 (1971) 171–81. For this same interpretation of the parable as a scheme of rewards, cf. Origen, *Hom in Jos* 2.1.

14. The restraint Cyprian shows in portraying both the delights of the saved and the punishments of the damned can be underscored by comparing it with the vivid description of both in the contemporary Ps.-Cyprianic treatise, *De Laude Martyrii*, esp. 20–21.

15. See P. Jay, "Saint Cyprien et la doctrine du purgatoire," *RThAM* 27 (1960) 133–36.

5 A school for souls: Alexandrian eschatology and its critics (185–300)

1. Cf. J. A. Fischer, "Μελέτη Θανάτου. Eine Skizze zur früheren griechischen Patristik," in E. C. Suttner and C. Patock (eds.), *Wegzeichen* (= Festschr. H. M. Biedermann [Würzburg 1971]) 43–54.

2. On the use of ἀποκατάστασις by second-century authors, see A. Méhat, "'Apocatastase': Origène, Clément d'Alexandrie, Act 3.21," *VigChr* 10 (1956) 196–214. See also the qualifying comments of P. Siniscalco, "'Ἀποκατάστασις, ἀποκαθίστημι nella tradizione della grande chiesa fine ad Ireneo," *StPatr* 3 (= TU 78 [Berlin 1961]) 380–96. For the idea that the sun represents the future abode of all the just in a single body of light, see Origen, *In Matt* 10.3 (*SC* 162.153).

3. See M. Mees, "Jetzt und Dann in der Eschatologie Klemens von Alexandrien," *Aug* 18 (1978) 127–37.
4. On the use of the phrase πῦρ φρόνιμον in Clement, Origen and other ecclesiastical authors, and its origin in Stoic philosophy, see W. C. Van Unnik, "The 'Wise Fire' in a Gnostic Eschatological Vision," in P. Granfield and J. A. Jungmann (eds.), *Kyriakon* (= Festschr. J. Quasten [Münster 1970]) 1. 277–88.
5. Without such mature knowledge of God, Clement seems to assume, no human creature can be fully happy. So he quotes with approval a verse from the *Apocalypse of Peter*, which promises that aborted infants will be given to the care of an angel-guardian, "that they may obtain knowledge and so receive a better dwelling-place, suffering what they would have suffered if they had been born bodily" (*Ecl Proph* 48). The mercy of God, in Clement's view, allows even to the unborn the painful growth necessary for salvation.
6. Cf. G. Anrich, "Clemens und Origenes als Begründer der Lehre vom Fegfeuer," *Theologische Abhandlungen für H. J. Holtzmann* (Tübingen/Leipzig 1902) 95–120; T. Spacil, "La dottrina del purgatorio in Clemente Alessandrino ed Origene," *Bess* 23 (1919) 131–45; K. Schmöle, *Läuterung nach dem Tode und pneumatische Auferstehung bei Klemens von Alexandrien* (Münster 1974).
7. So *Comm Ser in Matt* 49 (*GCS* 11.102.9–15); *ibid.*, 50 (112.11–14); etc. On Origen's treatment of the Lucan Apocalypse, see A. Lauras, "Le Commentaire patristique de Lc 21.25–33," *StPatr* 7 (1966) 505–12.
8. For Origen's use of the term *parousia*, see R. Trevijano Etcheverría, "'Επιδημία y παρουσία en Origenes," *ScrVict* 16 (1969) 313–37.
9. For a defense of the plausibility of the notion of a "son of the devil" who is opposite to Christ in all respects, see *Cels* 6.45f.
10. See A. Monaci, "Apocalisse ed escatologia nell'opera di Origene," *Aug* 18 (1978) 139–51. On the authenticity of the fragments ascribed to a commentary by Origen on the Johannine Apocalypse in later catenae, see C. Diobouniotis and A. v. Harnack, *Die Scholien-kommentar des Origenes zur Apokalypse Johannis* (= TU 38 [Leipzig 1911]); A. de Boyssen, "Avons-nous un commentaire d'Origène sur l'Apocalypse?", *RB* 10 (1913) 555–67; D. Strathmann, "Origenes und die Johannesoffenbarung," *NKZ* 34 (1923) 228–36, esp. 231.
11. For a thorough discussion of Origen's conception of the resurrection body, see H. Crouzel, "La Doctrine origénienne du corps résuscité," *BLE* 81 (1980) 175–200; 241–66. Cf. H. Chadwick, "Origen, Celsus and the Resurrection of the Body," *HThR* 41 (1948) 83–102; A. Le Boulluec, "De la croissance selon les Stoïciens à la résurrection selon Origène," *REG* 88 (1975) 143–55. Origen himself wrote a treatise on the resurrection in two books, as well as two dialogues on the subject (*Cels* 6.20; *Princ* 2.10.1; Eusebius, *HE* 6.24.3), but only fragments have been preserved (in Pamphilus, *Apol pro Origene* 1.7; *PG* 17.594A6–597A6).
12. See H. Crouzel, "Mort et immortalité selon Origène," *BLE* 79 (1978) 19–38; 81–96; 181–96. The last two parts of this study deal directly with Origen's understanding of immortality.
13. The fullest discussion of Origen's underlying anthropological and metaphysical assumptions about the human person is H. Cornélis, "Les Fondements cosmolo-

giques de l'eschatologie d'Origène," *RSPhTh* 43 (1959) 32–80; 201–27; cf. Crouzel, "La Doctrine origénienne."

14. The assertion of Origen's later critics, that he believed the risen body will be spherical in shape (Justinian, *Ep ad Menam*, Anathema 5: ed. E. Schwartz, *ACO* III 213.25f.; Council of 553, Anathema 10 against the Origenists: ed. J. Straub, *ACO* IV.1, 249.19–22), is either totally unfounded or rests on a confusion of the speculations of sixth-century Origenists with some statements of the master about the spherical form of the "heavenly bodies" (e.g., *Or* 31.3). See A. M. Festugière, "Le Corps glorieux 'sphéroïde' chez Origène," *RSPhTh* 43 (1959) 81–86; J. Bauer, "Corpora orbiculata," *ZKTh* 82 (1960) 333–41. In several places, Origen does speak of the risen body – Jesus' and ours – as "ethereal" (*Cels* 3.41f.), but he also denies that this "ether" is a distinctive kind of matter (*Princ* 3.6.6). It is simply the quality of "purity and integrity" appropriate for a body living in the immediate presence of God (*Princ* 1.6.4). Cf. Crouzel, "La Doctrine origénienne" 192ff.

15. Jerome, *Ep* 124 *ad Avitum* 5, 9f.; Theophilus, *Ep Pasch* 1 (cited by Jerome, *Ep* 96.9, 13, 15), *Ep Syn* (cited by Jerome, *Ep* 92.2); Council of 553, Anathema 11 (ed. J. Straub, *ACO* IV.1, 249).

16. See J. Rius-Camps, "La suerte final de la naturaleza corpórea según el Peri Archōn de Origenes," *StPatr* 14 (=TU 117 [Berlin 1976]) 167–79; cf. the fragment of the commentary on Ps 15 quoted by Pamphilus, *Apol* 1.7 (*PG* 17.600A1–B5). Crouzel, "La Doctrine origénienne" 262ff., points out that none of Origen's extant Greek works suggests the glorified body will eventually disappear; Crouzel also observes that Rufinus is at least as credible a witness to Origen's doctrine as Jerome or Theophilus. Cf. Cornélis, "Les Fondements cosmologiques" 225–32; for a defense of Jerome's interpretation, see F. H. Kettler, *Der ursprüngliche Sinn der Dogmatik des Origenes* (Berlin 1966) 16 and n. 73.

17. See H. Crouzel, "La 'première' et la 'seconde' résurrection des hommes d'après Origène," *Didaskalia* 3 (1973) 3–20.

18. For Origen's conception of Hades, see H. Crouzel, "L'Hadès et la Géhenne selon Origène," *Gr* 59 (1978) 293–309. For his understanding of death, see H. Crouzel, "Mort et immortalité" 19–38; E. Früchtel, "Der Todesgedanke bei Origenes," in *Forma Futuri* (=Festschr. M. Pellegrino [Turin 1975]) 993–1002.

19. See H. Crouzel, "Le Thème platonicien du 'véhicule de l'âme' chez Origène," *Didaskalia* 7 (1977) 225–37.

20. For Origen's understanding of Gehenna and punishment after death, see Crouzel, "L'Hadès et la Géhenne" 309–31.

21. For a discussion of this interpretation of punishment and its apparent origin in Stoic psychology and ethics, see H.-J. Horn, "Ignis aeternus: une interprétation morale du feu éternel chez Origène," *REG* 82 (1969) 76–88; H. J. Horn, "Die 'Hölle' als Krankheit der Seele in einer Deutung des Origenes," *JAC* 11/12 (1968/69) 55–64. This metaphorical line of interpretation seems to have particularly scandalized Jerome: see *Ep* 124 *ad Avitum* 7; *Comm in Eph* 3 (on Eph 5.6); *Apol adv Ruf* 2.7.

22. See Crouzel, "L'Hadès et la Géhenne" 300. Cf. *Or* 27.15; *Comm in Matt* 15.31.

Origen himself comments on the ambiguity of the word αἰώνιος in *Comm in Rom* 6.5 (*PG* 14.1066c10–1067b1), but his conclusion is unambiguous: "eternal life should be thought of as not having an end."

23. A favorite text of Origen's in this connection is I Cor 3.11–15. For his interpretation of this Pauline reference to "purifying fire," see H. Crouzel, "L'Exégèse origénienne de I Cor 3.11–15, et la purification eschatologique," in J. Fontaine and C. Kannengiesser (eds.), *Epektasis* (= Festschr. J. Daniélou [Paris 1972]) 273–83.

24. For Origen's interpretation of these biblical fire images as denoting purgative punishment after death, see C.-M. Edsman, *Le Baptême de feu* (Uppsala 1940) 1–15. In the *Commentary on Matthew* 13.17, Origen applies the same "medicinal" interpretation to Jesus' statement in Matt 18.6, that "it would be better" for the one who causes "little ones" to sin " to have a great millstone fastened round his neck and to be drowned in the depth of the sea": "The one who gives scandal will be bound, as fits him for the healing (θεραπεία) of his sin . . . So, paying sufficient penalty in the sea (where the 'dragon' is, whom 'God made to sport in it'), and thus suffering to the full what is right for him, the one punished will from then on be free of suffering what he has endured in the depths of the sea, weighed down by the millstone."

25. This conception of the "end" (τέλος) of history is particularly strong in the *Commentary on John*: see, e.g., 1.36 (41) 264; 2.8 (4) 62; 6.59 (38) 302–303; 13.57 (56) 391–92; 19.14 (3) 87–88; 28.18 (14) 152–55. Cf. P. Némeshégyi, *La Paternité de Dieu chez Origène* (Paris/Tournai 1960) 203–24; J. Rius-Camps, "La hipótesis origeniana sobre el fin último (peri telous). Intento de valoración," in U. Bianchi and H. Crouzel (eds.), *Archè e Telos* (Milan 1981) 58–117. For Origen's exegesis of I Cor 15.24–28, see esp. E. Schendel, *Herrschaft und Unterwerfung Christi* (Tübingen 1971) 81–110.

26. See A. Méhat, "'Apocatastase': Origène, Clément d'Alexandrie, Act 3.21," *VigChr* 10 (1956) 201f.; G. Müller, "Origenes und die Apokatastasis," *ThZ* 14 (1958) 174–90.

27. See H. Crouzel, "L'Hadès et la Géhenne" 325, who argues that Origen considered the ἀποκατάστασις πάντων "non comme une certitude, mais comme un grand espoir."

28. The possiblity of future falls, after "all things are subjected to Christ," and of consequent future worlds of material existence, is suggested in two passages attributed to Origen by Justinian (*Ep ad Menam*, fr. 16: ed. Schwartz, *ACO* III, 211.24–27; fr. 20: *ibid.*, 212.15–19), as well as by two fragments translated by Jerome, *Ep* 124 *ad Avitum* 5 (*CSEL* 56, 101.13–103.6) and 10 (*ibid.*, 111.13–112.9). These sources can certainly be regarded as "hostile witnesses." In *Cels* 8.72 and *Jo* 1.16.91, Origen confidently predicts that God will ultimately triumph over evil. Cf. H. Chadwick, "Origen, Celsus and the Stoa," *JThS* 48 (1947) 34–49, esp. 41f.; Némeshégyi, *La Paternité de Dieu* 217–24; J. Rius-Camps, "La hipótesis origeniana." Origen explicitly rejects the theory of an endless cycle of falls and redemptions in *Comm in Rom* 5.10 (*PG* 14.1052b7–1053c2). This work, however, is preserved only in a translation by the "friendly witness" Rufinus.

29. For a discussion of this letter, and of the ambiguity of Origen's position on the

salvation of the devils, see C. C. Richardson, "The Condemnation of Origen," *ChH* 6 (1937) 50–64; H. Crouzel, "A Letter from Origen 'to Friends in Alexandria,'" in D. Neiman and M. Schatkin (eds.), *The Heritage of the Early Church* (= Festschr. G. Florovsky: OrChrA 195 [Rome 1973]) 135–50, esp. 145ff.

30. See the "Letter to Friends in Alexandria" mentioned above; also the sixth-century *Replies of Barsanuphius and John* 600 (tr. C. Regnault and P. Lemaire [Solesmes 1971] 391–94); Justinian, *Ep ad Menam*, Anathema 9 (E. Schwartz, *ACO* III, 214).

31. *Metaphrasis in Ecclesiasten* 12.1–7 (*PG* 110.1016C1–1017A7). Cf. S. Leanza, "Eccl 12.1–7: L'interpretazione escatologica dei Padri e degli esegeti medievali," *Aug* 18 (1978) 191–99.

32. See M. Simonetti, "Il millenarismo in oriente da Origene a Metodio," in *Corona Gratiarum* (= Festschr. E. Dekkers; Instrumenta Patristica 10 [Bruges 1975]) 1.37–58.

33. *Ibid.*, 51f.

34. J. B. Pitra (ed.), *Analecta Sacra* 4 (Paris 1933) 193f. and 429; cf. L. B. Radford, *Three Teachers of Alexandria: Theognostus, Pierius and Peter. A Study in the Earlier History of Origenism and Anti-Origenism* (Cambridge 1908) 76–86. For a full study of the extant evidence on Peter, see T. Vivian, *St. Peter of Alexandria, Bishop and Martyr* (Philadelphia 1988).

35. Cf. H. Crouzel, "Les critiques adressées par Méthode et ses contemporains à la doctrine origénienne du corps ressuscité," *Gr* 53 (1972) 679–716, esp. 682.

36. *Ibid.*, 695.

37. Although he nowhere alludes to Athenagoras' *De Resurrectione*, and only a handful of times to his *Legatio*, Methodius shows a similar conception of the human composite to that of Athenagoras. So M. Pohlenz remarks ("Griechische Philosophie im Dienste der christlichen Auferstehungslehre," *ZWTh* 47 [1904] 250) that Methodius is "einer der wenigen Männern der alten Zeit . . . die Athenagoras kennen." Perhaps the apparent familiarity of Gregory of Nyssa with Athengoras is due to his own reading of Methodius.

38. Cf. T. H. C. Van Eijk, "Marriage and Virginity, Death and Immortality," in *Epektasis* (= Festschr. J. Daniélou [Paris 1972]) 221–24; A. C. Rush, "Death as Spiritual Marriage: Individual and Ecclesial Eschatology," *VigChr* 26 (1972) 91–100.

6 The dawn of the final conflict: Latin eschatology in the Great Persecution (303–313)

1. Jerome points this dependence out several times: *Epp* 61.2; 84.7; *Apol adv Ruf* 3.14; *Comm in Eccl* 4.13. In general, he is respectful towards Victorinus as a martyr and man of the Church, and only criticizes his poor Latin style (*De Vir Ill* 74) and his foolish readiness (*simplicitas*) to be dazzled by the great Alexandrian (*Apol adv Ruf* 1.2).

2. Cf. C. Curti, "Il regno millenario in Vittorino di Petovio," *Aug* 18 (1978) 419–33, esp. 431.

3. "Anonymi Chiliastae in Matthaeum XXIV Fragmenta," *Varia Sacra* (= StT 11 [Rome 1903]) 3–45.

4. "An Exegetical Fragment of the Third Century," *JThS* 5 (1904) 218–27.

5. Serafino Prete, *La Escatologia e parenesi negli scrittori cristiani Latini* (Bologna 1966) 38, has characterized Lactantius as "an intellectual rather than a biblical Christian." In this sense, suggests Prete, his interpretation of the apocalyptic tradition is "suffocated" by his own learning (*ibid.*, 102). "Egli . . . dimostra, a nostro avviso, come l'apocalittismo fosse caro a gruppi religiosi, a cercoli eruditi, ma non riusce a penetrare nelle communità cristiane, delle quale solo alcune l'avevano accolto per tradizione" (*ibid.*). This judgment, however, fails to notice the effect on later Latin eschatology of Lactantius' schematization of the apocalyptic and millenarian traditions in *Inst* 7.

6. See B. Kötting, "Endzeitprognosen zwischen Lactantius und Augustinus," *HJ* 77 (1958) 125–39.

7. For a discussion of the qualities of this fire, and of the sources of Lactantius' conception of it, see M. Perrin, *L'Homme antique et chrétien: l'anthropologie de Lactance – 250–325* (Paris 1981) 529ff. For the sources of his theory of the ability of an immortal soul to suffer pain (20), see J. Doignon, "Le 'Placitum' eschatologique attribué aux Stoïciens par Lactance ('Institutions divines' 7.20)," *RPh* 51 (1977) 43–55.

8. See L. J. Swift, "Lactantius and the Golden Age," *AJP* 89 (1968) 144–56; V. Fabrega, "Die chiliastische Lehre des Laktanz. Methodische und theologische Voraussetzungen und religionsgeschichtlicher Hintergrund," *JAC* 17 (1974) 126–46.

9. On this document, see J. R. Hinnells, "The Zoroastrian Doctrine of Salvation in the Roman World: A Study of the Oracles of Hystaspes," in E. J. Sharpe and J. R. Hinnells (eds.), *Man and his Salvation* (= Studies in Memory of S. G. F. Brandon [Manchester 1973]) 125–48. On the sources of *Inst* 7, see especially H. W. A. Van Rooijen-Dijkman, *De vita beata. Het zevende Boek van de Divinae Institutiones van Lactantius. Analyse en Bronnenonderzoek* (Assen 1967).

7 Facing death in freedom: Eastern eschatology in the age of Nicaea (325–400)

1. In one of the Coptic versions of the *Life of Pachomius* (Bo 82), the saint gives a long explanation of the role angels play in the death of a human person. They receive the righteous soul on to a large white cloth and escort it to its merited resting-place with mysterious songs; but the sinner's soul they tear out of his body with a fishhook, and drag it off to hell tied to the tail of an angelic horse. On the role of angels in the soul's departure from this life, see J. Rivière, "Le rôle du démon au jugement particulier chez les Pères," *RevSR* 4 (1924) 43–64; A. Recheis, *Engel, Tod und Seelenreise. Das Wirken der Geister beim Heimgang des Menschen in der Lehre der alexandrinischen und kappadokischen Väter* (Rome 1958), esp. 169–77 (desert Fathers).

2. For an anecdote about Paul the Simple, in which the faithful are urged to pray for the dead who are being purged of their sins, since the dead are powerless to help themselves, see M. Jugie, "Un apophthègme des Pères inédit sur le

purgatoire," *AOC* 1 (= Mémorial Louis Petit [Bucharest 1948]) 245–53.

3. On the theme of the "sleep of souls" in Aphrahat and Ephrem – a theme that was to become a commonplace in the Syriac theological tradition – see F. Refoulé, "Immortalité de l'âme et résurrection de la chair," *RHR* 163 (1963) 44–49.

4. See the introduction by F. Graffin to R. Lavenant's translation of these hymns in *SC* 137 (Paris 1968) 14. See also the English translation by Sebastian Brock, *Saint Ephrem, Hymns on Paradise* (New York 1990).

5. See J. Teixidor, "Muerte, cielo y šeol en S. Efrén," *OrChrP* 27 (1961) 82–114.

6. On the details of Ephrem's description of Paradise, see E. Beck, "Eine christliche Parallele zu den Paradiesjungfrauen des Korans?" *OrChrP* 14 (1948) 398–405; I. Ortiz de Urbina, "Le Paradis eschatologique d'après saint Ephrem," *OrChrP* 21 (1955) 457–72. On the background of these hymns and their conception of heaven in Jewish theology, see N. Séd, "Les Hymnes sur le Paradis et les traditions juives," *Muséon* 81 (1968) 455–501.

7. For references to these allusions, see F. Trisoglio, "Eusebio di Cesarea e l'eschatologia," *Aug* 18 (1978) 174–77.

8. H. Eger, "Kaiser und Kirche in der Geschichtstheologie Eusebius' von Cäsaräa," *ZNW* 38 (1939) 97–115; cf. H. J. Opitz, "Eusebius als Theologe," *ZNW* 34 (1935) 1–19, esp. 15; D. S. Wallace-Hadrill, *Eusebius of Caesaraea* (London 1960) 168–89. Opitz clearly exaggerates in saying, "Die ganze Eschatologie des früheren Christentums . . . wird von Euseb überhaupt nicht beachtet" (7). Trisoglio (see n. 7 above) comes closer to the truth in speaking of Eusebius' "sordità escatologica" (181). Eusebius simply failed to perceive the radical questioning of the historical order that is implied in all Christian hope for a future salvation.

9. M. Tetz, "Die Theologie des Markell von Ankyra III: Die pseudo-athanasianische *Epistula ad Liberium*, ein Markellisches Bekenntnis," *ZKG* 83 (1972) 188.

10. The fragments of Marcellus' works are assembled in Erich Klostermann's edition of Eusebius' anti-Marcellan corpus: *GCS, Eusebius' Werke IV* (rev. G. C. Hansen [Berlin 1972]) 185–215.

11. See A. Grillmeier, *Jesus der Christus im Glauben der Kirche* I (Freiburg ²1979) 414–39, esp. 422f. (= *Christ in Christian Tradition* I [Oxford ²1975] 274–96, esp. 281f.). See also the literature cited there, esp. M. Tetz, "Die Theologie des Markell von Ankyra I–III," *ZKG* 75 (1964) 217–70; 79 (1968) 3–42; 83 (1972) 145–94.

12. This work, ascribed in the manuscripts to Athanasius, has been identified as the work of Marcellus by Tetz, "Zur Theologie des Markell von Ankyra I."

13. On the eschatology of Cyril's *Catecheses*, see G. A. Nicolae, "Învaţatura despre invierea morţilor in 'Catechezele' Sfintului Chiril al Ierusalimii," *StTeol* (Bucharest) 19 (1967) 629–39; G. Hellemo, *Adventus Domini. Eschatological Thought in Fourth-Century Apses and Catecheses* (Leiden 1989) 146–98.

14. See J. Gribomont, "L'Origénisme de Basile de Césarée," in *L'Homme devant Dieu* (= Festschr. H. de Lubac [Paris 1963]) 1.281–94.

15. See P. J. Fedwick, *The Church and the Charism of Leadership in Basil of Caesaraea* (Toronto 1979) 149–52.

16. Basil is careful to point out, however, that each person will be judged according

to the knowledge of God's law that was available in his or her circumstances; so pagan barbarians like the Scythian nomads will be judged by a more lenient standard than will those who have had the benefit of biblical moral teaching: *In Ps* 7.5 (*PG* 29.240C10–D4). On Basil's doctrine of divine judgment, see M. Girardi, "Il giudizio finale nella omiletica di Basilio di Cesarea," *Aug* 18 (1978) 183–90.

17. Cf. *In Ps* 48.3 (*PG* 29.437B12–C9), where Basil alludes to the theory of the devil's "rights" over the fallen human race, prior to redemption by Christ. In the *Commentary on Isaiah* 3.116f. (*PG* 30.305B14–308C3) – a work of doubtful authenticity – Satan is portrayed as the "bailiff" of Lk 12.58, who will seize us and accuse us of our unpaid debts before Christ the judge; this commentary is probably not an authentic work of Basil, however, although it seems to be Cappadocian and roughly contemporary (see Fedwick, *The Church* 154). On Basil's representation of Satan as an accuser in eschatological passages of his homiletic works, see A. D'Alès, "Le Prince du siècle scrutateur des âmes d'après saint Basile," *RSR* 23 (1933) 325–28.

18. The *Commentary on Isaiah* attributed to Basil (see n. 17 above) consistently conceives of the judgment of sinners as the internal, purgative process of recalling one's own sins: e.g. 1.43 (*PG* 30.201A15–B14). It also asserts that those who voluntarily commit sin and fail to repent before death will have to be "purged by fire" afterwards (4.4:*PG* 30.341B1–C5), a notion that seems to have no parallel in Basil's authentic works.

19. Cf. J. Mossay, "Perspectives eschatologiques de Saint Grégoire de Nazianze," *QLP* 45 (1964) 320–39, esp. 328: "On ne peut donc s'attendre à rencontrer dans l'œuvre de notre auteur ce qu'on pourrait appeler une thanatologie systématique." For a broad study of Gregory's treatment of eschatological themes see J. Mossay, *La Mort et l'au-delà dans saint Grégoire de Nazianze* (Louvain 1966); see also H. Althaus, *Die Heilslehre des heiligen Gregor von Nazianz* (Münster 1972).

20. See J. Daniélou, "L'Apocatastase chez Saint Grégoire de Nysse," *RSR* 30 (1940) 328–47; *L'Etre et le temps chez Grégoire de Nysse* (Leiden 1970) 205–26; B. Salmona, "Origene e Gregorio di Nissa sulla risurrezione dei corpi e l'apocatastasi," *Aug* 18 (1978) 383–88.

21. See M. Alexandre, "Protologie et eschatologie chez Grégoire de Nysse," in H. Crouzel and U. Bianchi (eds.), *Archè e telos: L'antropologia di Origene e di Gregorio di Nissa. Analisi storico-religiosa* (Milan 1981) 122–59.

22. See C. Tsirpanlis, "The Concept of Universal Salvation in Saint Gregory of Nyssa," *Greek Patristic Theology: Basic Doctrine in Eastern Church Fathers* I (New York 1979) 41–56.

23. The existence of textual variants to this passage, which omit all reference to universal salvation, testifies to the scandal felt by later Greek readers at Gregory's espousal of this position: see the note of J. Daniélou in his edition, *ad loc* (*SC* 1.155); also his article, "L'Apocatastase" 329–37. The same uneasiness of later scribes on Gregory's espousal of the *apokatastasis* theory is attested by glosses and variants in a number of manuscripts of his *De Anima et Resurrectione*, which has unfortunately not yet been critically edited.

24. On this notion of the "limits" of evil in Gregory's work, see J. Daniélou, "Le

Notes to pages 87–90

Comble du mal et l'eschatologie de S. Grégoire de Nysse," in E. Iserloh and P. Manns (eds.), *Festgabe Joseph Lortz* (Baden-Baden, 1958) 2.27–45; cf. Daniélou, *L'Etre et le temps* 186–204.

25. Note, for example, the bold statement of *De An et Res* (*PG* 148A1f.): "So then, if we were to try to describe this mystery [i.e., the resurrection] by defining it, we would say this: resurrection is the restoration of our nature to its pristine state." On Gregory's understanding of the resurrection, see J. Daniélou, "La Résurrection des corps selon saint Grégoire de Nysse," *VigChr* 7 (1953) 154–70.

26. In a number of passages, Gregory describes the process of purification necessary for human salvation by using the image of putting off the "coats of dead skin" that were given to Adam and Eve after the fall (Gen 3.21). If a Christian has led a holy life, death itself brings such a removal, "for there is no need of such coats for those who live in Paradise" (*In Meletium: GNO* 9.454.13f.). It is clear, however, that Gregory – unlike Didymus and other "strict" Origenists – does not interpet this process as the destruction of corporeality, but as the restoration of the entire human composite nature to its original "angelic" form (*De Hom Opif* 17.2; 22.4). So he interprets the "coats of dead skin" variously as "the wisdom of the flesh" (*De Virg* 12), as mortality (*Or Catech* 8), or as the passions (*De Mort: GNO* 9.56.1–3); he never simply equates them with bodies.

27. For the theological perspectives and purposes of Gregory's funeral orations, see R. C. Gregg, *Consolation Philosophy: Greek and Christian Paideia in Basil and the Two Gregories* (Cambridge, Mass. 1975), esp. 243–53; A. Spira, "Rhetorik und Theologie in den Grabreden Gregors von Nyssa," *StPatr* 9 (1966) 106–14. For Gregory's theology of death, see L. F. Mateo Seco, "La teología de la muerte en la Oratio catechetica magna di San Gregorio di Nyssa," *ScrTh* 1 (1969) 453–73; L. F. Mateo Seco, "La muerte y su más allá en el Dialogo sobre el almo y la resurrección," *ScrTh* 3 (1971) 75–107; J. Daniélou, *L'Etre et le temps* 154–85.

28. On Gregory's notion of purification after death, see especially M. Alexandre, "L'Interprétation de Lc 16.19–31 chez Grégoire de Nysse," *Epektasis* (= Festschr. J. Daniélou [Paris 1972]) 425–41.

29. The principal account of this synod is contained in Theophilus' synodal letter, preserved in Latin translation by Jerome: *Ep* 92. For the historical circumstances of the condemnation and the role played in the controversy by the four Origenist monks known as the "tall brothers," see Socrates, *HE* 6.7; Sozomen, *HE* 8.11–14. For a reflection of violent anti-Origenist sentiment in the Egyptian monastic milieu of the late fourth and early fifth century, see the First Greek *Life of Pachomius* 31, and the Pachomian *Paralipomena* 7.

30. Cf. Palladius, *Hist Laus* 11 (Ammonius).

31. In the *Anakephalaiosis* or summary of the *Panarion*, Epiphanius adds to the list of Origen's putative errors the theory that "the Kingdom of Christ will have an end," based probably on Origen's exegesis of I Cor 15.24–28 in the *De Principiis*. As in the arguments of Marcellus' critics, one can see here a point where concern for Christological and concern for eschatological orthodoxy overlap. Epiphanius is as unsympathetic to Origen, and as ill informed about his true position, as Eusebius had been about Marcellus. On the history of the Origenist

controversies in the fourth century and later, see A. Guillaumont, *Les 'Kephalaia Gnostica' d'Evagre le Pontique et l'histoire de l'origénisme chez les grecs et chez les syriens* (Paris 1962).

32. Cf. C. Riggi, "Catechesi escatologica dell' 'Ancoratus' di Epifanio," *Aug* 18 (1978) 163–71.

33. For Didymus' notion of divinization, see J. Gross, *La divinisation du chrétien d'après les pères grecs* (Paris 1938) 250ff.

34. This work is known, as a whole, only in Syriac versions, of which the second – unedited until A. Guillaumont's edition of 1958 (*PO* 28.1)– seems to represent the Greek original more closely; cf. Guillaumont, *Les 'Kephalaia Gnostica'* (above, n. 31) 15–43.

35. Ed. W. Frankenberg, *AGWG.PH*, NF 13.2 (1912) 609. Significantly, Evagrius makes this comment in the course of interpreting the parable of Dives and Lazarus (Lk 16.19–31), to explain why even Dives in hell is concerned about his brothers on earth. See also A. Guillaumont, "De l'eschatologie à la mystique. Histoire d'une sentence d'Evagre," *Ecole des langues orientales anciennes de l'Institut Catholique de Paris: Mémorial du cinquantenaire 1914–1964* (Paris 1964) 187–92.

36. On Synesius' eschatological reservations, see C. Lacombrade, *Synésios de Cyrène, hellène et chrétien* (Paris 1951), esp. 167ff., 259; H.-I. Marrou, "Synesius of Cyrene and Alexandrian Neoplatonism," in A. Momigliano (ed.), *The Conflict between Paganism and Christianity in the Fourth Century* (Oxford 1963) 126–50, esp. 147; J. Bregman, *Synesius of Cyrene* (Berkeley 1982) 159f.; S. Vollenweder, *Neuplatonische und christliche Theologie bei Synesios von Kyrene* (Göttingen 1985) 183–87.

37. Lacombrade 209.

8 *Redemptio Totius Corporis*: Latin eschatology in the fourth century

1. Cf. A. Vecchi, "Il rovescimento dell' escatologismo," *ADSPM* (Modena) 5.1⁵ (1957) 84–87.

2. Cf. J. Doignon's introduction to his edition of Hilary's *Commentary on Matthew* 1 (*SC* 254 [Paris 1978]) 32ff.

3. Hilary shows his original style of exegesis in applying to the activities of the Antichrist Jesus' parable of the fig-tree (Matt 24.32). Since the time of Adam, he suggests, the fig-leaf has been, "as it were, sin's clothing" (*tamquam peccati vestis*); so the flourishing of sinners, under the leadership of the Antichrist, who is "a son of the devil, an inheritor of sin," is a sign that the "summer" of judgment – with the "heat" of eternal fire – is drawing near (*In Matt* 26.2). Cf. *In Matt* 33.2, where Hilary takes Barabbas ("son of his father," i.e., Satan) as a type of the Antichrist.

4. See G. Blasich, "La risurrezione dei corpi nell' opera esegetica di S. Ilario di Poitiers," *DT* (P) 69 (1966) 72–90.

5. Cf. J.-P. Pettorelli, "Le Thème de Sion, expression de la théologie de la rédemption dans l'œuvre de saint Hilaire de Poitiers," in *Hilaire et son temps*

(= Actes du Colloque de Poitiers, 29 September–3 October 1968 [Paris 1969])
213–33.

6. For Hilary's notion of the divinization of human nature, in relationship to his
anthropology, see M. J. Rondeau, "Remarques sur l'anthropologie de saint
Hilaire," *StPatr* 6 (1962) 197–210; also P. T. Wild, *The Divinization of Man
according to Saint Hilary of Poitiers* (Diss. Mundelein College, Mundelein, Ill.,
1951).

7. For the influence of Neoplatonism on Ambrose's eschatology, see H. Dörrie,
"Der Seelenaufstieg bei Porphyrius und Ambrosius," in A. Stuiber and A.
Hermann (eds.), *Mullus* (= Festschr. Th. Klauser: JAC Ergänzungsband 1
[Münster 1964]) 79–92; also G. Madec, *Saint Ambroise et la philosophie* (Paris
1974). On Ambrose's Origenism, see especially H. Crouzel, "Fonte prenicene
della dottrina di Ambrogio sulla risurrezione dei morti," *ScC* 102/4 (1974)
373–88.

8. For the eschatology of Ambrose's baptismal catecheses, the *De Sacramentis* and
De Mysteriis, see G. Hellemo, *Adventus Domini. Eschatological Thought in Fourth-
Century Apses and Catecheses* (Leiden 1989) 269–80.

9. So, too, in the *Exp in Luc* 5.61, Ambrose identifies the "first Kingdom of Heaven"
with death, and the "second" with the union of individuals with Christ after the
resurrection. See J. Derambure, "Le Millénarisme de S. Ambroise," *REA* 17
(1910) 545–56,

10. In *De Bono Mortis* 11.48, Ambrose presents a different scheme of the gradual
advancement of the saved in beatitude, derived from *4 Ezra* 7.91–99, which he
here cites as Scripture.

11. This notion is also of apocalyptic origin; here, too, Ambrose cites *4 Ezra* 7.32f. as
Scripture, to support his position.

12. This last-mentioned passage is one of several in which Ambrose comments on
what had become, by his time, the classical biblical reference to the soul's
"interim" state, the parable of Dives and Lazarus (Lk 16.19–31). In other
passages, he offers different interpretations of the parable: in *In Ps* 118.3.17,
Ambrose suggests the rich man has already been consigned to eternal fire (see
also *De Nabuthe* 52); later in the same series of homilies (20.23) he states that
"the rich man in the gospel, even though he is a sinner, is tried by hardships,
that he might escape from them sooner."

13. *Jerome. His Life, Writings and Controversies* (London 1975) 334.

14. See T. Larriba, "El Comentario de San Jerónimo al Libro de Daniel. Las profecías
sobre Cristo y Anticristo," *ScrTh* 7 (1975) 7–50,

15. In his concern to do justice to the text of Daniel and the Johannine Apocalypse,
however, Jerome does conjecture that a period of peace, a *silentium*, will
intervene between the defeat of the Antichrist and the judgment (*In Dan*
4.12.12; *In Matt* 4.24.37f.). Cf. R. E. Lerner, "Refreshment of the Saints: The
Time after Antichrist as a Station for Earthly Progress in Mediaeval Thought,"
Tr 32 (1976) 101ff.

16. Y. Duval has pointed out convincingly Jerome's dependence, in this passage, on
Tertullian's *De Carnis Resurrectione*: "Tertullien contre Origène sur la résurrec-

tion de la chair dans le *Contra Johannem hierosolymitanum* 23–36 de saint Jérome," *REAug* 17 (1971) 227–78.

17. In commenting on Eccl 9.4, Jerome respectfully reports the theory that it will still be possible to change morally, for better or for worse, after death, but his interpretation of the passage is opposed to such a view. His *Commentary on Ecclesiastes* was probably composed in 389.

9 Grace present and future: Greek eschatology in the fifth century

1. See F. Leduc, "L'Eschatologie, une préoccupation centrale de saint Jean Chrysostome," *POC* 19 (1969) 109–34.
2. The attempt of E. Michaud ("St. Jean Chrysostome et l'apokatastase," *RITh* 18 [1910] 672–96) to argue that Chrysostom's eschatology was fundamentally Origenist was massively refuted by S. Schiewietz, "Die Eschatologie des hl. Johannes Chrysostomus und ihr Verhältnis zu der origenistischen," *Kath* 4.12 (1913) 445–55; 4.13 (1914) 45–63, 200–16, 271–81, 370–79, 436–48.
3. Cf. J. Gross, *La Divinisation du chrétien d'après les pères grecs* (Paris 1938) 289–94; G. Langevin, "Le Thème de l'incorruptibilité dans le commentaire de saint Cyrille d'Alexandrie sur L'Evangile selon saint Jean," *ScEc* 8 (1956) 295–316.
4. In one of his answers to the questions proposed in *De Dogmatum Solutione*, Cyril denies that the just will be capable of progress in knowledge after the resurrection, since all change is characteristic of an earthly, materially circum- scribed existence (5 [= *Adv Anthrop* 7]). This seems to be a repudiation of Gregory of Nyssa's version of the Origenist theology of beatitude.
5. Cf. G. Koch, *Die Heilsverwirklichung bei Theodor von Mopsuestia* (Munich 1965) 150f.; J. M. Dewart, *The Theology of Grace of Theodore of Mopsuestia* (Washington, D.C. 1971) 147f.
6. On the eschatology of Theodore's catechetical homilies, see G. Hellemo, *Adventus Domini* (see above, chap. 8, n. 8) 208–31.
7. Dewart, *Theology of Grace* 117f.
8. W. de Vries, "Das eschatologische Heil bei Theodor von Mopsuestia," *OrChrP* 24 (1958) 325–28, and Koch, *Die Heilsverwirklichung* 149ff., see the grounds for Theodore's reluctance in his Christology, which preserves a lasting distinc- tion between the person of Jesus and the Logos dwelling in him. This Christology does not offer a model for salvation that involves any substantial identification of the human person with God. Joanne Dewart rightly sees the origin of Theodore's conception of salvation, as well as his Christology, in his more general opposition to any theological idea that blurs the border between God and creation: "Theodore is utterly opposed to any mixing of the divine and the human, to any erasure of the gulf between Creator and created. That gulf can be bridged only by grace, and grace does not change nature" (*Theology of Grace* 147, n. 50).
9. "Das eschatologische Heil" 309f., 322–28.
10. See Koch, *Die Heilsverwirklichung* 143, 149–52, 157.
11. See de Vries, "Das eschatologische Heil" (above, n. 8) 330–34, for references.

12. Cf. R. Devreesse, *Essai sur Théodore de Mopsueste* (= StT 141 [Rome 1948]) 103, n. 2.

13. See G. Koch, *Strukturen und Geschichte des Heils in der Theologie des Theodoret von Kyros. Eine dogmen- und theologiegeschichtliche Untersuchung* (Frankfurt 1974) 242. Koch suggests, however, that the citations containing such concepts, which appear in Theodoret's works, "können zeigen, dass der Begriff (der Vergöttlichung) und die Begriffsworte Theodoret nicht völlig unannehmbar erschienen."

14. On Hesychius' theological style and method, see especially K. Jüssen, *Die dogmatischen Anschauungen des Hesychius von Jerusalem* (Munich 1931, 1934); and L. Perrone, *La Chiesa di Palestina e le controversie cristologiche* (Brescia 1980) 64–72.

15. Published (with a Latin translation) by M. van Esbroeck, "L'Homélie géorgienne d'Hesychius de Jérusalem sur la résurrection des morts," *Muséon* 87 (1974) 1–21.

16. On the authorship and background of the Ps.-Macarian homilies, see especially L. Villecourt, "La Date et l'origine des homélies spirituelles attribuées à Macaire," *CRAI* (1920) 250–58; H. Dörries, *Symeon von Mesopotamien. Die Überlieferung der Messalianischen Makarios-schriften* (= TU 55.1 [Bonn 1941]); J. Meyendorff, "Messalianism or Anti-Messalianism? A Fresh Look at the Macarian Problem," in P. Granfield and J. A. Jungmann (eds.), *Kyriakon* (= Festschr. J. Quasten [Münster 1970]) 1.585–90. On the origin of the sect, see J. Gribomont, "Le Dossier des origines du messalianisme," in J. Fontaine and C. Kannengiesser (eds.), *Epektasis* (= Festschr. J. Daniélou [Paris 1972]) 193–205.

17. For a summary of this influence, see especially the remarks of E. des Places in the introduction to his edition of Diadochus' works, *SC* 5 bis (Paris 1955) 66ff.; also *DSp* 3.832ff.

18. See F. Dörr, *Diadochus von Photike und die Messalianer. Ein Kampf zwischen wahrer und falscher Mystik im fünften Jahrhundert* (Freiburg 1937); E. des Places, "Diadoque de Photicé et le Messalianisme," *Kyriakon* II.591–95.

19. The best survey of the contents and historical circumstances of these works is still H. Weinel, "Die spätere christliche Apokalyptik," in H. Schmidt (ed.), *ΕΥΧΑΡΙΣΤΗΡΙΟΝ* (= Festschr. H. Gunkel: Göttingen 1923) II.141–73. Cf. the introductions of W. Schneemelcher and H. Duensing, *NtA* II.533–39 (Engl. edn. 2.751–59).

20. Cf. E. Peterson, "Die 'Taufe' im Acherusischen See," *Vig Chr* 9 (1955) 1–20, esp. 9f. (= *Frühkirche, Judentum und Gnosis* [Rome 1959] 310–32), esp. 319f.

21. See I. Lévi, "Le Repos sabbatique des âmes damnées," *REJ* 25 (1892) 1–13; 26 (1893) 131–35; S. Merkle, "Die Sabbatruhe in der Hölle," *RQ* 9 (1895) 489–506.

22. So P. Bihlmeyer, "Un Texte non interpolé de l'Apocalypse de Thomas," *RBén* 28 (1911) 270–82; see M. R. James, *The Apocryphal New Testament* (Oxford 1924) 555–62, for a translation of both versions; A. de Santos Otero, *NtA* II.568–72 (Engl. edn. II.798–803), for introductory remarks and a translation of the shorter version.

23. This conception of the "fire enclosing Paradise" has parallels in Priscillianist

literature from about the same time: see D. de Bruyne, "Fragments retrouvés d'apocryphes Priscillianistes," *RBén* 24 (1907) 323. Bihlmeyer also points out similarities in the work to Manichaean themes: "Un Texte" 281f.

10 Signs of a Church triumphant: Latin eschatology in the fifth century

1. See Marcellinus Comes, *Chronicon* 2.62–74, for a narrative of the apocalyptic "signs" of the years 390–420, including a reported appearance of Jesus in a cloud over the Mount of Olives in 419; cf. Augustine, *Serm* 19.6 and *Ep* 228.8. Augustine also reports an apocalyptic panic in Constantinople from about the same time: *Sermo de Urbis Excidio* 6.7 (*PL* 40.732). For a survey of popular eschatological expectations of the late fourth century West, see B. Kötting, "Endzeitprognosen zwischen Lactantius und Augustinus," *HJ* 77 (1957) 125–39.
2. For Gaudentius' conception of the direction of history, see G. M. Bruni, *La teologia della storia secondo Gaudenzio* (Vicenza 1967).
3. For Severus' pessimistic view of his own time, see, e.g., *Chron* 2.46.1; 2.51.7–10; for his acceptance of the old belief that Nero had not died, and would come again as a precursor of the Antichrist, see also *Chron* 2.29.5f.; cf. G. K. van Andel, *The Christian Concept of History in the Chronicle of Sulpicius Severus* (Amsterdam 1976) 118–28.
4. The notion that Severus was a millenarian was proposed by A. Biamonti, "L'escatologia di Sulpicio Severo," *Bollettino di studi storico-religiosi* 1 (1921) 55–68, but has been rightly denied by S. Prete, "Sulpicio Severo e il millenarismo," *Convivium* 26 (1958) 394–404. On Severus' eschatology, see S. Prete, "Degenerazione e decadenza morale nell'escatologia di Sulpicio Severo," *Aug* 18 (1978) 245–56.
5. See P. Monceaux, *Histoire littéraire de l'Afrique chrétienne* (Paris 1901–23) VI.249–58.
6. For this belief in Africa at the start of the fifth century, see Augustine, *De Trin.* 4.5.9.
7. For the history, in Christian literature, of this rabbinic tendency to identify the day of creation and the eschaton with the Pasch, see V. Loi, "La tipologia dell'Agnello pasquale e l'attesa escatologica in età patristica," *Sal* 33 (1971) 187–204.
8. On the details of Tyconius' life and work, see G. Bardy, "Tyconius," *DThC* 15.1932ff. His commentary on the Apocalypse is no longer preserved in its entirety. Much of it, however, can be recovered from the Apocalypse-commentary of Beatus of Liebana, an eighth-century Spanish monk; this work is essentially a compilation of the interpretations of earlier Latin authors, notably Tyconius, with additional borrowings from Victorinus of Pettau, Ambrose, Augustine, Jerome, Gregory the Great and Isidore of Seville (see T. Hahn, *Tyconius-Studien. Ein Beitrag zur Kirchen- und Dogmengeschichte des 4. Jahrhunderts* [Leipzig 1900; repr. Aalen 1971] 10ff., for a tabulation of Beatus' quotations). Beatus' commentary has been edited critically by H. A. Sanders, *Beati in Apocalypsin libri duodecim* (Rome 1930). Part of a condensed and

theologically "purified" text of Tyconius' work, commenting on Apoc 2.12–4.1 and 7.16–12.6, exists, under the author's own name, in a Turin manuscript: see F. Lo Bue (ed.), *The Turin Fragments of Tyconius' Commentary on Revelation* (Cambridge 1963), and the edition of the monks of Monte Cassino, reprinted in *PLS* 1.622–52. For reflections on the textual problems of this commentary, as well as on the broad lines of Tyconius' theology that may guide the scholar towards its reconstruction, see especially Lo Bue's introduction to his edition, 19–38; Hahn, *Tyconius-Studien*; and I. M. Gomez, "El perdido comentario di Ticonio al Apocalipsis. Principios de critica literaria y textual para su reconstrución," in R. M. Diaz (ed.), *Miscellanea biblica B. Ubach* (Montserrat 1953) 387–411.

9. Tyconius' famous remark about the vision of the 144,000 assembled before the throne of the Lamb, in Apoc 7.9ff. – "Nihil est enim quod praeter ecclesiam describat" (Beatus 4.6.50: Sanders 399) – could easily summarize most of his scriptural exegesis. See Hahn 22; also Hahn 98: "Die Gegenwart beschäftigt Tyconius mehr als die Zukunft." Tyconius's *Liber regularum* (ed. F. C. Burkitt: *TaS* 3.1 [Cambridge 1894]; *PL* 18.15–66) is summarized approvingly, although with reservations, by Augustine in *De Doctrina Christiana* 3.30(42)–37(56).

10. Although Tyconius accepts the tradition foreseeing a human Antichrist, a *rex novissimus* (*Lib reg* 1: Burkitt 5.22; *Lig reg* 7: Burkitt 75.12, 77.12) who will rule alongside the "ten kings" who control the Roman world (Beatus 9.2.59: Sanders 567), he speaks of him more often as a personification of unbelief or of false Christianity, just as active in the present world as he will be in the end-time (see, e.g., *Lib reg* 6: Burkitt 68.27ff.; 69.25–70.3). "Ubique antichristi sunt," Tyconius remarks in passing (Beatus 2.6.83: Sanders 243). So he is "amazed at the presumption" of those who attempt to identify the Antichrist more exactly – e.g., with *Nero redivivus* (Beatus 6.7.28–31: Sanders 508). As Hahn remarks, "Den Tyconius interessiert nur das Antichristentum, *nicht der* Antichrist" (98).

11. This *mysterium facinoris* – a phrase taken from II Thes 2.7 – seems to be, in Tyconius' language, the reality of diabolic evil presently concealed among Christian institutions. In the final revelation, the true Church will "emerge from their midst" like a bolt of lightning (*Lib reg* 7: Burkitt 84.32–85.1). Cf. Beatus 11.5.9 (Sanders 604): "and from the first coming of the Lord until his second coming this mystery of evil exists, in the form of the beast, because it has always been both Church and beast . . ."

12. Tyconius expands his ecclesiological interpretation of this passage a few lines further on: "[The author] speaks of these thousand years with reference to this world, not to the everlasting age during which they shall rule with Christ. A thousand, after all, is a perfect number; but although a perfect number is mentioned, it is understood to have an end. When the Spirit writes this, he tells us that the Church will reign for 'a thousand years': in other words, until the end of this world" (Beatus 11.5.18f.: Sanders 605).

13. Eg., *De Doctr Christ* 3.42; *Ep* 93.43; Augustine's treatise *Contra epistolam Parmeniani* is a defense of Tyconius' ecclesiology against Donatist criticism. For a brief outline of Augustine's theological debt to Tyconius, see Hahn, *Tyconius-Studien* 115.

14. For Augustine's distinction between eternity, which is God's way of existing, and time, which is the measure of the experience of finite, embodied spirits, see especially *Conf* 11.10f. and 14–28. See also: J. Guitton, *Le Temps et l'éternité chez Plotin et Saint Augustin* (Paris 1933); H.-I. Marrou, *L'Ambivalence du temps de l'histoire chez S. Augustin* (Paris/Montreal 1950); J. Chaix-Ruy, *Saint Augustin. Temps et histoire* (Paris 1956); M. E. Ravicz, "St. Augustine: Time and Eternity," *Thom* 22 (1959) 542–54; U. Duchrow, "Der sogenannte psychologische Zeitbegriff Augustins im Verhältnis zur physikalischen und geschichtlichen Zeit," *ZThK* 63 (1966) 267–88; R. Teske, "'Vocans temporales, faciens aeternos': St. Augustine on Liberation from Time," *Tr* 41 (1985) 29–48.

15. For Augustine's sober exposition of the scriptural prophecies of the Antichrist, see *De Civ Dei* 20.19 and 23; cf. H. D. Rauh, *Das Bild des Antichrist im Mittelalter. Von Tyconius zum deutschen Symbolismus* (Münster 1973) 121–30. For an example of Augustine's skepticism about the dire apocalyptic prophecies made by both pagans and Christians in his time, see J. Hubaux, "Saint Augustin et la crise cyclique," *AugM* 2 (Paris 1954) 943–50; J. Hubaux, "Augustin et la crise eschatologique de la fin du IVe siècle," *BCLAB* 40 (1954) 658–73; J. Hubaux, "L'Enfant d'un an," in *Hommages à J. Bidez et à F. Cumont* (Collection Latomus 2; Brussels 1948) 143–58.

16. For a thorough study of the background of this scheme in both pagan and Christian literature, see K. H. Schwarte, *Die Vorgeschichte der augustinischen Weltalterlehre* (Bonn 1966). See also the useful article of O. Rousseau, "La Typologie augustinienne de l'Hexaemeron et la théologie du temps," in E. Iserloh and P. Manns (ed.), *Festgabe Joseph Lortz* (Baden-Baden 1958) 47–58; and A. Luneau, *L'Histoire du salut chez les Pères de l'église. La Doctrine des âges du monde* (Paris 1964) 285–356.

17. For the dating of this part of the *Tractatus in Johannis Evangelium*, see A.-M. La Bonnardière, *Recherches de chronologie Augustinienne* (Paris 1965) 50–53. Besides the usual reference works, other publications used here for the dating of Augustine's works include: S. Zarb, "Chronologia operum Sancti Augustini," *Ang* 10 (1933) 50–110; 359–96; 478–512; 11 (1934) 78–91; S. Zarb, *Chronologia Enarrationum S. Augustini in Psalmos* (Malta 1948); and A. Kunzelmann, "Die Chronologie der Sermones des hl. Augustinus," *Miscellanea Agostiniana II* (Rome 1931) 417–520. In this section, the dates of Augustine's works, when known, are given in square brackets with references.

18. On Augustine's early use of the millenarian tradition and his abandonment of it after 394, see G. Folliet, "La Typologie du 'sabbat' chez saint Augustin. Son interprétation millénariste entre 389 et 400," *REAug* 2 (1956) 371–91.

19. For a discussion of the importance of *De Civ Dei* 20.9, and of the various interpretations given to the passage in modern scholarship, see B. Lohse, "Zur Eschatologie des älteren Augustin (De Civ Dei 20.9)," *VigChr* 21 (1967) 221–40. See also R. A. Markus, *Saeculum: History and Society in the Theology of St. Augustine* (Cambridge 1970), esp. 1–21. For Augustine's non-millenarian interpretation of the "Sabbath rest" promised to the saints, see Folliet, "La Typologie du 'sabbat.'"

20. See E. Lamirande, *L'Eglise céleste selon saint Augustin* (Paris 1963) 204, who

differs on this point from D. J. Leahy's apologetic attempts, in *Saint Augustine on Eternal Life* (London 1939) 104–18, to bring Augustine's theology into conformity with medieval Catholic teaching on the immediate enjoyment of the beatific vision by the just after death.

21. Surely the force of the expression *poenae temporariae* here is derived from its contrast with *sempiternae poenae*, and its parallelism with *poenae temporales* in the next sentence. Characteristic of the sufferings experienced by any souls after death is that they are "in time," not yet "in eternity," because the eschatological transformation of the resurrection has not yet been accomplished. As a result, like all else that is within history (*temporale*), such sufferings are "temporary" or transitory. But their qualitative difference from "eternal punishments" comes from the historical situation of the soul being punished, rather than from the nature of its sins.

22. *L'Evolution de la doctrine du purgatoire chez saint Augustin* (Paris 1966) 11f.

23. For this same point, see *De Cura pro Mortuis Gerenda* 1.2[424/25]; *Quaest Evang* 2.38.3; *De Civ Dei* 21.24. As J. Ntedika has pointed out, Augustine generally recognizes three categories of sinner: those guilty of very serious sins, which cannot be forgiven or expiated after death (*crimina, facinora, flagitia, scelera*), such as apostasy, heresy, schism, adultery, fornication or murder; those who have committed "light" sins, which Augustine does not specify any further but which presumably do not exclude a person from grace; and an intermediate class of sinner, whose deeds are *nec tam bona nec tam mala* and who has thus at least deserved to benefit from prayer and expiation (see esp. *De Civ Dei* 21.27; see Ntedika 14f. for further references). On Augustine's classification of sins, see E. F. Durkin, *The Theological Distinction of Sins in the Writings of St. Augustine* (Mundelein, Ill., 1952).

24. For the various judgments passed by modern authors on this question, see Ntedika 7f.; for a judicious summary of Augustine's thought on purgative suffering after death, see also J. Le Goff, *La Naissance du Purgatoire* (Paris 1981) 92–118).

25. See A. Lehaut, *L'Eternité des peines de l'enfer dans S. Augustin* (Paris 1912) 161–64.

26. On Augustine's exegesis of I Cor 3.10–15 and his understanding of "purgatorial" suffering, see J. Gnilka, *Ist I Cor 3.10–15 ein Schriftzeugnis für das Fegfeuer? Eine exegetisch-historische Untersuchung* (Düsseldorf 1955) 78–82; see also 58f., 68.

27. For the sources and argument of this work, see J. A. Mourant, *Augustine on Immortality* (Villanova 1969) 3–13, and C. W. Wolfskeel, "Ist Augustin in 'De Immortalitate Animae' von der Gedankenwelt des Porphyrios beeinflusst worden?," *VigChr* 26 (1972) 130–45.

28. Augustine finds himself unable to decide whether fetuses aborted from the womb will rise again, because of the acknowledged difficulty of deciding when a genuine human life begins. His position seems to be that once fetal development is far enough advanced to allow the identification of a human body within the womb, we are justified in including the aborted fetus among the human dead, and therefore among those who will rise (*Enchir* 23.85; *De Civ Dei* 22.13). In a

somewhat more developed argument, Gregory of Nyssa similarly urges that any human being who can be said to have lived at all has a right to share in the resurrection and in the life of growing union with God that is the natural goal of human existence (*De An et Res: PG* 46.149B14f.; *De infantibus praemature abreptis: GNO* 3.2.82.17ff.).

29. So no one escapes death, according to Augustine. In *De Civ Dei* 20.20 [425/26], he explains Paul's prediction, in I Thes 4.17, that those who are alive at Christ's second coming will be "caught up . . . to meet the Lord in the air," by suggesting that they also will pass through death to risen life, *mira celeritate*, as they are being raised to the apocalyptic clouds. "Not even they will be given life through immortality," he insists, "unless they die beforehand, however briefly" (*ibid.*). In *Retractationes* 2.59 (33).3 [426/27], he corrects the earlier opinion, expressed cautiously in *De Peccatorum Meritis et Remissione et de Baptismo Parvulorum* 2.31.50 [411], that some will be allowed, at the end of time, to enter eternal life without experiencing death.

30. On Augustine's hope for a re-creation of the whole cosmos at the moment of resurrection, see T. E. Clarke, *The Eschatological Transformation of the Material World according to St. Augustine* (Woodstock, Md. 1956); T. E. Clarke, "St. Augustine and Cosmic Redemption," *TS* 19 (1958) 133–64.

31. On the philosophical implications of the vision of God for Augustine, see L. Cilleruelo, "Deum videre en San Agustin," *Sal* 12 (1965) 1–31.

32. Although Augustine's soteriology stresses the healing, liberating and reconciling activity of God in fallen human nature more than God's glorification and elevation of it to share in the divine nature, there are a number of passages where he also speaks of human fulfillment as deification. See J. Stoop, *De deificatio hominis in de Sermones en Epistulae van Augustin* (Leiden 1952); V. Capánaga, "La deificación en la soteriología agustiniana," *AugM* 2 (Paris 1954) 745–54.

33. See A. Di Giovanni, "La partecipazione alla 'immortalità' di Dio, *eschaton* dell' uomo, in sant' Agostino," *Aug* 18 (1978) 229–36.

34. For further references, see Lamirande, *L'Eglise céleste* 234 and nn. 1 and 3.

35. *Ibid.*, 243ff.

36. In his anti-Manichaean work *De natura boni* 39 [399], Augustine observes that the "eternal fire" of Gehenna is not eternal in the same sense as God is, "because although it is without end, it is not without a beginning." Augustine also points out here that this fire is not an evil thing in itself, but "has its proper limits and form and order, unspoiled by any moral evil" (38). The instruments of eternal punishment are, in other words, also creatures of God, made to achieve his just purpose, and are therefore in themselves good.

37. On this theme of the soul's journey back to its original home, its pilgrimage to "Jerusalem, my country," as the central, organizing theme of the *Confessions*, see R. J. O'Connell, *St. Augustine's Confessions. The Odyssey of Soul* (Cambridge, Mass. 1969), esp. 11f., 142ff., 151–54. Cf. Lamirande, *L'Eglise céleste*, for further references.

38. The text of this work, which appears also in *PL* 20.1071–1166, has been critically edited by G. Morin, *FlorPatr* 39 (Bonn 1935). Morin suggested

Firmicus Maternus as the author, but this view has not generally been shared. For the most plausible discussion of its authorship and date, see P. Courcelle, "Date, source et génèse des Consultationes Zacchaei et Apollonii," *RHR* 146 (1954) 174–93 (= P. Courcelle, *Histoire littéraire des grandes invasions germaniques* [Paris 1964] 261–75).

39. See especially H.-I. Marrou, "Saint Augustin, Orose, et l'augustinisme historique," *La storiografia altomedievale* 1 (Spoleto 1970) 59–87.

40. Orosius attributes the Origenist doctrines he criticizes to two fellow Spaniards, both named Avitus, and to "Sanctus Basilius Graecus" (*CSEL* 18.155.3, 19f.); perhaps he has confused Basil with his brother, Gregory of Nyssa, on the subject of universal salvation.

41. Critically edited now by R. Braun, *SC* 101–102 (Paris 1964); *editio major*, *CCL* 60 (Turnhout 1976). For an evaluation of the controversy over Quodvultdeus' authorship, and for additional arguments in favor of the attribution, see Braun's introduction, *SC* 101.88–113.

42. See Braun, *SC* 101.17f.

43. The number 153 is, of course, inspired by the 153 fish brought to the risen Christ in Peter's net, in Jn 21.11, which represent, in the first instance, the unknown number of human beings whom God plans to save: see part 3 (*Gloria Sanctorum*) 15 (ed. Braun, *SC* 102.664.7–12).

44. This unusual phrase seems to be derived from Daniel 7.25, Daniel 12.7 and Apoc 12.14, where the suffering of the saints at the end of time is depicted as lasting half a "week" of years. It may also reflect the fact that the author presents only half the number of "predictions" and "promises" here that he gives for each of the three periods (*tria tempora*) of salvation-history covered in the previous chapters of the work – the periods *anti legem* and *sub lege*, taken from the Old Testament and the period *sub gratia*, which comprises the life of Christ. See Braun, *SC* 101.25ff.

45. *Ibid.*, 36.

46. The most recent critical edition of Salvian's works is that of G. Lagarrigue, *SC* 176 (Paris 1971) and 220 (Paris 1975).

47. The best and most recent critical edition of Prudentius's work is that of M. P. Cunningham, *CCL* 127 (Turnhout 1966). In quotations from his poems I am using here the English verse-translation of M. C. Eagan, *FC* 43 (Washington, D.C. 1962) and 52 (Washington, D.C. 1965).

48. For a discussion of the different conceptions of immortality woven together by Prudentius in one of the hymns of the *Cathemerinon*, see K. Thraede, "'Auferstehung der Toten' im Hymnus ante cibum des Prudentius (Cath 3, 186/205)," in *Jenseitsvorstellungen in Antike und Christentum* (= Gedenkschrift A. Stuiber: JAC Ergänzungsband 9 [Münster 1982]) 68–78.

49. In *Perist* 6.97ff., Prudentius allows the martyr Fructuosus to speak of the liberating effect of the fire of his martyrdom in terms that may also be meant to suggest the "purgative fire" available after death to less heroic Christians:

> Blest indeed are these souls to whom is given
> To mount upwards through fire to heights celestial;
> Fires eternal shall flee from them hereafter.

50. For a sensitive analysis of three of these passages on Paradise, see J. Fontaine, "Trois variations de Prudence sur le thème de Paradis," in W. Wimmel (ed.), *Forschungen zur römischen Literatur* (= Festschr. K. Büchner [Wiesbaden 1970]) 96–115. For a striking example of Prudentius' ability to blend the bucolic idiom with biblical themes – in this case, the story of Dives and Lazarus – see *Hamartigenia* 856–62.

51. The only modern critical edition of Paulinus' letters and poems is that of W. von Hartel, *CSEL* 29–30 (Vienna 1894). In quoting from his works here I have made some use of the English translation of P. G. Walsh, *ACW* 35–36, 40 (New York 1966–67, 1975).

52. For this notion of the "flight upwards" of the spiritualized, single-minded Christian at the time of resurrection, see Prudentius, *Cath* 10.25–44. P. G. Walsh notes that it is a "striking synthesis of the Pauline vision (cf. I Thes 4.16ff.) with the Neoplatonist notion of God resident in the upper air" (*The Poems of St. Paulinus of Nola* [*ACW* 40] 366, n. 38).

53. This letter also appears among Augustine's letters as *Ep* 94. Augustine's reply to it (*Ep* 95) contains his own reflections on the same subjects.

54. Paulinus alludes here to the Italian practice of burying one's own dead near the tombs of the martyrs, in order to increase their effectiveness as heavenly intercessors by associating them with patrons of proven power (607–10). A letter of his to Augustine, asking for Augustine's views on the appropriateness of this practice, prompted Augustine's treatise *De Cura pro Mortuis Gerenda* [421].

55. See E. Griffe, *La Gaule chrétienne à l'époque romaine* II (Paris 1957) 9f., 220f.; A. Solignac, *DSp* 11 (Paris 1982) 903f. The *Commonitorium* and a few other poems attributed to Orientius have been edited several times: by R. Ellis (*CSEL* 16 [Vienna 1888] 191–261), by L. Bellanger (Paris 1903), and most recently by C. A. Rapisarda (Catania 1958–1960; rev. edn. 1970).

56. See Courcelle, *Histoire littéraire* 98–101. Another shorter Latin poem, ascribed in its manuscripts to Prosper of Aquitaine (d. after 455) and published by Hartel in an appendix to his edition of Paulinus of Nola, reflects the same sense of despair in the face of war and social collapse that we find in Orientius, and probably comes from the same Gallic milieu (*CSEL* 30.344–48). Addressing his wife in tender phrases, the unknown poet observes that even if the world should not be coming to an end, still the certainty of their own death should move them to deeper dedication to Christ and to each other.

57. *Commodiani Carmina*, ed. J. Martin: *CCL* 128 (Turnhout 1960) 1–113.

58. For the most detailed presentation of this thesis, see J. Martin, "Commodianus," *Tr* 13 (1957) 1–71; see also the introduction to his edition, *CCL* 128.x–xiii. Other attempts to situate Commodian in the late third century have recently been made by K. Thraede, "Beiträge zur Datierung Commodians," *JAC* 2 (1959) 90–114 (on the grounds of his polemic against Judaizers) and J. Gagé, "Commodien et la crise millénariste du IIIe siècle (258–62 ap. J-C)," *RHPhR* 41 (1961) 355–78 (on the grounds of a supposed "millenarian moment" in Christian theology around the year 260). In addition to making questionable suppositions about the third century, however, none of these articles takes

sufficient account of the resemblances between Commodian's eschatology and that of known fifth-century Latin writers. For a good critical evaluation of the abundant, often polemical literature on the date and nationality of Commodian, see Thraede 91–96, and Courcelle, *Histoire littéraire* 319–37.

59. The fullest and most recent elaboration of this thesis is by Courcelle, *Histoire littéraire* 319–37; cf. his earlier article, "Commodien et les invasions du Ve siècle," *REL* 24 (1946) 227–46. Of the two ancient sources that mention Commodian, one (the so-called *Decretum Gelasianum*, from the end of the fifth century) gives no clear indication of a date; the other (Gennadius of Marseille's continuation of Jerome's *De Viris Illustribus* [*c.* 480]) includes him among fifth-century authors (*c.* 15, *PL* 58.1068f.).

60. *Autonomisme et christianisme dans l'afrique romaine de Septime Sévère à l'invasion vandale* (Paris 1958) 378–410, esp. 390–94.

61. On Commodian's language and meter, see J. Martin, *CCL* 128.xiii–xviii.

62. See esp. *Instr* 2.35, a section entitled *Nomen gazaei* (= "the name of the treasurer"), in which the first letters of each line, read backwards, form an acrostic identifying the author as *Commodianus mendicus Christi*. The last line of the work ("The curiosity of the learned will find a name here") underlines the riddle-like quality of the section. The title of every section of the work, however, is spelt out acrostically in its lines.

63. For a discussion of this passage, its sources and historical significance, and for further bibliographical references, see Courcelle, *Histoire littéraire* 326–34.

64. See A. J. Visser, "Een of twee antichristen bij Commodianus," *NAKG* 47 (1965/66) 131–36. Visser suggests the *Carmen* represents Commodian's earlier view; in the light of the more common tradition, he then combined the two Antichrists into one figure in the *Instructiones*.

65. The *Instructiones* seems to envisage *two* fiery judgments by God, one before the millennial kingdom of the saints and another after it (*Instr* 1.42.42ff.; 1.43.9–19). The *Carmen* speaks of only a single judgment, after the millennium: a fiery process that will last seven months (995–1041).

66. So *Instr* 1.44.3; in the *Carmen*, however, the millennial kingdom will first belong to the just who are still alive at history's end. Free from disease and death, they will live on, awaiting the resurrection, and will pray that others, already dead, may rise and join them (991f.).

67. These have recently been critically edited by A. Olivar, *CCL* 24–24B (Turnhout 1975–82).

68. F. J. Peters has called it "nüchtern und besonnen"; *Petrus Chrysologus als Homilet* (Cologne 1918) 70. For a survey of Peter's eschatological doctrine see *ibid.*, 69–75, 83f.

69. If he does not have Ambrose's *De Bono Mortis* directly in mind, Peter is certainly thinking of Christian consolation-literature here, as well as of the Stoic and Platonic tradition of elaborating the benefits death confers on a soul weary of life in this world of sense.

70. For Peter's doctrine of the resurrection, see J. Speigl, "Petrus Chrysologus über die Auferstehung der Toten," *Jenseitsvorstellungen in Antike und Christentum* (= Gedenkschrift A. Stuiber: JAC Ergänzungsband 9 [Münster 1982]) 140–53.

71. The most common scholarly opinion today is that the author of this work was an Arian bishop, writing in Northern Italy, Illyricum or Pannonia, sometime in the fifth or early sixth century: see M. Simonetti, "Arianesimo Latino," *StMed* 8 (1967) 691ff. Michel Meslin has recently tried to revive an older theory that the author is the Arian bishop Maximinus, writing between 395 and 427: *Les Ariens d'occident* (Paris 1967) 150–80. Pierre Nautin, who has sharply criticized Meslin's arguments (*RHR* 177 [1970] 74–77), himself supports J. Stiglmayr's thesis that the work is a translation of a Greek commentary by a Constantinopolitan presbyter named Timothy, written in the 430s: "L' 'Opus imperfectum in Matthaeum' et les Ariens de Constantinople," *RHE* 67 (1972) 381–408, 745–66. Neither argument has won wide acceptance, nor has the earlier contention of G. Morin that the same author also made our extant Latin translation of Origen's commentary on Matthew ("Quelques aperçus nouveaux sur *Opus imperfectum in Matthaeum*," *RBén* 37 [1925] 239–62). For a balanced review of scholarly discussion of the commentary, see H.-J. Sieben, *DSp* 8 [1974] 362–69. The most accessible text is that in *PL* 56.611–946, but a critical edition, by J. van Banning, is in preparation.

11 *Apokatastasis* and apocalyptic: Eastern eschatology after Chalcedon

1. The *History*, of which the *Teaching* comprises cc. 259–715, has been edited by K. Ter Mkrtč'ean and S. Kanayeanc' (Tiflis 1909); an annotated English translation of the *Teaching* has been published by R. W. Thomson, *The Teaching of Saint Gregory: An Early Armenian Catechism* (Cambridge, Mass. 1970). All my references here are to paragraph numbers in Thomson's translation.
2. Thomson 32ff.
3. In his *Life of Mashtotz* 16.7, the fifth-century Armenian writer Koriun points out that the Catholicos often used "similarities and examples from our transitory world" to present the hope of the resurrection to his hearers. Thomson (p. 37) finds in the *Teaching*'s treatment of the resurrection confirmation of his own theory that the work "was composed in conscious imitation of Mashtotz's known style as an epitome of Christian teaching."
4. The fifth-century Coptic *Life of Schenute* has been published in *CSCO* 41 (tr. 129); homilies, letters and hymns attributed to him have been collected so far in *CSCO* 42 (tr. 96) and 73 (tr. 108).
5. Schenute states clearly, in his "Apocalypse," that "the universe, by divine decree, is governed by angels" (*Op.* 82.1: *CSCO* 73.199; tr. 108.121).
6. On this passage, see S. Morenz, "Altägyptischer und hellenistisch-paulinischer Jenseitsglaube bei Schenute," *MIOF* 1 (1953) 250–55. Morenz points out similarities between Schenute's emphasis on the promise of physical integrity in the resurrection and ancient Egyptian concern that the body be kept intact in death.
7. See P. Gignoux, "Les Doctrines eschatologiques de Narsai," *OrSyr* 11 (1966) 324. Gignoux's article (*ibid.*, 321–52; 461–88; 12[1967] 23–54) is the most thorough available study of Narsai's eschatology, and extensively cites works not otherwise published. It will be the basis of my own summary here. The most

complete edition of Narsai's works to date is that of A. Mingana, in two volumes (Mossoul 1905). This is not a critical edition, however ; it contains only forty-seven of the homilies, and is now rare. For the most recent bibliography of editions and translations of Narsai's works, as well as secondary literature, see F. G. McLeod, "Narsai's Metrical Homilies on the Nativity, Epiphany, Passion, Resurrection and Ascension," *PO* 40.1 (Turnhout 1979) 7–10.

8. See Gignoux 323ff.

9. In several passages, Narsai stresses the exceptional, even miraculous nature of this annihilation. By nature, the soul is indestructible, he observes, but "the power of the Creator will make the soul of a single human being perish, so that others may learn how evil his wickedness is" (*Hom.* 44: Mingana 2.64.12–65.16). To the Antichrist alone, God will "shut the door of the resurrection," forcing him to remain in Sheol – the state of death – forever (*Hom.* 18: Gignoux 462). God will thus not even allow him to join his master Satan in the torments of Gehenna (*Hom.* 34: Mingana 1.322.24f.).

10. A few passages in Narsai's homilies suggest that since all will rise equally in beauty and integrity, even the distinction between the sexes will disappear – a theory he may have derived from Aphrahat. Cf. Gignoux 486f.

11. This emphasis on the spatial difference between the present and future worlds recalls, once again, the two-stage eschatology of Theodore of Mopsuestia, as well as its more crudely material version in the *Christian Topography* of Theodore's sixth-century disciple, Cosmas "Indicopleustes" (see pp. 196ff.).

12. On Narsai's conception of this "sleep of souls," see P. Krüger, "Le Sommeil des âmes dans l'œuvre de Narsai," *OrSyr* 4 (1959) 193–210, including the introductory reservations expressed by the editor, G. Khouri-Sarkis. Cf. Gignoux 332ff.

13. See the remarks of G. Khouri-Sarkis, *OrSyr* 4 (1959) 194ff.

14. There are two published collections of the corpus attributed to Isaac of Antioch, neither complete and neither a critical edition: that of P. Bedjan (Paris 1903) and that of G. Bickell (2 vols.; Giessen 1873–77).

15. So F. Graffin, *DSp* 7.2 (Paris 1971) 2010f.

16. See P. Krüger, "Gehenna und Scheol in dem Schrifttum unter dem Namen des Isaak von Antiochien," *OstKSt* 2 (1953) 270–79.

17. Although only a few of Jacob's writings have been edited critically, P. Bedjan published 212 of his 300 extant *memrē* (5 vols.; Paris/Leipzig 1905–10). For bibliographical details of more recent editions of individual works, see F. Graffin, *DSp* 8.1 (Paris 1974) 56–59. The metrical homily on Alexander the Great attributed to Jacob (ed. E. A. W. Budge, *ZA* 6 [1891] 357–404), which contains a long apocalyptic description of the wars preceding the end of the world, is now agreed to be unauthentic: see P. Peeters, *AnBoll* 66 (1948) 195f.

18. The orthodoxy of Jacob's writings has been discussed at some length, especially with reference to his Christology. See esp. P. Peeters, "Jacques de Sarug appartient-il à la secte monophysite?," *AnBoll* 66 (1948) 134–98; P. Krüger, "War Jakob von Serugh Katholik oder Monophysit?," *OstKSt* 2 (1953) 199–208; T. Jansma, "The Credo of Jacob of Serugh, A Return to Nicaea and Constantinople," *NAKG* 44 (1960) 18–36; R. Chesnut, *Three Monophysite*

Christologies (Oxford 1976) 119–41. For further references, see F. Graffin, *DSp* 8.10 (Paris 1974) 59.

19. See M. D. Guinan, "The Eschatology of James of Sarug" (Diss. Catholic University of America, 1972), on which this summary largely depends.

20. Syriac text in G. Olinder (ed.), *Jacobi Sarugensis Epistolae Quotquot Supersunt* (*CSCO* 110 [Louvain 1952]) 2–11; English translation in A. L. Frothingham, *Stephen Bar Sudaili, The Syrian Mystic, and the Book of Hierotheos* (Leiden 1886) 10–27.

21. Olinder 8ff.; Frothingham 20–25.

22. Quoted by A. de Halleux, *Philoxène de Mabbog: sa vie, ses écrits, sa théologie* (Louvain 1963) 394, n. 4.

23. Fragment on Jo 2.19, cited by de Halleux, *ibid.*, 159.

24. Comm. on Matt 3.1–16: de Halleux 394, n. 4. See also another quotation from the same passage, 427, n. 16: "When bodies (*gushmē*) will have been renewed in the flesh (*pagrā*), they will become spiritual and rejoin their souls and the incorporeal powers, to exist in God in an ineffable manner."

25. *Ibid.*, 427, n. 16; see also 136.

26. *Letter to Abraham and Orestes*: ed. Frothingham, *Stephen Bar Sudaili* 28–48 (Engl. tr. 29–49), esp. 32f.

27. De Halleux 426f., n. 16.

28. See Philoxenus' comments on Jo 2.19: de Halleux 159.

29. Comm on Matt 3.1–16: de Halleux 428, n. 21.

30. A. Guillaumont, *Les "Kephalaia Gnostica" d'Evagre le Pontique et l'histoire de l'origénisme chez les grecs et chez les syriens* (Paris 1962) 207–13, argues persuasively that Philoxenus may well be the translator of the theologically "moderated" Syriac version of Evagrius' *Kephalaia Gnostica* that Guillaumont refers to as S_1. Philoxenus' views on asceticism and contemplative prayer also owe a great deal to Evagrius' writings. None the less, the Syrian bishop points out to the priests Abraham and Orestes that some of Stephen Bar Sudaili's dangerous eschatological ideas were derived from "the monk Evagrius": see Guillaumont 208. De Halleux refers to Philoxenus' eschatology as an "évagrianisme adouci" or "évagrianisme mitigé" (*Philoxène* 394, n. 3; 428, n. 21).

31. See Guillaumont, *Les "Kephalaia Gnostica"* 302–306, and *DSp* 4.2 (Paris 1961) 1481–84, for a reconstruction of Stephen's life.

32. For Jacob's letter to Stephen, see Guinan, *The Eschatology*; for Philoxenus' description of Stephen's career and doctrines, and for his own criticism of them, see his *Letter to Abraham and Orestes*, ed. Frothingham, *Stephen Bar Sudaili* 28–48 (Engl. tr. 29–49).

33. Ed. F. S. Marsh, *The Book of the Holy Hierotheos* (London 1927; repr. 1969); see Frothingham, *Stephen Bar Sudaili* 49–68, for a discussion of Stephen's career and a comparison of his known teachings and those of "Hierotheos." Stephen's authorship of this work is now generally accepted: see Guillaumont, *Les "Kephalaia Gnostica"* 311–18.

34. According to Philoxenus (*Letter to Abraham and Orestes*: Frothingham, *Stephen Bar Sudaili* 32.14ff.), Stephen was also influenced by a certain "John the Egyptian," whose doctrine was heretical. Several scholars have suggested this

may be John of Apamaea, a Syrian monk of Gnostic sympathies whose books Philoxenus caused to be publicly burnt; see Guillaumont, Les "Kephalaia Gnostica" 316f.

35. Frothingham, Stephen Bar Sudaili 32.19–23; 34.12–16; 36.4f. Cf. Guillaumont, Les "Kephalaia Gnostica" 307f., 318.

36. Frothingham, Stephen Bar Sudaili 30.12.f.; cf. The Chronicle of Michael the Syrian 9.30.2 (ed. J. B. Chabot [Paris 1900–10] 4.312 b29–313a2), who refers to this final equality of all as "confusion" (ḥultānā). Cf. also Guillamont, Les "Kephalaia Gnostica" 308.

37. Frothingham, Stephen Bar Sudaili 32.23–34.1.

38. Ibid., 34.3–7.

39. Ibid., 34.12–16.

40. Tr. Marsh, The Book of the Holy Hierotheos 133. The author's "Origenist" conception of hell as temporary and medicinal punishment is made still clearer in one of the twenty-four syllogistic aphorisms of the following chapter: "For if Hell be for the sake of correction, and evildoing be not corrected (thereby), then Hell is in vain; but if Hell be not in vain, then evildoing is corrected, and if evildoing be corrected, demon is no longer demon" (5.3.10; tr. Marsh, ibid., 136).

41. The Armenian text has been edited, with a German translation, by G. Kalemkiar, WZKM 6 (1892) 109–36, 227–40; French translation by F. Macler, RHR 17 (1896) 290–309. For comments on this text and further bibliography, see H. Weinel, "Die Spätere christliche Apokalyptik," in H. Schmidt (ed.), 'EYXAPIΣTHPION: Studien zur Religion und Literatur des Alten und Neuen Testaments (= Festschr. H. Gunkel [Göttingen 1923]) 160f.; P. J. Alexander, The Oracle of Baalbek: The Tiburtine Sibyl in Greek Dress (Washington, D.C., 1967) 118f.

42. The various textual forms of this work have been edited and commented on in detail by H. Erbse, Fragmente griechischer Theosophien (Hamburg 1941); for the contents of the work's "brief chronicle," see 167.15ff. The best discussion of the complicated history of the collection is still that of K. von Fritz, "Theosophia," RE 2.5A (Stuttgart 1934) 2248–53.

43. Commentary on Daniel 4.23f.; cf. P. J. Alexander, The Oracle of Baalbek 119f.

44. P. J. Alexander, The Oracle of Baalbek: The Tiburtine Sibyl in Greek Dress (Washington, DC, 1967).

45. Alexander, The Oracle of Baalbek 41–47. The various Latin versions of the "Tiburtine Sibyl" are edited by E. Sackur, Sibyllinische Texte und Forschungen (Halle 1898; repr. Turin 1963). Cf. H. D. Rauh, Das Bild des Antichrist im Mittelalter. Von Tyconius zum deutschen Symbolismus (Münster 1973) 138–45.

46. For the political turbulence and natural disasters recorded for Leo's reign, which may have prompted this assertion, see Alexander, The Oracle of Baalbek 91, 111. The text's references to the "blasphemous words against the nature of the Son" spoken by Leo and his successor Zeno (145f.) suggest that the author saw in the growing opposition to the Chalcedonian Christology, which began in the East under these two emperors, a theological indication that the age of final apostasy had begun.

47. Alexander, *The Oracle of Baalbek* 120. For a careful comparison of the details of this Apocalypse with earlier examples of the genre, see *ibid.*, 120f.

48. Ed. H. C. Hoskier (Ann Arbor, Mich., 1928). Severus wrote at least five letters to the Count Oecumenius; two of them, along with a fragment of a third – all on Christological subjects – are still extant (*PO* 12.2.175–94). Liberatus, *Breviarium* 19 (written 560–66), refers to letters from Severus to "Oecumenium scholasticum Isauriae," which suggests both his place of origin and his reputation for secular learning. Although the manuscripts of the *Commentary* do not explicitly identify the author with Severus' friend, two of them (Messina 99 and Vat. Fr. 1426) call him "philosopher and rhetor," and a seventh-century Syriac florilegium, of monophysite origin, includes an excerpt from the commentary attributed to "Oecumenius, a diligent man and one who is very orthodox, as the letters of the Patriarch Mar Severus which are written to him show" (BL MS Syr. Add. 17214, f. 72v). See J. Schmid, "Die griechischen Apokalypse-Kommentare," *BZ* 19 (1931) 237f.; A. Spitaler and J. Schmid, "Zur Klärung des Oikoumenios-problems: zusätzliche Bemerkungen," *OrChr* 3.9 (1934) 208–18. The author of the *Commentary*, however, clearly speaks the Christological language of the centrist, "neo-Chalcedonian" party, rather than that of the anti-Chalcedonian or "monophysite" group led by Severus: see Hoskier 32.3–9; 255.10–18. If he is the recipient of Severus' extant letters – one of which can be dated 508–12, another 512–18 – they would represent the continuing attempts of the monophysite leader to persuade a learned and influential kindred spirit to join his anti-Chalcedonian camp.

49. Oecumenius reports three suggestions for deciphering the "number" that conceals the Antichrist's name in Apoc 13.18: "Lampetis," "Benediktos" and "Titan." Although the last of these is familiar since Irenaeus (*AH* 4.30.3), the others do not appear in our known sources.

50. In one passage, Oecumenius cites Gregory of Nyssa and Evagrius in support of his theory that God's punishment will be less severe than people think: Hoskier 122.19–25. For his reflection of the Origenist tradition on the question of punishment, see F. Diekamp, "Mitteilungen über den neugefundenen Commentar des Oecumenius zur Apokalypse," *SPAW* 43 (1901) 7f.

51. For a review of the long discussion of the identity of the Pseudo-Dionysius, see R. Roques, *DSp* 3 (Paris 1957) 245–57.

52. On the sources and main themes of Pseudo-Dionysius' theology, see *ibid.*, 264–86, and R. Roques, *L'Univers dionysien. Structure hierarchique du monde selon le Pseudo-Denys* (Paris 1954).

53. In *Eccl. Hier.* 3.3.7, 11, Pseudo-Dionysius suggests that the present negative conditions of human life, including mortality, the passions and the struggles of bodily existence, are the result of humanity's free apostasy from God's original gift: a share in the divine nature. Whether the body is simply part of that fallen, corruptible state, as the Evagrian system held, is unclear; see J. Gross, "Ur- und Erbsünde in der Theosophie des Pseudo-Dionysius Areopagita," *ZRGG* 4 (1952) 32–42.

54. The *scholia* on Pseudo-Dionysius attributed to Maximus the Confessor identify this remark as a repudiation of the millenarian tradition (*PG* 4.176c5–d3).

55. See T. L. Campbell, *Dionysius the Pseudo-Areopagite: The Ecclesiastical Hierarchy* (Lanham, Md. 1981) 211, n. 372.

56. A native Greek speaker, Severus seems to have had no acquaintance with the Syrian eschatological tradition, and repeatedly cites Athanasius, the Cappadocian Fathers, John Chrysostom and Cyril of Alexandria as his authorities, in eschatology as in Christology. For a general discussion of Severus' eschatological doctrine, see W. de Vries, "Die Eschatologie des Severus von Antiochien," *OCP* 23 (1957) 354–80.

57. *Johannis Caesariensis Opera* (ed. M. Richard and M. Aubineau): *CCG* 1 (Louvain 1977) 131ff. For a discussion of the authorship of the syllogisms, see *ibid.*, liv–lviii.

58. *Ibid.*, lvif.

59. For the probable reconstruction of Leontius' life and an interpretation of the accusation of Origenism against him, see B. E. Daley, "The Origenism of Leontius of Byzantium," *JThS* 27 (1976) 333–69; for his eschatology, see *ibid.*, 357f.

60. The main narrative sources for this controversy are the lives of the Palestinian monks by Cyril of Skythopolis, especially his *Life of Sabas* 36, 72, 84–90, and *Life of Cyriacus* 12ff. (ed. E. Schwartz, TU 49.2 [Leipzig 1939] 124f., 175f., 189–200, 229f.]). For a reconstruction of the complicated details of the Origenist controversy in the sixth century, see F. Diekamp, *Die Origenistischen Streitigkeiten im sechsten Jahrhundert und das fünfte allgemeine Concil* (Münster 1899); L. Duchesne, *L'Eglise au sixième siècle* (Paris 1925) 156–218; E. Stein, *Histoire du Bas-Empire* II (Paris 1949) 392–95, 654–83; Guillaumont, *Les "Kephalaia Gnostica"* 124–70; Daley, "Origenism of Leontius," 362–69.

61. Cyril of Skythopolis, *Vita Sabae* 83; Barsanuphius of Gaza, *Responsio* 604.

62. No complete modern edition of these questions and answers is yet available; there is, however, a convenient French translation by L. Regnault and P. Lemaire: *Barsanuphe et Jean de Gaza: Correspondance* (Solesmes 1972). Questions 1–124 have been edited, with English translation, by D. J. Chitty (*PO* 31 [Paris 1966] 449–616).

63. The text of the letter has been edited by E. Schwartz, *ACO* III (Berlin 1940) 189–214.

64. Although there is nothing in the extant writings of Origen, Didymus or Evagrius to suggest they themselves held such a conception of the risen body, sixth-century witnesses agree in including it among the Origenist doctrines of the time. For various explanations of its source, see A.-J. Festugière, "De la doctrine 'origéniste' du corps glorieux sphéroïde," *RSPhTh* 43 (1959) 81–86; J. Bauer, "Corpora Orbiculata," *ZKTh* 82 (1960) 333–41. Cf. Guillaumont, *Les "Kephalaia Gnostica"* 143, n. 74.

65. The sixth-century historian Evagrius Scholasticus preserves a saying attributed to Theodore Askidas: "If the apostles and martyrs perform wonderful works now, and live now in such honor, what kind of *apokatastasis* will there be for them unless, in the *apokatastasis*, they become equal to Christ?" (*Hist. Eccl.* 4.38). For the sources of such a notion in the writings of Evagrius Ponticus, see Guillaumont, *Les "Kephalaia Gnostica"* 155f.

66. For the names of these factions within the Origenists, see Cyril of Skythopolis, *Vita Sabae* 89 (ed. Schwartz 197.15ff.). Cf. Guillaumont, *Les "Kephalaia Gnostica"* 149.

67. The text of these anathemas, known since the seventeenth century but long considered unrelated to the Council of 553, was re-edited by Franz Diekamp (*Die Origenistischen Streitigkeiten* 90–96) and included by J. Straub in *ACO* IV, I (Berlin 1971) 248f. For a discussion of their authenticity and dating, see Diekamp 131f.; Straub xxvi–xxix.

68. For the text of this letter see Diekamp, *Die Origenistischen Streitigkeiten* 90–97; also *PG* 110.780c6–784B10.

69. For references, see Guillaumont, *Les "Kephalaia Gnostica"* 136–40; Straub, *ACO* IV, I xxviiif. For correspondences in Evagrius' writings, cf. Guillaumont 147–59.

70. This work has been edited critically for the first time by M. E. Colonna (Naples 1958). For a general study of the aim and arguments of the dialogue, see M. Wacht, *Aeneas von Gaza als Apologet: seine Kosmologie im Verhältnis zum Platonismus* (Bonn 1969). For an attempt to reconstruct the author's life, see E. Legier, "Essai de biographie d'Enée de Gaza," *OrChr* 7 (1907) 349–69.

71. Aenas later emphasizes, however, that "immortality was given to them [i.e., souls] not by necessity but as a gift" (ed. Colonna 50.13f.); his meaning, perhaps, in the context is that the creation of the natural world, both mortal and immortal, is itself an act of grace.

72. For Aeneas' dependence on Gregory of Nyssa, see especially S. Sikorski, *De Aenea Gazaeo* (Brescia 1909) 34–40.

73. For a discussion of the content and background of this passage, see Wacht, *Aeneas von Gaza* 105–33. The contention of M. Baltes, in his review of Wacht's study (*Gn* 42 [1970] 550), that the "rational substances" referred to in the passages are fallen angels, not human souls, is not justified by the context. Cf. E. Gallicet, "La risurrezione dei morti in Enea di Gaza e in Zacaria Scolastico," *Aug* 18 (1978) 274f.

74. The only critical edition of this work is by M. Minniti Colonna (Naples 1973), with introduction, translation and commentary; see also *PG* 85.1012–1144. For a reconstruction of the life and works of Zachary, who is probably identical with Zacharias "Rhetor," the historian, and Zacharias "Scholasticus," biographer of Severus of Antioch and others, see Colonna 15–32.

75. For the relationship of the *Ammonius* to the *Theophrastus*, see M. E. Colonna, "Zacaria Scolastico. Il suo *Ammonio* e il *Teofrasto* di Enea di Gaza," *Annali della Facoltà di Lettere e Filosofia dell' Università di Napoli* 6 (1956) 107–18; Gallicet, "La risurrezione dei morti" 275–78.

76. See the note of M. Minniti Colonna, *ad loc.*

77. The epithet "Philoponus," which literally means "industrious," apparently identifies John with a group of aggressive young anti-Chalcedonians active in the Alexandrian Church in the late fifth and early sixth centuries: see Zachary of Mytilene, *Life of Severus* (PO 2.1.24).

78. *De Aeternitate Mundi contra Proclum* (ed. H. Rabe; Leipzig 1899).

79. *Responsio ad Aristotelem de Aeternitate Mundi*. Philoponus refers to this work in

De Aeternitate Mundi 6.6, 7.6 and 10.5; fragments are preserved in Simplicius' commentaries on Aristotle's *De Caelo* and *Physics*. See I. P. Sheldon-Williams, "The Greek Christian Platonist Tradition from the Cappadocians to Maximus and Eriugena," in A. H. Armstrong (ed.), *The Cambridge History of Later Greek and Early Medieval Philosophy* (Cambridge 1967) 479.

80. These yet unpublished fragments, contained in BL MS Syr. Add. 14538, f. 148ʳᵛ, are summarized and translated in part by Th. Herrmann, "Johannes Philoponus als Monophysit," *ZNW* 29 (1930) 216f., n. 1; cf. 211, n. 7.

81. BL MS Syr. Add. 14538, f. 148ʳ; tr. Herrmann 216f., n. 1. For his expectation of a wholly new world, see Nicephorus Kallistos, *Eccl. Hist.* 18.47 (*PG* 147.425A2ff.).

82. Timotheus Presbyter, *De Receptione Haereticorum* (*PG* 86.44A10ff.); Photius, *Bibliotheca*, cod. 21 (ed. R. Henry 1 [Paris 1959] 13).

83. *De Haeresibus et Synodis* 33 (*PG* 98.69D4f.). This accusation is apparently anticipated by Cosmas Indicopleustes, *Top. Christ.* 7.95.

84. Cosmas' work has been carefully edited and commented on by W. Wolska Conus, *SChr* 141 (Paris 1968), 159 (Paris 1970) and 197 (Paris 1973). For a full study of the sources and arguments of the work, see W. Wolska, *La "Topographie Chrétienne" de Cosmas Indicopleustes. Théologie et Science au VIᵉ siècle* (Paris 1962). For passages in the *Topography*, and in Philoponus' *De Opificio Mundi* (written at about the same time), in which the authors seem to be referring to each other, see Wolska, *La "Topographie Chrétienne"* 163–92. Cosmas seems to have been drawn to the Antiochene Christology and exegesis by the preaching of Mar Aba, the "Nestorian" Catholicos of Persia, who visited Alexandria during the 540s; see M. V. Anastos, "The Alexandrian Origin of the Christian Topography of Cosmas Indicopleustes," *DOP* (1946) 72–80, esp. 76f.

85. See, for example, *Top. Christ.* Hypothesis 4f.; 1.1–4; 5.180; 7.94ff.

86. Cosmas' surname, "Voyager to India," was apparently created by medieval scribes; his works make no claim that he traveled to Asia himself (see Wolska, *La "Topographie Chrétienne"* 11). For his use of other sources for his geographical information, see *ibid.*, 3ff.; for his acquaintance with contemporary Alexandrian natural science, see M. V. Anastos, "Aristotle and Cosmas Indicopleustes on the Void. A Note on Theology and Science in the Sixth Century," in ʽΕλληνικά (= Festschr. S. P. Kyriakides: Σύγγραμμα περιόδικον τῆς ʽΕταιρείας Μακεδονικῶν Σπουδῶν 4 [1953]) 35–50 = *Studies in Byzantine Intellectual History* (London 1979) xiv.

87. For parallels to this conception of the universe in the writings of earlier theologians of the Antiochene school, see Wolska, *La "Topographie Chrétienne"* 43ff.

88. Illustrations formed an important part of Cosmas' exposition: see Wolska Conus, *SChr* 141.124–231. One particularly clear drawing of his two-tiered universe, preserved in Vat.Gr. 699 (see *SChr* 197.151 and n. 2; also *ibid.*, 53), labels the lower region of the "cosmic box" as "this world, in which angels and human beings and the present state now exist." The upper region is identified as follows: "The second tabernacle, the holy of holies, the Kingdom of heaven, the world to come, the second state, the place of the just." Cosmology and eschatology are closely identified in this conception of salvation-history.

89. For a briefer but similar description of the "great and wonderful hopes" of Christians, see *ibid.*, 5.251.

90. See F. Diekamp, "Das Zeitalter des Erzbischofs Andreas von Cäsarea," *HJ* 18 (1897) 1–36. For the text of Andrew's *Commentary*, see J. Schmid, *Studien zur Geschichte des griechischen Apokalypse-Textes, 1 Teil: Der Apokalypse-Kommentar des Andreas von Kaisareia* (Munich 1955); cf. *PG* 106.207–486.

91. G. Podskalsky, *Byzantinische Reichseschatologie. Die Periodisierung der Weltgeschichte in den 4 Grossreichen (Dan 2 und 7) und des 1000jährigen Friedensreiches (Apok 20). Eine motivgeschichtliche Untersuchung* (Munich 1972) 88.

92. *Analecta Patristica* (OCA 117 [Rome 1938]) 161–72.

93. Although this treatise is not yet published in its entirety, part of the Greek text was published, with Latin translation, by Leo Allatius in *De Utriusque Ecclesiae Occidentalis atque Orientalis Perpetua in Dogmate de Purgatorio Consensu* (Rome 1655), 336–580; Allatius' Latin translation was republished by J.-P. Migne, *Theologiae Cursus Completus* XVIII (Paris 1841) 465–514. Eustratius was a disciple and biographer of the Patriach Eutychius, who died in 582; nothing further about his dates is certain. The *Refutation* is summarized by Photius, *Bibliotheca* 171.

94. For a critical text of this poem, along with a thorough discussion of its structure, meter and literary parallels, see J. Grosdidier de Matons, *Romanos le Mélode: Hymnes* v (SChr 283 [Paris 1981]) 209–67. For an earlier discussion of the work and its parallels in the Greek corpus of Ephraemic hymns, see T. M. Wehofer, "Untersuchungen zum Lied des Romanos auf die Wiederkunft des Herrn," *SAWW.PH* 154–55 (1906–1907).

95. See J. Grosdidier de Matons, *Romanos le Mélode et les origines de la poésie religieuse à Byzance* (Paris 1977) 243.

96. Proposed originally by E. Michaud, "S. Maxime le confesseur et l'apocatastase," *RITh* 10 (1902) 257–72, this interpretation was adopted more recently by H. U. von Balthasar, *Kosmische Liturgie* (Einsiedeln ²1961) 355–59, and has gained wider currency as a result. For the arguments against it, see P. Sherwood, *The Earlier Ambigua of St. Maximus the Confessor and his Refutation of Origenism* (= StAns 36 [Rome 1955]) 205–22; and B. E. Daley, "Apokatastasis and 'Honorable Silence' in the Eschatology of Maximus the Confessor," in F. Heinzer and C. Schönborn (ed.), *Maximus Confessor* (Fribourg 1982) 309–39. Balthasar remained unconvinced by the critique of his interpretation: see *Was dürfen wir hoffen?* (Einsiedeln 1986) 51f., n. 38.

97. The *Sermo de iis, qui in Fide Dormierunt* (PG 95.247–78), which has been circulated under John's name, is now generally regarded as unauthentic, and may be the work of Michael Synkellos (d. 846); see J. M. Hoeck, "Stand und Aufgaben der Damaskenos-Forschung," *OrChrP* 17 (1951) 39f.

12 The end of all flesh: eschatology in the sixth-century West

1. According to the ancient *Life* of Caesarius (1.4–7, 9: ed. G. Morin 2), the future bishop withdrew from Julianus' tutelage after a short while, because he had been warned in a dream against reading secular literature. This incident

suggests something of Julianus' humanistic reputation among his contemporaries, and is given credibility by the moderate and philosophical tone of his eschatology, compared with that of Caesarius' preaching.

2. This treatise (*PL* 59.415–520) was usually attributed to Prosper of Aquitaine, from Carolingian times until the seventeenth century. Some of the earliest manuscripts of the work, however, attribute it to Julianus Pomerius, an attribution confirmed by Isidore of Seville's allusion to a treatise of Julianus by this title (*De Viris Illustribus* 25.31; cf. the continuation of Gennadius, *De Vir. Ill.* 98).

3. After almost fifty years of exhaustive study of Caesarius and the homiletic collections associated with him, G. Morin published, in 1937–42, the first critical edition of the 238 sermons he considered to be authentic products of Caesarius' scholarly "atelier": *Sancti Caesarii Arelatensis Opera Omnia* (Maredsous 1937–42); repr. as *CCL* 103–104 (Turnhout 1953). My references here will be to this edition. For a discussion of the problems involved in determining the extent and form of the Caesarian corpus, and for an account of its origin, see G. Morin, "Mes principes et ma méthode pour la future édition de Saint Césaire," *RBén* 10 (1893) 62–77; G. Morin, "Les Editions des sermons de saint Césaire d'Arles du XVIe siècle jusqu'à nos jours," *RBén* 43 (1931) 23–37; G. Morin, "The Homilies of Saint Cesarius of Arles," *Orate Fratres* 14 (1939–40) 481–86. Dom Morin also edited, as a work of Caesarius, the *Expositio in Apocalypsim* attributed in ancient manuscripts to Augustine: *Caesarii Opera* 2.209–77. Morin considers this rather confused document to be a series of notes prepared by Caesarius or his staff for a projected series of homilies on the Johannine Apocalypse. Its sparse commentary is largely dependent on Victorinus of Pettau and Tyconius, and offers no new eschatological perspectives. See G. Morin, "Le Commentaire homilétique de S. Césaire sur l'Apocalypse," *RBén* 45 (1933) 43–61.

4. Ed. J. Leroy, *CCL* 101.67–73.

5. It is ironic that Latin theologians at the Council of Ferrara (1437) tried to support their arguments for the Western medieval doctrine of Purgatory with excerpts from these sermons of Caesarius. See P. Jay, "Le Purgatoire dans la prédication de saint Césaire d'Arles," *RThAM* 24 (1957) 5–14. Cf. J. Le Goff, *La Naissance du Purgatoire* (Paris 1981) 118–21.

6. Ed. W. Hartel, *CSEL* 3.3 (1871) 308–25; J. H. Waszink, *FlorPatrSuppl* 1 (Bonn 1937). See also J. H. Waszink, "Einige Bemerkungen über den Text des Carmen de resurrectione mortuorum et de iudicio Domini," *Jenseitsvorstellungen in Antike und Christentum* (= Gedenkschrift A. Stuiber: JAC Ergänzungsband 9 [Münster 1982]) 79–85.

7. *PL* 68.793–934, with omissions supplied in *PLS* 4.1207–21.

8. *PLS* 4.1221–48.

9. For Beatus' commentary, see above, chap. 10, n. 8.

10. On Gregory's relentlessly theological way of interpreting natural and historical events, see the excellent study of P. Boglioni, "Miracle et nature chez Grégoire le Grand," *Cahiers d'études médiévales* 1 (Montreal/Paris 1974), esp. 14–70.

11. Gregory was cautious in schematizing his understanding of the shape of history,

in one passage (*Hom. in Ev.* 1.19.1) speaking of five great "ages," in others (e.g., *Mor. in Job* 35.8.17) using the Augustinian scheme of seven; see P. Siniscalco, "L'età del mondo in Gregorio Magno," in J. Fontaine, R. Gillet and S. Pellistrandi (eds.), *Grégoire le Grand* (Chantilly Colloquium, 1982 [Paris 1986]) 377–86.

12. Gregory, following the tradition of the Ambrosiaster and Jerome, conceived of the Antichrist as literally an incarnation of Satan: see H. Savon, "L'Antéchrist dans l'œuvre de Grégoire le Grand," in Fontaine *et al.* 389–404.

13. See G. Cracco, "Gregorio e l'oltretomba," in Fontaine *et al.* 255–65.

14. Gregory recounts a number of dramatic anecdotes to illustrate this traditional belief: e.g., *Hom. in Ev.* 1.19.7: *PL* 76.1158f. (repeated in 2.38.16: 1292f.; and *Dial.* 4.40.3ff.: *SC* 265.140ff.); *Hom. in Ev.* 1.12.7: *PL* 76.1122 (repeated in *Dial.* 4.40.6ff.: *SC* 265.142ff.); *Dial.* 4.19: *SC* 265.72ff. See A. C. Rush, "An Echo of Christian Antiquity in St. Gregory the Great: Death a struggle with the Devil," *Tr* 3 (1945) 369–80.

15. Gregory interprets reports of new volcanoes in the islands near Sicily as proof that the entrances to hell are being multiplied, now that the end of the world is approaching: *Dial.* 4.36.12: sc 265.122. For colorful stories of contemporary visions of hell, see *Dial.* 4.31–33: *SC* 265.104–12 and 38.3f.: 136f.

16. On this disputation with Eutychius and its significance for Gregory's eschatology, see Y.-M. Duval, "La Discussion entre l'apocrisiaire Grégoire et le patriarche Eutychios au sujet de la résurrection de la chair," in Fontaine *et al.* 347–65.

17. For an evaluation of Gregory's contribution to the developing doctrine of Purgatory, see Le Goff, *Naissance du Purgatoire* 121–31; on other effects of his conception of life after death, see C. Vogel, "Deux conséquences de l'eschatologie grégorienne: la multiplication des messes privées et les moines-prêtres," in Fontaine *et al.* 267–76.

18. So Boglioni, "Miracle et nature" 63, n. 129.

19. Ed. J. N. Hillgarth, *CCL* 115.11–126.

BIBLIOGRAPHY

Preliminary bibliography

(1) Patristic eschatology in general

L. Atzberger, *Geschichte der christlichen Eschatologie innerhalb der vornicänischen Zeit* (Frankfurt 1896); R. Frick, *Die Geschichte des Reich-Gottes-Gedankens in der alten Kirche bis zu Origenes und Augustin* (Giessen 1928); E. Staehelin, *Die Verkündigung des Reiches Gottes in der Kirche Jesu Christi I–II* (Basle 1951–53); G. W. H. Lampe, "Early Patristic Eschatology," *Scottish Journal of Theology Occasional Papers* 2 (London 1953) 17–35; G. Florovsky, "Eschatology in the Patristic Age," *GOTR* 2 (1956) 27–40 (= *StPatr* 2 [Berlin 1957] 235–50); S. Prete, *La escatologia e parenesi negli scrittori cristiani latini* (Bologna 1966); H. Rondet, *Fins de l'homme et* ✓ *fin du monde* (Paris 1966); A. J. Visser, "A Bird's-eye View of Ancient Christian Eschatology," *Numen* 14 (1967) 4–22; A. R. Marmorstein, "Marking Well the End: Eschatological Solutions to Dilemmas Faced by the Ante-Nicene Church" (Diss. University of California, Davis, 1988).

(2) Christian apocalyptic

(a) Jewish origins

D. S. Russell, *The Method and Message of Jewish Apocalyptic, 200 B.C.–A.D. 100* (Philadelphia 1964); W. Schmithals, *The Apocalyptic Movement. Introduction and Interpretation* (Nashville 1975); P. D. Hanson, *The Dawn of Apocalyptic* (Philadelphia 1979); C. Rowland, *The Open Heaven. A Study of Apocalyptic in Judiasm and Early Christianity* (New York 1982); J. J. Collins, *The Apocalyptic Imagination. An Introduction to the Jewish Matrix of Christianity* (New York 1984).

(b) Christian apocalyptic literature

H. Weinel, "Die spätere christliche Apokalyptik," in H. Schmidt (ed.), *'EYXAPIΣTHPION: Studien zur Religion und Literatur des Alten und Neuen Testaments* (= Festschr. H. Gunkel [Göttingen 1923]) 2.141-73; E. Hennecke (rev. W. Schneemelcher), *Neutestamentliche Apokryphen* (2 vols.; Tübingen

Bibliography

1959–64; English edition ed. R. McL. Wilson, London 1963–65); B. McGinn, *Visions of the End* (New York 1979).

(c) *End of the world, history*

E. Mangenot, "Fin du monde," *DThC* 5.2 (1939) 2504–52; H. A. Wolfson, "Patristic Arguments against the Eternity of the World," *HThR* 59 (1966) 351–68; L. G. Patterson, *God and History in Early Christian Thought* (London 1967).

(d) *The Antichrist*

W. Bousset, *Der Antichrist in der Überlieferung des Judentums, des Neuen Tetaments und der alten Kirche* (Göttingen 1895; Engl. edn. London 1896); H. D. Rauh, *Das Bild des Antichrist im Mittelalter. Von Tyconius zum deutschen Symbolismus* (Münster 1973).

(e) *Millenarianism*

L. Gry, *Le Millénarisme dans ses origines et son développement* (Paris 1914) 87–129; G. Bardy, "Millénarisme," *DThC* 10.2 (1929) 1760–63; A. Wikenhauser, "Die Herkunft der Idee des tausendjährigen Reiches in der Johannes-Apokalypse," *RQ* 45 (1937) 1–24; "Weltwoche und tausendjähriges Reich," *ThQ* 127 (1947) 399–417; W. Bauer, "Chiliasmus," *RACh* 2 (1954) 1073–78; W. Nigg, *Das ewige Reich* (Zurich ²1954); H. Bietenhard, *Das tausendjährige Reich* (Zurich ²1955); A. Luneau, *L'Histoire du salut chez les pères de l'église. La Doctrine des âges du monde* (Paris 1964); P. Bissels, "Die frühchristliche Lehre vom Gottesreich auf Erden," *TrThZ* 84 (1975) 44–47.

(3) *The "last things"*

(a) *Death*

J. Rivière, "Mort et démon chez les Pères," *RevSR* 10 (1930) 577–621; A. C. Rush, *Death and Burial in Christian Antiquity* (Washington, D.C., 1941); "Death as Spiritual Marriage: Individual and Ecclesial Eschatology," *VigChr* 26 (1972) 81–101; J. Daniélou, "La Doctrine de la mort chez les Pères de l'Eglise," in *Mystère de la mort et sa célébration* (Lex Orandi 12 [Paris 1951]) 134–56; J. C. Plumpe, "Mors secunda," in *Mélanges J. de Ghellinck* 1 (Gembloux 1951) 397–403; J. A. Fischer, *Studien zum Todesgedanken in der alten Kirche* (Munich 1954); A. Recheis, *Engel, Tod und Seelenreise. Das Wirken der Geister beim Heimgang des Menschen in der Lehre der alexandrinischen und kappadokischen Väter* (Rome 1958); J. Pelikan, *The Shape of Death. Life, Death and Immortality in the Early Fathers* (Nashville 1961).

(b) *Coming of Christ*

J. Timmermann, *Nachapostolisches Parusiedenken* (Munich 1968).

Bibliography

(c) *Judgment*

J. Rivière, "Le Rôle du démon au jugement particulier chez les Pères," *RevSR* 4 (1924) 43–64; "Jugement," *DThC* 8.2 (1947) 1765–1804.

(d) *Heaven*

P. Bernard, "Ciel," *DThC* 2.2 (1932) 2478–99; B. Lang and C. McDannell, *Heaven: a History* (New Haven, Conn. 1988).

(e) *Hell*

I. Lévi, "Le Repos sabbatique des âmes damnées," *REJ* 25 (1892) 1–13; S. Merkle, "Die Sabbatruhe in der Hölle," *RQ* 9 (1895) 489–506; P. Richard, "Enfer," *DThC* 5.1 (1939) 47–83; A. Michel, "Feu de l'enfer," *DThC* 5.2 (1939) 2200–8.

(f) *Purgatory*

A. Michel, "Purgatoire," *DThC* 13.1 (1936) 1190–1227; "Feu de purgatoire," *DThC* 5.2 (1939) 2250–59; J. Le Goff, *La Naissance du Purgatoire* (Paris 1981; Eng. tr. Chicago 1984).

(4) *Christian fulfillment*

(a) *Immortality*

W. Götzmann, *Die Unsterblichkeitsbeweise in der Väterzeit und Scholastik bis zum Ende des dreizehnten Jahrhunderts* (Karlsruhe 1927); H. A. Wolfson, "Immortality of the Soul and Resurrection in the Philosophy of the Church Fathers," *Harvard Divinity School Bulletin* 22 (1956/57) 5–40 (= K. Stendahl [ed.], *Immortality and Resurrection* [New York 1965] 54–96); J. Coman, "L'Immortalité de l'âme dans le 'Phédon' et la resurrection des morts dans la littérature chrétienne des deux premiers siècles," *Helikon* 3 (1963) 17–40; P. Bissels, "Die Unsterblichkeitslehre im altchristlichen Verständnis," *TrThZ* 78 (1969) 296–304.

(b) *Resurrection*

A. Chollet, "Corps glorieux," *DThC* 3.2 (1939) 1889–98; A. Michel, "Résurrection des morts," *DThC* 13.2 (1939) 2520–44; H. Cornélis, J. Guillet, Th. Camelot and M.-A. Genevois, *La Résurrection de la chair* (Paris 1962) 123–214; F. Refoulé, "Immortalité de l'âme et résurrection de la chair," *RHR* 163 (1963) 11–52; A. Fierro, "Las controversias sobre la resurrección en los siglos ii–v," *RET* 28 (1968) 3–21; G. Kretschmar, "Auferstehung des Fleisches. Zur Frühgeschichte eines theologischen Lehrformel," in *Leben angesichts des Todes* (= Festschr. H. Thielicke [Tübingen 1968]) 101–37; A. H. C. Van Eijk, "'Only that can rise

Bibliography

which has Previously Fallen.' The History of a Formula," *JThS* 22 (1971) 517–29.

(c) *Divinization*

J. Gross, *La Divinisation du Chrétien d'après les pères grecs* (Paris 1938).

(d) *Universal salvation (apokatastasis)*

A. Theodorou," '*H περὶ ἀποκαταστάσεως τῶν πάντων ἰδέα*," *Θ* 29 (1958) 530–40; 30 (1959) 20–50, 179–200; G. Müller, '*Ἀποκατάστασις πάντων*. A Bibliography (Basle 1969).

(5) *Scriptural exegesis*

K. H. Schelkle, "Biblische und patristische Eschatologie nach Röm. 13.11–13," *Sacra Pagina* 12–13 (1959) 357–72 (= K. H. Schelkle, *Wort und Schrift* [Düsseldorf 1966] 239–50); A. Strobel, *Unterschungen zum eschatologischen Verzögerungsproblem, auf Grund der spätjüdisch-urchristlichen Geschicte von Habakuk 2.2ff* (Leiden 1961); A. Lauras, "Le Commentaire patristique de Lc 21.25–33," *StPatr* 7 (1966) 503–15; P. Lebeau, *Le Vin nouveau du Royaume. Etude exégétique et patristique sur la Parole eschatologique de Jésus à la Cène* (Paris/Bruges 1966) (on Matt 26.29); E. Schendel, *Herrschaft und Unterwerfung Christi* (Tübingen 1971) (on I Cor 15.23–28); E. Pietrella, "'Caro et sanguis regnum Dei possidere non possunt' (I Cor 15.50)," *Aevum* 49 (1975) 36–76; F. Altermath, *Du corps psychique au corps spirituel. Interprétation de I Cor 15.35–49 par les auteurs chrétiens des quatres premiers siècles* (Tübingen 1977); S. Leanza, "Eccl. 12.1-7: l'interpretazione escatologica dei Padri e degli esegeti medievali," *Aug* 18 (1978) 191–99; J. Doignon, "La Lecture de I Thessaloniciens 4.17 en Occident de Tertullien à Augustin," in *Jenseitsvorstellungen in Antike und Christentum* (= Gedenkschrift A. Stuiber: JAC Ergänzungsband 9 [Münster 1982]) 98–106.

(6) *Related subjects*

(a) *Eschatology and Spirituality*

T. H. C. Van Eijk, "Marriage and Virginity, Death and Immortality," in J. Fontaine and C. Kannengiesser (eds.), *Epektasis* (= Festschr. J. Daniélou [Paris 1972]) 209–35; D. de Pablo Maroto, "Repercussiones espirituales de la escatología primitiva," *Revista de Espiritualidad* 33 (1974) 207–32.

(b) *Eschatology and liturgy*

H. B. Swete, "Prayer for the Departed in the First Four Centuries," *JThS* 8 (1907) 500–14; B. Botte, "Prima resurrectio. Un vestige de millénarisme dans les

Bibliography

liturgies occidentales," *RTAM* 15 (1948) 5–17; J. Ntedika, *L'Evocation de l'au-delà dans la prière pour les morts. Etude de patristique et de liturgie latines (IV–VII s.)* (Louvain 1971); G. Martinez y Martinez, *La escatología en la liturgía romana antigua* (Salamanca/Madrid 1976); G. Wainwright, *Eucharist and Eschatology* (New York ²1981).

(c) *Eschatological themes in early Christian archaeology and art*

L. von Sybel, *Christliche Antike* 1 (Marburg 1906); F. Van der Meer, *Maiestas Domini. Theophanies de l'apocalypse dans l'art chrétien* (Rome 1938); J. Quasten, "Der gute Hirte in der frühchristlichen Toten-liturgie und in der Grabeskunst," in *Miscellanea Giovanni Mercati* 1 (= StT 121 [Rome 1946]) 373–406; I. A. Richmond, *Archaeology and the After-life in Pagan and Christian Imagery* (Oxford 1950); L. Réau, *Iconographie de l'art chrétien* 2.2 (Paris 1957) 638–754; A. Stuiber, *Refrigerium Interim. Die Vorstellungen vom Zwischenzustand und die frühchristliche Grabeskunst* (Bonn 1957); B. Brenk, *Tradition und Neuerung in der christlichen Kunst des ersten Jahrtausends. Studien zur Geschichte des Weltgerichtsbildes* (Vienna 1966); C. Murray, *Rebirth and Afterlife: A Study of the Transmutation of Some Pagan Imagery in Early Christian Funerary Art* (Oxford 1981); G. Hellemo, *Adventus Domini. Eschatological Thought in Fourth-Century Apses and Catecheses* (Leiden 1989).

I Early Semitic Christianity

(1) *Early Semitic Christianity*

W. Staerk, "Der eschatologische Mythos in der altchristlichen Theologie," *ZNW* 35 (1936) 83–95; O. Cullmann, "Quand viendra le royaume de Dieu? Le Témoignage des écrivains chrétiens du II siècle jusqu'en 150," *RHPhR* 18 (1938) 174–86; J. Daniélou, *Theologie du judéo-christianisme* (Paris 1958) 341–66 (Engl. tr.: J. A. Baker, *The Theology of Jewish Christianity* [London/Chicago 1964]); E. Baert, "Het thema van de zalige godsaanschouwing in de griekse patristiek tot Origenes," *Tijdschrift voor Theologie* 1 (1961) 289–308; A. P. O'Hagan, *Material Re-Creation in the Apostolic Fathers* (= TU 100 [Berlin 1968]); D. E. Aune, *The Cultic Setting of Realized Eschatology in Early Christianity* (Leiden 1972); F. F. Bruce, "Eschatology in the Apostolic Fathers," in D. Neiman and M. Schatkin (eds.), *The Heritage of the Early Church* (Festschr. G. V. Florovsky: OrChrA 195 [Rome 1973]) 77–89; T. H. C. Van Eijk, *La Résurrection des morts chez les Pères Apostoliques* (Paris 1974); A. Fernandez, "La escatología en los escritos de los Padres Apostólicos," *Burg* 20 (1979) 9–55; *La escatología en el siglo II* (Burgos 1979).

(2) *I Clement*

W. C. Van Unnik, "Le nombre des élus dans la première Epître de Clément," *RHPhR* 42 (1962) 237–46; O. Knoch, *Eigenart und Bedeutung der Eschatologie im*

Bibliography

theologischen Aufriss des ersten Clemensbriefes (Bonn 1964); B. Weiss, "Amt und Eschatologie im I Clemensbrief," *ThPh* 50 (1975) 70–83.

(3) *Epistle of Barnabas*

A. Hermans, *Le Pseudo-Barnabé est-il millénariste?* (Bruges/Paris 1960).

(4) *Didache*

A. Agnoletto, "Motivi etico-escatologici nella Didachè," in *Convivium Dominicum: Studi sull' Eucaristia nei Padri della Chiesa* (Catania 1959); O. Giordano, "La escatologia nella Didachè," in *Oikoumene* (Catania 1964) 121–39; R. Trevijano Etcheverría, "Discurso escatológico y relato apocalíptico en Didakhe 16," *Burg* 17 (1976) 365–94.

(5) *Ignatius of Antioch*

H. Schlier, *Religionsgeschichtliche Untersuchungen zu den Ignatius-Briefen* (Giessen 1928); K. Bommes, *Weizen Gottes: Untersuchungen zur Theologie des Martyriums bei Ignatius von Antiochien* (Karlsruhe 1976); H. Paulsen, *Studien zur Theologie des Ignatius von Antiochien* (Göttingen 1978).

(6) *Polycarp*

A. Bovon-Thurneysen, "Ethik und Eschatologie im Philipperbrief des Polycarp von Smyrna," *ThZ* 29 (1973).

(7) *Hermas*

R. Van Deemter, *Der Hirt des Hermas, Apokalypse oder Allegorie?* (Delft 1929); A. P. O'Hagan, "The Great Tribulation to Come in the Pastor of Hermas," *StPatr* 4 (1961) 305–11; R. J. Bauckham, "The Great Tribulation in Hermas," *JThS* 25 (1974) 27–40.

(8) *Montanism*

K. Aland, "Bemerkungen zum Montanismus und zur frühchristlichen Eschatologie," *Kirchengeschichtliche Entwürfe* (Gütersloh 1960) 105–48.

II The Apologists

(1) *Justin*

E. R. Goodenough, *The Theology of Justin Martyr* (Jena 1923); F. R. Montgomery Hitchcock, "Loofs' Asiatic Source (IQA) and the Ps.-Justin De Resurrectione," *ZNW* 36 (1937/38) 35–60; W. Delius, "Ps.-Justin, Uber die Auferstehung: ein

Bibliography

Werk Melitons von Sardes?," *ThViat* 4 (1952) 181–204; E. Christen, *Thanatos und die ihm Zugeordneten beim hl. Justin* (Diss. Gregoriana [Rome 1963]); L. W. Barnard, "Justin Martyr's Eschatology," *VigChr* 19 (1965) 86–98; *Justin Martyr. His Life and Thought* (London 1967); A. O. Wieland, "Die Eschatologie Justins des Philosophen und Märtyrers" (Diss. Innsbruck 1969); E. F. Osborn, *Justin Martyr* (Tübingen 1973).

(2) Athenagoras

L. W. Barnard, *Athenagoras. A Study in Second Century Christian Apologetic* (Paris 1972). On the *De Resurrectione*: L. Chaudouard, *La Philosophie du dogme de la résurrection de la chair au IIe siècle: étude sur le περὶ ἀναστάσεως d'Athénagore* (Lyons 1905); R. M. Grant, "Athenagoras or Ps.-Athenagoras?," *HThR* 47 (1954) 121–29; E. Bellini, "Atenagora e il trattato sulla risurrezione dei morti," *ScC* 101 (1973) 511–17; L. W. Barnard, "Athenagoras' De Resurrectione. The Background and Theology of a Second-Century Treatise on the Resurrection," *StTh* 30 (1976) 1–42; J.-M. Vermander, "Celse et l'attribution d'un ouvrage sur la résurrection des morts," *MSR* 35 (1978) 125–34.

III The Gnostic crisis (150–200)

(1) Gnosticism

E. Schweizer, "Die Gegenwart des Geistes und eschatologische Hoffnung bei Zarathustra, spätjüdischen Gruppen, Gnostikern und den Zeugen des Neuen Testaments," in W. D. Davies and D. Daube (eds.), *The Background of the New Testament and its Eschatology* (= Festschr. C. H. Dodd [Cambridge 1956]) 482–508; H. J. Schoeps, "Bermerkungen zu Reinkarnationsvorstellungen der Gnosis," *Numen* 4 (1957) 228–32; R. Haardt, "Das universal-eschatologische Vorstellungsgut in der Gnosis," in K. Schubert (ed.), *Vom Messias zum Christus* (Vienna 1964) 315–30; M. L. Peel, "Gnostic Eschatology and the New Testament," *NT* 12 (1970) 141–65; W. C. Van Unnik, "The 'Wise Fire' in a Gnostic Eschatological Vision," in P. Granfield and J. A. Jungmann (eds.), *Kyriakon* (= Festschr. J. Quasten [Münster 1970]) 1.277–88; A. González Blanco, "Misticismo y escatología en el 'Corpus Hermeticum,'" *Cuadernos de Filología* 5 (1973) 313–60; A. Méhat, "Apocatastasis chez Basilide," in *Mélanges H.-C. Puech* (Paris 1974) 365–73; E. H. Pagels, "'The Mystery of the Resurrection': A Gnostic Reading of I Corinthians 15," *JBL* 93 (1974) 276–88; K. Rudolph (ed.), *Gnosis und Gnostizismus* (Darmstadt 1975); K. Rudolph, *Die Gnosis: Wesen und Geschichte einer spätantiken Religion* (Göttingen 1977; tr. R. McLaren Wilson, *Gnosis: The Nature and History of Gnosticism* [San Francisco 1984]); D. Devoti, "Temi escatologici nello gnosticismo valentiniano," *Aug* 18 (1978) 47–61; G. Filoramo, "Rivelazione ed escatologia nello gnosticismo cristiano del II secolo," *Aug* 18 (1978) 75–88.

On the *Epistle to Rheginos* (= "Letter on the Resurrection"): R. Haardt, "'Die Abhandlung über die Auferstehung' des Codex Jung aus der Bibliothek gnostischer koptischer Schriften von Nag Hammadi: Bemerkungen zu

Bibliography

ausgewählten Motiven," *Kairos* 11 (1969) 1–5; M. L. Peel, *The Epistle to Rheginos. A Valentinian Letter on the Resurrection* (London 1969) (text, translation and commentary); H.-G. Gaffron, "Eine gnostische Apologie des Auferstehungsglaubens," in G. Bornkamm and K. Rahner (eds.), *Die Zeit Jesu* (= Festschr. H. Schlier [Frankfurt 1970]) 218–27; B. Dehandschutter, "L'Epître à Rhéginos. Quelques problèmes critiques," *OLoP* 4 (1973) 101–11; J.-E. Ménard, "La Notion de 'résurrection' dans l'Epître à Rhéginos," in M. Kraus (ed.), *Essays . . . in Honor of Pahor Labib* (Leiden 1975) 110–24; E. Peretto, "L'Epistola a Rheginos: il posto del corpo nella risurrezione," *Aug* 18 (1978) 63–74.

(2) *Irenaeus*

E. Buonaiuti, "Il millenarismo di Ireneo," *Saggi sul cristianesimo primitivo* (Rome 1923) 79–96; N. Bonwetsch, *Die Theologie des Irenäus* (Gütersloh 1925); V. Crewers, "Het millenarisme van Irenaeus," *Bijdragen van de philosophische en theologische Faculteiten der Nederlandsche Jezuiten* 1 (1938) 28–80; E. Scharl, *Recapitulatio mundi. Der Rekapitulationsbegriff des hl. Irenaeus und seine Anwendung auf die Körperwelt* (Frankfurt 1941); M. Aubineau, "Incorruptibilité et divinisation selon Saint Irénée," RSR 44 (1956) 25–52; A. Bengsch, *Heilsgeschichte und Heilswissen. Eine Untersuchung zur Struktur und Entfaltung des theologischen Denkens im Werk "Adversus Haereses" vom hl. Irenäus von Lyon* (Leipzig 1957); A. Benoit, *Saint Irénée. Introduction à l'étude de sa théologie* (Paris 1960); J. Arroniz, "La immortalidad como deificación en S. Ireneo," *ScrVict* 8 (1961) 262–87; "La salvación de la carne en S. Ireneo," *ScrVict* 12 (1965) 7–29; W. C. Van Unnik, "Der Ausdruck, 'In den letzten Zeiten,' bei Irenäus," in W. C. Van Unnik (ed.), *Neotestamentica et Patristica* (= Festschr. O. Cullmann [Leiden 1962]) 293–304; G. Joppich, *Salus Carnis. Eine Untersuchung in der Theologie des hl. Irenäus von Lyon* (Münsterschwarzach ²1967); M. O'Rourke Boyle, "Irenaeus' Millennial Hope. A Polemical Weapon," *RThAM* 36 (1969) 5–16; A. S. Wood, "The Eschatology of Irenaeus," *EvQ* 41 (1969) 30–41; G. Jossa, *Regno di Dio e chiesa. Ricerche sulla concezione escatologica ed ecclesiologica dell' Adversus haereses di Ireneo di Lione* (Naples 1970); "Storia della salvezza ed escatologia nell' Adversus Haereses di Ireneo di Lione," *Aug* 18 (1978) 107–25; E. Norelli, "Il duplice rinnovamento del mondo nell'escatologia di San Ireneo," *ibid.*, 89–106.

IV Eschatology in the West: 200–250

(1) *Tertullian*

A. Quacquarelli, "Antropologia ed escatologia secondo Tertulliano," *RSFil* 2.2 (1949) 14–17; J. Pelikan, "The Eschatology of Tertullian," *ChH* 21 (1952) 108–22; R. Franco, *El final del reino de Cristo en Tertuliano* (Granada 1956); H. Finé, *Die Terminologie der Jenseitsvorstellungen bei Tertullian: ein semasiologischer Beitrag zur Dogmengeschichte des Zwischenzustandes* (Bonn 1958); C. Tibiletti, "Il senso escatologico di 'pax' e 'refrigerium' e un passo di Tertulliano (De Exhort. Cast. 1.1)," *Maia* 10 (1958) 209–20; "Inizi del millenarismo di Tertulliano,"

Bibliography

Annali della Facoltà di lettere e filosofia dell' Università di Macerata 1 (1968) 195–213; "San Ireneo e l'escatologia nel De Testimonio Animae di Tertulliano," *AAST* 94 (1959–60) 290–330; P. Siniscalco, "Il motivo razionale della risurrezione della carne in due passi de Tertuliano," *AAST* 78 (1960/61) 195–221; *Ricerche sul "De Resurrectione" di Tertulliano* (Rome 1968); R. Sider, "Structure and Design in the *De Resurrectione Mortuorum* of Tertullian," *VigChr* 23 (1969) 177–96; F. Cardman, "Tertullian on the Resurrection" (Diss. Yale University 1974); J. Daniélou, *The Origins of Latin Christianity* (= *History of Early Christian Doctrine III*; Eng. tr. London 1977) 390–404.

(2) Hippolytus

A. d'Alès, *La Théologie de S. Hippolyte* (Paris 1906); A. Donini, *Ippolito di Roma* (Rome 1925); D. Ritschl, "Hippolytus' Conception of Deification," *SJTh* 12 (1959) 388–99.

(3) Cyprian

P. Jay, "Saint Cyprien et la doctrine du purgatoire," *RThAM* 27 (1960) 133–36; B. de Margerie, "L'Intérêt théologique du *De mortalitate* de S. Cyprian," *ScEc* 15 (1963) 199–211; J. Daniélou, *The Origins of Latin Christianity* (= *History of Early Christian Doctrine III*; Eng. tr. London 1977) 251–58.

V Alexandrian eschatology and its critics (185–300)

(1) Clement of Alexandria

G. Anrich, "Clemens und Origenes als Begründer der Lehre vom Fegfeuer," in *Theologische Abhandlungen für H. J. Holtzmann* (Tübingen/Leipzig 1902) 95–120; T. Spacil, "La dottrina del purgatorio in Clemente Alessandrino ed Origene," *Bess* 23 (1919) 131–45; A. Méhat, "'Apocatastase': Origène, Clément d'Alexandrie, Act. 3.21," *VigChr* 10 (1956) 196–214; *Etude sur les Stromates de Clément d'Alexandrie* (Paris 1960), esp. 456–74; M. Berciano, *Kairos. Tiempo humano e historico-salvifico de Clemente de Alexandria* (Madrid 1974); K. Schmöle, *Läuterung nach dem Tode und pneumatische Auferstehung bei Klemens von Alexandrien* (Münster 1974); M. Mees, "Jetzt und Dann in der Eschatologie Klemens von Alexandrien," *Aug* 18 (1978) 127–37.

(2) Origen

G. Anrich, "Clemens und Origenes als Begründer der Lehre vom Fegfeuer," in *Theologische Abhandlungen für H. J. Holtzmann* (Tübingen/Leipzig 1902) 95–120; T. Spacil, "La dottrina del purgatorio in Clemente Alessandrino ed Origene," *Bess* 23 (1919) 131–45; W. Völker, *Das Vollkommenheitsideal bei Origenes* (Tübingen 1931), esp. 125–36; H. Koch, *Pronoia und Paideusis. Studien über Origenes und sein Verhältnis zum Neuplatonismus* (Berlin 1932); H. Chadwick, "Origen, Celsus and

the Resurrection of the Body," *HThR* 41 (1948) 83–102; A. Méhat,
"'Apocatastase': Origène, Clément d'Alexandrie, Act. 3.21," *VigChr* 10 (1956)
196–214; M. M. Branişte, "Eshatologia în concepţia lui Origen," *StTeol* 10 (1958)
440–53; H. Cornélis, "Les Fondements cosmologiques de l'eschatologie
d'Origène," *RSPhTh* 43 (1959) 32–80, 201–47; A. M. Festugière, "Le Corps
glorieux 'sphéroïde' chez Origène," *RSPhTh* 43 (1959) 81–86; J. Bauer, "Corpora
orbiculata," *ZKTh* 82 (1960) 333–41; P. Némeshégyi, *La Paternité de Dieu chez
Origène* (Paris/Tournai 1960); G. Gruber, *ZΩH. Wesen, Stufen und Mitteilung des
wahren Lebens bei Origenes* (Münster 1961); H. Crouzel, *Origène et la philosophie*
(Paris 1962); "L'Exégèse origénienne de I Cor 3.11–15, et la purification
eschatologique," in J. Fontaine and C. Kannengiesser (eds.), *Epektasis* (=
Festschr. J. Daniélou [Paris 1972]) 273–83; "La 'Première' et la 'Seconde'
Résurrection des hommes d'après Origène," *Didaskalia* 3 (1973) 3–20; "Les
Prophéties de la résurrection chez Origène," *Forma Futuri* (= Festschr. M.
Pellegrino [Turin 1975]) 980–92; "Le Thème platonicien du 'véhicule de l'âme'
chez Origène," *Didaskalia* 7 (1977) 225–37; "L'Hadès et la Géhenne selon
Origène," *Gr* 59 (1978) 291–331; "Mort et immortalité selon Origène," *BLE* 79
(1978), 81–96, 181–96; "La Doctrine origénienne du corps résuscité," *BLE* 81
(1980) 175–200, 241–66; "L'Anthropologie d'Origène: de l'arché au telos," in U.
Bianchi and H. Crouzel (eds.), *Archè e Telos: l'antropologia di Origene e di Gregorio di
Nissa. Analisi storico-religiosa* (Milan 1981), 36–49; "Différences entre les
résuscités selon Origène," *Jenseitsvorstellungen im Antike und Christentum* (=
Gedenkschr. A. Stuiber: JAC Ergänzungsband 9 [Münster 1982]) 107–16; *Origène*
(Paris 1985; Eng. tr. Edinburgh/San Francisco 1989); F. H. Kettler, *Der
ursprüngliche Sinn der Dogmatik des Origenes* (Berlin 1966); H.-J. Horn, "Die 'Hölle'
als Krankheit der Seele in einer Deutung des Origenes," *JAC* 11/12 (1968/69)
55–64; "Ignis aeternus: une interprétation morale du feu éternel chez Origène,"
REG 82 (1969) 76–88; R. Trevijano Etcheverría, "'Επιδημία y παρουσία en
Origenes," *ScrVict* 16 (1969) 313–37; B. Weiss, "Die Unsterblichkeit der Seele als
eschatologischer Heilsgut nach Origenes," *TrThZ* 80 (1971) 156–69; A. Le
Boulluec, "De la croissance selon les Stoïciens à la résurrection selon Origène,"
REG 88 (1975) 143–55; J. Rius-Camps, "La suerte final de la naturaleza corpórea
según el Peri Archon de Orígenes," *StPatr* 14 (= TU 117 [Berlin 1976]) 167–79;
"La hipótesis origeniana sobre el fin último (peri telous)," in U. Bianchi and H.
Crouzel (eds.), *Archè e Telos: l'antropologia di Origene e di Gregorio di Nissa. Analisi
storico-religiosa* (Milan 1981) 58–117; A. Monaci, "Apocalisse ed escatologia nell'
opera di Origene," *Aug* 18 (1978) 139–51; L. R. Hennessey, "The Place of Saints
and Sinners after Death," in C. Kannengiesser and W. L. Petersen (eds.), *Origen of
Alexandria: his World and his Legacy* (Notre Dame 1988) 295–312.

(3) *Methodius*

N. Bonwetsch, *Die Theologie des Methodius von Olympus* (AGWG.PH 7/1 [1904]);
E. Buonaiuti, "The Ethics and Eschatology of Methodius of Olympus," *HThR* 14
(1921) 255–66; A. Biamonti, "L'escatologia di Metodio di Olimpo," *Rivista di*

studi filosofici e religiosi 4 (1923) 182–202; L. G. Patterson, "The Anti-Origenist Theology of Methodius of Olympus" (Diss. Columbia Univ. 1958); "*De Libero Arbitrio* and Methodius's View of Origen," *StPatr* 14 (= TU 117 [Berlin 1976]) 160–66; "Notes on *De cibis* and Methodius's View of Origen," in R. P. C. Hanson and H. Crouzel (eds.), *Origeniana Tertia* (Rome 1985) 233–43; "Who are the Opponents in Methodius's *De resurrectione?*," *StPatr* 19 (forthcoming); H. Crouzel, "Les Critiques addressées par Méthode et ses contemporains à la doctrine origénienne du corps résuscité," *Gr* 53 (1972) 679–716; M. Simonetti, "Il millenarismo in oriente da Origene a Metodio," in *Corona Gratiarum* (= Festschr. E. Dekkers: Instrumenta Patristica 10 [Bruges 1975]) 1.37–58.

VI Latin eschatology in the Great Persecution (303–313)

(1) *Victorinus of Pettau*

C. Curti, "Il regno millenario in Vittorino di Petovio," *Aug* 18 (1978) 419–33.

(2) *Anonymous Commentary on Matthew 24*

G. Mercati, "Anonymi Chiliastae in Matthaeum XXIV Fragmenta," *Varia Sacra* (= StT 11 [Rome 1903]) 3–45; C. H. Turner, "An Exegetical Fragment of the Third Century," *JThS* 5 (1904) 218–27.

(3) *Lactantius*

P. J. Couvee, *Vita beata en vita aeterna bij Lactantius, Ambrosius en Augustinus* (Baarn 1947); B. Kötting, "Endzeitprognosen zwischen Lactantius und Augustinus," *HJ* 77 (1958) 125–39; H. W. A. Van Rooijen-Dijkman, *De vita beata. Het zevende Boek van de Divinae Institutiones van Lactantius. Analyse en Bronnenonderzoek* (Assen 1967); L. J. Swift, "Lactantius and the Golden Age," *AJP* 89 (1968) 144–56; V. Loi, *Lattanzio nella storia del linguaggio e del pensiero teologico pre-niceno* (Zurich 1970); V. Fabrega, "Die chiliastische Lehre des Laktanz. Methodische und theologische Voraussetzungen und religionsgeschichtlicher Hintergrund," *JAC* 17 (1974) 126–46; J. Doignon, "Le 'Placitum' eschatologique attribué aux Stoïciens par Lactance ('Institutions divines' 7.20)," *RPh* 51 (1977) 43–55; M. Perrin, *L'Homme antique et chrétien: l'anthropologie de Lactance – 250–325* (Paris 1981).

VII Eschatology in the fourth-century East:
the age of Nicaea (325–400)

(1) *The Desert Fathers*

F. Refoulé, "Immortalité de l'âme et résurrection de la chair," *RHR* 163 (1963) 44–49.

Bibliography

(2) Ephrem

E. Beck, "Eine christliche Parallele zu den Paradiesjungfrauen des Korans?" *OrChrP* 14 (1948) 398–405; I. Ortiz de Urbina, "Le Paradis eschatologique d'après saint Ephrem," *OrChrP* 21 (1955) 457–72; J. Teixidor, "Muerte, cielo y šeol en S. Efrén," *OrChrP* 27 (1961) 82–114; N. Séd, "Les Hymnes sur le Paradis et les traditions juives," *Muséon* 81 (1968) 455–501.

(3) Eusebius of Caesaraea

H. J. Opitz, "Eusebius als Theologe," *ZNW* 34 (1935) 1–19; H. Eger, "Kaiser und Kirche in der Geschichtstheologie Eusebius' von Cäsaräa," *ZNW* 38 (1939) 97–115; D. S. Wallace-Hadrill, *Eusebius of Caesaraea* (London 1960), esp. 168–89; F. Trisoglio, "Eusebio di Cesarea e l'escatologia," *Aug* 18 (1978) 174–77.

(4) Marcellus of Ancyra

M. Tetz, "Die Theologie des Markell von Ankyra I–III," *ZKG* 75 (1964) 217–70; 79 (1968) 3–42; 83 (1972) 145–94.

(5) Cyril of Jerusalem

G. A. Nicolae, "Invaţatura despre invierea morţilor in 'Catechezele' Sfintului Chiril al Iersusalimii," *StTeol* 19 (1967) 629–39. G. Hellemo, *Adventus Domini. Eschatological Thought in Fourth-Century Apses and Catecheses* (Leiden 1989) 146–98.

(6) Cappadocian Fathers

A. Recheis, *Engel, Tod und Seelenreise. Das Wirken der Geister beim Heimgang des Menschen in der Lehre der alexandrinischen und kappadokischen Väter* (Rome 1958); R. C. Gregg, *Consolation Philosophy: Greek and Christian Paideia in Basil and the Two Gregories* (Cambridge, Mass. 1975).

(a) Basil of Caesaraea

J. Gribomont, "L'Origénisme de Basile de Césarée," in *L'Homme devant Dieu* (= Festschr. H. de Lubac [Paris 1963]) I.281–94; M. Girardi, "Il giudizio finale nella omiletica di Basilio di Cesarea," *Aug* 18 (1978) 183–90.

(b) Gregory of Nazianzus

J. Mossay, "Perspectives eschatologiques de Saint Grégoire de Nazianze," *QLP* 45 (1964) 320–39; *La Mort et l'au-delà dans saint Grégoire de Nazianze* (Louvain 1966).

Bibliography

(c) Gregory of Nyssa

J. B. Aufhauser, *Die Heilslehre des hl. Gregors von Nyssa* (Munich 1910): J. Daniélou, "L'Apocatastase chez saint Grégoire de Nysse," *RSR* 30 (1940) 328–47; "La Résurrection des corps selon saint Grégoire de Nysse," *VigChr* 7 (1953) 154–70; "Le Comble du mal et l'eschatologie de s. Grégoire de Nysse," in E. Iserloh and P. Manns (eds.), *Festgabe Joseph Lortz* (Baden-Baden 1958) II.17–45; "Le Traîté 'Sur les enfants morts prématurément' de Grégoire de Nysse," *VigChr* 20 (1966) 159–82; *L'Etre et le temps chez Grégoire de Nysse* (Leiden 1970); "Metempsychosis in Gregory of Nyssa," in D. Neiman and M. Schatkin (eds.), *The Heritage of the Early Church* (= Festschr. G. Florovsky: OrChrA 195 [Rome 1973]) 228–43; H. Merki, ʽΟμοίωσις Θεῷ. *Von der platonischen Angleichung an Gott zur Gottähnlichkeit bei Gregor von Nyssa* (Frankfurt 1952); J. Gaith, *La Conception de la liberté chez Grégoire de Nysse* (Paris 1953); D. L. Balas, Μετουσία Θεοῦ. *Man's Paraticipation in God's Perfection according to St. Gregory of Nyssa* (Rome 1966); A. Spira, "Rhetorik und Theologie in den Grabreden Gregors von Nyssa," *StPatr* 9 (1966) 106–14; L. F. Mateo Seco, "La teología de la muerte en la Oratio catechetica magna di San Gregorio di Nyssa," *ScrTh* 1 (1969) 453–73; "La muerte y su más allá en el Diálogo sobre el almo y la resurrección," *ScrTh* 3 (1971) 75–107; M. Alexandre, "Le *De mortuis* de Grégoire de Nysse," *StPatr* 10 (1970) 35–43; "L'Interprétation de Lc 16.19–31 chez Grégoire de Nysse," in J. Fontaine and C. Kannengiesser (eds.) *Epektasis* (= Festschr. J. Daniélou [Paris 1972]) 425–41; "Protologie et eschatologie chez Grégoire de Nysse," in H. Crouzel and U. Bianchi (eds.) *Archè e telos: L'antropologia di Origene e di Gregorio di Nissa. Analisi storico-religiosa* (Milan 1981) 122–59; B. Salmona, "Origene e Gregorio di Nissa sulla risurrezione dei corpi e l'apocatastasi," *Aug* 18 (1978) 383–88; C. Tsirpanlis, "The Concept of Universal Salvation in Saint Gregory of Nyssa," in *Greek Patristic Theology: Basic Doctrine in Eastern Church Fathers* 1 (New York 1979) 141–56; M. Harl, "La Croissance de l'âme selon le *De infantibus* de Grégoire de Nysse," *VigChr* 34 (1980) 237–59; M. Alexandre and T. J. Dennis, "Gregory [of Nyssa] on the Resurrection of the Body," in A. Spira and C. Klock (eds.), *The Easter Sermons of Gregory of Nyssa* (Cambridge, Mass. 1981) 55–80.

(7) Epiphanius

C. Riggi, "Catechesi escatologica dell' 'Ancoratus' di Epifanio," *Aug* 18 (1978) 163–71.

(8) Evagrius

A. Guillaumont, "De l'eschatologie à la mystique. Histoire d'une sentence d'Evagre," in *Ecole des langues orientales anciennes de l'Institut Catholique de Paris: Mémorial du cinquantenaire 1914–1964* (Paris 1964) 187–92.

Bibliography

(9) *Synesius of Cyrene*

C. Lacombrade, *Synésios de Cyrène, hellène et chrétien* (Paris 1951); H.-I. Marrou, "Synesius of Cyrene and Alexandrian Neoplatonism" in A. Momigliano (ed.), *The Conflict between Paganism and Christianity in the Fourth Century* (Oxford 1963) 126–50; S. Vollenweider, *Neuplatonische und christliche Theologie bei Synesios von Kyrene* (Göttingen 1985), esp. 183–87.

VIII Latin eschatology in the fourth century

(1) *Hilary of Poitiers*

P. Galtier, *S. Hilaire de Poitiers, le premier docteur de l'église latine* (Paris 1960); G. Blasich, "La risurrezione dei corpi nell'opera esegetica di S. Ilario di Poitiers," *DT(P)* 69 (1966) 72–90; J.-P. Pettorelli, "Le Thème de Sion, expression de la théologie de la rédemption dans l'œuvre de saint Hilaire de Poitiers," in *Hilaire et son temps* (Actes du Colloque de Poitiers, 1968 [Paris 1969]) 213–33; M. Durst, *Die Eschatologie des Hilarius von Poitiers: ein Beitrag zur Dogmengeschichte des vierten Jahrhunderts* (Bonn 1987).

(2) *Ambrose*

J. E. Niederhuber, *Die Lehre des hl. Ambrosius vom Reiche Gottes auf Erden* (Mainz 1904); *Die Eschatologie des hl. Ambrosius* (Paderborn 1907); J. Derambure, "Le Millénarisme de S. Ambroise," *REA* 17 (1910) 545–56; P. J. Couvee, *Vita beata en vita aeterna bij Lactantius, Ambrosius en Augustinus* (Baarn 1947); H. Dörrie, "Der Seelenaufstieg bei Porphyrius und Ambrosius," in A. Stuiber and A. Hermann (eds.), *Mullus* (= Festschr. Th. Klauser: JAC Ergänzungsband 1 [Münster 1964]) 79–92; P. Scazzoso, "Osservazioni intorno al 'De Bono Mortis' di S. Ambrogio," *DT(P)* 71 (1968) 276–307; R. Iacoangeli, "La catechesi escatologica di S. Ambrogio," *Salesianum* 41 (1979) 403–17; A.-L. Fenger, "Tod und Auferstehung des Menschen nach Ambrosius' 'De excessu fratris' II," *Jenseitsvorstellungen in Antike und Christentum* (= Gedenkschr. A Stuiber: JAC Ergäzungsband 9 [Münster 1982]) 129–39; G. Hellemo, *Adventus Domini. Eschatological Thought in Fourth-Century Apses and Catacheses* (Leiden 1989) 269–80.

(3) *Jerome*

J. P. O'Connell, *The Eschatology of Saint Jerome* (Mundelein, Ill. 1948); Y. Duval, "Tertullien contre Origène sur la résurrection de la chair dans le *Contra Johannem Hierosolymitanum* 22–36 de saint Jérôme," *REAug* 17 (1971) 227–78; J. N. D. Kelly, *Jerome. His Life, Writings and Controversies* (London 1975); T. Larriba, "El comentario de San Jerónimo al Libro de Daniel. La profecías sobre Cristo y Anticristo," *ScrTh* 7 (1975) 7–50.

Bibliography

IX Greek eschatology in the fifth century

(1) John Chrysostom

E. Michaud, "St. Jean Chrysostome et l'apokatastase," *RITh* 18 (1910) 672–96; S. Schiewietz, "Die Eschatologie des hl. Johannes Chrysostomus und ihr Verhältnis zu der origenistischen," *Kath* 4.12 (1913) 445–55; 4.13 (1914) 45–63, 200–16, 271–81, 370–79, 436–48; F. Leduc, "L'Eschatologie, une préoccupation centrale de saint Jean Chrysostome," *POC* 19 (1969) 109–34.

(2) Cyril of Alexandria

E. Weigl, *Die Heilslehre des hl. Cyrill von Alexandrien* (Mainz 1905); G. Langevin, "Le Thème de l'incorruptibilité dans le commentaire de saint Cyrille d'Alexandrie sur l'Evangile selon saint Jean," *ScEc* 8 (1956) 295–316.

(3) Theodore of Mopsuestia

W. de Vries, "Das eschatologische Heil bei Theodor von Mopsuestia," *OrChrP* 24 (1958) 309–38; R. A. Greer, *Theodore of Mopsuestia, Exegete and Theologian* (London 1961); U. Wickert, *Studien zu den Pauluskommentaren Theodors von Mopsuestia als Beitrag zum Verständnis der antiochenischen Theologie* (Berlin 1962); G. Koch, *Die Heilsverwirklichung bei Theodor von Mopsuestia* (Munich 1965); J. M. Dewart, *The Theology of Grace of Theodore of Mopsuestia* (Washington, D.C. 1971). G. Hellemo, *Adventus Domini. Eschatological Thought in Fourth-Century Apses and Catecheses* (Leiden 1989) 208–31.

(4) Theodoret of Cyrus

G. Koch, *Strukturen und Geschichte des Heils in der Theologie des Theodoret von Kyros. Eine dogmen- und theologiegeschichtliche Untersuchung* (Frankfurt 1974).

(5) Later apocalyptic

D. de Bruyne, "Fragments retrouvés d'apocryphes Priscillianistes," *RBén* 24 (1907) 323; P. Bihlmeyer, "Un texte non interpolé de l'Apocalypse de Thomas," *RBén* 298 (1911) 270–82; H. Weinel, "Die spätere christliche Apokalyptik," in H. Schmidt (ed.), *ΕΥΧΑΡΙΣΤΗΡΙΟΝ* (= Festschr. H. Gunkel [Göttingen 1923]) 2.141–73; E. Peterson, "Die 'Taufe' im Acherusischen See," *VigChr* 9 (1955) 1–20 (= *Frühkirche, Judentum und Gnosis* [Rome 1959] 310–32).

X Latin eschatology in the fifth century

(1) Gaudentius

G. M. Bruni, *La teologia della storia secondo Gaudenzio* (Vicenza 1967).

Bibliography

(2) Sulpicius Severus

A. Biamonti, "L'escatologia di Sulpicio Severo," *Bollettino di studi storico-religiosi* I (1921) 55–68; S. Prete, "Sulpicio Severo e il millenarismo," *Convivium* 26 (1958) 394–404; "Degenerazione e decadenza morale nell'escatologia di Sulpicio Severo," *Aug* 18 (1978) 245–56; G. K. Van Andel, *The Christian Concept of History in the Chronicle of Sulpicius Severus* (Amsterdam 1976).

(3) Tyconius

T. Hahn, *Tyconius-Studien. Ein Beitrag zur Kirchen- und Dogmengeschichte des 4. Jahrhunderts* (Leiden 1900; repr. Aalen 1971); A. Pincherle, "Da Ticonio a S. Agostino," *Ricerche Religiose* 1 (1925) 443–66; I. M. Gomez, "El perdido comentario di Ticonio al Apocalipsis. Prinicipios de critica literaria y textual para su reconstrución," in R. M. Diaz (ed.), *Miscellanea biblica B. Ubach* (Montserrat 1953) 387–411; F. LoBue (ed.), *The Turin Fragments of Tyconius' Commentary on Revelation* (Cambridge 1963); H. D. Rauh, *Das Bild des Antichrist im Mittelalter. Von Tyconius zum deutschen Symbolismus* (Münster 1973) 102–21.

(4) Augustine
(a) General works

E. Portalié, "Saint Augustin," *DThC* 1.2 (Paris 1902) (Eng. tr.: *A Guide to the Thought of Saint Augustine* [Chicago 1960]); H. Eger, *Die Eschatologie Augustins* (Greifswald 1933); E. Dinkler, *Die Anthropologie Augustins* (Stuttgart 1934); G. F. D. Locher, *Hoop, Eeuwigkeid en Tijd en de Predeking van Augustin* (Wageningen 1961); L. Ballay, *Der Hoffnungsbegriff bei Augustin* (Munich 1964); A. Benoit, "Remarque sur l'eschatologie de S. Augustin," in M. Geiger (ed.), *Gottesreich und Menschenreich* (= Festschr. E. Stähelin [Basle 1969]) 1–9.

(b) Time and history

J. Guitton, *Le Temps et l'éternité chez Plotin et Saint Augustin* (Paris 1933); W. Verwiebe, *Welt und Zeit bei Augustin* (Leipzig 1933); E. Lewalter, "Eschatologie und Weltgeschichte in der Gedankenwelt Augustins," *ZKG* 53 (1934) 1–51; W. von Loewenich, *Augustinus und das christliche Geschichtsdenken* (Munich 1947); H.-I. Marrou, *L'Ambivalence du temps de l'histoire chez S. Augustin* (Paris/Montreal 1950); J. Chaix-Ruy, *Saint Augustin. Temps et histoire* (Paris 1956); O. Rousseau, "La Typologie augustinienne de l'Hexaémeron et la théologie du temps," in E. Iserloh and P. Manns (eds.), *Festgabe Joseph Lortz* (Baden-Baden 1958) 47–58; M. E. Ravicz, "St. Augustine: Time and Eternity," *Thom* 22 (1959) 542–54; U. Duchrow, "Der sogenannte psychologische Zeitbegriff Augustins im Verhältnis zur physikalischen und geschichtlichen Zeit," *ZThK* 63 (1966) 267–88; K. H. Schwarte, *Die Vorgeschichte der augustinischen Weltalterlehre* (Bonn 1966); R. A. Markus, *Saeculum: History and Society in the Theology of St. Augustine* (Cambridge

Bibliography

1970); R. Teske, "'Vocans temporales, faciens aeternos': St. Augustine on Liberation from Time," *Tr* 41 (1985) 29–48.

(c) *End of the world, millenarianism*

J. Hubaux, "L'Enfant d'un an," in *Hommages à J. Bidez et à F. Cumont* (Collection Latomus 2 [Brussels 1948]) 143–58; "Augustin et la crise eschatologique de la fin du IVe siècle," *BCLAB* 40 (1954) 658–73; "Saint Augustin et la crise cyclique," *AugM* 2 (Paris 1954) 943–50; G. Folliet, "La Typologie du 'sabbat' chez saint Augustin. Son interprétation millénariste entre 389 et 400," *REAug* 2 (1956) 371–91; B. Kötting, "Endzeitprognosen zwischen Lactantius und Augustinus," *HJ* 77 (1957) 125–39; J. Lamotte, "Saint Augustin et la fin du monde," *Aug* 12 (1962) 5–26; B. Lohse, "Zur Eschatologie des älteren Augustin (De Civ Dei 20.9)," *VigChr* 21 (1967) 221–40.

(d) *Death and interim state*

J. J. Gavigan, "Sancti Augustini doctrina de Purgatorio, praesertim in 'De Civitate Dei,'" *CD* 167.2 (1956) 283–97; J. Ntedika, *L'Evolution de la doctrine du purgatoire chez saint Augustin* (Paris 1966); P. Jay, "Saint Augustin et la doctrine du purgatoire," *RThAM* 36 (1969) 17–30; S. Kowalczyk, "La Mort dans la doctrine de saint Augustin," *EstAg* 10 (1975) 357–72.

(e) *Resurrection and immortality*

P. Goñi, *La resurrección de la carne según San Agustín* (Washington, D.C. 1961); H.-I. Marrou, *The Resurrection and Saint Augustine's Theology of Human Values* (Villanova 1966) (cf. *REAug* 12 [1966] 111–36); K. E. Börresen, "Augustin, interprète du dogme de la résurrection. Quelques aspects de son anthropologie dualiste," *StTh* 23 (1969) 141–55; J. A. Mourant, *Augustine on Immortality* (Villanova 1969); C. W. Wolfskeel, "Ist Augustin in 'De Immortalitate Animae' von der Gedankenwelt des Porphyrios beeinflusst worden?," *VigChr* 26 (1972) 130–45; R. Areitia, "Tiempo, inmortalidad y resurrección en San Agostino," *Estudios de Deusto* 21 (1973) 277–342; A. Di Giovanni, "La partecipazione alla 'immortalità' di Dio, *eschaton* dell'uomo, in sant' Agostino," *Aug* 18 (1978) 229–36.

(f) *Eternal life, beatitude and damnation*

A. Lehaut, *L'Eternité des peines de l'enfer dans S. Augustin* (Paris 1912); D. J. Leahy, *St Augustine on Eternal Life* (London 1939); P. J. Couvee, *Vita beata en vita aeterna bij Lactantius, Ambrosius en Augustinus* (Baarn 1947); J. Stoop, *De deificatio hominis in de Sermones en Epistulae van Augustin* (Leiden 1952); V. Capánaga, "La deificación en la soteriología agustiniana," *AugM* 2 (Paris 1954) 745–54; T. E. Clarke, *The Eschatological Transformation of the Material World according to St.*

Bibliography

Augustine (Woodstock, Md. 1956); "St. Augustine and Cosmic Redemption," *TS* 19 (1958) 133–64; R. Holte, *Béatitude et sagesse. Saint Augustin et le problème de la fin de l'homme dans la philosophie ancienne* (Paris 1962); E. Lamirande, *L'Eglise céleste selon saint Augustin* (Paris 1963); L. Cilleruelo, "Deum videre en San Agustin," *Sal* 12 (1965) 1–31; P. Sessa, "Desiderio dell'eternità e della vita eterna secondo la dottrina di S. Agostino," *RAMi* 11 (1966) 161–71.

(5) *"Consultationes Zacchaei et Apollonii"*

G. Morin, *FlorPatr* 39 (Bonn 1935) (critical edition, with introduction); P. Courcelle, "Date, source et génèse des Consultationes Zacchaei et Apollonii," *RHR* 146 (1954) 174–93 (= *Histoire littéraire des grandes invasions germaniques* [Paris 1964] 261–75).

(6) *Orosius*

B. Lacroix, *Orose et ses idées* (Montreal/Paris 1965); H.-I. Marrou, "Saint Augustin, Orose, et l'augustinisme historique," *La storiografia altomedievale* 1 (Spoleto 1970) 59–87; H.-W. Goetz, *Die Geschichtstheologie des Orosius* (Darmstadt 1980).

(7) *Prudentius*

J. Fontaine, "Trois variations de Prudence sur le thème de Paradis," in W. Wimmel (ed.), *Forschungen zur römischen Literatur* (= Festschr. K. Büchner [Wiesbaden 1970]) 96–115; K. Thraede,"'Auferstehung der Toten' im Hymnus ante cibum des Prudentius (Cath 3, 186/205)," in *Jenseitsvorstellungen in Antike und Christentum* (= Gedenkschrift A. Stuiber: JAC Ergänzungsband 9 [Münster 1982]) 68–78.

(8) *Commodian*

P. Courcelle, "Commodien et les invasions du Vᵉ siècle," *REL* 24 (1946) 227–46; *Histoire littéraire* (above, sec. 5) 319–37; J. Martin, "Commodianus," *Tr* 13 (1957) 1–71; K. Thraede, "Beiträge zur Datierung Commodians," *JAC* 2 (1959) 90–114; J. Gagé, "Commodien et la crise millénariste du IIIᵉ siècle (258–62 ap. J.-C)," *RHPhR* 41 (1961) 355–78; A. J. Visser, "Een of twee antichristen bij Commodianus," *NAKG* 47 (1965/66) 131–36.

(9) *Peter Chrysologus*

F. J. Peters, *Petrus Chrysologus als Homilet* (Karlsruhe 1918), esp. 69–75, 83f.; J. Speigl, "Petrus Chrysologus über die Auferstehung der Toten," in *Jenseitsvorstellungen in Antike und Christentum* (= Gendenkschrift A. Stuiber: JAC Ergänzungsband 9 [Münster 1982]) 140–53.

Bibliography

XI Eastern eschatology after Chalcedon

(1) "Agathangelos"

R. W. Thomson, *The Teaching of Saint Gregory: An Early Armenian Catechism* (Cambridge, Mass. 1970).

(2) Schenute

S. Morenz, "Altägyptischer und hellenistisch-paulinischer Jenseitsglaube bei Schenute," *MIOF* 1 (1953) 250–55.

(3) Narsai

P. Krüger, "Le Sommeil des âmes dans l'œuvre de Narsai," *OrSyr* 4 (1959) 193–210; P. Gignoux, "Les Doctrines eschatologiques de Narsai," *OrSyr* 11 (1966) 321–52, 461–88; 12 (1967) 23–54.

(4) Isaac of Antioch

P. Krüger, "Gehenna und Scheol in dem Schrifttum unter dem Namen des Isaak von Antiochien," *OstKSt* 2 (1953) 270–79.

(5) Jacob of Sarug

M. D. Guinan, "The Eschatology of James of Sarug" (Diss. Catholic University of America 1972).

(6) Sixth-century Greek apocalyptic

P. J. Alexander, *The Oracle of Baalbek: The Tiburtine Sibyl in Greek Dress* (Washington, D.C. 1967); G. Podskalsky, *Byzantinische Reichseschatologie. Die Periodisierung der Weltgeschichte in den 4 Grossreichen (Dan 2 und 7) und des 1000 jährigen Friedensreiches (Apok 20). Eine motivgeschichtliche Untersuchung* (Munich 1972); "Marginalien zur Byzantinischen Reichseschatologie," *ByZ* 67 (1974) 351–58.

(7) Greek commentaries on the Apocalypse of John

(a) Oecumenius

F. Diekamp, "Mitteilungen über den neugefundenen Commentar des Oecumenius zur Apokalypse," *SPAW* 43 (1901) 7f.; J. Schmid, "Die griechischen Apokalypse-Kommentare," *BZ* 19(1931) 228–56; A. Spitaler and J. Schmid, "Zur Klärung des Oikoumenios-problems: zusätzliche Bemerkungen," *OrChr* 3.9 (1934) 208–18.

Bibliography

Text: ed. H. C. Hoskier (Ann Arbor, Mich. 1928).

(b) *Andrew of Caesaraea*

F. Diekamp, "Das Zeitalter des Erzbischofs Andreas von Cäsarea," *HJ* 18 (1897) 1–36.
Text: J. Schmid, *Studien zur Geschichte des griechischen Apokalypse-Textes, 1 Teil: Der Apokalypse-Kommentar des Andreas von Kaisareia* (Munich 1955).

(8) *Pseudo-Dionysius*

O. Semmelroth, *Das ausstrahlende und emporziehende Licht. Die Theologie des Pseudo-Dionysius Areopagita in systematischer Darstellung* (Bonn 1947); R. Roques, *L'Univers dionysien. Structure hierarchique du monde selon le Pseudo-Denys* (Paris 1954); M. Schiavone, *Neoplatonismo e cristianesimo nello Pseudo-Dionisio* (Milan 1963); B. Brons, *Gott und die Seienden. Untersuchungen zum Verhältnis von neuplatonischer Metaphysik und christlicher Tradition bei Dionysius Areopagita* (Göttingen 1976).

(9) *Severus of Antioch*

W. de Vries, "Die Eschatologie des Severus von Antiochien," *OCP* 23 (1957) 354–80.

(10) *Aeneas of Gaza*

S. Sikorski, *De Aenea Gazaeo* (Brescia 1909); M. Wacht, *Aeneas von Gaza als Apologet: seine Kosmologie im Verhältnis zum Platonismus* (Bonn 1969); E. Gallicet, "La risurrezione dei morti in Enea di Gaza e in Zacaria Scolastico," *Aug* 18 (1978) 273–78.
Text: ed. M. E. Colonna (Naples 1958).

(11) *Zachary of Mytilene*

M. E. Colonna, "Zacaria Scolastico. Il suo *Ammonio* e il *Teofrasto di Enea di Gaza*," *Annali della Facoltà di Lettere e Filosofia dell'Università di Napoli* 6 (1956) 107–18; E. Gallicet, "La risurrezione dei morti in Enea di Gaza e in Zacaria Scolastico," *Aug* 18 (1978), 273–78.
Text: ed. M. Minniti Colonna (Naples 1973).

(12) *Cosmas "Indicopleustes"*

M. V. Anastos, "The Alexandrian Origin of the Christian Topography of Cosmas Indicopleustes," *DOP* (1946) 72–80; "Aristotle and Cosmas Indicopleustes on the Void. A Note on Theology and Science in the Sixth Century," Ἑλληνικά (= Festschr. S. P. Kyriakides: Σύγγραμμα περιόδικον τῆς Ἑταιρείας Μακεδονικῶν

Bibliography

Σπουδῶν 4 [1953]) 35–50 (= *Studies in Byzantine Intellectual History* [London 1979] xiv); W. Wolska, *La "Topographie Chrétienne" de Cosmas Indicopleustes. Théologie et Science au VIe siècle* (Paris 1962).
Text: ed. W. Wolska Conus, *SChr* 141 (Paris 1968), 159 (Paris 1970) and 197 (Paris 1973).

(13) *Romanos "the Melodist"*

T. M. Wehofer, "Untersuchungen zum Lied des Romanos auf die Widerkunft des Herrn," *SAWW.PH* 154–55 (1906–1907); J. Grosdidier de Matons, *Romanos le Mélode et les origines de la poésie religieuse à Byzance* (Paris 1977).
Text: ed. J. Grosdidier de Matons, *SChr* 99 (Paris 1964), 110 (Paris 1965), 114 (Paris 1965), 128 (Paris 1967), 283 (Paris 1981).

(14) *Maximus the Confessor*

E. Michaud, "S. Maxime le confesseur et l'apocatastase," *RITh* 10 (1902) 257–72; P. Sherwood, *The Earlier Ambigua of St. Maximus the Confessor and his Refutation of Origenism* (= StAns 36 [Rome 1955]), esp. 205–22; H. U. Von Balthasar, *Kosmische Liturgie* (Einsiedeln ²1961), esp. 355–59; B. E. Daley, "Apokatastasis and 'Honorable Silence' in the Eschatology of Maximus the Confessor," in F. Heinzer and C. Schönborn (eds.), *Maximus Confessor* (Fribourg 1982) 309–39.

XII Eschatology in the sixth-century West

(1) *Caesarius of Arles*

G. Morin, "Le Commentaire homilétique de S. Césaire sur l'Apocalypse," *RBén* 45 (1933) 43–61; P. Jay, "Le purgatoire dans la prédication de saint Césaire d'Arles," *RThAM* 24 (1957) 5–14.
Text: ed. G. Morin (Maredsous 1937–42; = CCL 103–104 [Turnhout 1953]).

(2) *Carmen ad Flavium Felicem*

J. H. Waszink, "Einige Bemerkungen über den Text des Carmen de resurrectione mortuorum et de iudicio Domini," in *Jenseitsvorstellungen in Antike und Christentum* (= Gedenkschr. A. Stuiber: JAC Ergänzungsband 9 [Münster 1982]) 79–85.
Text: ed. J. Waszink, *FlorPatr* Suppl 1 (Bonn 1937).

(3) *Gregory the Great*

N. Hill, "Die Eschatologie Gregors des Grossen" (Diss. Freiburg 1942); R. Manselli, "L'escatologismo di Gregorio Magno," *Atti del 1° Congresso internazionale di Studi Longobardi* (Spoleto 1952) 383–87; "L'escatologia di Gregorio Magno,"

Bibliography

Ricerche di storia religiosa 1 (1954) 72–83; J. P. McClain, "The Doctrine of Heaven in the Writings of St. Gregory the Great" (Diss. Catholic University of America 1956); R. Wasselynck, "La voix d'un Père de l'Eglise: l'orientation eschatologique de la vie chrétienne d'après S. Grégoire le Grand," *ASeign* 2 (Bruges/Paris 1962) 66–80; C. Dagens, "La Fin des temps et l'église selon Grégoire le Grand," *RSR* 58 (1970) 273–88; P. Boglioni, "Miracle et nature chez Grégoire le Grand," *Cahiers d'études médiévales* 1 (Montreal/Paris 1974), esp. 14–70; G. Cracco, "Gregorio e l'oltretomba," in J. Fontaine, R. Gillet and S. Pellistrandi (eds.), *Grégoire le Grand* (Chantilly Colloquium, 1982 [Paris 1986]) 255–65; Y. Duval, "La Discussion entre l'apocrisiaire Grégoire et le patriarche Eutychios au sujet de la résurrection de la chair," *ibid.*, 347–65; H. Savon, "L'Antéchrist dans l'œuvre de Grégoire le Grand," *ibid.*, 389–404; P. Siniscalco, "L'età del mondo in Gregorio Magno," *ibid.*, 377–86; C. Vogel, "Deux conséquences de l'eschatologie grégorienne: la multiplication des messes privées et les moines-prêtres," *ibid.*, 267–76.

INDEX

Index

Index

Index

Index

Ephrem (*c*. 306–373), 74–76
Epiphanius of Salamis (*c*. 315–403), 89–90
Epistle of the Apostles, see Epistula Apostolorum
Epistula Apostolorum, 7–9
Epistle of Barnabas, 11
Epistle to Rheginus (Valentinian tract on the resurrection), 26–28
eschatology, meaning of term, 1
  and Christology, 2
  and ethical behavior, 12, 23, 161, 162–63
  and salvation, 2, 4
  and theodicy, 2
  continuing questions, 221–23
  evolution of (general lines), 216
  realism of, 218
  "realized," 10, 12, 15–16, 43, 71–72, 77–78, 120, 130, 218
  relation to theology as whole, 2
  sources of, 4
eternity of creation, 91, 191
Eucharist
  eschatological dimension, 12, 13
  offered for the dead, 138–9, 200, 214
  promise of resurrection of flesh, 30
Eugenius of Seleucia (late sixth century), 196
Eusebius of Caesaraea (d. 339), 77–78
Eustathius of Antioch (d. before 337), 77
Eustratius of Constantinople (late sixth century), 200
Eutychius of Constantinople, Patriarch (d. 582), 213
Evagrius of Pontus (346–399), 90–91, 188–90
evil, finitude of, 86–87
Evodius of Uzala (early fifth century), 150
Ezra, Fifth and Sixth Books of, 7–9

fire, cosmic, 26, 38
fire, eternal, 9, 12, 84, 89 (*see also* Gehenna, punishment of sinners)
fire, "wise," 38, 46, 57, 209, 231 n. 5
fire of destruction (at end of world), 15
fire of Gehenna
  immaterial, 203
  invisible, 56, 107
  needs no fuel, 67, 186
  preserves and replenishes what it burns, 187, 209
  psychological interpretation, 56, 152, 207
  single, 213
fire of judgment, 9, 21, 67, 93, 135–36, 141, 153, 159, 163, 169, 173, 199–200, 202, 209
fire of purification, 21, 84, 88, 91, 151, 158, 199, 209, 214
"fire of testing" (during present life), 119
Firmicus Maternus, Julius (first half of fourth century), 93–94
Firminus, monastery of (Palestine, sixth century), 189
fulfilment, human (*see also* beatitude, rewards of just)
  "commingling" of minds with each other and God, 177–78
  divinization, *see* divinization
  knowledge uniting believer to God, 45–46, 113, 119, 183, 210, 221
  immortality, incorruptibility, 113
  likeness to God, 45, 82, 84
  social, ecclesial, rather than individual, 55, 128
  transformation, 113, 198, 201

Gaudentius of Brescia (d. after 406), 124–25
Gehenna
  absence of Christ, 107
  darkness, 82, 125, 175, 187, 210
  exclusion from presence, notice of God, 181, 209
  fire, eternal, 36, 42, 82, 84, 107, 125, 148, 161, 170, 175, 181, 186, 187, 209, 210, 213; "rivers of fire," 121; "sea of fire," 40, 107
  pit, 82
  present earth, 173
  reality of, 156
  silence, 70
  worm, 70, 82, 84, 98, 148, 160, 161, 207
generosity to poor, norm for future judgment, 154–56, 208
George Hamartolos (ninth century), 190
Germanus of Constantinople (*c*. 634–*c*. 733), 196
ghosts, appearances of, 55, 97, 137, 200

Index

"Gnostic, true" (Christian), 44–45
Gnosticism
  conception of human body, 25–26
  conception of world, 25–26, 218
  idea of salvation, 26
goal of God, perfection of human creature,
  86, 116, 201
Gog and Magog, 180
Gospel of Nicodemus, 123
Gospel of Philip (Valentinian treatise), 26–28
Gospel of Truth (Valentinian treatise), 27–28
Goths, invasion by as sign of end, 163
Gregory of Nazianzus (329/30–c. 390),
  83–85
Gregory of Nyssa (c. 335–394), 85–89,
  192, 194, 196
Gregory the Great, Pope (c. 540–c. 604),
  211–15
Gregory the Illuminator (early fourth
  century), 169
Gregory the Wonderworker
  (Thaumaturgus) (d. c. 270), 60
growth towards salvation, in this life,
  29, 44

Hades (*see also* Sheol)
  classless society, 227 n. 21
  realm of the dead, 36, 40, 83
  "storehouse of souls," 6, 100, 138, 199
  to be opened at second coming of
    Christ, 8
Hamartolos, George (ninth century), 190
heaven, *see* beatitude, Paradise, rewards of
  just
Hegesippus, 6
Heliopolis, king from, 179
hell, *see* Gehenna, Hades, Sheol,
  punishment of sinners
Hermas, author of *The Shepherd*, 16–17
Hesychius of Jerusalem (d. after 450),
  117
Hesychius of Salonae (correspondent of
  Augustine), 132, 135
Hilarianus, Quintus Julius (late fourth
  century), 127
Hilary of Poitiers (c. 315–367), 94–96
Hippolytus (d. c. 235), 38–41
history
  cyclic view, 91
  limit of six thousand years, 39, 41, 61,

67, 93, 94, 117, 124, 125–27, 163,
  169, 178–79, 231–32 n. 8
  linear view, 219
  progress towards salvation under
    Christian emperors, 77–78, 152
  two "ages," 6
Holy Spirit
  allows believers to taste "first fruits" of
    eschatological transformation, 15,
    112, 115, 119
  source of souls's immortality, 22–24
  "homeland" of human person with God,
    149–50, 186, 206, 208
hope
  link between faith and love, 217
  work of Holy Spirit, 217
Hystaspes, Oracles of (Hellenized Zoroastrian
  treatise), 68

Ignatius of Antioch (d. c. 110), 12–13
immortality, human
  makes retribution possible, 157
  participation in immortality of God,
    24
  reward to just, 24
immortality of soul
  changelessness, 193
  gift of God (not due to nature), 22–23,
    29, 46, 194
  leads to resurrection of body, 23–24, 51,
    194
  natural to humans, 51, 142, 161, 191,
    200, 220
  theory criticized as pagan, 40, 220
immutability, as eschatological gift, 116
incorruptibility (of risen body), 8, 40, 46,
  95, 110, 116, 143, 146, 191, 201
initiation liturgy, as type of eschatological
  salvation, 27
intercession of just for sinners, at
  judgment, 9
"interim state" (between death of individual
  and end of history)
  anticipation by soul of future rewards
    and punishments, 36–37, 85, 100,
    117, 137, 142, 160, 165
  limited enjoyment of God's presence, 120,
    137, 142, 185, 213, 220
  "sleep of souls," 73, 74, 95, 114, 165
  souls aware of each other, 117

Index

resurrection of dead (*cont.*)
    restoration to original human state,
        85–86, 97, 210
    soul bestows its qualities on body, 85,
        87–88, 95
    spiritual interpretation, 90–91
    totally new creation of body, 195–96
    universal, 95, 110, 115, 116
Revelation, Book of: see *Apocalypse of John*
revelation, central to human salvation, 29
rewards for just (*see also* beatitude,
        fulfilment, Paradise)
    access to hospitable universe, 40
    banquet, everlasting, 9
    "commingling" of minds with each other
        and God, 177–78
    crowns, 14, 16, 117; of flowers, 160,
        169
    different degrees of bliss and glory, 42,
        45, 206, 208
    divinization, *see* divinization
    enhanced by companionship, 103, 213
    equality of all, 73
    fellowship, friendship with God, 22, 29,
        32, 40, 182, 206
    fellowship with angels, 114, 199, 206,
        208
    fellowship with the other saved, 41, 71,
        114, 171, 206
    festival, eternal, 108
    freedom from earthly concerns and
        desires, 9, 73, 82
    glory, share in God's, 32, 76
    growth, possibility of, 31, 88
    immediately after death, 42, 101, 103,
        109, 161, 165, 213
    immortality, incorruptibility, 13, 22, 114
    inability to sin, 206, 208
    Kingdom of God, realized in resurrection
        96, 114
    knowledge of God, 82, 114, 173, 176,
        182, 204
    light, 9, 16, 27, 32, 73, 160, 184
    likeness, assimilation to God, 45, 82, 84,
        153
    merit, dependent on, 42, 71, 206
    Paradise, *see* Paradise
    place of, *see* Paradise
    rest, 9, 16, 27, 138, 191, 208
    radiance, radiant garments, 9, 16, 117,

153, 161, 171, 226–27 n. 17
    return to original state of humanity,
        85–86
    vision of Christ, 114, 173, 203
    vision of God, 29, 45, 108–109, 114,
        153
    union with God, 27, 83, 115–16,
        176–77, 177–78, 204
risen body
    adapted to environment of eternity, 52,
        144
    beauty, freedom from disfigurements,
        144
    ease and speed of perception and
        movement, 144, 206
    ethereal, immaterial, 87, 176, 213
    form different from present body, 169
    free form burdens of present life, 146,
        194, 206, 208, 214
    identical materially with present body,
        23, 35, 62, 64, 87, 95, 102, 106,
        143, 169, 180, 187, 191, 197,
        213–14, 222
    immutable, 116
    incorruptible, 8, 40, 46, 95, 110, 116,
        143, 146, 191, 201
    integrity of organs, 35, 144, 171,
        185–86, 206
    lightness of, 192
    like angels, 6, 35, 95, 103, 122, 146–47
    mind will be known to all thorough body,
        144
    penultimate stage of human perfection
        (?), 54
    perfectly subject to spirit, 143, 214
    radiance, 199, 208
    real flesh, 30, 35, 143, 157, 185–86,
        188
    same as present body, for sinners, 22
    sexes, differentiation of (?), 88, 103, 117,
        144, 206
    size of mature person, 144, 153
    spherical (?), 188–90, 199
    spiritual character, 95, 143, 176, 197
    subtle but palpable, 214
    transformed into light, 6
    uniformity of all, 95
    will need other creatures to exist, 116–17
Romanos "the Melodist" (d. *c.* 560),
    200–201

Index

Sabbath
    age of rest at end of history, 11, 39, 61,
        63, 66, 119, 124, 127, 132–33,
        134, 169, 177
    periodic rest for damned, 122
sacraments of Church, types of future
    salvation, 112
saints, revealed at resurrection, 10
salvation, of all believers ("misericordism"),
    104, 126
salvation, universal, *see apokatastasis*
salvation-history, 29, 78–79, 176–77
Salvian of Marseilles (d. after 470), 154–55
Satan
    accuser of the dead, 82, 208
    to be saved in the end (?), 58–59, 117
Schenute (*c.* 348–466), 170–71
Scripture, eschatological texts used by
    Fathers:
    Ezek. 37, 53–54
    Ps 1.5, 53, 62
    Ps 18.6, 45
    Matt 3.1–16, 176
    Matt 5.26, 37
    Matt 8.12, 53–54
    Matt 10.28, 53
    Matt 18.6, 237 n. 24
    Matt 24, 48–49, 66, 132, 134, 155, 167
    Matt 25.31–46, 208
    Luke 16.19–31, 36, 165, 242 n. 28, 243
        n. 35, 244 n. 12
    Luke 23.43, 137–38
    Acts 1.7, 134
    Acts 3.21, 79
    Rom 8.11, 53
    I Cor 3.10–15, 141, 214
    I Cor 15, 52, 58, 90, 96, 115–16, 143,
        164–65
    I Pet 3.19–4.6, 36, 139
    II Pet 1.4, 113
    Apoc 9.5f., 182
    Apoc 10.4, 182
    Apoc 20.1–21.5, 66, 98, 130–31, 180
senectus mundi ("old age" of world), 41, 48,
    67, 98, 101–102, 133, 152, 161, 166,
    211
Seventh Vision of Daniel (fifth–sixth century),
    178
Severan period (193–235), Christian life in,
    33

Severus of Antioch (*c.* 465–538), 184–87
Sheol (*see also* Hades), 73, 74, 174, 175
    place of equality, 74
    place of sleep, 73, 74, 174
Shepherd of Hermas, 16–17
Sibyl, Tiburtine (late fourth century), 179
Sibylline Oracles VII and VIII, 8–9, 68, 153
"sleep of souls," 73, 74, 95, 114, 165, 174
Solomon, Odes of, 15–16
soul
    continuing form of changing body,
        51–54, 191
    immortality of, *see* immortality of soul
    incapable of change after death, 108,
        203–204
    material nature of, 232 n. 3
    not same as form of material body, 195
souls
    active in world after death, 200
    pre-existence and fall of, 191, 192–93
    transmigration of, *see metempsychosis*
    "states of existence" (*katastaseis*), two,
        111–12, 172, 197
Stephen Bar-Sudaili (*c.* 480–*c.*543),
    176–78
Stoicism, influence on Christian
    eschatology, 53, 91
"storehouse of souls," 6, 100, 138, 199
Sulpicius Severus (d. *c.* 420), 126–27
symbols, liturgical, 28
Synesius of Cyrene (*c.* 370–413/14), 91–92
Syria, 12, 171–72, 174–78

tabernacle, Old Testament, as model of
    cosmos, 197
Tabernacles, Feast of (typological
    interpretation), 62
Tartarus, 27, 46, 121, 126
Tatian, 22–23
Teaching of St. Gregory (i.e., the Illuminator),
    168–70
Teaching of the Twelve Apostles, see Didache
Tertullian (Quintus Septimius Florens
    Tertullianus, *c.* 160–*c.* 220), 34–37
"Tetradites" (Origenist group, sixth-century
    Palestine), *see* "Protoktistoi"
Theodore Askidas (bishops of Caesaraea in
    Cappadocia; d. after 553), 189
Theodore of Mopsuestia (*c.* 352–428),
    111–15, 172, 197

Index